Messianism, Zionism, and

Jewish Religious

Radicalism

CHICAGO STUDIES IN THE HISTORY OF JUDAISM

A series edited by William Scott Green

Aviezer Ravitzky

Messianism, Zionism, and Jewish Religious Radicalism

Translated by
Michael Swirsky and
Jonathan Chipman

THE UNIVERSITY OF CHICAGO PRESS
Chicago & London

Originally published as

הקץ המגולה
ומדינת היהודים:
משיחיות, ציונות ורדיקליזם דתי בישראל

© Am Oved Publishers Ltd Tel Aviv 1993

The University of Chicago Press, Chicago 60637
The University of Chicago Press, Ltd., London
© 1996 by The University of Chicago
All rights reserved. Published 1996
Printed in the United States of America
16 15 14 13 12 11 10 09 08 07   3 4 5 6 7

ISBN-10: 0-226-70578-1 (paper)
ISBN-13: 978-0-226-70578-1 (paper)

Library of Congress Cataloging-in-Publication Data
Ravitzky, Aviezer.
[ha-Ḳets ha-meguleh u-medinat ha-Yehudim. English]
Messianism, Zionism, and Jewish religious radicalism / Aviezer
Ravitzky ; translated by Michael Swirsky and Jonathan Chipman.
    p.   cm.—(Chicago studies in the history of Judaism)
Includes bibliographical references and index.
    1. Zionism and Judaism.   2. Religious Zionism—Israel.
3. Messianic era (Judaism)   4. Orthodox Judaism—Israel.
5. Judaism and state—Israel.   I. Title.   II. Series.
DS149.R32313   1996
296.3′3—dc20   96-249
                                                CIP

To Ruthie

אשת בריתי

CONTENTS

Introduction

THE MESSIANIC DEMAND

It was a dream of utter perfection: the day would come when the entire Jewish people, the whole Congregation of Israel, would reassemble as one in an undivided Land of Israel, reconstituting its life there according to the Torah in all its aspects. The Jewish people would free itself completely from its subjugation to the great powers. It would then be a source of blessing for all nations, for its redemption would bring about the redemption of the world as a whole, "For the land shall be filled with devotion to the Lord as water covers the sea" (Isa. 11:9). Thus did the messianic dream persist in its pristine purity for a hundred generations.

Compared with this dream, the actual historical realization that has taken place in our own time seems truncated. Only a part of the Jewish people has gathered together into a Jewish state, and only in certain areas of the country. Only some of the returnees observe the precepts of the Torah. Political and military strife has not vanished from the land. Peace is elusive and morality compromised. Universal redemption seems even more remote than before. In short, the concrete fulfillment wrought by Zionism remains relative and contingent, stopping well short of the absolute terms of the classical vision. As the rabbis said, the End of Days continues to "tarry."

What is the status of this imperfect reality in Jewish religious consciousness? Does what has been achieved constitute a part of the process of final redemption or an abortion of that process? Is this the beginning of the End, a step toward the fulfillment of the prophetic promises, or is it rather a violent betrayal of those promises in all their perfection?

Traditional Jewish sources generally speak in terms of two polar concepts: exile and redemption. After the destruction of the Temple, Jewish existence could not be conceived in any other terms. Can Jewish religious thought now acknowledge an intermediate or hybrid model that is neither exile nor redemption? Can it make room for a notion of Jewish historical existence that hovers somewhere between these two poles without clearly belonging to either? If not, where within that framework is the present historical return to be placed? Can a Jewish people once more sovereign in the Holy Land still be said to be in exile? On the other hand, can we speak of a redemption or even a "beginning of redemption" of this people that is not founded on the Torah and religious repentance and not the result of supernatural intervention? Alternatively, can the return to Zion and the recovery of Jewish independence be conceived in terms that deviate completely from the classical conceptual framework?

Two generations prior to the Zionist reawakening, "the Hatam Sofer" (Rabbi Moses Sofer, d. 1839), the rabbi of Pressburg and leader of Hungarian Orthodox Jewry, addressed this issue in a sensitive and instructive way: "There may have been times in the past when we could have been partially redeemed [or given peace with the nations of the world in whose shadow we live] or even granted such redemption as [were our forebears] in the days of the Second Commonwealth . . . But it would have been pointless, for even had we compromised and accepted that sort of redemption for ourselves, our holy ancestors could never have reconciled themselves to anything less than full redemption. Thus it is worthwhile for the people of Israel to suffer prolonged exile in order to attain such redemption in the end."[1] In other words, the Jewish people finds itself in a profound dilemma, torn between an urgent desire for historical, existential salvation in the here and now and uncompromising devotion to an all-encompassing ultimate destiny and hope, a devotion that is inherently antiexistential. The Hatam Sofer knew well his own heart and that of his people. The Jews who live in the distress of exile might "compromise" and rejoice at the tidings of a partial salvation, he wrote. They might be tempted to make do with a restoration of the ancient past (sovereignty in the Land of Israel), forsaking utopian hopes. But the full messianic claim does not permit the Jew to follow such heart promptings and accept such existential options. The Congregation of Israel is committed, both historically and metahistorically, to its ultimate hope. It cannot be satisfied with a part, but only with the whole, the appearance of the Redeemer of Israel in all his power.

In time, the Zionist movement was to proclaim partial, concrete salvation in the here and now. Moreover, it sought to carry out its plan in secular fashion and by means of ordinary human political initiative. Thus, the Zionist awakening, besides raising in intensified form the classical question of the relationship between partial historical realization and the vision of utopian perfection, confronted the religious tradition with two other urgent issues, in the form of secular Jewish nationalism and Jewish activism.

Would the Congregation of Israel be ready at last to heed such a call? Could it see its way clear to distinguishing between the whole and the part, the sacred and the secular, the theological and the political? Could modern activism on the historical plane coexist with persistent metahistorical claims, and not by its very nature deny the basic concepts of Jewish faith?

"THE APOCALYPTIC STING"

Parallel to these questions that confronted Orthodox religious thought, some non-Orthodox Zionists urgently adduced the question of "the price of messianism." Gershom Scholem, who coined this phrase, repeatedly posed to his listeners and readers the following question: "Can Jewish history manage to re-enter concrete reality without being destroyed by the messianic claim which [that reentry is bound to] bring up from its depths."[2] Scholem set down these words rather late in his career, but as early as 1926, in a letter written to Franz Rosenzweig and only recently published, he raises a similarly penetrating question regarding the renewal and "secularization" of the Hebrew language: "The Land is a volcano. It provides lodging for the language . . . [But] what will be the result of the updating of Hebrew? Will the abyss of the holy tongue which we have implanted in our children not yawn wide? People here do not realize what they are doing. They think they have made Hebrew into a secular language, that they have removed its apocalyptic sting. But that is not so . . . Every word which is not simply made up but rather taken from the treasurehouse of well-worn terms is laden with explosives . . . God will not remain dumb in the language in which He has been adjured so many thousands of times to come back into our lives."[3] The "explosives" and "apocalyptic sting" are to be found in such classical expressions as *memshalah u-mamlakhah* (rulership and kingdom), *kibbutz galuyot* (the ingathering of the exiles), *yeshuah* (salvation), *shalom* (peace), *tzur yisrael* (Rock of Israel), and *ge'u-lah la-aretz* (redemption of the land)—expressions that have found their way into the modern Hebrew vernacular. Similarly, a "volcano" lies dormant in many terms whose original religious meaning has been radically altered or altogether lost in modern Hebrew. For example, *bittaḥon*, which now denotes military security, originally referred to trust in God; *ha'ap-alah*, which is used to refer to the prestate "illegal" immigration, originally denoted a forbidden and catastrophic breakthrough (Num. 14:44);[4] *keren kayemet*, the name of the modern-day Jewish National Fund, is taken from a Talmudic reference to "credit" for good deeds accumulated for the after-life (M Pe'ah 1:1; BT Shabbat 127a); and one often hears in a secular context such antique phrases as *zekhut avot* (the merits of [our] ancestors). But that is not all. The very name given to the State of Israel, *Medinat Yisrael,* presents just such a phenomenon. Although not drawn directly from ancient sources, so that one might believe it to be free of historical and eschatological hopes, it too is encumbered by the freight of the past and the accompanying tensions between part and whole, the political and the theological. Indeed, this particular example, so central to our subject, hovers between the sacred and the profane.

In what context did the phrase "the State of Israel" first appear? Ninety years ago, at the outset of the Zionist movement, a distinguished rabbi of the time, Elyakum Shlomo Shapira of Grodno, published a sharp criticism of the Zionists' ideas and activities. In particular, he was outraged by the secular character of the Zionist movement and the hollow presumption of its leaders in seeking to reconstitute Jewish life on a national basis, devoid of Torah and commandments. He wrote: "For I know the devastation they are wreaking upon the Congregation of Israel. My heart sinks within me, my eyes grow dark, and my ears wax heavy at what is being done and said. Their valor in the land is not for the sake of the true faith, nor is it for this that they wave their banners (while we raise the banner of God). What sort of 'nation' can they have if they throw over our holy Torah and its precepts (perish the thought)? *How can I bear that something be called 'the State of Israel' without the Torah and the commandments (heaven forbid)?*"[5] To the best of my knowledge, this is the first use of the expression "the State of Israel" in Hebrew literature in direct reference to the new national movement and its goals. How ironic that this coinage should appear in a text sharply critical of Zionism that draws on terms of biblical reproof and echoes the lament of Queen Esther: "How can I bear to see the disaster which will befall my people! And how can I bear to see the destruction of my kindred!" (Esther 8:6).[6]

Of course, Theodor Herzl's utopia, *Der Judenstaat* (The Jewish state), had been published five years earlier. But Dr. Herzl's phrase "the state of the Jews" has a rather different connotation than Rabbi Shapira's "the State of Israel." By speaking of "the Jews," Herzl evokes the sociological dimension, populated by living men, women, and children. "The state of the Jews" thus refers to concrete people in concrete distress, to their individual and collective lot and to the question of their concrete political freedom. "Israel," on the other hand, is a term laden with metahistorical, theological associations. It refers to the eternal Congregation of Israel and the Divine Presence, which hovers over it, regardless of time or space. Thus the term "State of Israel," as used here, cannot be detached from the spiritual vocation of the Jewish people: "How can I bear that something be called 'the State of Israel' without the Torah and the commandments?"

Less than twenty years later (ante 1920), "the State of Israel" appears once again, in an essay by Rabbi Abraham Isaac Kook,[7] an ardent supporter of the movement for national revival and a mentor of its redemptive-religious wing (see below, chapter 3). Kook, too, links the term with the transcendent destiny of the people of Israel, but unlike his predecessor, he does not see the new movement as a betrayal or denial of that destiny. Rather, he envisages Zionism as paving the way to ultimate religious and national fulfillment. Will Zionism not restore assimilated, alienated Jews to their people, to the Holy Land and the holy tongue? Thus, for Kook, the future "State of Israel" has a sacred basis as well. It will be completely different from any ordinary state which is grounded solely in mutual interests and is to be judged according to utilitarian criteria. The "State of Israel" will have messianic, metaphysical standards to live up to: "An ideal state, one that has the highest of all ideals engraved in its being . . . the most sublime happiness of the individual . . . this shall be our state, the State of Israel, *the pedestal of God's throne in this world,* for its only aim shall be that the Lord be acknowledged as one and His name one, which is truly the highest happiness."[8] The exalted stature Kook confers on the state-to-be is not a mere rhetorical flourish; it is based on an ancient dispute. In one of Daniel's apocalyptic visions (7:9), the kingdom of heaven is revealed as resting upon "thrones" (*kharsavan*). In a discussion of this passage in the Mishnah, Rabbi Akiva offers a daring interpretation. Two supreme thrones, he says, exist side by side; one is meant for the kingdom of God, the other for the kingdom of David, that is, the messianic kingdom. Rabbi Yose the Galilean objects, rebuking Akiva for mingling the sacred and the profane, the kingdom of heaven and that of flesh and blood: "Akiva, how long will you persist in making the Divine Presence a worldly thing?"[9]

One may assume that Rabbi Kook was aware of this text, but it obviously did not deter him from blatantly identifying the political with the theological. "The State of Israel," he says, is to be no less than the foundation of God's presence in the world.[10] The political embodiment of the Congregation of Israel is to be revealed to us like Jacob's ladder, standing upon the earth with its top reaching the heavens. This is Kook's expectation, and it is his religious and political agenda for the new settlement movement in the Land of Israel.

In 1948, on the eve of the proclamation of the Jewish state, the members of the National Council and the framers of the Proclamation of Independence pondered what name to give it.[11] When they finally chose the name "State of Israel," it is very doubtful that they were aware that a sage named Shapira had already weighed that term down with all the theological baggage of the name "Israel," or that a sage named Kook had imbued it with the theological connotations of "the Kingdom of Israel" and the "Congregation of Israel" on high. Yet these religious notions, with their messianic overtones, had not been expunged from the classical texts or from Jewish consciousness. They merely retreated temporarily so as to re-emerge and make their claim at another time.[12] "They think they have made Hebrew into a secular language, that they have removed its apocalyptic sting," wrote Gershom Scholem. "But that is not so . . . God will not remain dumb in the language in which He has been adjured so many thousands of times to come back into our lives."

"A SATANIC ACT"? "A DIVINE STATE"?

A single thread thus runs through the pre-Zionist messianic expectation of the Hatam Sofer, the anti-Zionist messianic expectation of Rabbi Shapira, and the messianic Zionist hope of Rabbi Kook: it is the uncompromising demand for utopian perfection—"Our holy ancestors could never have reconciled themselves to anything less than full redemption" (in the above-cited language of the Hatam Sofer). Moreover, both Rabbi Shapira and Rabbi Kook would agree that the only legitimate Jewish state is "one that has the highest of all ideals engraved in its being"; and both based these ideas upon Torah and the religious commandments. However, they differed deeply as to the actual significance of the new nationalist awakening and made contradictory predictions concerning its future.

What is the meaning of the Zionist revival? Is it simply a rebellion—abandonment of Torah and covenant, with the mundane replacing the piritual and the national claiming to take the place of the religious? Or is it, perhaps, first and foremost, a return to and a reforged link with our origins, a worldly national return (*shivah*) leading ultimately to a religious-spiritual return (*teshuvah*)? What would this "State of Israel" of the distant future look like, if it were to come into being? One may assume that today, almost two generations after the rise of the Jewish state, we have sufficient perspective to assess which of the two theses has been vindicated and which disproved—the forecast of the anti-Zionist ultra-Orthodox Jew, or the religious-Zionist forecast of Rabbi Kook's school. Or may it be that both alike have been disproved? One might answer, let the simple facts speak for themselves, let them decide between the contending positions. In the spiritual realm, however, firmly held a priori positions tend to be slow in giving way to "uncooperative realities." They assess events according to their own perspectives, regard developments in their own image, and at times go so far as to impose yesterday's forecasts on a recalcitrant current reality. All the more so when the realization of a vision, both spiritual and mundane, is relative and not absolute, partial and not complete, as is the case with every historical fulfillment. Indeed, during the past generation, controversy has deepened and ideological polarities have continued to sharpen. A variety of intermediate positions have also evolved. What seems to one person the attainment of destiny may seem to another a betrayal of that same destiny; what to some appears in the light of the Messiah will appear to others in the dark image of the anti-Messiah.

In fact, contemporary Orthodoxy offers a wide range of attitudes toward the State of Israel, from radical delegitimation to virtual beatification. It is said to be a "Satanic act," an "anti-Jewish state," a "regime which calls itself Israel," a "state ruled by Jews," "the state of the Jews," "the state of the Jewish people," "the state of the Congregation of Israel," "the pedestal of God's throne in this world," and, finally, "a divine state"![13] Moreover, the question of how to relate to Zionism and the Jewish state—no less than the older issue of how to relate to modern culture—is today a key issue dividing the various Orthodox factions. Indeed, the question of the State of Israel has proven even more divisive than the issue of modernity.

In the following study, I attempt to uncover the theological roots of the intense controversy within Israel concerning questions of religion, nation, and state; to trace the ideological sources of the various Orthodox positions; and to place these positions within a general conceptual framework. I emphasize particularly the process of radicalization that has taken place in different ideological groups in relation to the questions of Zionism and messianism. Thus the contours of our discussion and its division into chapters are shaped neither by political frameworks nor by ethnic viewpoint, but first and foremost by models of religious thought. The first chapter explains the historical and conceptual framework of the question of Zionism and messianism as it was presented to Jewish Orthodoxy at the beginning of the twentieth century. This chapter is primarily intended to set the necessary background for the discussion of contemporary phenomena that follows, rather than to challenge or refute conventional views or to break new paths in research.

The second chapter examines the radical anti-Zionist position: Neturei Karta, Satmar Hasidim, and the Edah Haredit of Jerusalem. These groups regard Zionism as a demonic, antimessianic eruption. To them, the Jewish political entity represents a collective rebellion against heaven and a betrayal of the unique Jewish destiny. As such, it is unworthy of the name "Israel." Consequently, the Zionist enterprise is foredoomed, and the full and miraculous redemption will eventually arise on its ruins. Chapter 2 traces the sources of the radical Haredi (ultra-Orthodox) ideology as it gradually evolved in Munkács, in Jerusalem, and in New York: beginning with an unprecedented demonization of the Land of Israel and culminating in a unique theology of separatism and zealotry.

The third chapter is devoted to the radical religious Zionism of the disciples of Rabbi Kook and the religious leadership of Gush Emunim. These groups regard the history of Zionism and the State of Israel as a clearly messianic process. The state is inherently holy. Indeed, human beings act within it as agents of Divine Providence. They are not "forcing the End," but rather being propelled and guided by it to act on the plane of history. The ultimate success of the enterprise—Israel's repentance and final redemption—is thus guaranteed in advance, despite temporary setbacks and reversals. The discussion traces the impact of the harmonious and deterministic conceptions in shaping this position, and stresses the radicalization that its devotees have undergone over the past two generations. I conclude chapter 3 by describing certain far-reaching messianic outbursts that have taken place at the margins of these groups.

The fourth chapter deals with the view most prevalent today among ultra-Orthodox (Haredi) Jews. For them, the era of exile persists despite the existence of the Jewish state, and indeed, even the Jews living there are still in exile, "the exile of Israel in the Holy Land." The appropriate attitude toward the state is a pragmatic, accommodating one. The state is recognized only de facto, and cooperation with it is reserved. Nevertheless, these circles have increasingly found themselves caught on the horns of a dilemma: what to make of this strange historical hybrid of Jewish sovereignty over the Holy Land prior to the dawn of the messianic age, led by transgressors of the Law. Chapter 4 focuses on the tension between the declared theology of these groups and their concrete existential reality within the Jewish state, that is, the consciousness of "exile," on the one hand, and the "danger" of messianic realization, on the other. I also consider their immanent difficulty to propose a coherent model for a legitimate, premessianic Jewish state, and examine the ideological confrontation of these groups with secular society.

The fifth and final chapter concerns the Ḥabad Hasidic movement and the profound changes it has undergone in recent generations—in light of the modern experience and within the State of Israel. While this Hasidic grouping is among the central contemporary Haredi streams, as described in chapter 4, the recent intense messianic ferment within this group—the like of which has not been known in Jewish history since the seventeenth century—is deserving of attention and requires a separate discussion. In this discussion I will thus focus on the transformation within Habad Hasidism, from conservatism to radical messianism.

Finally, since any Jewish religious ideology must base itself upon classical, authoritative sources, the present work may also be read as an attempt to uncover a series of new "midrashim" (contemporary interpretations) of the classical Jewish sources; these different readings all grew out of the encounter and confrontation between Jewish religious tradition and the modern Jewish-national revolution.

I

Messianism, Zionism, and Orthodoxy: Historical and Conceptual Background

The Zionist movement has from its inception appeared to the Orthodox religious leadership as a threatening paradox. It seemed to be a modernist Jewish movement that sought to overthrow the traditional way of life and rebelled against the imperatives of the past. Yet at the same time it looked backward: it employed the sacred symbols of the past and aspired to fulfill ancient Jewish hopes. The Zionist awakening was perceived by the rabbinic authorities as a secular human initiative, undertaken by heretics and freethinkers, which at the same time pretended to achieve goals traditionally associated with messianic hopes, and as such deeply grounded in religious faith. Note: Zionism wished to bring about the return to Zion and the ingathering of the exiles away from such classical, metaphysical concepts as reward and punishment, exile and redemption, covenant and promise, sin and atonement. The Zionists were eager to bring about a human, worldly redemption for their people. Their goal was to render the "Eternal People" a historical people, temporally and spatially bound; to transform the "Chosen People" into a "normal people," like other nations. Moreover, they claimed to offer national salvation against the background of the deepest spiritual rebellion (Enlightenment, reform, secularization) in Jewish exilic history. Did not Zionism thus threaten to breach into the holy sanctum, to "ravish the queen"—the messianic expectation, historical memory, and holy tongue— "in my own palace" (Esther 7:8)—in the Holy Land and the Holy City?

"THE CHARACTER OF MY PEOPLE"

In 1770 a certain non-Jew, "a man of rank," wrote to Moses Mendelssohn with a proposal for the establishment of a Jewish state in Palestine.[1] Mendelssohn, in a polite reply, expressed his esteem for this "great idea," lauding the courage of this individual, "who speaks of the realization of such a bold project." Not surprisingly, however, he rejected the idea on different grounds. Mendelssohn noted certain external, practical elements that would hinder the implementation of the plan.

However, he wrote, the decisive obstacle was in fact the mental makeup of the Jews themselves—their passivity and spirituality which, over the course of generations, had stamped itself on the Jewish people until it had become virtually second nature. Thus the Jewish people would ipso facto be incapable of executing a historical breakthrough or of undertaking a political initiative on a national scale. In the words of this Jewish philosopher: "The greatest obstacle in the way of this proposal is the character of my people. It is not ready to attempt anything so great. The pressure under which we have lived for centuries has removed all vigor from our spirit . . . the natural impulse for freedom has ceased its activity within us. It has been changed into a monkish piety, manifested in prayer and suffering, not in activity."[2] Mendelssohn thus ascribed the Jews' submissiveness and political impotence to their difficult straits and the travails of exile. Interestingly, on a different occasion, when Mendelssohn wished to reassure Gentiles as to the Jews' absolute civic loyalty, he offered a very different explanation for their apolitical behavior. The traditional Jewish passivity, he observed, was grounded in the binding provisions and stipulations of the Jewish religion—ab initio, not ex post facto—reflecting the common sense of the ancients, who deferred collective, national activity until the advent of the Messiah, thus enabling the Jews to adjust to a life of dispersion and exile. "The hoped-for return to Palestine," argued Mendelssohn, is reserved only "for synagogue and prayer," for the Jews' inner religious feeling alone, but "it has no influence on our conduct as citizens." "The Talmud forbids us to even think of a return to Palestine by force [to hasten the End by human effort]. Without the miracles and signs mentioned in the Scripture, we must not take the smallest step in the direction of forcing a return and a restoration of our nation. The Song of Songs expresses this prohibition in a somewhat mystical, yet captivating way, in the verse (2:7): 'I adjure you, O maidens of Jerusalem, by gazelles and by hinds of the field: do not wake or rouse love until it please [to come of itself].' "[3]

In brief, whether we speak about an acquired Jewish trait—the suppression of the "natural impulse toward freedom," engendered by hardship and oppression—about which Mendelssohn complained; or about an inherent Jewish viewpoint—the Talmudic injunction against "forcing the End," a viewpoint praised by Mendelssohn—in either case, the traditional political passivity of the Jews is perceived by this thinker as a basic characteristic marking the Jewish people in the time of exile.

Actually, a full century before Mendelssohn, Benedict Spinoza bemoaned the same mental trait of the Jews, which denies them the ability to engage in political initiative (and in military activity). He, too, held that this trait was the barrier to the renewal of their kingdom. Spinoza, however, did not consider this Jewish attribute to be the result of either hardship and distress or of any particular religious interdiction. He ascribed it to the overall nature of the Jewish religion—a religion that renders its adherents obeisant and servile: "If the foundations of their religion have not emasculated their minds, [the Jews] may even, if occasion offers—so changeable are human affairs—raise up their empire afresh, and God may a second time elect them."[4] (This last phrase is, of course, intended metaphorically, as a way of saying that the Jews will ultimately achieve a normal political existence.)[5] Spinoza's criteria for examining Jewish history are historical and sociological categories, not theological or metaphysical ones. Scholars have already noted that the conclusion to be inferred is that the Jews must make a fateful choice between two alternative paths. They may continue following their religion, with all its inherent traits, thereby forfeiting any prospect of a national-political revival. Or they may abandon their ancient faith and customs, thus reacquiring the greatness of spirit that is a sine qua non for their future national rebirth. In any event, according to Spinoza, the hypothetical rebuilding of the Jewish commonwealth is incontrovertibly dependent upon the prior secularization of the Jewish people.[6]

The brief remarks of these two philosophers, Spinoza and Mendelssohn, may be seen as adumbrating and incarnating an array of questions that, in time, would be at the center of the religious controversy concerning Zionism and messianism: What is the nature of the prohibited "forcing of the End"? How is one to interpret a nonmessianic Jewish national renewal, which occurred at a historically propitious moment ("if occasion offers") and not at the End of Days? Is a naturalistic return to Zion possible— "without miracles and great wonders"—that does not inherently flaunt Jewish uniqueness and abjure the metaphysical dimension of Jewish history? Furthermore, does the traditional Jewish passivity reflect a historical "accident" and decline, which then evolved under the hardships of the Exile? Or should it be seen as the result of the judicious practical guidance of the Sages of Israel? Alternatively, is that passivity rooted in a substantive religious principle and a binding imperative? Finally, what is the true aim of Zionism? Do the Zionists rebel only against the Jewish fate and Jewish passivity, or does their revolt entail the eradication of Judaism itself—that is, the uprooting of the entire religious tradition, which (like Spinoza before them) they blamed for the national disposition to political submission and historical inaction?

MESSIANISM AND PASSIVITY

In light of all the above-mentioned problems, the majority of Orthodox leaders condemned Zionism from its very outset. Needless to say, their criticism was leveled first and foremost at the secularity of the national idea and the Zionist leaders' and settlers' repudiation of religious practice. Some prominent rabbis also opposed the Zionist initiative for pragmatic reasons, depicting the enterprise as hopelessly deluded and unrealistic. It was on theological grounds, however, that some of the most important critics took the new movement to task, striking its root from the standpoint of traditional messianic faith.

Even when they did not say so explicitly, the Orthodox opponents of Zionism saw it as a direct threat to traditional ways of thought—to nothing less, that is, than the theological interpretation of Jewish history—and not only to traditional practices. No wonder, then, that the issue of the relationship between Zionism and messianism soon became a central question: no longer confined to the realm of intuitive aversion and protest, it now became a subject for direct debate and eloquent ideological formulation.

To some, even the earliest initiatives of the Hibbat Zion movement—a precursor to political Zionism—evoked old echoes of false messianism. "They are a new sect like that of Shabbatai Zevi, may the names of evildoers rot"—fulminated the rabbi of Brisk, Joseph Baer Soloveichik (1889).[7] Ten years later, following in his father's footsteps, his great son, Rabbi Hayyim Soloveichik, was equally unsparing in his castigation of the new Zionist movement: "Regarding the 'Zionist sect,' which has now banded and united together by force . . . Have they not a bad reputation in their own places, and is not their purpose to uproot the fundaments of [our] religion—and to this end also to take control of all the Jewish communities . . . The people of Israel should take care not to join a venture that threatens their souls, to destroy religion, and is a stumbling block to the

House of Israel."[8] True, this admonition was primarily directed against the secular nationalist agitation rather than against Zionism's messianic aspect. Nevertheless, to the traditional Jew, the trenchant phrase—"the Zionist sect, which has now banded and united together by force"—might well bring to mind the ancient warning against forcing the End: "The Holy One, blessed be He, has adjured Israel 'not to ascend the wall,'" the Talmud states (BT Ketubbot 111a; see below); and Rashi glosses, "'Not to ascend,' together, by force!"

Such was the rebuke of some Lithuanian rabbinic authorities (the Mitnaggedim). Harsh imprecations against Zionism were also voiced in this period by many Orthodox leaders in Western Europe. But the latter, in their distinctive ideological tone, had already addressed the messianic question explicitly. Thus, on the eve of the First Zionist Congress in 1897, the National Organization of German Rabbis denounced "the efforts of the so-called Zionists to establish a Jewish national state in the Land of Israel," representing these efforts as "conflicting with the messianic goals of Judaism, as these are expressed in the Scriptures and in other religious sources."[9] David Vital has already noted that no other national Jewish organization was so far-reaching in its public repudiation of Zionism. Indeed, such a public declaration cannot be viewed apart from the open desire of Germany's rabbis to demonstrate their civic loyalty (as seen above in Mendelssohn's remarks). This element, however, does not negate the declaration's basic, authentic theological approach.

But it was above all the castigation of Zionism by the Hasidic Rebbes of Eastern Europe that focused this discussion on the messianic issue. It was these religious leaders, never content with formal halakhic criteria and always seeking to delve into the theological significance of events and deeds, who placed the question of messianic redemption and the metaphysical singularity of Israel at the forefront of the Orthodox polemic against Zionism.

Such tendencies are discernible as early as the 1860s, in the initial Hasidic responses to the call of the "Harbingers of Zionism." These critical reactions intensified as Zionism evolved a formal organization and made inroads in the social and political realm. Recent research[10] suggests that the traditional fear of "forcing the End" and of rebelling against the exilic decree was far deeper and more widespread in Hasidic circles than historians have thought. The Zionist enterprise thus rendered these anxieties more concrete. To illustrate this point, we shall examine the polemical writings of the contemporaneous Lubavitcher Rebbe, the highly influential leader of the Habad movement during the early period of Zionism.

Starting in 1899, the Lubavitcher Rebbe, Rabbi Shalom Dov Baer

Schneersohn, laid the cornerstone of a principled ultra-Orthodox (Haredi) critique of Zionism.[11] Schneersohn gave extensive attention to the messianic argument, devoting considerable energy to implanting the idea that a political Zionist awakening as such—quite apart from the movement's secular character—was a denial of messianism, both because of Zionism's arrogance in seeking to bring redemption through human efforts, and because it stopped short of the perfection of the original messianic vision. I shall present these two arguments more fully, as an archetype of the Orthodox anti-Zionist theological polemic.

Forcing the End

Schneersohn attacked the Zionist aspiration of changing the condition of the Jewish people during the epoch of exile through a collective incursion into history. National reawakening and a return to the Land of Israel in order to achieve political sovereignty are not, in this view, religiously neutral acts. They represent a human effort to realize decidedly messianic expectations—the ingathering of the exiles, liberation from "subjugation to the great powers"—expectations whose fulfillment should depend solely on the transcendental and miraculous intervention of the Savior of Israel. Zionism thus appears to be a blatant violation of the oath sworn by the Jewish people to wait patiently until the End of Days, a betrayal of the religious norm of exile.

Schneersohn placed particular stress on the latter argument. Even if the other two arguments against the national movement were to lose their validity—that is, if all the Zionists were to become "submissive to the Lord and His Torah," and a real possibility arose of achieving their goal—"we must not heed them in their call to achieve redemption on our own, for we are not permitted to hasten the End even by reciting too many prayers,[12] much less so by corporeal stratagems, that is, to set out from exile by force."[13] The theological argument against Zionism thus stands on its own.

At times Schneersohn went even further, portraying the messianic question as the very pivot upon which the entire secular national idea turned. As we have seen, he regarded Zionism as a clear-cut secularization of the traditional messianic concept, that is, a transfer of initiative from divine to human hands. Now secularization cannot be partial; since the messianic vision has always been rooted in a comprehensive religious matrix, the Zionists are compelled to destroy that matrix, denying traditional religious faith in its entirety. That is, the Zionists' desire to throw off the yoke of passive messianism kindles in them a desire to liberate the Jewish people from the strictures of religion in general: they are trying to escape

Jewish destiny, and to do so they must first abandon the Torah and faith of Israel. Schneersohn explains: "In order to infuse our brethren with the idea of being a 'nation' and an independent polity . . . the Zionists must give nationalism precedence over the Torah, because it is known that those who cling to the Torah and the commandments are not likely to change and accept another identity, especially such as is implied in leaving exile by force and redeeming themselves by their own power . . . Hence, in order to implement their idea, the Zionists must distort the essence [of Jewishness] in order to get [the Jews] to assume a different identity."[14]

These remarks can be read as a mirror image of statements made by some of the most vociferous secular authors in condemnation of passive messianic belief and of the entire Jewish tradition that fostered that belief. At the same time, the Rebbe did not hesitate to argue against the Zionist pretension that "we are rendered incapable of this by our [Jewish!] trait."[15] In other words, the very nature of the Jews during the epoch of exile is inconsistent with a life of worldly activity and political initiative. In contrast to Spinoza, Mendelssohn (in one context), and the radical Zionist writers—who deplored this "Jewish trait"—the Lubavitcher Rebbe considered it a positive virtue. As he put it: "Our God-fearing brethren know that they are under the yoke of the Exile and that they need to be submissive in every situation . . . For this [reason], even after the heavy yoke that has been imposed upon them at various times, and despite all the persecutions and oppressions they have suffered, they are able to find themselves an [existential, internal] 'place.' [Paradoxically,] it is the nature of the soft to resist the hard [and to overcome it]."[16]

In short, from the viewpoint of the ultra-Orthodox leader, "softness of soul" and political submissiveness are the guarantee of Jewish existence in nonmessianic times. In the final analysis, physical inferiority is a source of strength and tenaciousness. As Rabbi Maimon the Dayan (Maimonides' father) observed long before, in his "Letter of Consolation" written in the twelfth century: "While the current destroys walls and sweeps along rocks, the soft thing remains standing. Thus the Exile destroys and breaks and uproots great pillars and enormous walls, but the Holy One, blessed be He, saves the weak and soft nation, that the current not sweep it along."[17] Nevertheless, to the Lubavitcher Rebbe, all such practical considerations are subordinate to the crucial theological principle: the Jew's traditional passivity most faithfully expresses devotion to the final redemption. Israel, the singular people, retreat from mundane history to immerse themselves in the four cubits of religious practice and faith.

Stopping Short of Perfection

Schneersohn had a further criticism of Zionism vis-à-vis messianism. All human activity is ipso facto incomplete, relative, and transient, and therefore must fall short of the yearned-for messianic redemption. Only by drawing a clear distinction between the two and removing the latter as far as possible from the realm of worldly salvation can the fullness of the final redemption be assured. Schneersohn stresses the utopian character of such redemption, rejecting the restoration under Cyrus and even the Exodus from Egypt (!)[18] as models: "The redemption that took place through Moses and Aaron was also not a full one, for the Jewish people were once again [to be enslaved, to Babylonia]; and even less so was the redemption at the hands of Hananiah, Mishael, and Azariah [i.e., the creation of the Second Commonwealth] . . . In the present exile we must expect redemption and salvation only at the hands of the Holy One, blessed be He, Himself, not by flesh and blood, and thus will our redemption be complete."[19]

The view proposed by the Hatam Sofer in a more abstract context (see the introduction) was now sharpened and aimed directly at the concrete phenomenon of Zionism. It is noteworthy that Schneersohn also rejected out of hand the prevalent religious-Zionist view (see below) that the ingathering of the exiles and the rebuilding of Jerusalem were to be part of a gradual process, to be initiated "little by little" by human beings but completed by God. Basing himself on certain classical religious texts, he declared that the ingathering of the exiles to Zion would depend entirely on a miraculous, revolutionary, and decisive messianic revelation, and would therefore take place only after the transcendent rebuilding of Jerusalem and the Temple ("which will be built from Above").[20] The redemption of Israel would thus be both initiated and completed by heavenly powers.

Schneersohn thus combines two classical messianic tenets—the requirement of human passivity and the quest for perfection—and makes them interdependent. Zionism is the antithesis of both these principles; it represents both activism and the acceptance of partial fulfillment, and is therefore doomed to failure. Thus he pronounced in a 1904 epistle: "Their presumptuous goal of gathering [the exiles] together on their own will never come to pass [!], and all their strength and their many stratagems and efforts will be of no avail against the will of the Lord. They will try one idea after another, like garments, but it is the counsel of the Lord that will prevail. He alone, may He be blessed, will gather us up and assemble us from the four corners of the earth."[21]

As previously noted, the fear that the Zionist enterprise would uproot messianic faith was articulated at that time by other Eastern European Hasidic Rebbes as well. Some of them stressed other aspects of the danger: they warned their followers against the radical transformation that Zionism was wreaking on the Jewish hope of redemption, and on Jewish faith in general—from the spiritual and miraculous to the earthly and natural. For example, the Bialer Rebbe, Yitzhak Ya'akov Rabinowitz, argued shortly after the emergence of Zionism:

> [Zionism represents] the struggle of the Evil Urge and its assistants, who wish to bring us down, heaven forbid, by false and harmful opinions, claiming that, if Israel will not perform some concrete action to settle in the Holy Land and to actually work the land, then they will be unable to leave this bitter exile, heaven forbid . . . This falsified view has strengthened in our time, due to our great sins . . . The Zionists likewise wish to join together and to unite against God and His Messiah. In fact, Israel have no greater foe and enemy, who wish to deprive them of their pure faith, that our salvation and redemption transcends the way of nature and human intelligence; that He, may He be blessed, watches over us with a sharp eye in our exile, and "in all our troubles He is troubled" [Isa. 63:9], so to speak.[22]

Not long afterward (1902), Rabbi M. N. Kahane-Shapira of Kishunez wrote in a similar vein: "Heaven forbid that we walk in the way of these sinful people, who strive for natural redemption. This striving is forbidden . . . The act of *teshuvah* (repentance) alone is a legitimate means to hasten the End, but acts of ingathering [the exiles] and of bringing [Israel to their land] depend solely upon the hand of God: 'Unless the Lord builds the house, its builders labor in vain on it; unless the Lord watches over the city, the watchman keeps vigil in vain' [Ps. 127:1]."[23]

It bears stressing that the fear of "forcing the End" and of using natural means to trespass in the realm of the messianic was not an anti-Zionist innovation of a particular school. It has deep roots in classical Jewish literature, and left its clear mark in the medieval and modern eras. The generations preceding the emergence of Zionism saw numerous sages who urged the Jewish people to abide by the principle of passivity and accept the yoke of the Exile. As I shall argue later on, this motif had a far greater impact historically than recent scholarship would indicate.

But it was the Lubavitcher Rebbe, the highly influential Hasidic leader during the early years of Zionism, who made this traditional motif the focal point of the ultra-Orthodox struggle against the Jewish national movement. (Other rebbes generally confined themselves to the sermons addressed to an inner circle of Hasidim;[24] hence their ideas did not reach the general public.) To illustrate Schneersohn's crucial impact, I shall compare two polemical works that appeared around this time. The first is *Or la-yesharim,* published in Warsaw in 1900, a well-known collection of letters condemning Zionism. The contributors include some of the greatest rabbis of the day, but of these, only Schneersohn sees fit to present the messianic argument in detail.[25] The others generally focus their criticism on the Zionists' antireligiosity. Two years later, however, in *Da'at ha-Rabbanim,* a second collection in the same spirit published in Warsaw, the messianic argument has become central, and the writers dwell on it at length. For example, Rabbi Yerahmiel Minzberg of Likiva, in a direct paraphrase of Maimonides' admonition against the messianic agitation in Yemen, wrote: "The Zionist movement is a massive entreaty to terminate the Exile before the appointed time."[26] Furthermore, Rabbi Minzberg argued: "Even if the king of the Turks—may he be honored—or any rulers should permit the people of God to go up to their holy land, their patrimony, as was the previous redemption in the time of Ezra; if this redemption will not stem from the Great Redeemer Himself in His Glory . . . we shall say: This is not the path to the true salvation, or the long-desired goal. We shall not even consider it for temporal and incidental redemption, but only as a fly in the ointment."[27] As we have already found, the partial and the transitory contradict the perfect; the natural, historical realization does not pave the way to utopia, but denies it outright. Theologically, therefore, even the assent of the Gentile rulers and their desire to restore the Jewish people to its home are immaterial.[28] That return, too, is to be considered a trespass by human hands against the ultimate messianic redemption. Others in this collection (*Da'at ha-Rabbanim*) wrote in a similar spirit. Indeed, one must not ignore the fact that this latter collection, unlike *Or la-yesharim,* primarily represents the views of Hasidic rabbis, who could be expected to show greater sensitivity to theological matters that transcend the formal halakhic sphere. For these rabbis, the metaphysical domain is all-pervasive and leaves no "empty space," no religiously neutral realm of human activity. In any case, the question of Zionism is henceforth frequently examined in the light of messianism.

ASPECTS OF REDEMPTION

The messianic idea in Judaism has always been marked by inner tension and profound disagreement.[29] As early as the Talmudic era, we find significant differences of opinion on the subject of eschatology. Among the issues are, What is the role of human action in preparation for the messianic era?

Will the yearned-for redemption occur gradually ("little by little") or break forth all at once ("in the wink of an eye")? Will the time of redemption depend solely upon the Jews' repentance or also upon a divine decree? Is redemption necessarily to revolve around the human figure of a personal Messiah? Will the messianic age usher in a change in the Torah and the Halakhah?

Disagreements over the nature of the final redemption occasionally become acute and fundamental. At one end of the spectrum is the limited notion of political emancipation, the liberation of the Jewish people from "subjugation to the great powers." At the other extreme is the hope for cosmic redemption and a profound change in nature itself, leading to an entirely new world order, literally "a new heaven and a new earth" (Isa. 65:17). Moreover, there were those who yearned for redemption in a concrete, immediate way, while others stressed the dreadful "birth pangs," the apocalyptic suffering and catastrophe, to precede the advent of the Messiah. For the latter, fear sometimes outweighed desire, an attitude expressed by several *amoraim:* "Let him come, but let me not see him in my lifetime!" (BT Sanhedrin 98a).

The sharpness of these disagreements was not diminished by the passage of time. To the contrary, mystics and philosophers, preachers and halakhists, doomsayers and eschatological visionaries, all continued to elaborate new notions of redemption or stressed different aspects of the old notions. For example, one may note a severe narrowing of messianic expectations in Maimonides' *Code,* which describes national redemption in purely natural, historical, worldly terms: "Let no one think that in the days of the Messiah any of the laws of nature will be set aside or any innovation introduced into creation . . . Do not think that the King Messiah will have to perform signs or wonders or bring anything new into being."[30] In the teachings of Rabbi Isaac Abrabanel and Rabbi Judah Löw, the Maharal, of Prague, on the other hand, a far more apocalyptic view is expressed.[31] These scholars look forward to the end of history and yearn for a radical change in the nature of the cosmos and man. As the Maharal puts it: "This world is the world of nature, the material world; but the Messiah stands above this world, on another plane . . . Let there be a new world, let there be a world separate [from matter]."[32] These two examples suffice to indicate how wide is the range of Jewish messianic beliefs.

Any attempt to define messianism, then, entails a process of (not necessarily conscious) choice among the differing views found in the sources. This is also true of the Haredi theological position in its arguments against Zionism. As noted above, that position accords primacy to utopian messianism—"no eye has seen it" (Isa. 64:3)—over the restorative variety—"renew our days as of old" (Lam. 5:21). It comprehends messianism in miraculous and supernatural terms rather than in concrete, political terms. It yearns for a transcendent redemption that arrives all at once—"and the Lord whom you seek shall come to His temple suddenly" (Mal. 3:1)—rather than that gradual redemption whose light dawns "little by little."[33] By the same token, this view makes redemption dependent on repentance, on preparation of an exclusively spiritual nature, detached from all mundane human activity. Consequently, it favors the traditional quietism and historical passivity, as opposed to the attitude that permits certain kinds of activism. And when it comes to the question of the Holy Land—the conflict between its powerful attraction and the fear of not living up to the severe religious demands entailed in dwelling there (see chapter 2)—this view gives greater weight to the fear.

A clear pattern emerges from these choices: the vision of redemption is exalted as far as possible above "the present time," and in many cases the Land of Israel, in its holiness, rises along with it, far above "the present place." Thus a great barrier is erected between concrete historical reality and high hopes for the future. Such separations make it possible to avert an outburst of acute messianic enthusiasm in the here and now, protecting the given social order from being overthrown. The End of Days is postponed, denying the legitimacy of any concrete messianic pretension and fending off any threat to the status quo and to public tranquility during the era of exile.

Historical precedents show that it is precisely the effort to restrain the hope of redemption and confine it within mundane and realistic bounds that is liable—when the time is ripe—to bring messianic tension to a head.[34] In a seemingly paradoxical way, it is precisely the moderate image of redemption that, seizing upon a suitable personality or circumstance, is most likely to provoke a tempest of messianic fervor. In contrast, it is the miraculous, supernatural, utopian vision of redemption that, in many cases, succeeds in blocking the way, preserving and defending the status quo.

Of course the latter model, as exemplified in the Haredi theological response to Zionism, does not reflect merely polemical needs or an ad hoc choice. Involved here are fundamental tendencies and patterns of thought, anchored in a long-standing tradition. In fact, they faithfully reflect the messianic view prevalent among Jewish believers for many generations in exile. Note that even in the popular images of a Messiah who descends from on high as a living, accessible figure, a personality known almost intimately who stands at the gate ("outside our wall") waiting to enter our city, it is not we ourselves or any conveyance of ours that will bring him in. On the contrary, these depictions usually deny the value of any practical human action, any mundane causal process, in preparing the Messiah's way. Only by studying the Torah today can we bring about his sudden coming tomorrow. Indeed, according to one perspicacious Talmudic saying, the Messiah is numbered among those things that come when one is not particularly expecting them (BT Sanhedrin 97b: "Three things come unawares: the Messiah, a found object, and a scorpion!"). Or, as we find in an insightful parable attributed to Rabbi Hayyim of Volozhin (d. 1821), the founder of the Lithuanian yeshivot: "Thus will be the advent of the Messiah: you will be sitting in your room alone studying, and your wife will suddenly enter and say, 'Oy, Hayyim! You are sitting here studying? Don't you know the Messiah has come?' Startled, you will spit three times and say to her, 'Who told you?' And she will say to you, 'Go outside and see for yourself: not a soul is left in the city, not even the babes in their cradles, for everyone has gone out to greet [him].' "35

In sum, both the intimate and the more remote images of redemption display a marked tendency toward passive, miracle-centered messianism. This strong emphasis is thus not peculiar to any one school, and is certainly not a new idea. Undoubtedly, however, the direct confrontation with Zionism greatly contributed to sharpening this traditional passive posture and raising it to consciousness, bringing it from the margins to the center, at times transforming it from a mere folk image into a well-defined concept.

What about the fear of "forcing the End" or of mass immigration to the Land of Israel? As we have seen, many of the Zionists' Orthodox adversaries actually made the traditional attitude of passivity into a binding religious demand, an absolute norm of the epoch of exile. Not only, they maintained, could the return to Zion not succeed if initiated naturally, by human beings, but it was also forbidden by decree and by oath. Of course, this view, too, originated in the classical sources: it is based on the primeval myth of the children of Ephraim, who went up from Egypt prematurely, "transgressed the End and the oath," and fell by the sword.36 Beyond this, it is rooted in the oaths that the Jewish people were made to swear—according to the Midrash and the Talmud—"that Israel not ascend the wall" from the exile, "that they not rebel against the nations of the world," and that "they not force the End" (although another version has "that they not postpone the End"—*yirḥaku* rather than *yidḥaku!*) (Cant. R. 2:7; BT Ketubbot 111a). The Talmudic midrash goes on to tell of a parallel oath imposed upon the nations of the world: "that they not oppress Israel overly much." It is as though the Exile were based on a status quo between Israel and the nations—between the oppressed and the rulers—in which both sides are called upon to maintain stability and not violate the other's boundaries.

What accounts for the revival enjoyed by these sources in recent generations? Did the religious critique against Zionism, by clinging to a few forgotten midrashim, imbue them, in the heat of debate, with a new content such as they never before possessed? This indeed is the picture that seems to emerge from recent historical studies on the question of Zionism and religion. According to these works, the use of the "oaths" as an argument against *aliyah* was mainly, or even wholly, an innovation of Western European proponents of the Emancipation and of Zionism's opponents in Eastern Europe. Contemporary scholars explain that throughout Jewish history this motif was perceived as something aggadic and nonbinding. While at times it was cited to justify the duration of the Exile, it was never adduced in a normative, practical sense as a warning against immigration to and settlement in the Land of Israel. Even when organized groups actually settled in the Land of Israel, this prohibition was not voiced.[37]

This approach needs to be revised. As I noted in the introduction, this chapter does not endeavor to challenge conventional views or to break new paths in research; it is meant to set the ideational background for an understanding of contemporary religious trends. Since my conclusions on the subject of the oaths differ from the prevailing scholarly ideas, however, I shall now briefly summarize those conclusions. An appendix to this book sets forth the matter in detail and cites the relevant evidence in medieval and modern Jewish literature.

It is true that the "three oaths" were more widely used in the twentieth century than in the nineteenth, and in the nineteenth century more than in the eighteenth. Indeed, they were more widespread in the modern era than in the Middle Ages. Naturally, during those long centuries in which neither Land of Israel nor "ascending the wall" (i.e., collectively) from exile was a concrete social option, the very fear of such actions was overcome and repressed by the Jewish nation, and with them the importance of the "oaths" also faded. In contrast, when the Land of Israel was perceived as a substantive possibility, and Jews actually settled there, the warning was again frequently voiced—especially when acute messianic agitation was involved.

This is quite clear in material from the medieval period. For example, in the early thirteenth century several groups of French-Jewish sages (from the school of the Tosaphists) settled in the Land of Israel. Their action was soon emulated by other sages in the West, thus making *aliyah* to the land an accepted pattern of behavior among scholarly circles. Interestingly enough, at that very time, not far away, some distinguished figures among the medieval German pietists (*Hasidei Ashkenaz*) explicitly warned people against *aliyah*. Thus it was said that those who went to the land would not expiate their sins: on the contrary, they "further multiply transgression." Another writer railed against any Jew who would burst into the Holy Land, making tremendous effort to block the way there by a fortified wall: "'Beware of going up the mountain' [Exod. 19:12]—for He has adjured Israel not to force the End and not go up to the Land of Israel prematurely . . . Whoever hastens shall not live—whoever goes up before the End—for while the Exile persists they shall not go free."

The remoteness of the Land of Israel, and the recoil from transgressing the edict of the oaths, subsequently reappeared among the Gerona Kabbalists—the very same circle from which would later come the most famous figure among those who settled in the Land of Israel in that period, Moses Nahmanides. His own *aliyah* was set against clear disagreements with his colleagues concerning the mystical and halakhic status of the land. The warning against *aliyah* would again be voiced in fifteenth-century Spain, in the face of the mass immigration by the Jews of Castile: "Let all those making this move turn back, let every person return home in peace, and not hasten the End as the children of Ephraim did, heaven forbid." The oaths were heard again, in surprising contexts, in the aftermath of the expulsions from Spain and Portugal. A similar protest was sparked by the *aliyah* of messianic groups such as that of Judah he-Hasid, which "ascended the wall to the Land of Israel" in 1700, and by the famous *aliyah* of the Perushim in the early nineteenth century. Paradoxically, then, the appearance of the adjurations of passivity acts like a seismograph, revealing concrete historical traces of the Land of Israel and its genuine presence in the life of different communities. Differently put, the repeated emergence of this idea is indicative of the profound tension, in Jewish texts and in Jewish life alike, between the attraction and fascination exercised by the land, and its power to frighten and deter.

Of course, our primary concern here is with theological and existential motifs, rather than Halakhic prohibition. Nevertheless, it bears noting that in the later Middle Ages, in the wake of concrete questions concerning *aliyah,* the edict of the oaths seeped into saliently halakhic literature too. Thus Rabbi Isaac ben Sheshet Perfet, "Ribash," who saw *aliyah* as an ongoing commandment, took care to qualify his views by citing the oath that "they not ascend in the wall" from the Exile against the will of the ruling nations. In the same spirit, Rabbi Solomon ben Simeon Duran, "Rashbash," likewise ruled: "It is incumbent upon every individual to go up to live there . . . However, this is not an all-inclusive commandment for all of Israel in their exile . . . for it is one of the oaths that the Holy One, blessed be He, has adjured Israel, that they not hasten the End, and not go up in the wall." The words of these sages reveal an interesting new metamorphosis of the classical tension generated by the question of the Land of Israel: on the one hand, the attractive power of the land is reflected in the halakhic argument, that is, in the commandment to settle the Land of Israel; on the other hand, its repellent power is reflected in the theological argument, namely, the decree of exile imposed upon the Congregation of Israel. Thus, even in these halakhic responses, precisely the appearance of the "oaths" demonstrates most clearly how *aliyah* had become a concrete social issue at the time, which the leading authorities of the era were called upon to consider in halakhic terms.

I will not survey here the many transformations undergone by the oaths in the generations that followed, eventually acting as an admonition against Sabbateanism and its later manifestations. "For at that time [the period of Sabbatai Zvi]," Rabbi Moses Hagiz wrote in the early eighteenth century, "the plague began. Nearly all the people of Israel were exposed to the danger . . . and they were on the brink of death, heaven forbid, to be judged as rebels and violators of the oath which the Holy One, blessed be He, imposed upon Israel, while they are in exile among Edom [Christianity] and Ishmael [Islam]." Or, in the words of the great combatant against Sabbateanism and its secret believers, Rabbi Jacob Emden: "It was then a time of grace; redemption was imminent, had the Sabbateans not forced the hour and violated the oath."

These few examples are sufficient to illustrate the living presence of the idea of the oaths and the fear it aroused in the sages across the generations, finally intensifying in the nineteenth century, to the point where it became a become a central motif in Hasidic thought in Eastern Europe and in Western European Orthodox thought.

Of course, we must not unduly exaggerate the historical significance of these "oaths," and certainly not their Halakhic status; they clearly never enjoyed the crucial standing with which they were imbued in the aftermath of the Holocaust by the radical opponents of Zionism (see chapter 2). But they were always lurking just off the main road of Jewish history, bursting in from time to time to block the path that ascended to the Holy Land.

No wonder, then, that the advent of the Zionist national movement should again arouse, and more strongly still, the traditional fear of human trespassing of the "End" and against mass migration to the Land of Israel.

Compounding this attitude, of course, was the basic resistance to Zionism's secular character and to the way in which the movement's leaders and settlers ran roughshod over the halakhah. The upshot was that the modern Jewish national revival actually brought about a heightening of the passive ideology, together with a previously unknown emphasis on the heavenly and spiritual character of the messianic redemption.

As these developments are nowhere more striking than in Lubavitch Hasidism, I shall conclude the discussion, as I opened it, by considering that movement. During the first generations of the Ḥabad movement very little was written about the messianic question (this was true of Hasidism generally at the time).[38] Ḥabad's spiritual leaders were far more concerned with the question of the ongoing Divine Presence in the world[39] than with that of a transcendent breakthrough in the future. But such a neutralizing silence could no longer hold sway against a real movement of national reawakening, clearly perceived as "forcing the End" and usurping the messianic prerogative. Here a direct and explicit response became necessary, and indeed such is to be found in Shalom Dov Baer Schneersohn's writings (see above). This matter is taken up in greater depth in chapter 5, which deals also with the manifest discontinuity between the silence of the earlier generations of Ḥabad leadership and the acute messianic tension that has characterized Ḥabad Hasidism in the past two generations.

MESSIANISM AND ACTIVISM

During the nineteenth century, a few Orthodox ideologues began to articulate a different, more activistic and worldly vision of redemption. Some even called upon the Jewish public to take a messianic initiative: to begin a gradual process of immigration to and agricultural settlement in the Land of Israel, as a necessary and organic step toward full redemption. They also tried to develop practical programs, some quite far-reaching, for furthering this enterprise. These figures, including Rabbi Judah Alkalai (Serbia, d. 1878), Rabbi Zvi Hirsch Kalischer (Prussia, d. 1874), and other "Lovers of Zion" who espoused these views (such as Rabbi Eliyahu Golomb and Rabbi Nathan Friedland), succeeded in attracting a modest following, and were later known as the "Harbingers of Zionism."[40]

It is noteworthy that in earlier sources as well, particularly those connected with the name of the Vilna Gaon, one finds allusions to the possibility of redemption coming by a natural process and various hints connecting this possibility with concrete settlement in the Land of Israel.[41] However, the thrust of these ideas was primarily mystical, and they were restricted to elite circles of eschatologists. This was not the case with the comprehensive ideas and practical public goals of the Harbingers. We will therefore examine their distinctive doctrine of redemption in some detail.

Where did this doctrine originate? As we have seen, classical messianic faith was marked by inner tensions and disagreements, but for many generations the passivist tendency had enjoyed the upper hand. However, it should not have been surprising if source texts and ideas relegated to obscurity were to emerge at some opportune moment and demand their due. That is, more activistic, realistic messianic views might, in certain circles, come to reassert their appeal and be rehabilitated as living, authentic options. Indeed, just such a revival did occur in the circles we are discussing.

For one thing, it was just the right historical moment for activist ideas to come to the fore. The Harbingers' vigorous efforts to turn messianic hopes once again into a force for change were closely connected with events taking place around them, for these men were clearly influenced by the national struggles then raging in Europe. The profound changes they observed taking place in the condition of the Jews—Emancipation, on the one hand, and renewed persecution, on the other—significantly shaped their views. Moreover, they had largely internalized the dynamism and receptiveness to innovation that characterized modernity, and took a more practical, rational attitude toward historical change than was usual in their traditional surroundings. As Alkalai put it: "The spirit of the times has freed all the inhabitants of the earth to live where they wish and granted them freedom to travel from country to country; it calls upon us 'to say to the prisoners [the Jewish people], "Go free!"' [Isa. 49:9]. The spirit of the times summons every [people] to reclaim its sovereignty and raise up its language; so too does it demand of us that we reestablish [Zion], the center of our life, and raise up our holy language and revive it."[42] The "spirit of the times" affecting the peoples of Europe was sounding its call to the Jewish people as well. Of course, from the author's point of view this was none other than the call of Divine Providence, directing history toward a messianic turning point.

At the same time, these new ideas were deeply immersed in the reservoir of classical Jewish concepts and sources, stirring up long dormant messianic elements, and causing the ancient seeds of activism to germinate and grow. These thinkers thus challenged the prevailing passive concept of messianism with confidence in their grounding in tradition. They went so far as to castigate the popular view of the Messiah as heretical, an obstacle in the nation's path. Kalischer warned, "If a man should come before you and sanctimoniously declare, orally or in writing, that the Messiah will be sent from heaven at one stroke, you should pour coals upon his head, saying, 'You are a denier of prophecy!' "[43] In the same spirit, his ally Alkalai writes: "Our holy rabbis are delaying the consolation of our land . . . The people expect a man to come from heaven in a fiery horse-drawn chariot and gather up the scattered remnant of Israel . . . [But] this outworn idea has become a stumbling block to the people of Israel."[44]

The two are thus forced to delve into Jewish literature and either extract from it an activistic, practical approach (as does Kalischer) or at least find in it sanction for such an approach (as does Alkalai). As we shall see, they thereby contribute greatly to the creation of a new, Zionist midrash (i.e., homiletical reworking) of the classical messianic texts. In time, this new midrash would confront that propounded by the ultra-Orthodox camp and compete with it for the people's hearts.

Disregarding certain personal differences between them, what are the basic assumptions underlying the messianic views of these rabbis? How do their views differ from the traditional tenets of Orthodoxy?

To begin with, the Harbingers see messianic redemption not as a one-time event but as a process, not as revolution but as evolution. Redemption will not burst forth as full-blown perfection, but will unfold gradually. "Israel's salvation will come little by little; slowly will the horn of redemption flower" (Kalischer).[45] Indeed, the Jerusalem Talmud and various midrashim compare redemption to the light of the morning star, which shines higher and higher each day: "Thus will be the redemption of Israel . . . first it will glimmer, then sparkle, then shine forth more and more brightly" (Cant. R. 6:16).[46] This early source became the archetype and credo of the new messianism, sweeping other traditional sources aside. (The same is still true: not for naught did the present Lubavitcher Rebbe find it necessary to assert that Maimonides had ruled conclusively against this midrash (!) and that "redemption will not come little by little.")[47]

Thus the messianism of the Harbingers, in contrast to the prevalent Haredi one, no longer regards partial national reconstruction as a phenomenon that shatters, uproots, and destroys the whole, but rather as an organic link in the very development of that whole. As such, partial redemption becomes legitimate. By the same token, this doctrine neutralizes certain revolutionary elements that have accompanied the messianic idea, removing from it the paradoxical tone of crisis with which it has always been overlaid. On the contrary, it assumed a decidedly optimistic stand toward historical events: the messianic process had its beginning in the Emancipation of European Jewry (especially according to Kalischer and Friedland); it would continue to advance with the help of the enlightened nations, which would assist in the restoration of the Jewish people to its land; and it would culminate in full, universal human redemption. Redemption, then, no longer comes out of the depths or in the wake of cataclysm, but rather by a gradual, step-by-step process.

Second, a clear distinction is drawn between the messianic process, which is a concrete historical development, and the messianic goal, a utopia that transcends history. Although redemption moves forward along a natural, human course—the gradual ingathering of the exiles and resettlement of the land—it is to be completed with a miraculous divine revelation that bursts beyond the boundaries of both man and nature. This distinction between the ongoing process and the final goal allows the believer to regard the present as an open field for mundane human activity and voluntary communal initiative, and it sparks a decidedly activistic element within the traditional messianic faith. "We must build houses and dig wells and plant vineyards and olive groves," Alkalai writes. The Jews must redeem the land and use the political process; a firm economic basis for agricultural settlement must be prepared; and the like— "for one cannot behave in this world as though it were the world to come"![48] Rabbi Hayyim David Hazzan, the Sephardic rabbi (*Hakham Bashi*) of Jerusalem, wrote in a similar spirit, enthusiastically supporting Rabbi Kalischer's initiative to resettle the land: "We shall receive the good from God following the proper preparation . . . through acts of flesh and blood . . . We shall succeed in bringing redemption to the Holy Land by plowing and reaping, and by performing the commandments related to the land. The salvation of the Lord thus shall spring forth from the land . . . from which come blessings of life and food to all who are therein. May God bring from on high the [final] redemption close to the redemption of the land."[49] Kalischer and Alkalai did not hesitate to carry this line of thought to its logical conclusion. Both, for example, considered the philanthropic act of establishing *batei maḥseh* (shelter houses) in the Old City of Jerusalem of secondary importance, urging that the focus be instead on agricultural settlement. Manifestly, the sharp differentiation between the historical act and the utopian goal effectively brought about a religious "shift of values": the act of earthly building—the creation of a firm material infrastructure in the Land of Israel—assumed an immediate urgency, taking precedence over spiritual and social tasks: "For when we redeem the land on earth, so shall the horn of salvation spring up from heaven."

The conceptual transformation that the Harbingers sought to initiate from within the traditional sources is evident in their daring efforts to "translate" traditional spiritual concepts into earthly terms and endow them with concrete content. For example, the repentance (*teshuvah*) upon which the redemption of Israel depends (BT Sanhedrin 97b) means none other than the actual, voluntary return (*shivah*) of the Jewish people to its land. In Alkalai's words, "*Teshuvah* means they should return [*yashuvu*] to the land . . . for [the Jew] who dwells elsewhere is like one who has no God; hence there is no repentance greater than this."[50] He thus imbues the concept of repentance, like that of redemption, with a physical meaning. Alkalai takes this idea from his teacher Judah Bibas,[51] making wide programmatic use of it. For him, repentance-return no longer takes place only in the life of the individual; it is now understood as a collective act of the Jewish people as a whole, a historic event and common task.[52] It is this return to the land that will bring the hoped-for messianic turning point.

This exegetical line also makes use of early aggadic symbols. For example, certain classical Jewish sources make a well-known distinction between the figure of the Messiah ben Joseph, who symbolizes the last historical battle at the onset of the messianic age, and the Messiah ben David, who will bring the ultimate, utopian redemption.[53] Alkalai identifies the former messiah with an assembly of Jewish sages (or with its leader) that is to arise to guide the Jewish people toward redemption.[54] The aggadic symbol is henceforth to be embodied in a social institution!

Creative midrash was thus employed to reinterpret concepts and symbols that had been bound up with collective passivity. Henceforth man was summoned, on various levels of activity, to prepare the historical foundations with his own hands. In this fashion, "the awakening from below"—another old spiritual concept that is given social meaning—"will bring about an awakening from above."[55]

Indeed, early in his career Kalischer does not hesitate to advocate the renewal of sacrifice,[56] which he also sees as a concrete redemptive act. Thus modern activism and traditional symbols are merged in his consciousness in a complementary fashion.

As I have said, gradualistic messianism, for all its modern realism and activism, does not abandon the absolute expectation of a metahistorical future age. It holds that the earthly process will ultimately lead to a miraculous prophetic revelation, in which human history is to reach its fulfillment and spiritual goal. A utopian picture of redemption is thus retained: "And afterward the true Messiah will be revealed, together with all the promised beneficences; and the Evil Urge will be destroyed, for the earth will be filled with knowledge [of the Lord] at the sight of these wonders . . . For He shall cause the evil kingdom to pass from the earth" (Kalischer).[57] In this view, in contrast to the prevalent traditional outlook, human activity does not preclude the yearning for ultimate perfection.

Finally, how did this approach overcome the question of the "three oaths" and the barrier it placed between the people and its land? As one might anticipate, the Harbingers and their allies spared no efforts to neutralize the traditional passive doctrine inherent in these oaths.[58] But they went even further, seeking to extract from the oath itself the doctrine of redemption articulated in their school. Indeed, it was here that the creative exegetical moment was revealed in its full power.

The injunction "not to ascend the wall"—that is, that Israel not burst into the land as one—was interpreted by Alkalai in an original manner, as itself expressing his own approach of realistic messianism! Does not the realistic approach depict the return to Zion as a gradual, evolving process, in contrast to the approach that speaks of "ascending" collectively in a sudden, revolutionary thrust? "Thus is the redemption of Israel," he wrote. "At first little by little, for we are adjured not to go up all together!"[59] The traditional edict of passivity is thus turned on its head, finding a place of honor in the school of active messianism: "The Holy One, blessed be He, wishes the redemption to take place in a dignified and orderly way; therefore He adjured us not to all go up together, not to be scattered about the face of the field like tent dwellers, but [to go] little by little, until our land is [completely] rebuilt and established."[60]

Second, with regard to the oath "not to force the End," Kalischer asked, Does not the activist messianic approach also leave the miraculous, utopian end in the hands of heaven? Originally the oath referred only to the final messianic end, to the notion of hastening the "End," but left plenty of room for an actual historical "beginning," for the active preparation of the soil of redemption by human hands![61] Hence the second basic distinction in the Harbingers' doctrine—between the goal and the process—is also consistent with the ancient doctrine of the oaths.

As for the third injunction—"not to rebel against the nations of the world"—both Alkalai and Kalischer argued that this had nothing to do with the contemporary return to Zion. Obviously, this return would be a wholly political, not military, matter, carried out with the assent of the nations of the world and the support of their rulers[62]—and no sword shall pass through our land. (This approach, according to which the agreement of the nations releases Israel from the fear of the oaths, is indeed grounded in classical Judaic sources.) Kalischer also proposed, at the time, to request permission from the Turkish sultan for extensive settlement in the Land of

Israel; although this was of course a pragmatic proposal—a kind of precursor of the policy later pursued by political Zionism—it was also in harmony with his religious conviction.

Finally, "God did not adjure us other than not to attempt 'to ascend to the top of the mountain' [Num. 14:44] by force; but to 'take delight in its stones' [Ps. 102:15] and to act for its settlement—"there is no greater commandment than this.' "[63] It is noteworthy that the confrontation with the question of the oaths recurs consistently in the writings of the Harbingers' allies,[64] and subsequently occupied a substantial place in the period of Hibbat Zion.[65] The doors of exegesis were not shut: they were once more opened wide to meet the needs of the imminent national revival.

THE SEPARATION OF REALMS

The Harbingers' doctrine of redemption had very limited influence at the time. It failed to gain significant support among the rabbinical leadership or among the majority of Orthodox Jewry. During the 1870s and 1880s certain messianic overtones could still be heard in the speeches and writings of such rabbis as Shmuel Mohilever, Nathan Friedland, and Mordecai-Gimpel Jaffe, but the messianic justification of settlement in the Land of Israel gradually waned.[66] Even those religious leaders who supported the Lovers of Zion and the organized settlement movement tended to base their position on other arguments, such as the unity of the people and the sanctity of the land, while repressing messianic motives or rejecting them out of hand. In fact, several of the chief rabbinical advocates of settling the Land of Israel, such as Rabbi Naftali Zvi Judah Berlin, "the Netziv," of Volozhin and Rabbi Isaac Jacob Reines, expressed explicit reservations regarding the Harbingers' doctrine of redemption.[67]

Rabbi Naftali Zvi Judah Berlin, the famous *rosh yeshivah* of Volozhin, attributed the messianic outlook of Rabbi Kalischer to the false hopes Kalischer had pinned on the Emancipation: "For he based himself upon a deceptive light that he saw in the countries of the West." Berlin objected in principle to the pretense of setting forth a well-defined messianic theory predicting the actual course of the redemption. In the political sphere, he also feared a sharp Gentile backlash to Jewish messianic agitation (1891). Clearly, the differences of time and place between the Harbingers and Berlin led to the considerable disparity between the optimism of the former and the pessimism of the latter concerning the actual situation of European Jewry. In Berlin's words: "All of this [messianic] talk came to pass only because the Gaon [Kalischer] thought that the light of redemption had begun in his day; but in our own time, in which we are subjugated in the Exile and subject to new edicts, we must not bring up any idea of redemption in connection with the settlement of the land."[68]

The most systematic critique of the Harbingers at that time was published by Rabbi Isaac Jacob Reines, who later founded the Mizrachi (religious-Zionist) movement. As early as the 1880s, Reines spoke out against the confusion of practical, present-day settlement in the Land of Israel with the hoped-for future messianic redemption. He was also critical of the new concepts of redemption and repentance that had been taught by the Harbingers: "Those who were enthusiastic about this idea [of settling the Land of Israel] were not content to explain the merit of the idea in itself, but saw fit to preach it as bearing droplets of redemption and beads of salvation, so that some of them, in their naïveté and excitement, predicated the final redemption upon this return . . . Indeed, they frequently twisted quotations from the Bible and the rabbis to fit their opinion, and it is understandable that by so doing they aroused controversy and strife."[69] Reines's rejection of the doctrine of natural, worldly redemption did not derive solely from apologetic needs, from a tendency toward cautious defensiveness in the face of Haredi criticism. His extensive writings afford ample evidence that this was his principled religious position. Surprising as it may seem today, a century later, the founder of religious Zionism clung throughout his life to the traditional passive, miracle-centered view of the Messiah. Like his forefathers and teachers, he drew a firm line between transcendental redemption and any collective initiative or physical action performed by flesh and blood. "Redemption in itself is above nature and human effort," wrote Reines in the early article quoted above. "It is only in the heights of miracle and wonder that it is to be established!" In his later, more comprehensive writings, he remained faithful to this view, depicting the future messianic redemption in decidedly revolutionary and utopian fashion.[70] He went even further in this direction than many traditional sources, making the redemption of Israel dependent upon "the elimination of human corruption" and "the utter extirpation of evil." Reines thus envisioned Jewish national redemption as coming only after the reforming of humanity as a whole.[71] Expectably, this position also rejects out of hand any "forcing of the End" by human initiative. How then is such a theological position to be reconciled with the Zionist fervor manifested by its author and the historical activism advocated by him and his colleagues?

The key to this problem lies in the explicit separation between the domain of legitimate Zionist activity, which is close at hand, and that of messianic hope, which is ideal and distant. Reines writes: "Zionist ideology is devoid of any trace of the idea of redemption . . . In none of the Zionists' acts or aspirations is there the slightest allusion to future redemption. Their sole intention is to improve Israel's situation, to raise their stature and accustom them to a life of happiness . . . [If so,] how can one compare this idea with the idea of redemption?"[72] Clearly, action in the present day does not trespass upon utopian hopes for the Time to Come.

This separation of realms between Zionism and messianism, which was both ideological and pragmatic, molded the formative stage of religious-Zionist thought. We shall therefore examine the separation in the larger context of that movement and its aims.

In 1900 a number of rabbis, under Reines's leadership, published an open letter in support of the new Zionist movement. They wished to separate the controversy over Zionism among religious circles as far as possible from the issue of messianic redemption.

> Anyone who thinks the Zionist idea is somehow associated with future redemption and the coming of the Messiah and who therefore regards it as undermining our holy faith is clearly in error. [Zionism] has nothing whatsoever to do with the question of redemption. The entire point of this idea is merely the improvement of the condition of our wretched brethren. In recent years our situation has deteriorated disastrously, and many of our brethren are scattered in every direction, to the seven seas, in places where the fear of assimilation is hardly remote. [The Zionists] saw that the only fitting place for our brethren to settle would be in the Holy Land . . . And if some preachers, while speaking of Zion, also mention redemption and the coming of the Messiah and thus let the abominable thought enter people's minds that this idea encroaches upon the territory of true redemption, only they themselves are to blame, for it is their own wrong opinion they express.[73]

Zionism does not propose to fulfill or to replace messianic expectations. It offers a partial, relative solution for the here and now. It operates in an unredeemed world and does not trespass upon the realm of the perfect or the absolute. Of course, the gradual resettlement of the Land of Israel is worthy of the highest religious esteem in itself, just as the entire national revival must be accorded positive religious value.[74] However, that value and esteem are to be registered in the chronicles of history, not in accounts of the End of Days. Religious significance need not be solely messianic! The religious Zionist thus lends a hand to current efforts on behalf of the national and religious restoration of the people and the elevation of their present fortunes. But he continues to cling unreservedly to the utopian, messianic vision of the Time to Come. This dual loyalty is possible due to the clear separation of realms: that of concrete human history, to which Zionism relates, and that of "the anticipated, miraculous redemption," "the sphere of pure faith, faith in the Messiah" (S. J. Rabinowitz).[75]

It must be recalled that the founders of the religious-Zionist movement, unlike their precursors the Harbingers, had to relate to the concrete emergence of secular Zionism and secular settlements in Palestine, a fundamentally new reality that was bound to raise serious questions of principle for them. In Kalischer's and Alkalai's time, almost all the country's Jewish inhabitants (known as the Old Yishuv) had been Orthodox, and these thinkers naturally assumed that any new settlement activity would likewise be conducted in the spirit of the Torah. But beginning in the 1880s there was a radical change:[76] the Zionist rabbis were now called upon to join forces with freethinkers, heretics, and sinners, and to issue rulings allowing others to do so. Any confusion of Zionism with traditional messianism was liable to impede such cooperation, for the latter could only be permitted if it were limited to well-defined practical goals and did not deviate into areas that might be sensitive from a religious point of view.[77] Public activity that focused on finding an immediate solution for the distress and humiliation of the Jews in exile did not appear to endanger religious faith. But if cooperation were expanded to include cultural and spiritual, and especially theological, matters,[78] there would be reason to fear a betrayal of principles and perhaps even a sliding into false messianism. The distinction between Zionist activity and messianic redemption thus suited the overall purpose of fostering coexistence between Orthodox and secular Zionists.

As already noted, some major secular writers were also concerned to maintain a strict separation between Zionism and traditional messianism.[79] In their minds the religious concept of redemption was bound up with Jewish helplessness and passivity; hence, only if religious aspirations were sharply demarcated and the heavy weight of absolute, metahistorical messianism set aside could the field be freed for concrete activity in the here and now. Zionism had to be "protected" from messianism. The more polemically inclined coined such sayings as "Israel has no Messiah, so set to work!" and "Let us rise up and live without a Messiah!" (Joseph Hayyim Brenner).[80] While the spokesmen of religious Zionism likewise sought to keep the two ideas separate, they did so as much to protect their messianism from Zionism as the other way around. They wanted to preserve the perfection and purity of their religious vision of redemption from the new nationalistic aspirations to which they were also devoted. For them, the present national task did not compromise the vision of future fulfillment, but left its original innocence intact.

Of course, there was a blatantly apologetic element in all these arguments: the desire to erect a defense against Haredi criticism. The high barrier that the religious Zionists set up between their Zionism and their messianism was partly intended to refute any claim that they were forcing the End; they could thereby get rabbinical approval for Zionism and make it permitted to the faithful.

Thus the well-known writer Peretz Smolenskin had good reason to warn his fellow Lovers of Zion, as early as 1881, "If you strive to establish colonies in the Land of Israel, may you go from strength to strength! . . . But if you say it is your intention in doing so to clear the way for the Messiah, you will be attacked by both the believers and the enlightened."[81] The separation of realms was viewed by this Lover of Zion as an effective means of appeasing both the Orthodox and the secular. It would circumvent and neutralize the problem of messianism, making it possible to attract many good people from both camps to the new settlement movement.

MESSIANIC AND ANTIMESSIANIC PROCESSES

We have thus far examined three options regarding the issue of messianism and Zionism which presented themselves to Orthodox Jews at the turn of the century. One of these options, well expressed by Shalom Dov Baer Schneersohn, the Lubavitcher Rebbe, adhered unreservedly to the traditional ideal of waiting passively for the ultimate redemption. According to this view, Zionist activity was antimessianic because it sought to "force the End" prematurely. The second option, developed by the Harbingers of Zionism and popularized in various forms, was both messianic and activist. It welcomed the new national movement as a contribution to the final redemption, "an awakening from below." The common ground shared by both these approaches was that Zionism was ultimately viewed in the perspective of messianic faith, and so they looked for a connection between the actions of the former and the hopes of the latter. By contrast, the third option, formulated by the founders of the Mizrachi movement, was careful to isolate Zionism from messianic expectations and to measure its actions by the yardstick of ordinary historical achievement.[82]

Sociologists of religion might use the following terminology:[83] The first option adopted, in the name of messianic faith, a position of "rejection" vis-à-vis modern Zionism. The second option, by contrast, took a stance of "expansion," seeking to broaden the traditional boundary of messianism to encompass, ab initio, modern nationalism. The third option adduced an approach of "compartmentalization," wholly separating the realm of Zionism from that of messianism.

Could such a clear separation between Zionism and messianism survive over time? Could believing Jews consistently distinguish between historical action and metahistorical hope? We know that this distinction, however effective and fruitful it may have been in its time, was in fact not sustained, nor has it affected decisively the mainstream ideologies that emerged in the Orthodox world. On the one hand, it has never become the dominant viewpoint of religious Zionism, which has increasingly interpreted historical events in the Land of Israel in messianic terms. On the other hand, it has also failed to elicit much of a response from Haredi circles or to legitimize the Zionist enterprise in their eyes. On the contrary, ideological polarization over the question of Zionism, and later the question of the status and destiny of the State of Israel, have increasingly been bound up with the issue of messianism, the various ideological positions being articulated around the interpretation of classical rabbinic texts on redemption.

This development is most striking in the case of two radical groups on opposite sides of the ideological divide. The disciples of Rabbi Abraham Isaac Kook and the leadership of Gush Emunim have interpreted the Zionist enterprise as a decidedly messianic process: the State of Israel was conceived in holiness and is itself an embodiment of redemption. By contrast, the Satmar Hasidim, the Edah Haredit in Jerusalem, and the Neturei Karta have interpreted the Zionist enterprise as the polar opposite, as an antimessianic rebellion: the State of Israel was conceived in sin, and represents a violent betrayal of classical faith in redemption. Both views, though, evaluate Zionism in the perspective of messianic perfection. As we shall see, the two more moderate Orthodox schools of thought also failed to disentangle themselves completely from the issue under consideration here, and they too felt the need to define themselves in the classical terms of exile and redemption.

This should be no cause for surprise. We have already seen that Zionism did not appear in a vacuum, religiously speaking, nor was its message neutral with respect to traditional Jewish messianic hopes. Zionism called for Jewish immigration to the Land of Israel just as messianism promised the return to Zion and the ingathering of the exiles. As the former movement sought to attain political independence for the Jewish people, the latter hoped for the liberation of the Jews from "subjugation to the great powers." Zionism worked to make the land fruitful, to "conquer the waste places"; it even spoke explicitly of "redeeming the land." Employing a somewhat different idiom, messianism taught (in the words of the Talmud) that "there is no other revealed End than this, as it is said, 'But you, O mountains of Israel, shall yield your produce and bear your fruit for My people Israel, for their return is near'" (Ezek. 36:8), or, in Rashi's gloss, "When the Land of Israel gives its fruit generously, the End is at hand" (BT Sanhedrin 98a). Likewise, both messianism and Zionism sought the social reform of the Jewish people in their land.[84] The religious Zionists, indeed, were inclined to believe from the start that the national reawakening would ultimately give rise to spiritual renewal as well, stirring the people to comprehensive repentance. Even Reines, who had advocated limiting Zionist activity to the pursuit of material objectives, firmly hoped that a return to the people and the land would ultimately bring about a return to God. Here too we can detect what appear to be echoes of traditional messianism.[85]

In short, the religious mind found it difficult to view Zionism and messianism as two unrelated, parallel phenomena; rather, it tended to see them as overlapping. Too many elements in Zionist activity and rhetoric evoked the classical vision of redemption for a view that unwaveringly distinguished between the two to capture people' imaginations for long.

From a different standpoint, however, the Zionist enterprise seemed to challenge messianic faith. Worldly salvation by human means, purely secular activity, redemption without any need for repentance—these elements were too significant for the religious mind to regard them with indifference. While Zionism and messianism both seemed to be playing in the same arena, were they not playing by different rules? What was the connection between the historical and the utopian, the natural and the miraculous, the mundane and the spiritual, between the political and the theological? How to interpret the dramatic events of Zionist history, from the Balfour Declaration through the Six-Day War? Were these signs of salvation from heaven or rebellion against heaven; the first stirrings of redemption or the work of the Devil?

As I shall later argue, the trauma of the destruction of the Jews of Europe reinforced the growing tendency within the religious camp to link Zionism with messianism. I refer in particular to the two radical positions, the one viewing the State of Israel as an unmistakably messianic phenomenon, the other as egregiously antimessianic. Both schools try to formulate a religious response to the Holocaust, seeking to supply a "reason" or a "meaning" to counter the abyss that yawned in that great destruction. The one sees in the Zionist enterprise a metaphysical counterpoise to the gaping ruin, while for the other Zionism is the collective sin, the demonic rebellion against heaven, that actually precipitated the destruction.

Hence, the more the Zionist idea was translated into reality, the more insistently were messianic claims made for it by the religious-Zionist camp, on the one hand, and its legitimacy called into question by the Haredi camp, on the other. "The present time" and "the present place" were seen by many *sub specie aeternitatis*—in the perspective of the messianic age and the Temple—while the earthly State of Israel was summoned to give account before the ideal Kingdom of Israel and the ideal Congregation of Israel.

"Forcing the End": Radical Anti-Zionism

THE SATAN WHO CHOOSES JERUSALEM

In "A Whole Loaf," one of the stories in Agnon's *Book of Deeds*, the narrator introduces us to two of his oldest and closest friends. One is Dr. Yekutiel Neeman, who clearly symbolizes Moses, the faithful one (*ne'eman*) of the House of the Lord; the other, Mr. Gressler, is the very image of Satan, the embodiment of the Evil Urge and its seductions.[1] The narrator experiences many personal reversals and finds himself buffeted back and forth repeatedly between these two. But when Gressler, the demonic friend, causes the narrator's home and all of his possessions to go up in smoke, he decides to put an end to Gressler's seductive mischief. He breaks off the friendship, "buries himself in the book of Yekutiel Neeman," and finally packs up and leaves for Eretz Israel (Palestine).[2]

"As soon as I set off for Eretz Israel," he continues, "who should I run into first but Gressler; for he was traveling on the same ship, albeit on the upper deck, which is reserved for the rich, whereas I rode on the lower deck with the poor." The two characters thus carry their flirtation to the Holy Land, where their paths frequently cross. Some time later, the two are traveling in a carriage (an allusion to that of Mephistopheles), which overturns, casting them to the ground. Rolling in the dirt, they soil the important letters which Yekutiel Neeman had asked the narrator to deliver.

"As soon as I set off for Eretz Israel, who should I run into first but Gressler." Even in the Holy Land there is no respite from the unceasing struggle between the two giants, the Torah of Moses and the chariot of Satan. It is not only the Shekhinah (the Divine Presence) that, as tradition would have it, dwells in Eretz Israel; the Sitra Ahra (the Other Side, i.e., the force of evil) is there too, ready to pounce upon a Jew as soon as he sets foot on the sacred soil; and at times this force proves more virulent there than it ever was in the alien land from which the Jew came.

Agnon seems to have utilized here a parable from an earlier source. And indeed, the same motif was once used by the Rebbe of Munkács, Rabbi Hayyim Eleazar Shapira, in a letter sent to his followers in Jerusalem following his visit to Eretz Israel in 1930. In an ironical and penetrating passage, he wrote:

> When I journeyed to the Holy Land, I said to the Adversary before embarking at Istanbul, "A billet costs a great deal of money . . . You decide: either you go to the Holy Land and I stay here . . . or you stay here and I go alone to the Holy Land . . . And he chose to stay there . . . and I rejoiced in my voyage. But when I reached the Holy Land, I immediately caught sight of the Adversary standing there in the port, and I cried out in anguish, "What are you doing here? Did I not leave you in Istanbul with the understanding that you would stay there?" And he . . . answered me, saying, "You ask me what I am doing here? 'The fellow came here as an alien, and already he acts the ruler' [Gen. 19:9]. Why, this is my regular abode, and the one . . . with whom you spoke in Istanbul was just my overseas emissary!"[3]

Here, too, the narrator boarded a ship bound for Eretz Israel, imagining that he was leaving Satan and his temptations behind; but he came in for a rude surprise, for his old tempter latches onto him there with even greater vigor and tenacity.

But unlike Agnon, Shapira goes on to spell out the meaning of the parable: today's Satan, who makes his home in the Holy Land, is none other than the new Zionist settlement movement. Zion, Shapira argued, has always been the focus of a great struggle between light and darkness, between God, on the one hand, and the Evil Urge, on the other. So it is, too, in our own time with its dreadful events. It is not only God who delights to dwell in the Holy Land and the Holy City, but also the "new ones, who came but lately" (Deut. 32:17), those who seek to force Zion to submit to them and make it the center of their sacrilegious enterprise. Shapira goes on to interpret Zechariah 3:2 in this spirit. It is not, "May the Lord who has chosen Jerusalem rebuke you, O Satan," but rather, "May the Lord rebuke you, O Satan who chooses Jerusalem."[4]

Rabbi Hayyim Eleazar Shapira of Munkács (1872–1937) was one of the most prominent Hasidic leaders of Hungarian Jewry in his era, re-

nowned both for his halakhic erudition and his mastery of Kabbalistic doctrine. In many respects, he represents the prototypical teacher of the most
conservative, radical wing of ultra-Orthodoxy. Shapira conducted a merci-
less battle against Zionism and the new settlement movement in Palestine,
developing an original and unique ideological stance concerning this question, based on both Halakhic and theological arguments. Indeed, Shapira
carried his protests against the new settlements further than all of his predecessors (and apparently even his successors) in the Orthodox camp. He
in fact formulated a distinctly demonological conception of the Holy Land
and of the dark forces nesting within it and threatening its inhabitants.

Shapira challenged not only the leadership of the Zionist movement,
but also contemporary Orthodox leadership. His wrath was primarily directed against Agudat Israel, the more middle-of-the-road Haredi (i.e.,
ultra-Orthodox) group that settled strictly observant Jews in Eretz Israel.
Such Jews might take pride in their beards and piety, he claimed, but they
were in effect tacit partners of the Zionists, and "in their hypocrisy they
have done us more harm than all the wicked of the earth."[5] Accordingly,
Shapira waged a vigorous struggle against them. Over the course of the
years, he took many important steps toward the establishment of the separatist, militantly orthodox camp within Orthodox Jewry, for both his and
our own generation.

DENUNCIATION AND ISOLATION

In 1922 a gathering was held in Csap, Slovakia, of distinguished rabbis and
Hasidic leaders. Those in attendance, constituting the leadership of the
radical ultra-Orthodox wing of Hungarian Jewry, sought to stem the tide
of secularization and "sacrilege" that seemed to threaten religious education in Eastern Europe and Jewish life in the Holy Land. But on this occasion, their criticism was not aimed directly at the Maskilim (proponents of
the Enlightenment), the Zionists, or the Reform movement: it was primarily aimed at Agudat Israel, whose rabbis and leaders they perceived as com-
promisers, accommodationists, and, ultimately, collaborators with the
secular adversary. The Munkaczer Rebbe, who had assembled and chaired
the meeting, rose to enumerate, one by one, the sins of the Agudah and its
leaders: from the way they conducted yeshivah education, through their
approach to the Land of Israel and to messianism.[6]

First, Shapira charged, the Agudists were allowing themselves to be influenced by the new, suspect currents of thought sweeping Western Eu-

ropean Orthodoxy. In their schools, they were permitting the purity of genuine sacred study to be tainted with "admixtures of secular learning," combining Torah and worldly knowledge. (Many Agudah supporters in western Slovakia, who had been educated in the yeshivah of Pressburg, had indeed been exposed to the influence of German neo-Orthodoxy; Rabbi Shapira feared that this line of influence would penetrate his own circles.) Thus the yeshivah newly established in Warsaw by the Gurer Rebbe deviated gravely, in Shapira's view, from what was acceptable: it was nothing more than an imitation of the misguided modern rabbinical seminaries set up by the German "doctor-rabbis" (university-trained rabbis) and *rabanim* (literally, "evil sons": a play on the Hebrew *rabbanim*, "rabbis," used to designate the errant Reformers). This development might spread to other places, including the holy city of Jerusalem, where these people might attempt to establish a world rabbinical seminary, a technical school, and the like: "a stock sprouting poison weed and wormwood" (Deut. 29:17).[7]

Second, although the Agudists pretended to fight the Zionists, the two groups increasingly revealed a similarity of thought and action. Like the Zionists, the Agudah was developing Eretz Israel physically and preaching settlement "through [the tilling of] fields and vineyards." Such actions were contrary to the traditional view that the Holy Land is intended only for prayer and sacred study.[8] In the final analysis, the Agudists were collaborating with the Zionists and even infecting innocent schoolchildren with the Zionist ethos and style. "They are defiling the children's minds and hearts with foolishness that leads to levity and heresy, God forbid, and with songs that speak of the settlement of the land, the fields and the vineyards of Eretz Israel—just like [those of] the Zionist poets."[9] Moreover, the Agudists were sabotaging the economic basis of Torah study in the Holy Land, because their words and deeds were diverting funds from the academies and yeshivot of Eretz Israel to agricultural settlement and material development. In this way, they were taking food from the mouths of the students of Torah. "Sages and saints who were spending their lives in holiness and purity in our Holy Land have now suddenly and unaccountably fallen prey to the wickedness of the Zionists, the Mizrachi [religious Zionists], and the Agudists."[10]

Third, Shapira found that the Agudah literature contained statements that could be construed as directly challenging the traditional belief in the Messiah and subverting the traditional Jew's simple, passive yearning for divine salvation. He cited expressions that allegedly echoed the false Zionist doctrine that Israel would inherit the land through its own physical efforts—aided by the other nations—rather than through profound penitence and exclusive devotion to the study of Torah. According to Shapira, the spokesmen of Agudah even place messianic faith in the actions of what they call "the exalted government of England."[11] Thus, in this area as well, the Agudists had adopted the Zionist myth and ethos.

In brief, the Agudists had deviated from the correct path in their approach to education, the Land of Israel, and messianism. Therefore, "[the Agudists] are for all practical purposes Zionists . . . They pour fuel on the fire, claiming they are trying to put it out, but in the end the Agudists and the Zionist will be joined arm in arm."[12]

Of course, this was not an objective reflection of the views or activity of Agudat Israel at the time. In fact, the Agudah came into existence through its struggle against the Zionist movement; from the outset, it declared all-out war on secular Jewish nationalism and the new Zionist ideas about revival and redemption. Although the Agudah ideologues approved of settling the land, they believed that only the faithful should undertake such activity under conditions conducive to piety, and they forbade any collaboration with the Zionist enterprise. Likewise, although they sometimes allowed the limited introduction of secular studies into the curriculum of their schools, they did so merely to meet their students' practical needs as future job holders; the Agudists had no enthusiasm for the ideal of a secular national revival.

Nevertheless, the dispute between the Munkaczer rebbe and his camp, on the one hand, and Agudat Israel, on the other, must be taken seriously. Although the depiction of Agudah voiced at the rabbinic meeting was inaccurate, it clearly reflected the self-image of the radical Haredi camp. This camp sensed itself to be at odds with the great majority of Orthodox Jews in Poland and Lithuania and, of course, in Western Europe.[13] Indeed, other speakers on that occasion supported the views expressed by the Munkaczer rebbe, and the meeting ended with a unanimous ban on any association with Agudat Israel.[14]

The first name on the list of signatories to the ban was that of a young rabbi, scion of one of the Hasidic dynasties, who was presiding at that time over the small community of Orsova. Of all the speakers, he was the most vehement in his support of Shapira's separatist, antisettlement views. This man, Rabbi Joel Moshe Teitelbaum, was destined to become the Satmarer rebbe, the adored leader of tens of thousands of Hasidim and the most vigorous opponent that Zionism and the State of Israel were ever to know in the Haredi camp.[15] Basic ideas and principles developed within the

Munkaczer school were transformed by the Satmarer Rebbe into a detailed, full-fledged theory, which he elaborated in numerous writings and speeches. This theory was concretized in reaction to dramatic historical events—the Holocaust and the establishment of the State of Israel—and eventually came to guide the political (or rather, antipolitical) reactions of a large Haredi community.

Thus the opposition to mass *aliyah* and settlement that had existed all along grew over the years into an uncompromising struggle led by Teitelbaum against the sovereign Jewish state and all its works. Under his guidance, the time-honored call for the establishment of separate "holy communities" turned into an insistence on total self-segregation by the new "remnant of Israel" and the delegitimation of all those who continued to falsely consider themselves part of the Jewish people—from the secularists to Agudat Israel. Moreover, the classical fear of "forcing the End" and undermining faith in divine redemption grew in Teitelbaum's doctrine into a metahistorical demonization of the Zionist enterprise as the ongoing antimessianic work of Satan himself.

Teitelbaum echoed the Munkaczer Rebbe's reading of the verse from Zechariah ("May the Lord rebuke you, O Satan who chooses Jerusalem"), which he interpreted in relation to actual events in the Land of Israel: "May the Lord rebuke Satan, for [the latter] has chosen Jerusalem in order better to overcome those who dwell there . . . to seduce and corrupt the entire world wrapped in the mantle of Jerusalem's glory . . . And 'outrages have been committed by the enemy in the sanctuary' [Ps. 74:3] in the hallowed land . . . for vicious people have come there and defiled it with their heretical government, may God protect us."[16] In Teitelbaum's view, the Holocaust and the establishment of the State of Israel were not contrary developments, destruction versus construction, but a single continuous process: the final eruption of the forces of evil as a prelude to redemption.

A detailed comparison of the writings of Rabbis Shapira and Teitelbaum reveals the decisive influence of the former upon the latter and, consequently, upon the entire school of radical ultra-Orthodoxy in our time. Were it not for the severe personal dispute that later erupted between the two figures concerning the territorial boundaries of their rabbinical jurisdiction, and the breakdown in relations ensuing from this dispute, the intense conceptual affinity between the two rabbis might have become common knowledge. To be sure, both Shapira and Teitelbaum were following their respective family traditions, which rejected emigration and physical settlement of Eretz Israel. (The Teitelbaum tradition can be traced back at least four generations!) Yet only now, in response to the Zionist movement, was this tradition bolstered theoretically, and made paramount in the consciousness of this radical separatist community.

THE RELIGIOUS RETREAT FROM THE LAND OF ISRAEL

First I shall clarify the fundamental approach underlying all of Rabbi Shapira's sermons and writings about the settlement of the Land of Israel. I shall thereafter portray the radical, mythic breakthrough to be found in his later writings.

Naturally, Shapira takes a stand against development of the Holy Land by secular means and at the hands of sinners. Accordingly, he seeks to deprive the licentious Zionists of any foothold in the Land of Israel.[17] But he insists that Eretz Israel is no place for ordinary Jews either. Here he elaborates upon a much earlier tradition, dating back to the medieval era, which sought—on halakhic and ideological grounds—to discourage people from settling in the Holy Land. This trend of thought emphasizes the frightening holiness and dangerous uniqueness of the Land of Israel, and points to the prodigious religious demands that the land makes upon its inhabitants: the extra degree of spirituality required and the extra punishment for those who violate the commandments there. Accordingly, the Munkaczer Rebbe would often cite the warning issued by the twelfth-century Rabbi of Rothenberg to every God-fearing Jew who wished to travel to the Land of Israel: "Let him be abstinent in the land and beware of any transgression, for if he sins there, he will be punished most severely. For God supervises the land and watches over its inhabitants [see Deut. 11:12]. He who rebels against the kingdom from within the king's palace is not the same as he who rebels outside it. This is the meaning of 'a land that consumes its inhabitants' [Num. 13:32]. As for those who go there and think they can get away with levity and reckless contentiousness, I would invoke the verses, 'But you came and defiled My land' [Jer. 2:7] and 'Who asked of you to trample My courts?' [Isa. 1:12]."[18] The Munkaczer Rebbe sought to develop this view and add to its sting. He explicitly depicted the Holy Land as fraught with religious danger, warning his followers of the terrible spiritual decline that would befall unworthy Jews who moved there. In fact, Shapira regarded the Land of Israel as the abode of the ideal Jew, not of the real, average Jew.[19] It is a place reserved for righteous zealots, for those who are prepared to sacrifice themselves in the service of God, not for ordinary run-of-the-mill persons. How much less should the new Zionist heretics and sinners, who unabashedly portray their undertaking as a revolt against God and His Torah, be permitted to set foot in the Land of Israel.

Moreover, the physical rebuilding of the Land of Israel entails, by definition, spiritual decay and destruction. Shapira vehemently denied the very legitimacy of agricultural work and other forms of manual labor in the Holy Land. He therefore forbade Jews, even God-fearing and observant ones, to devote themselves to material concerns in the land: "For those who travel to the Holy Land for worldly purposes, rather than to study Torah and to worship God, place themselves in 'the company of the insolent' [Ps. 1:1]. It is written of such persons: 'But you came and defiled My land' [Jer. 2:7]."[20] That is to say, the Land of Israel demands one's whole being and shapes one's entire life. The land was designed solely for prayer and spiritual activity. Therefore, "we must follow in the footsteps of our old rabbis and forefathers, by supporting only those residents of the land who devote themselves to the study of Torah and the worship of God . . . [Indeed,] the evil forces have become stronger in our Holy Land and they undermine its very foundation through their plowshares and agricultural colonies."[21] Shapira thus carried the idea of the land as a religious object to its most radical and dichotomous conclusion: "the Holy Land" sustains its holiness during the period of exile only by denying its very materiality.[22]

These ideas were also in keeping with Shapira's messianic outlook. Needless to say, the rebbe conceived any merely human attempt to bring the Jews collectively to the Land of Israel as a usurpation of the Messiah's role and an attempt to force the End of Days. The very effort to settle the land with human hands implies an abandonment of "faith in miraculous redemption from heaven."[23] Likewise, Shapira completely dismissed the Zionist hope to achieve diplomatic and political progress through the help of other nations, and vehemently dismissed the Balfour Declaration and its implications for the life of Israel.[24] Like many other ultra-Orthodox leaders, he upheld the value of Jewish political passivity and made it an ultimate religious norm of the exilic era: "One may not rely on any natural effort or on material salvation by human labor. One should not expect redemption from any source other than God."[25] Accordingly, Shapira would cite Rabbi Jonathan Eybeschütz's (eighteenth-century) sharp formulation of the oath taken by Israel not to hasten the End of Days: "The congregation of Israel shouted out their vow . . . For even if the whole people of Israel is prepared to go to Jerusalem, and even if all the nations consent, it is absolutely forbidden to go there. Because the End is unknown and perhaps this is the wrong time. [Indeed,] tomorrow or the next day they might sin, and will yet again need to go into exile, heaven forbid, and the latter [exile] will be harsher than the former."[26] The inevitable result of the new settlers' activity is thus not physical construction, but spiritual destruction. They threaten to bring upon the people of Israel a new and terrible exile.[27]

But what of the commandment to settle Eretz Israel? In his volume of Halakhic responsa, *Minhat Ele'azar,* the Munkaczer Rebbe argues, first, that this precept applies only to the messianic era, not to our own time; second, that even in the Time to Come, the responsibility for bringing about the return to Zion will be entirely in the hands of the Messiah. That is to say, the Jewish people are to play no active role, either collectively or as individuals, in the process of return. "For it will not be up to them to conquer [the land]; they will come rather from a commandment and an order imposed upon the holy King Messiah, who alone will do it . . . through strange and marvelous signs and wonders."[28] The question of settling in Eretz Israel is thus altogether removed from the normative realm: there is no possible historical situation in which the Jewish people as a collectivity would be called to go there.[29] On the contrary, any merely human effort in this direction, even if undertaken by pious Jews, would inevitably betray a lack of faith and the beginnings of heresy.

To summarize, Shapira distances the real Jewish people from the Holy Land, both by emphasizing its awesome spiritual demands and by depicting it exclusively in the most ultimate messianic categories. Indeed, in his later sermons, the Munkaczer Rebbe went even further and developed a bold new idea—in truth, a mythic breakthrough—which even his most radical successors did not dare to embrace in either letter or spirit. We shall now examine this development.

THE DEMONOLOGY OF THE HOLY LAND

Contemporary students of religion and religious consciousness tend to emphasize the inner tension characterizing the religious consciousness per se: the believer is attracted to the holy, he or she is fascinated by it, but at the same time withdraws from the holy in awe and fear.[30] The same dialectic applies to the holy place and the holy land: the religious person is intensely attracted to them, seeking to partake intimately in their metaphysical power, but simultaneously he or she is likely to retreat from the holy and to keep a distance from its threatening metaphysical force.[31]

Shapira's approach to the Land of Israel well exemplifies this tension. No doubt his direct confrontation with Zionism which, in his eyes, threatened to desecrate the Holy Land, tipped the scales entirely in the direction of separation and withdrawal. Interestingly enough, Shapira seeks to add a distinctly mystical, indeed demonic, dimension to this spiritual awe of the Land of Israel. In this context, he adopts extremely polarizing formulations, unparalleled in Jewish literature.

The Land of Israel's impurity is tantamount to its holiness. The land concentrates and expresses the ultimate manifestations of both direct divine revelation and satanic evil; these two influences are locked there in direct confrontation. On the one hand, Shapira emphasizes and amplifies the Divine Presence in the land. Not only is the land subject to God's direct Providence, unmediated by natural laws or supernatural forces[32]—"the Land of the Hart was not subjected to the rule of ministers, to the laws of the celestial spheres, or to the reign of heaven"—but rather it is directly supervised "under the Governance of the *Ein-Sof*, may His name be blessed, without the mediation of any minister or celestial sphere, and without any contraction [*tzimtzum*]."[33] The *Ein-Sof*, the supreme hidden face of God in Kabbalistic theory, is manifested in the land without any mediation or limitation and, so to speak, without the graduated contraction of God's abundant emanation through spheres and vessels! This manner of expression is unique in Kabbalistic literature. Even mystics like Nahmanides and Joseph Caro, who elevated the spiritual status of the Land of Israel and depicted it as a mystical gateway to the highest stages of the divine world (from *Tiferet* up to *Binah* and *Hokhmah*),[34] did not blaze a path all the way to the hidden Divine One. Even if one reads Shapira's words as rhetorical hyperbole, one cannot simply ignore such expressions when they are written by an authentic Kabbalist. In any case, Shapira's position raises a pressing question: Who is worthy of living in the land, and who would dare to do so?

The Land of Israel—the palace of the King—is, on the other hand, also a gateway to hell. There, in the Holy Land itself, "where the Canaanite of Palestine dwells, lies the source and inspiration of defilement."[35] Shapira makes liberal use of the traditional myth concerning the evil forces that attach themselves to holiness and try to transform and displace it. He intensifies this idea sevenfold in relation to the Holy Land. The Zionist's new foothold in the Land of Israel is interpreted entirely within this sinister framework: it is nothing but the external manifestation of the destructive forces that have always inhered in the inner sanctum of holiness: it demonstrates "that the adversary himself chose his dwelling in Jerusalem."[36] It follows that any God-fearing Jew who goes to the Land of Israel inevitably plunges into the arena of a struggle: immigration to Israel means, by definition, declaration of war against "the Evil Side" and against its concrete social manifestation or, alternatively, exposure to their detrimental influence.

And who is worthy or willing to face such danger? As the Munkaczer Rebbe warned his followers in the Diaspora several months before his death (1937): "Only our forefather, Abraham, was holy enough to withstand the ordeal [of going to the Land of Israel], but as for us, the present ordeals and conflicts are quite sufficient. Thus Abraham demanded that 'you will not take a wife for my son from the daughters of the Canaanites' [Gen. 24:3], so that his descendants would not, God forbid, fall under the influence of the Canaanites in Palestine . . . [As if Abraham was saying,] 'I alone can fight the forces of defilement and conquer them entirely, but I do not wish my children to engage in such a fight, for the journey there poses a great danger to them.'"[37] And as Shapira warned his followers, the denizens of Jerusalem, who resided in the focus of danger itself: "May the Lord rebuke you, O Satan, who seeks to overcome the righteous men of Jerusalem! . . . This is the secret of the verse: 'This city [of Jerusalem] has aroused My anger and My wrath' [Jer. 32:31]. The evil forces excite God's anger and fury; they are most powerful in the Land of Israel, particularly in Jerusalem. For, as Satan has his foothold in this very place, yet he desists from tormenting those who seek to eliminate them through [holy] deeds and studies. Thus the residents of Jerusalem must bolster and strengthen themselves with Torah."[38]

The evil force that festers in the Holy Land is endowed by Shapira with an autonomous status: this force came into existence long before it was concretely manifested through the new settlers of the land. Shapira thus took great pains to depict the Land of Israel as an arena of conflict, as a mythic and social battlefield, not as an abode or a homestead. The Land of Israel was suited to the spiritual strengths and qualities of the ancient forefathers; in the future, after the final messianic victory in the battle, it will also become the residence of the redeemed sons: "Only when the blessed God will appear 'to wreak judgment on Mount Esau' [i.e., to root out the forces of evil] and when 'dominion shall be the Lord's' [Obad. 1:21]—we will then walk [to the land] together with the righteous Messiah."[39] But at the present time, the land is designed only for warriors, for "zealous fearers of God" who set out "to fight the just war for the residue of God's heritage in the holy mount of Jerusalem" (Shapira consistently used such language in the messages he sent to his followers in the Land of Israel).[40] We have already seen that the land was designed for the truly righteous, not for simple householders: it is these righteous ones who are now depicted as "valiant men of war."[41] This also applies to their concrete religious-social struggle: "It is apparent how far things have gone these days, when the Land of Israel is full of defilement . . . The religious ordeals are especially difficult there, and it is extremely dangerous to dwell in the land since the new immigrants, who pretend to 'ascend' to the land, are in fact descending to the depths of hell. When they lived there in the Diaspora, they were already ruined by false ideas; but when they arrive in the Land of Israel, they lose all contact with Judaism, by violating the holy Sabbath and the Torah as a whole."[42] "It is now mortally dangerous to reside in the land. With all those who are defiling the land, the God-fearing Jews will be forced against their will to fight difficult battles."[43]

In conclusion, Shapira greatly intensified the spiritual fear of the land by emphasizing, on the one hand, the land's heightened holiness "under the governance of the *Ein-Sof*" and, on the other hand, by stressing the heightened impurity that festers "where the Canaanite of Palestine dwells." The original ideological rejection of the Zionist enterprise was thus transformed into a religious-existential terror, focusing upon the land's awesome powers.[44] True, the Munkaczer Rebbe skillfully integrates his teaching with the sayings of some later Kabbalists, but it is difficult to find parallels in Jewish literature to Shapira's overall, semignostic approach to the Land of Israel.

This daring approach later left its mark on the most radical, separatist stream of ultra-Orthodoxy. But it would appear that even a figure like Rebbe Teitelbaum, the great zealot who carried his predecessor's views to extremes in other areas, adopted a more moderate position than his predecessor in this question. It is true that Teitelbaum also spoke of "Satan's strong hand in the holy realm."[45] But Teitelbaum did not use this idea to instill fear of the very being of the land. Instead, he demonized the historical process—that is, the Zionist enterprise and achievements in the Land of Israel.

THE GUARDIANS OF THE WALLS

The extreme anti-Zionists in the Diaspora who chose to split off from the rest of the Haredi camp found faithful allies in the Holy City itself. This alliance has endured for two generations.

The Ashkenazic Old Yishuv (the pre-Zionist Jewish community) of Jerusalem had long been a stronghold of the most conservative attitudes toward education and religious practice. It served as a kind of refuge, particularly for Hungarian Jews, from the winds of change sweeping Europe. But at the turn of the century, this stronghold itself seemed to be threatened by the new waves of *aliyah*. The latter brought together in Jerusalem people of widely diverse beliefs and practices. More than in any other place, it was at this crossroad of the Jewish world that one could find the full spectrum of secularists, traditionalists, moderate Orthodox, ultra-Orthodox, and self-styled "zealots," all of whom had to live together in close quarters. What is more, they needed to deal with the question of institutional cooperation, a matter that was particularly troublesome for the non-Zionist ultra-Orthodox, and which arose repeatedly in a variety of settings: the city council, the Jewish Agency, the National Committee (which, among other things, collected voluntary taxes), the Chief Rabbinate, the prestate militia, and later, the Knesset (Israel's parliament), the government, and the army.

It is no wonder that, in the face of this social and political reality, the conservative forces should feel the need to barricade themselves behind an ideology that would permit them to attack the mounting threat at its root. And, of course, the extremists kept a close watch on their own camp for any signs of cooperation with the enemy institutions—cooperation that, if exposed, was promptly vilified. The most zealous would enter into conflict with the rabbinic leadership of the ultra-Orthodox community itself whenever it seemed insufficiently resolute in pursuit of its own stated values and goals.[46] It was thus natural that Munkács and Satmar should find allies in these circles in Jerusalem.

With the death in 1932 of Joseph Hayyim Sonnenfeld, rabbi of the Edah Haredit (Jerusalem's organized ultra-Orthodox community), the radicals pressed for the election of Teitelbaum (who had not yet become the Satmarer Rebbe) as his successor. The leaders of the community were frightened by Teitelbaum's close ties to the zealots, however, and the effort came to naught.[47] Three years later, in the wake of severe disagreements over matters of education and self-segregation, a group of radicals, led by Rabbi Amram Blau and Rabbi Aaron Katzenellenbogen, split off from the Edah Haredit to form a separate group that later became the Neturei Karta (Guardians of the Walls). In 1945 this group obtained a majority in the Council of the Edah Haredit, and thus took control of that body. The circle was closed in 1953, when the Satmarer Rebbe was chosen as the rabbi of the Edah. To be sure, the Rebbe continued to live in Williamsburg, Brooklyn, where tens of thousands of his followers were concentrated, and never exercised direct control over the lives of the Jerusalem zealots. Nevertheless, he placed his distinctive stamp, along with his halakhic backing, on their emerging ideology.

Thus all three interlocking groups—the Satmar Hasidim, the Neturei Karta, and the Edah Haredit—could henceforth be considered one ideological camp, despite the obvious differences among them.[48] (We shall note below that the small group of Munkaczer Hasidim in the United States also belongs today to this same camp.)

It was only after the Holocaust and the founding of the State of Israel that the worldview of this group was fully crystallized and set down in written form. Nevertheless, note must be taken of the significant contribution made to this process by the Jerusalem community during the preceding period. This contribution is well attested in the works of Rabbi Yeshayahu Asher Zelig Margolis, "one of the leaders of the hosts of the zealous Hasidim in Jerusalem,"[49] who wrote in the 1920s and 1930s.[50]

More than any other figure, Margolis represents the alliance between the zealots in Jerusalem and those in Hungary and Slovakia. One of the ardent Jerusalem followers of the Munkaczer Rebbe, Margolis corresponded with him regularly, and in 1930 arranged for Shapira to visit Jerusalem.[51] He was less successful in his efforts two years later to have the Satmarer Rebbe appointed rabbi of the Edah Haredit. But he kept up contact with Teitelbaum over a period of years[52] and, after the State of Israel was established, it was Rabbi Margolis who encouraged him to publish a comprehensive tract explaining his opposition to the state and boycott of the Knesset elections.[53] It was at this time that Teitelbaum's major work, Va-Yo'el Moshe, began to take shape.

Margolis, a rabbinic scholar well versed in the Kabbalah, sought to give depth to the ideology—one might even call it a theology—of zealotry and self-segregation and to ground this doctrine in earlier sources. A creative thinker in his own right, he also had a gift for anthologizing, editing, and polemics, and knew how to tap the potential for radicalism long dormant in his comrades. Indeed, Teitelbaum was later to eulogize him as "the great luminary who fought the Lord's battle and was zealous for the faith," the man "who was long close to my soul."[54]

The following is a summary of the principal components of the ideology of the Jerusalem separatists, as formulated by Margolis:

Conservatism. An extremely conservative attitude is taken toward all aspects of the Jewish way of life. Innovation is forbidden in all areas, from education and study to the details of dress, the cut of the beard, and the "impurity of waving the hair."[55] Seemingly external details take on a deep, inner, and often symbolic and mystical significance. Thus the slightest departure from accepted patterns is forbidden. "Care should be taken that the right lapel overlaps the left, so that the right hand of the Most High, 'the right hand of the Lord uplifted' in its exalted Love, predominates over the left side, which represents Power, the strength of the Evil Impulse." Whoever makes changes is presumed guilty; better that there be fewer yeshivah students than that boys be admitted "whose dress and deportment" deviate in the slightest from the established custom.[56]

An Embattled Minority. According to the worldview of Israel as an embattled minority, it is the zealot, who fights the Lord's battles, who is the normative Jew. Those few who are prepared to step into the breach and stand fast against the tide are the bulwark of Jewish survival down through the ages. Jewish history is thus not primarily the story of the people of Israel as such, but rather that of the repeated encounters between the "guardians of the walls" and the benighted masses. Similarly, the true leader is portrayed, not as he who leads the people, but rather as one who is prepared to oppose them without fear. In other words, Margolis's is a kind of counter-history pivoted entirely on the heroism of the zealous minority fighting for its Torah. It is noteworthy that, according to the Munkaczer Rebbe, the Land of Israel was destined for such warriors and zealots alone.

For example, the true distinction of the tribe of Levi was not its service in the Temple, but rather its zeal in the Lord's cause—slaying the multitudes of sinners—after the building of the Golden Calf.[57] Moses was first and foremost the one who stood up to his fellow Hebrews—the one who intervened in the fight between two Jews ("So he said to the offender, 'Why do you strike your fellow?'" [Exod. 2:13]), and who met single-handedly the challenge of Korah, Dathan, and Abiram. Even Aaron, portrayed in rabbinic sources as the archetypal "lover of peace and pursuer of peace," is seen by Margolis in this light: to "pursue" does not necessarily mean to seek; rather, "sometimes [Aaron] would drive peace away, for 'pursue [peace]' [Ps. 34:15] can also mean 'to drive something away.'" Similarly, to say that Aaron was a "lover of peace" does not necessarily mean that he would make peace among his fellow men. On the contrary, he would reprove Israel for its sins and thus "make peace between Israel and its heavenly Father"!

Thus zealotry, protest, and controversy for the sake of heaven are not special or exceptional responses, but rather the perennial Jewish norm. Moses and Phinehas son of Eleazar, the leader and the zealot, are no longer viewed as contrasting models of Jewish behavior: they belong to the same end of the continuum.[58] Furthermore, it makes no difference whether the battle is joined against the Jews who violate the Covenant, and thus bear falsely the name of Israel, or against the Gentile enemies of the Jewish people: it is all one battle.

Thus all those "who have not taken a false oath by My life" [Ps. 24:4] or indulged in deceit should go forth like the tribe of Levi. Moses our Teacher, of blessed memory, did not praise the Levites for the holiness and exaltation of their singing in the Temple but for "[saying] of [their] father and mother, 'I consider them not'" [Deut. 33:9] at the time of the sin of the [Golden] Calf, when they gave their full devotion to the sanctification of the Divine Name . . . From this we conclude that the Holy One, blessed be He, considers [such devotion] more important and precious even than the Temple service.

And thus would our forefathers always act when the wicked arose in the land . . . At the time of the Hasmoneans, the blessed Lord came to [their] aid, "delivering the mighty into the hands of the weak and the many into the hands of the few" [in the words of the Prayer Book] . . . Even if there be but one [righteous person] in the city, the old sage says, "Let him be strong as a tiger and light as an eagle, swift as a deer and courageous as a lion" [M Abot 5:23]; this is the true heroism that every God-fearing person should display . . . And indeed Phinehas stood up against Zimri, even though the latter was a prince of Israel and his tribe defended him . . . "Do not stand in dread of them, for the Lord your God is in your midst, a great and awesome God" [Deut. 7:21] . . . Thus did Elijah stand up to Ahab and the 450 prophets of Baal and the whole generation that followed them. And Hananiah, Mishael, and Azariah stood up to the wicked Nebuchadnezzar, a tyrant who made the great powers of the world tremble. And thus did the righteous Mordecai stand up to the evil Haman without quavering . . . It is therefore a sacred obligation for every Israelite to take up this holy war, as it is written, "The Lord will be at war with Amalek throughout the ages" [Exod. 17:16].[59]

Social and Metaphysical Separation. Margolis's ideology naturally demands that the "remnant of Israel" separate themselves completely from the community of the nonobservant and (in his view) incompletely observant. This demand, which originally arose from the purely pragmatic need to protect the faithful and shelter their children from the "evil winds" of the time, now takes on greater depth and is given a mystical grounding.

By joining forces with evil, the Jewish heretic proclaims that he is "not rooted in the soul of Israel" but belongs rather to "the external souls, the Amalekite spirits . . . These are descended from the mixed multitude [who came with Israel] out of Egypt."[60] The way such people end up proves their origins. Thus one must define boundaries to separate between the sacred and profane, light and darkness, Israel and so-called Israel.

Nor, in fact, can these Jewish infidels be expected to repent and truly change their ways. A Jew who transgresses as a result of momentary lapse can, of course, atone for the sin. But the wicked have made sin a positive ideology rather than just a lapse; their heresy is a faith in its own right. Thus their very personality and inner being are bound up with evil and impurity, and as a result, the gates of penitence are utterly closed to them.[61] (It should be noted that this distinction does have sound ground in halakhic and philosophical sources.) As for Zionism, then, "all who go to her cannot return" (Prov. 2:19).[62] The rebel who throws off the yoke can never go back. "If the Lord is God, follow Him; and if Baal, follow him!" (1 Kgs. 18:21). An ontological gulf has opened between those who continue to keep the embers of the faith glowing and the apostate seducers and corrupters, "the mixed multitude who mingled with the people of Israel . . . These, the offspring of Pharaoh, arise in every generation and every age in a different guise and with different names, seeking to undo us."[63] Any attempt to win these renegades back into the fold can only result in a blurring of boundaries and a confusion of value systems. Rather, let them carry on as before, and this will lead to the final parting of the ways between good and evil, pure and impure, on the eve of the ultimate redemption. "For the pruning of dead wood improves the tree," and, "when Israel is rid of these people, the Son of David will come."[64] Hence social self-segregation comes to symbolize, at bottom, a metaphysical separation. As in so many other instances in the history of religions, the embattled few come to see themselves as the "children of light," the elect who take their stand against a fallen society that is fundamentally debased.

Of course, such sharp formulations result at times from the heat of debate, as the speaker gets carried away with his own rhetoric. However, as Yehudah Leibes has pointed out, these particular ideas do have a basis in the Kabbalistic tradition, including the polemics of that self-styled "zealot and son of a zealot," Rabbi Jacob Emden, against the Sabbateans.[65]

Redemption and Its False Substitutes. Margolis repeatedly stresses the profoundly subversive effect of Zionism on traditional messianic beliefs, replacing as it does the supernatural with the natural, the religious with the secular, the passive with the active. In this, he adds little of substance to the views of the Munkaczer and Lubavitcher schools; he is only more sharply polemical. Like them, he warns against "forcing the End" by mass *aliyah* in advance of the final redemption, and he too goes to great lengths in his demonization of Zionism: "Samael [Satan] himself and all his host have come down to mislead and intoxicate the whole of Israel throughout the world . . . And this is the substitute they offer for [true] redemption: false idolatry of *tzarat Ba'al-Peor* [literally, the troubles of Baal Peor, a play on *hatzharat* Balfour, the Balfour Declaration] that, through our sins, has darkened the vision of Israel; and blind [*ivrim*] Hebrews ['*ivrim*] have arisen . . . saying, 'Redemption is coming!' . . . Verily, since the time of the first Golden Calf, Satan has never had such an opportunity to blind Israel (God forbid) as he has now."[66]

Most noteworthy in this context is that a doctrine of redemptive religious Zionism was being developed by Rabbi Abraham Isaac Kook in Jerusalem precisely during this interwar period. Margolis took note of this development and condemned it in the strongest terms. His principal grievance is with Kook's defense of the secular Zionists and his readiness to accord a religious meaning to the contemporary return to Zion: "He takes the Lord's sanctuary and recasts it in the idolatrous image of their national revival . . . He accords [the latter] all the traditional [*mesorasi*, in Ashkenazic pronunciation] albeit emasculated [*mesorasi*] splendor and depth . . . And 'he had a dream' [Gen. 37:5] and 'prophesied to you delusion and folly' [Lam. 2:14], [a vision] in which the 'angels' of redemption—wicked people called angels—'were going up and down on it' [Gen. 28:12]."[67] This criticism is doubtless directed against Rabbi Kook's letter to the Mizrachi movement, in which he wrote: "The source of Zionism is the most supreme source of holiness, the Bible, which affords all of the tradition's splendor and depth."[68] Margolis was well acquainted with Rabbi Kook's innovative theory of Jewish religious nationalism; a detailed examination of this polemic would carry us beyond the bounds of the present discussion. The gist of it is, according to Margolis, that what was taking place was neither redemption nor "the beginning of redemption," but the work of Satan, pure and simple.

We have thus far been examining the radical Haredi viewpoint as articulated by Yeshayahu Margolis of Jerusalem. His major contribution, it appears, lies in his development of the separatist zealot ideology, historically rooted in Hungarian Jewry.[69] These ideas were crystallized in accordance with Rabbi Shapira's approach to messianism and the Land of Israel. These two themes were later integrated, in the doctrines of the Satmarer Rebbe, into a detailed full-fledged theory, leaving a decisive imprint upon radical Haredi circles to this day.

Margolis was a close disciple of the elderly Sephardic sage Rabbi Solomon Eliezer Alfandari, known as the Holy Grandfather, who lived to be more than a hundred years old.[70] He often quoted Alfandari, received the latter's *haskamah* (imprimatur) for his book, and even cared for him personally on his sickbed. Margolis was certainly more extreme than his mentor, but Alfandari, too, adopted a radical approach to the issue of self-segregation. He wrote a tract attacking Rabbi Kook, and Jerusalem zealots attributed to him acerbic sayings such as "The Mizrachi and the Agudah differ in name alone; what binds them all together is money and power rather than [concern for] the honor of heaven."[71]

The Munkaczer Rebbe also looked to Rabbi Alfandari for guidance. Of all the sages of the Land of Israel, it was Alfandari whom Shapira revered as the leading saint of his generation. Various documents indicate that Margolis played a decisive role in mediating between his two mentors, and in engendering Rabbi Shapira's great admiration for Alfandari.[72]

In 1930 Shapira set out for the Holy Land, having refused to do so— "for great and secret reasons"[73]—for many years. His whole mysterious pilgrimage to Eretz Israel, attended by a considerable entourage, centered on Alfandari. Shapira insistently claimed: "My main concern is to meet and honor the Holy Grandfather . . . because the commandment to settle the Land of Israel is not applicable in our era."[74] Indeed, it seemed as though Shapira pinned his hopes for a speedy redemption on this man's stature and mystical virtues. Those of his companions who were privy to his meeting with Alfandari later reported it as follows. Basing himself on the rabbinic dictum that, "what the righteous decree, the Holy One, blessed be He, fulfills, . . . the Rebbe pleaded with the Holy Grandfather, as the leading saint of his generation, that he decree irrevocably, for the glory of the Shekhinah [Divine Presence] and the well-being of all Israel, that the Messiah ben David, come quickly in our own time, for we could no longer bear our plight . . . And the Holy Grandfather, in his humility, said, 'I am not a righteous man.' And our Rebbe stayed and pleaded with him for a long time."[75] It was as if the Holy Grandfather were the very antithesis of "the Satan who chooses Jerusalem." Rabbi Shapira's scribe recorded his own impression of this meeting in the following words: "From behind the curtains we heard them dealing with the issue of our total redemption, in the manner of the counsel of the holy angels. We who stood outside were seized with dread and horror, and to this day my pen trembles as I recall the great awe that gripped us that day."[76]

A few days later, Alfandari was afflicted with illness. The next day he was summoned to heaven, with Shapira and his followers standing by his bedside.[77]

Let us recall a marvelous story that Shapira used to tell his disciples: Rebbe Menahem Mendel of Rymanow once came to visit Rabbi Jacob, "the Seer," of Lublin, in order to work with him to hasten the redemption. But the demonic "counterforces" overcame them. Rebbe Menahem Mendel took ill, and "he did not have the strength to stay and fight the adversaries who were forcing him to leave. They thus sensed that this was a decree from heaven preventing them from doing anything [for the sake of redemption]."[78]

Did the counterforces also gain the upper hand over the forces of holiness emanating from Alfandari and Shapira? In any event, the very next day the Munkaczer Rebbe and his followers left the Holy Land.[79] Upon returning to Munkács, Shapira refused to attend the festive homecoming ceremony organized on his behalf, "nor did he allow his disciples to dance and sing."[80] Years later, his followers were said to have deciphered the hidden reason for the Rebbe's unusual behavior on that day, the second day of the month of Sivan. "The heart knows its own bitterness" (Prov. 14:10): they calculated that exactly seven years later, on the second of Sivan, the Munkaczer Rebbe was to die, his soul departing for the world to come; exactly seven more years thereafter, on the very same day, the grim reaper came to Munkács and sent its last sons to Auschwitz.[81]

Shapira's only daughter and his son-in-law were spared, for they had left for Palestine before the Holocaust.[82] The son-in-law, Rabbi Baruch Rabinowitz, strayed from the path charted by his father-in-law and was later appointed chief rabbi of the town of Holon in Israel. But the wheel continues to turn. His own son, Rabbi Moshe Leib, left Israel for the United States, placing himself under the tutelage of the Satmarer Rebbe, thereby attaining the title of Munkaczer Rebbe (while his father was still living!). In this way, the loyal remnant of the Munkács tradition have been attempting to restore the crown to its former glory.

"THE TRANSFORMATION"

The Holocaust and the rise of the State of Israel led the Neturei Karta, the Edah Haredit, and the Satmar Hasidim to formulate their views in a more systematic way. These dramatic events caused theological uneasiness in many quarters, raising fundamental questions about messianic redemption, Jewish passivity, political sovereignty, and the role of the Jewish people in the world. But the radical ultra-Orthodox groups were among the first to articulate a direct religious response.

There were major Haredi factions who tended to avoid these questions, denying that the events had any theological meaning. On the one hand, the Holocaust was seen as an instance of *Deus absconditus,* of an unfathomable mystery from which no conclusions could be drawn concerning the revealed ways of God in the world. On the other, the State of Israel was viewed as a purely secular, religiously neutral phenomenon with no bearing on the relation between the Jew and his or her Creator or between the people of Israel and its Torah. (We shall return to this issue in chapter 4.)

The self-segregated extremists, however, tended to view the concrete events of the day in a highly religious light, indeed, as being of an altogether metaphysical and demoniacal rather than a historical nature. The concrete occurrences represented for them the very hand of God, the higher Providence that hovers over history, judging all in order to reward and punish.

Statistically speaking, the phenomenon in question is marginal. All told, the extremists number today perhaps ten thousand in Israel and several tens of thousands in the United States.[83] But their indirect influence, the challenge posed by their radical views, is widely felt in the Haredi mainstream.[84] They project an image of consistency and unswerving faith, of a kind of avant-garde whose demands disturb the compliant bourgeois complacency of others. Though the views of the radicals are vehemently rejected by most of the ultra-Orthodox community, the former serve as a kind of gadfly, warning the community of the dangers of too much cooperation with the Zionists and their state. And they no doubt succeed in drawing the larger community into repeated confrontations with Israeli society and its institutions. It is a universal phenomenon that extreme, absolutist ideologies, untainted by complexity or ambivalence, frequently have an influence far beyond the circle of their own followers.

The same might have been said of the radiation of influence within the extremist camp itself, where the minuscule Neturei Karta, for example, long exerted an impact on the thinking of a larger group. But a change has taken place of late, and the most unbridled of the extremists have been expelled from the Edah Haredit. This development is related to a split within the Neturei Karta itself: the most militant faction, which numbers less than a hundred families, no longer accepts the authority of the Edah Haredit rabbinical court (*Badatz*).

It is this faction that expresses affinity for the Palestine Liberation Organization (PLO) and that refuses to participate in demonstrations that have police permits (since doing so would amount to indirect recognition of the authority of the state). In 1988 the dissension reached such a pitch that the leader of this faction, Rabbi Hayyim Katzenellenbogen, was formally excommunicated by the Edah Haredit court. The remaining faction, led by Rabbi Uri Blau, cooperates with the Edah, which continues to represent most of the radical groups.

But despite certain internal variations, the radical camp has taken a consistent ideological line for nearly two generations. We shall now examine the intellectual and spiritual roots of this ideology.

Let us begin with the key issue: the theological (antimessianic) import of the Zionist enterprise and of Jewish sovereignty. In 1938 the Yishuv imposed a head tax, called *kofer ha-yishuv,* on all Jewish residents of the country, in order to cover the cost of organized defense against Arab attacks. The Jerusalem separatists refused on principle to contribute to the military effort, taking the following Talmudic source as their watchword:

> Rabbi Judah the Prince sent Rabbi Hiyyah, Rabbi Assi, and Rabbi Ammi to appoint scribes and teachers in towns throughout Eretz Israel.[85] They came to a certain place where they could find neither a scribe nor a teacher. They said to [the townspeople]: "Bring us the guardians of the city [*neturei karta*]." They brought them the town watchmen. They said to them: "Are these then the guardians of the city? They are the destroyers of the city!" They said to them: "Who then are the guardians of the city?" They replied: "The scribes and teachers, as Scripture states: 'Unless the Lord builds the house, its builders labor in vain on it; unless the Lord watches over the city, the watchman keeps vigil in vain' [Ps. 127:1]." (JT Hagigah 2:7)

The name Neturei Karta, used to this day by the most radical of the ultra-Orthodox groups, was thus intended to connote a challenge to the new values, the new definitions of Jewishness and Jewish history, introduced by the Zionists. The separatists emphasized that the people of Israel, God's people, had stepped out of the stream of ordinary history when they entered the realm of the Torah. Israel had been commanded to show indifference and passivity toward all things political and military, but active devotion to things of the spirit. The Zionists now sought to upset this divinely established order and entice the people of Israel into a double betrayal of its destiny: calling on the Jews to force their way into the realm of earthly history, and thereby abandon the yoke of Torah and the Kingdom of Heaven.

Furthermore, in seeking the normalization of the Jewish people on a purely mundane, historical level, the national movement deliberately called into question the transcendent law that had governed all of Jewish history: the ahistorical law of divine reward and punishment, exile and redemption; the Divine Providence which had delivered Israel from the rule of physical causality prevailing in nature and "normal" human affairs. The covenant between Israel and the Creator had placed Jewish destiny on a purely religious plane. The catastrophes that had befallen the people had resulted, not from the aggressive intentions of its enemies, but, as the Prayer Book puts it, "because of our sins." Similarly, the future restoration of Jewish life would not be a matter of mere bricks and mortar; rather, in Maimonides' words, "Israel is to be redeemed by penitence alone." The political attempt to bring the Eternal People into the history of the nations is blasphemy, brazen defiance of Divine Providence.

What is more, the Zionists and those who had fallen under their spell were exposing the Jewish population to serious physical danger. Their nationalistic pretensions and arrogant political machinations were provoking the animosity of the Arabs, with whom the Old Yishuv had learned to live in peace over many generations. The passage cited earlier—"Are these then the guardians of the city? They are the destroyers of the city!"—seemed now to take on a double significance, both physical and spiritual, as the guardians of the walls (Neturei Karta) felt called upon "to rescue both our bodies and our souls from the rule of these wicked people." In the harsh words of Rabbi Amram Blau, leader of the Neturei Karta during the immediate prestate period,

> Over Israel there have arisen Zionists who adopt Gentile notions in an attempt to force the End, using a false idea of worldly redemption through power and the kindness of the other nations . . . They have come to the Holy Land and raised the flag of rebellion against the kingdom of heaven . . . They have connived by the most horrendous means to uproot our holy Torah, as well as all human morality . . . They have become entangled with our Arab neighbors to the point where the Yishuv is being subjected to riots and Jewish blood is being shed, heaven forfend . . . Our holy Torah teaches that we should take no interest in the political realm while in exile, until the coming of the Messiah, may he come speedily and in our own day, and there is nothing in this position to antagonize our Arab neighbors. While in exile we wish only to live and to fulfill the commandments of our Creator, may His name be blessed; and we have no interest in living in our Holy Land except to imbibe its holiness and to fulfill the commandments which can only be fulfilled here.[86]

(In this context "exile" is of course an expression of time and condition, rather than of place. Those living in Eretz Israel are as much in exile as Jews anywhere else.)

The closer Zionism came to realizing its goals, the more sharply focused became the ideology and historiosophy of Jewish passivity in opposition to it. Inactivity regarding mundane political matters was turned into the essential feature of Jewishness in the premessianic era. It is the Jews' patient expectation of complete, utopian redemption, a miraculous occurrence unconnected with any worldly effort on their part, that captures the fundamental nature of Judaism itself: acknowledgment of divine rule, of prophetic destiny, of the chosenness of Israel, and of the special laws governing Israel's fate.[87] It is no longer just the Jews' unique way of life that has religious significance; the very fact that they live in exile becomes a declaration of faith. Their very passivity represents a heroic decision that must daily be reaffirmed.

The Zionist claim that it can bring about salvation and national rebirth in advance of the messianic age expresses the exact opposite. Any attempt to realize messianic expectations by human means—the conquest of the land, political liberation, the ingathering of the exiles—is tantamount to blasphemy.[88] A sovereign Jewish state would thus be a new Tower of Babel, an insolent human attempt to usurp the prerogative of the Creator Himself. It is antimessianic hubris, "absolute apostasy, brazen arrogance, dreadful heresy that shakes the foundations of the world and hacks at the very root of the covenant linking [the children of] Israel and their Father in heaven."[89]

THE OATHS AND THE HOLOCAUST

It is in this context that a theological "explanation" is given for the Holocaust, an explanation unparalleled among Jewish reactions to this event in its categorical and oversimplified character: it is seen as a collective punishment for a collective offense, the Jewish people's rebellion against the rule of heaven, as reflected in the Zionist effort to force the End!

Chapter 1 discussed the function played in Jewish history by the "three oaths"—that is, the declaration of Jewish passivity during the period of exile (see the appendix also). As mentioned, during recent generations, in response to the ongoing controversy concerning *aliyah* and the rebuilding of the land, these oaths enjoyed a certain revival. However, it was only during the generation of the Holocaust and the founding of the State of Israel that this idea acquired the status of a supreme principle within the radical circles—becoming, so to speak, the very manifestation of the Jewish commitment to God, upon which rested the entire theological structure and legal system of Judaism.

The Satmarer Rebbe, Rabbi Joel Moshe Teitelbaum made the oaths the summation of a whole way of thinking and a binding halakhic norm. In his view, this norm was of such gravity that a Jew should be prepared to endure martyrdom rather than violate it! Teitelbaum scoured the literature looking for support for his notion of the supreme status of the oaths, demonstrating in the process how creatively the midrashic techniques of reinterpretation can still be used.[90] For example, having failed to find any mention of the oaths in so fundamental a halakhic work as Maimonides' *Code,* he does not conclude that Maimonides meant to be lenient in the matter, but to the contrary: forcing the End was of such gravity that it did not do to simply list it as one prohibition among many. "To force the End prematurely is worse than all other transgressions, even the most serious in the Torah!"[91] An act such as this, which undermines the very foundations of the faith and contradicts essential principles of Torah, cannot be dealt with adequately among ordinary halakhic prohibitions.

(One finds a surprising mirror image of this claim in the religious-Zionist notion of the commandment of resettling the land. The fact that this commandment is missing from Maimonides' enumeration of the 613 commandments is explained in terms of its being an overarching principle rather than a mere detail of the Law. [See chapter 3.])

From here, Teitelbaum turned to the terror of the Holocaust, giving it too a theological interpretation (he himself escaped the Nazis in Hungary aboard Rezsö Kasztner's evacuation train). His discussion of the three oaths is marked throughout by a far-reaching radicalism. The discussion actually proceeds from a single point of departure: the ultimate human experience, that of death. Speaking of the seriousness of the prohibition, he writes, "These oaths may not be violated even on pain of death; even if they [the Gentiles] threaten you with the cruelest torture, it is no less forbidden to leave the exile [en masse] than to commit apostasy!"[92] Or, in regard to the punishment for violating the prohibition, "Nowhere in the Scriptures do we find so dreadful a punishment as [that which is threatened here] for the sin of [forcing] the End and violating the oaths—[namely,] stripping away the flesh."[93]

Earlier instances in which Jews collectively betrayed their faith and destiny are seen in the same light. First and foremost is the classic case of the Bar Kokhba rebellion, in which Jews living in a time of exile seized freedom and sovereignty for themselves. Teitelbaum sees this episode as a clear instance of the violation of the oaths; hence the catastrophic consequences were inevitable: "When [Bar Kokhba] was slain, the enemies of Israel slew more Jews than they had at the time of the Destruction [of the Temple] . . . It was then that the horn of Israel was cast down, never to be raised up again until the coming of the Son of David."[94]

One theme emerges clearly from this whole fabric of extreme statements: the Jewish tradition offers us ample resources for coming to grips with the mass murder and collective destruction of our own day. For Teitelbaum the Holocaust should be interpreted within the same classic categories of reward and punishment, sin and repentance, guilt and reckoning, as have all other trials that Jews and other human beings have endured. The Holocaust should likewise be seen in light of Jewish experience down through the ages, from the Golden Calf through Bar-Kokhba down to Sabbatai Zvi. It was not an "eclipse of God" or an unintelligible jumble of events, but a revelation of divine judgment! The Nazi Auschwitz, with its bottomless evil, may have been on another planet, but the Jewish Auschwitz took place in this world, and hence must be understood in terms of traditional beliefs and the transcendent law that has always determined the fate of the people of Israel. In contrast to the belief of some modern religious thinkers, the Holocaust does not require a new religious orientation or usher in a new era in the covenantal relationship between God and His people (Irving Greenberg),[95] nor does it give rise to a new "614th commandment" (Emil Fackenheim).[96] On the contrary, it confirms the traditional norms and patterns of faith. The appropriate religious response to these events is the classic one, and the teachers of our day are duty-bound to reprove the people and call them to repentance. In Teitelbaum's words,

> Because of our sinfulness we have suffered greatly, suffering as bitter as wormwood, worse than any Israel has known since it became a people . . . In former times, whenever troubles befell Jacob, the matter was pondered and reasons sought—which sin had brought the troubles about—so that we could make amends and return to the Lord, may He be blessed . . . But in our generation one need not look far for the sin responsible for our calamity . . . The heretics have made all kinds of efforts to violate these oaths, to go up by force and to seize sovereignty and freedom by themselves, before the appointed time . . . [They] have lured the majority of the Jewish people into awful heresy, the like of which has not been seen since the world was created . . . And so it is no wonder that the Lord has lashed out in anger . . . And there were also righteous people who perished because of the iniquity of the sinners and corrupters, so great was the [divine] wrath.[97]

This is the gist of the argument laying the blame for the Holocaust at the doorstep of Zionism. It is interesting that, as early as the Second World War, harsh accusations were made by some ultra-Orthodox radicals concerning direct Zionist responsibility for what was happening: it was the Zionists' declarations that provoked the anger of the oppressor to the point of bloodshed; it was they who hindered the rescue effort; it was they who disturbed the tranquility of the Jews in the lands of their dispersion. Even the claim we are concerned with here, concerning sin and punishment, was voiced as early as the 1940s by the Neturei Karta, and since then has been repeated in many of their attacks.[98] But only in the writings of Teitelbaum did this idea became a fully developed doctrine, supported in detail by references to Jewish law and lore.

Actually, Teitelbaum's aim was to defend tradition and faith against a double assault: the theological incongruity of the Holocaust and the theological heresy implicit in Zionism. Both posed difficult challenges to the traditional passivity of the Exile;[99] by way of reaction, that passivity was turned into the very essence of Jewish faith and identity. It was not that the Exile had become untenable and brought about its own destruction, but that the Zionist betrayal of the Exile had brought catastrophe on the Jewish people. As the Zionists had "ascended the wall by force," rebelling against the nations and forcing the End, the nations in turn rose up and violated the one oath to which they had been adjured—"not to subjugate Israel overmuch." So Israel's flesh was stripped away and left to be devoured by wild beasts.[100] Moreover, just as the sin had been a collective one, involving the masses of the Jewish people, so was the punishment collective: once the assailant was given free rein to kill, he no longer distinguished between the righteous and the wicked. Thus was Teitelbaum's demonization of Zionism rendered complete. "Satan and the Angel of Death are one and the same" (BT Bava Batra 16a).

It is difficult here to avoid questioning, not only the image of Zionism reflected in this analysis, but also the image of God and of Divine Providence. Clearly, the God who had revealed Himself to Teitelbaum—a survivor of Bergen-Belsen whose family, community, and people were annihilated at Auschwitz—was the God of Judgment.

"THE TORAH STATE": A CONTRADICTION IN TERMS

The successful realization of the Zionist aspiration to create a Jewish state posed a painful dilemma for the Haredi camp. Until that point, the confrontation had been with a mere idea or vision; now there was the reality to contend with. It had been one thing to steer clear of a voluntary ideological movement, but it was quite another to remain separate from a living, comprehensive social structure with a full range of political, legal, economic, and military institutions. And in fact, the majority of ultra-Orthodox Jews chose to recognize the new historical reality, if only de facto, and were able to find ways of tolerating it, and even of cooperating with it to a limited degree.

The radicals, on the other hand, rejected outright any compromise with or reconciliation to the new polity, stubbornly refusing to accept the yoke of "the spirit of heresy armed with the power of the state."[101] The success of the evildoers on the material, political, or military level did not legitimate their iniquity. "The Amalekites, the 'mixed multitude,' take many forms," warned Rabbi Elyakum Schlesinger, head of the Ramah

Yeshivah in London. "What was once called Zionism and ostracized as such by all faithful Jews is now called a state. What was once the treasury of the Jewish National Fund is now the state treasury [*sic*]. The so-called pioneers, who were always considered beyond the pale, are now members of the Knesset." Even the apparent success of the evildoers in winning over observant Jews to their cause has no bearing on the essence of what they are about. "There are times when the 'mixed multitude' is clean-shaven and times when it is bearded, times when it seems boorish and ignorant and times when it takes the guise of the sage and the saint."[102] In other words, political or institutional cooperation between the Zionists and the Orthodox does not legitimate the former, but rather delegitimates the latter.

The Guardians of the Walls were determined not to budge from their fortress. Immediately after statehood was proclaimed, they imposed a ban on participation in elections to the Knesset, swore never to set foot in government institutions, and prohibited accepting any funds whatsoever from the state or its representatives, even for such sacred purposes as the support of yeshivot and communal activities. They redoubled their criticism of Agudat Israel, which ostensibly carried on its tradition of opposition to the Zionist movement yet accepted the benefits, financial and otherwise, of the Zionist state.[103] The separatists were particularly harsh in their condemnation of the Agudah's political "realism." Its leaders, they said, "were given the Torah of realism by the Evil Urge." Lacking in principle, the Agudah "used 'reality' and 'post-factum' [arguments] to make the criminal activities [of the Zionists] seem kosher" (Rabbi Elijah Porush).[104]

In the separatists' view, Agudat Israel represented treacherous pragmatism and opportunism, "[a bunch of] hypocrites and flatterers, latter-day renegades who are turning the world to lawlessness." Their deviance illustrated clearly the dangers that lay in wait for all God-fearing people now that Zionism had taken on a new, politically powerful, economically seductive guise. Logic and experience both teach that, "if [we] let up even to the slightest degree, God forbid, from our hatred of evil, of seducers and corrupters, [if we breach] the separateness to which our holy Torah obliges us . . . then the way is open to every forbidden thing, for we will have left the straight and narrow path for a crooked one (Rabbi Amram Blau)."[105]

The consolidation of the state thus led to an intensification of separatist protest and a deepening of the gulf between the "remnant of Israel" and "the regime that calls itself Israel." The more the Zionist undertaking took root in the Holy Land and the clearer it became that it was not merely a passing episode, the more inimical toward one another did external reality and internal principle seem. The former, the work of Satan, was utterly opposed to the latter, the word of God, and had to be totally ignored by the faithful. The radical position makes none of the pragmatic distinctions between ab initio and ex post facto, tactics and strategy, or short- and long-term objectives. It rejects concepts like partial realization, step-by-step progess, or accommodation to circumstances. It knows nothing of tacit consent, only of vocal protest.

As already noted, then, the traditional opposition of these groups to Zionism was directed not so much against the secular character of the movement as against its deeper theological meaning: the human attempt to usurp the messianic prerogative. The same logic was now at work in the castigation of the State of Israel: it is not that the state is secular or that it passes offensive laws, but that it exists at all; not that it behaves in one way or another, but that its very creation—by human, worldly, political initiative—is an affront. Yerahmiel Domb, the most extreme contemporary ideologue of the Neturei Karta, author of a dozen books and pamphlets, put it this way in an article in their newsletter, *Ha-Homah* (The wall, 1975):

> The Zionists profane the holy Sabbath, but that is profanation of the Sabbath, not Zionism, and there would be profaners of the Sabbath without them. The Zionists eat forbidden food, but that is not Zionism; there are many people in this world who eat forbidden food aside from the Zionists. The Zionists transgress and violate all [the teachings of] the Torah, but that is not Zionism; there were sinners in this world before Zionism came along. Zionism is one thing and one thing only: the state! *The State of Israel is the great defilement and the profound heresy that the Zionists have introduced* . . . In its very essence Zionism utterly denies the essentials of our faith, and it is an absolute denial that reaches down to the very depths, the very foundations, the very roots.

Or, as he put it in his wide-ranging work *Kuntres et nisayon* (Tract for a time of trial, 1972):

> Zionism in and of itself represents a negation of faith in the holiness of the Torah and the holiness of Israel, in the coming of the Messiah and the resurrection of the dead, in reward and punishment, in all things divine . . . Zionism, i.e., the notion that we [ought to] have a state, freedom, and independence, does not ostensibly contradict any explicitly [revealed] precept, positive or negative, yet it represents a dreadful heresy. The heresy of Zionism—leaving aside that of the Zionists themselves—amounts to a negation of all the principles of our faith . . . This Zionism, *[the idea] that we*

*[ought to be] a nation and have a state, is a pollution that encompasses all
other pollutions, a complete heresy that includes all other heresies.*[106]

Ironically, the author's view dovetails with that of a particular school of
thought within the Zionist movement, the one known as political Zionism.
In his view, what is essential to Zionism is not cultural or social revival or
even the ingathering of the exiles, but rather the achievement of Jewish self-
rule.

The upshot is that any form of Jewish historical (i.e., premessianic) existence that has the trappings of statehood is ipso facto invalid, whatever its
aims and however it conducts itself. Even if the state were to adopt the halakhah as its legal system and all its inhabitants became religious Jews, its
fundamental nature would not be affected, for there would still be the original sin of its having been established at all. "The very idea of the people of
Israel achieving independence before the coming of the Messiah represents
heresy against the ways of the Lord, may He be blessed, for it is He alone
who enslaves and redeems" (Teitelbaum).[107]

Thus the faithful should not strive for "religious legislation" or seek to
remake public life and institutions in the spirit of the Torah, as Israel's religious political parties boast of doing. The notion of a "Torah state" or a
"halakhic state" achieved by human beings is likewise no more than an
obscene slogan and a falsehood. Indeed, a "Torah state" would be a contradiction in terms, a vain attempt to realize the Torah by uprooting it.

These radical Haredi circles would seem, then, to be the most fervent
advocates of the separation of religion and state in Israel. Yet they call for
separation, not because the two realms have nothing to do with one another, but because they are in direct conflict. "It is not possible for one person to adhere to both faith in the state and faith in our holy Torah, for they
are complete opposites and cannot share a single crown."[108] Teitelbaum
put it most incisively: "Even if the cabinet ministers were 'all beloved [of
God], all pure,' even if they were all Talmudic sages, nevertheless, because
they have seized freedom and sovereignty before the appointed time, they
have committed heresy against our holy Torah and faith. The kingdom of
[Bar Kokhba] was, after all, ruled by the Torah . . . and his contemporaries
were all saints . . . Yet see how grievously they were punished, heaven spare
us the like, for [their actions, in rebelling against Rome] amounted to a
forcing of the End before the appointed time." "Even if the members of the
Knesset were saints, it would be a terrible crime to seize deliverance and
statehood, for the prohibition against violating the oaths and trying to advance the End applies to all Jews, however righteous."[109]

In summary, the State of Israel amounts to a perversion that cannot be rectified. It was conceived and born in sin, and hence the sole remedy is for the Jewish people as a whole to disengage itself from collective political activity and forgo entirely the sovereignty it so illicitly seized.

"RELIGIOUS LEGISLATION?"

The Neturei Karta are contemptuous of efforts made by the religious parties to pass "religious legislation" for another reason as well: the Torah and the commandments would be desecrated by the very fact of having been discussed and decided on by a secular legislature. This argument has important implications for public controversies now raging in Israel, far beyond the confines of the radical Haredi community in Jerusalem. We shall therefore examine it more closely. It involves, in fact, three interrelated claims.

First, with regard to the source of authority: in the radical view, any legislation regarding religious matters adopted by a secular body such as the Knesset makes the divine commandments seem human, thereby undermining the unique authority of the Torah as transcendent, revealed law. A citizen who obeys a Sabbath ordinance passed by the Knesset is obeying a "Zionist Sabbath law" rather than observing the holy Sabbath, even if the Knesset adopts the religious precepts of the Sabbath in their entirety. A religious law would thus have been converted into "a human, earthly, Gentile law of Zionism" that must be viewed as "a high-handed annulment of the Torah, by legal means, in favor of a human religion."[110] Secularization of the halakhah through its enactment into legislation is in fact desecration of the halakhah.

(There is an interesting analogy between this argument and Kant's well-known distinction between the moral imperative, rooted in an inward sense of duty, and the legal imperative, rooted in external authority. Here, too, what is decisive is not the resulting behavior but the intent, not the content of the law but the motivation for observing it. Of course, our concern here is with religious motivation rather than with the autonomous "categorical imperative," and thus what is at stake in the enactment of secular legislation is not just a downgrading, but a profanation.)

Second, even from a purely formal point of view, making questions of Torah and halakhah a matter of bargaining and voting in the legislature means subjecting the commandments—the word of God—to secular, human authority. Whatever the outcome, precedence is clearly given to the decisions of the legislature over the rulings of the halakhic codes, making for a "subversion of the Torah."[111] When the religious parties take part in such voting, they are implicitly accepting the right of the legislature and the electorate to accept or reject the Torah.

In the words of Rabbi Shimon Israel Posen, a leading halakhic authority of the Satmar community in New York: "Woe unto them for the shame of it, that people who put on phylacteries every day sit in that assembly [kinnus] of the wicked called the 'Knesset' and, signing their names to falsehoods, forge the signature of the Holy One, blessed be He, heaven forfend. For they think they can decide by majority vote whether the Torah of truth will be trampled upon even further or whether God's Torah will be granted authority; and they accept a reward from the enemies of the Lord, who embrace falsehood with all their might."[112]

Finally, even when it yields to the religious parties and passes such laws as a Sabbath ordinance, the Knesset adopts the laws selectively, and thus not in their halakhic form. It picks and chooses among the regulations and symbols as it sees fit, in reality creating its own version of the Sabbath. The public is thus grievously misled, for many innocent and seemingly innocent people take the Sabbath ordinance as an indication of what is permitted and forbidden by the Torah. The same criticism applies to a distinction made by the religious parties between the public domain, which should be governed by Jewish tradition, and the private domain, where each person should be free to do as he or she chooses. The Neturei Karta see this distinction as making a mockery of the Torah by depriving it of its authority in the private realm. Thus the Neturei Karta, in their polemical tract *Lehasir masveh* (Stripping away the mask), condemn Agudat Israel and its legislative initiatives: "According to the laws of our holy Sabbath, there is no difference between the severity of violation in private and that in public (except for the commandment to separate the violator from the community of Israel, which refers to the public realm), and it is no less forbidden to light a cigarette than to drive a train . . . [But once such a 'Sabbath ordinance' is passed,] everyone who obeys it will be considered a 'Sabbath observer,' even though they may commit violations [of the Sabbath] so serious that [in biblical law] capital punishment was ordained for them" (p. 12).

The conclusion of these three arguments is that observant Jews should not accept the rules of the parliamentary game or have any truck with such mischief. Their participation in the voting can only give a seal of religious approval to the decisions of the Knesset, thus precluding any future opposition. On the one hand, "the pious who enter the house of heresy enter into compromises regarding fundamentals of our holy Torah." On the other hand, "[their] power is thereby diminished": they forgo the right of protest, for their enemies can then always claim that "the pious have their representatives in the Knesset, but they are only an inconsequential minority who, as it were, haven't a leg to stand on, especially since they themselves are willing to concede essential points of Torah" (Teitelbaum).[113]

These arguments are all of a piece. Furthermore, they go hand in hand with the basic tenet of the Neturei Karta, which denies legitimacy to the Jewish state and to its appropriation of the name Israel. Let us be more concrete. Were the Edah Haredit, the Neturei Karta, or the Satmar Hasidim to accord the Israeli regime and the Israeli public the standing associated in religious tradition with *malkhut* (the kingdom), *nasi* (the prince), *kahal* (the community), or *klal Yisrael* (the Jewish people), would they then have to draw such a firm line between the religious and the political realms? They would then be halakhically in a position to grant juridical and religious authority to a consensus of the people or its representatives, to recognize the renewed validity of the classical distinction in Jewish tradition between, for example, individual and communal transgressions.

But such thinking, which characterizes many of the religious Zionists, is alien to them. Their demand that the Knesset keep out of matters of halakhah and religion is grounded not only in a fear of secularization but also in the theological denial of the legitimacy of the state itself, viewing it instead as an antimessianic attempt to force the End. It would not matter what form of government it had, democratic, monarchical, or even purely theocratic; the state cannot be improved. The only thing to do is to eliminate it.

One might well ask, Why, if the state is beyond repair, do the radical separatists continually mount street demonstrations rather than simply stay home? What point is there in sounding alarms and issuing denunciations if the effort is defined from the outset as being meaningless and futile? Indeed, if the Zionist public has in effect excluded itself from the historic Jewish people, are not the Lord's faithful released from all responsibility for its actions? To be sure, these demonstrations are avowedly not attempts to redress but mainly expressions of protest, declarations to all the world that the faithful remnant of Israel has no part in the machinations of the Zionists but rather utterly dissociates and separates itself from them.[114] The demonstrations call into question the right of the state and the majority of its people to use the name "Israel," or at least to monopolize it for themselves. This is the message for external consumption. At the same time, within their own community, the demonstrations function to "make the heretics smell bad," especially to the younger generation. A distinction is drawn, loudly and clearly, between the sacred and the profane, and all possible rapprochement with the unbelievers is ruled out. In this sense, confrontation per se, doing battle with the wicked, has a religious and educational value in its own right: "The duty to hate the wicked and combat them is a major principle of the Torah."[115] Or, in the words of the Psalmist, "O Lord, You know I hate those who hate You, and loathe Your adversaries" (Ps. 139:21).

Of course such ideological considerations do not exhaust the motivations that bring people into the streets. A Jew who cries "Shabbes! Shabbes!" in the streets of the Holy City is presumably doing more than making a symbolic gesture, and is not only concerned with the "world's" reaction or the education of his own children; no doubt he himself is actually pained by a concrete violation of the Sabbath he has witnessed. He is turning directly to the violators—typically, those who drive on the Sabbath—and demanding that they change their ways. He is motivated by the religious duty of reproof and the sense of responsibility all Jews are supposed to feel for one another, in spite of the oft-repeated assertion that the Zionists have excluded themselves from the Jewish people. Yet, as we have seen, the avowed purpose of these public demonstrations is to symbolize dissociation and withdrawal rather than involvement.

THE DEMONOLOGY OF VICTORY

When the Munkaczer Rebbe, some two generations ago, called the Zionist settlement movement the "Satan who chooses Jerusalem," his protest was directed against the national pretensions of the Zionists and their agricultural attempts in the Holy Land: their sinful efforts reflected the new, concrete embodiment of the demonic powers that have long hovered over the Land of Israel. But when the Satmarer Rebbe spoke about "the Satan who chooses Jerusalem to seduce and corrupt the entire world wrapped in the mantle of Jerusalem's glory," he was no longer speaking of mere beginnings and intentions of Zionism, but about its surprising historical success and its concrete political breakthrough. The Munkaczer Rebbe need only ask, "What is the source of their wickedness?" The Satmarer Rebbe, however, needed to go on to ask, "What is the source of their worldly success?" Naturally, the demonology of Zionism was now directed toward the actual historical process. That is, the material accomplishments of the collective rebellion against divine rule now manifest in the Holy Land testifies to the workings of the very real powers of evil that have arisen to challenge the Divine Presence in its own sanctuary. Only the literal intervention of Satan could have given the Zionists the strength to overcome holiness and drag an entire world down in their net.[116]

The demonological interpretation of Zionist history reached the height of its development following the Six-Day War, when the Zionists, saved from dire peril, stormed Judea and Jerusalem and entered the Temple Mount and the place of the Holy of Holies. This astounding military victory, seen by many Jews as a miraculous deliverance on a biblical scale, was a source of acute embarrassment to the radicals. After years of confidently awaiting the demise of the rebellious state, they were forced to bring their heightened religio-historical sensitivity to bear on a completely reversed situation. "Who can forget the darkness of the six days [in 1967] when, under the pretext of the [closing of the] Strait of Tiran, the Zionists arose, surveyed the earth, and declared war," the Neturei Karta's Rabbi Hayyim Katzenellenbogen said some time later: "And in the end they conquered all of Eretz Israel from the Arabs, reaching the place of our glorious Temple. And the thing led to confusion and uncertainty, which grew apace. During the first week after the conquest, the sages forgot their wisdom; the trail of successes and the [ostensible] miracles, as well as [their own] blindness, led them to dance around the [Golden] Calf. Perfectly pious Jews looked catastrophe in the face and could not cope with it."[117]

The religious mind has always wondered "why . . . the wicked prosper" (Job 21:7; Jer. 12:1), why Divine Providence fails to intervene in the natural order and defeat them. In this there is nothing new. But that the triumph of evil should actually be assisted by wonders? That fortune should actually smile on those who would force the End? Such a situation could only lead to what the social psychologists call cognitive dissonance.[118] On the one hand, there were the events themselves, which in the religious imagination evoked associations of the miraculous, "the deliverance of the Lord in the blink of an eye" and enter into the sacred precincts; on the other hand, there was the unworthiness of "the saved," those heretics and destroyers of the Covenant who should by all rights have been spurned rather than rescued by Providence.

The Satmarer Rebbe, who viewed this problem with utmost gravity, "spoke out with a voice that 'kindles flames' [Ps. 29:7]," according to one of his admirers, "calling out in the assembly of the believers, 'Whoever is for the Lord, come here!' [Exod. 32:26]. But as for him who believes [the Zionists'] successes are 'miraculous,' he has no place among us."[119] Teitelbaum understood very well which aspect of the new reality would be most seductive, and he strictly forbade his followers to go to the Western Wall, now made accessible by the Israeli victory. (In Jerusalem, Amram Blau seems to have issued such a ban even earlier.) The God-fearing must refrain from enjoying the forbidden fruits of the Zionist conquest. They were duty-bound to stay well out of earshot of the shofar blasts on the Temple Mount that defiled the holy places with a nationalistic, military myth.

Teitelbaum was urgently concerned with offering the public more systematic guidance as well, and within a short time he published a book entitled *Al ha-geulah ve-al ha-temurah* (On Redemption and its [illegitimate] Substitutes). Here he explains the deeper meaning of the events, calling on the remnant of Israel to summon all its strength for that fateful—perhaps final?—stand against the forces of evil that must precede the redemption. "[As for] the conquest of the Old City and the place of the Temple . . . how could anyone imagine that the Holy One, blessed be He, would perform miracles for idolators? [Such a notion] is pure heresy. The only possible explanation is that this is the work of [Satan] and his minions . . . [Satan] is sparing no effort to deceive the world [through these events], for in this trial our redemption is at stake."[120]

In other words, the people of Israel now face the greatest test of faith they have ever encountered. It is no longer the classic situation in which Jews, confronted with the gray reality of exile in an unchanging world, are asked to persevere in their belief in miraculous deliverance. The present trial is a more difficult one, a test of the faith that true redemption is yet to come in the face of a reality that has only the appearance of redemption, but is in fact the work of the Devil. It is this test that will separate the wheat from the chaff, purifying the God-fearing for their messianic destiny.

Teitelbaum had the wisdom to instill his followers with a sense of the momentous, heroic nature of their task, so as to counterbalance the feelings of heroic, historic achievement then current among the Zionists—"for we know from the sages and the holy books that each time thought is given above to our [true] redemption, Satan conspires to produce a mere appearance of redemption in its stead."[121]

FAITH AND DETERMINISM

The heady feeling in Israel following the Six-Day War was short-lived. The Yom Kippur War of 1973 and the Lebanon War of 1982, as well as the peace accords with Egypt, all decidedly diluted the sense of success; the excitement was dampened by doubt and gave way to a measure of realism.

These historic turns have not been without their effect on the Neturei Karta and their polemics, eliciting, in recent years, a certain ambivalence on their part. To be sure, these people have remained alienated from political and military power and have continued to stress the demonic character of the state's victories and successes. But at the same time, one begins to detect an opposite focus as well, reminiscent of views expressed by their spokesmen in the early years of independence—a focus upon the retreats, material failures, and political weaknesses of the state as decisive proof of its false, transitory character. In this view, external reality no longer appears as dissonant with, but rather as affirming, in many respects, deeply held beliefs and expectations about the future. Indeed, a number of writers in this camp (particularly in its periodical press) implicitly acknowledge this change when they speak of the various periods in recent history in terms of "the rise of the Zionist state" and "its decline."[122]

But whether current events favor the Zionist cause or not, the radicals are expected to stand aside and watch from the sidelines in utter passivity. Their assigned role is that of spectator and critic, not that of shaper and mover. In this sense, their approach differs profoundly from the revolutionary one of latter-day Muslim[123] and Western radicalism, as well as from that of contemporary Jewish political messianism. The zealotry of the Haredim entails protest and withdrawal, not an attempt to seize power. Indeed, the more militant this radicalism becomes, the less likely it is to use political power or physical force to achieve its ends.

It is unthinkable, for example, that the Neturei Karta would ever organize underground paramilitary activity against the State of Israel. This would turn them into "Zionists" themselves, as they see it, for they would then be furthering the normalization of the Jewish people. What do the Zionists want, after all, but to turn the Lord's people into a nation like all nations, to determine its fate through earthly means and by force. To fight them with their own "Gentile" weapons would be to concede the Zionists' victory, an act of surrender by the remnant of Israel.

The archmilitant Domb put it this way in his pamphlet *Al ha-nissim* (On miracles):

> We have no alternative political program to that of Zionism, nor do we have bombs or other weapons. We shall take no action against the heretical Jewish state, any more than against the Vatican or the Communist states. We are bound to oppose and protest, but responsibility for the course of history rests in the hands of God alone. Whether the Zionists are for the moment successful or not, we put no faith in them. They could build an empire and we would still deny their legitimacy and refuse their favors.[124]

The more extreme faction of the Neturei Karta has achieved notoriety by going so far as to profess affinity for the enemies of the State of Israel. Some have professed support for the PLO (or, in an earlier period, for the

Kingdom of Jordan) and have made symbolic gestures of solidarity with it. Does this not contradict the principle of political passivity? In their view it is simply an assertion of religious principle, not an attempt to change the course of political history. Jewish sovereignty in the "age of exile" must be negated, and the adherence of the Jewish people to its solemn oath to God must be publicly reaffirmed. God Himself has ordained that, for the time being, Jews should be ruled by Gentiles, and the Zionists have rebelled against this decree. The latter must therefore not be allowed to appear as the sole representatives of the Jewish people. Moreover, this position is seen as being very much within the classic tradition of submission to the powers that be, a pattern reflecting the Jewish instinct for survival in the age of exile. Assuming that the designs of the Devil are short-lived and that the Zionist regime is not long for this world, is it not wise to begin now to cultivate its successor? Should not steps be taken now to prevent this new ruler from seeing the Jewish people as his mortal enemy? The Neturei Karta are, as it were, simply looking out for long-range Jewish interests.

Hence what we have is both a declaration of religious conviction and an act of *shtadlanut* (diplomacy that curries favor with the authorities), in perfect accord with the requirements of Jewish existence in the exilic age and in perfect opposition to the Zionist attempt to bring that age to an end.

For all its passivity, this position, the Neturei Karta believe, will ultimately win out. The remnant of Israel will triumph, and the Jewish people as a whole will be reshaped in its image. Like radical groups everywhere, the Haredi extremists see themselves as the vanguard of the future, only temporarily biding their time as a deviant, separatist minority. Now on the margins of history, they are the true harbingers of history's promised and long-awaited fulfillment. The Neturei Karta are thus those who remain true, not only to the past but also to the future; who leave the camp, as it were, to scout ahead. As Domb writes in another of his pamphlets: "While yet under the rule of darkness, we shall know no victory, only struggle . . . We shall not triumph today, but it is crystal clear that triumph will ultimately be ours . . . The future belongs not to the [Golden] Calf or to those dancing [around it] but rather . . . to the Lord."[125]

Whatever their numerical weight, it is the faithful who provide the nucleus around which events are destined to unfold. Contemporary writers, like Margolis before them, point to the inner struggles in Jewish history in which those few who keep the spark alive muster the strength of spirit to stand up to the many who betray the Covenant. It is the former whom history vindicates, from the biblical instances of Joshua and Caleb in their dissent from the other ten scouts, or Elijah in his challenge to the prophets of

Baal, to the later struggles of Rabbi Jacob Sasportas against the Sabbateans and of Rabbi Jacob Emden, "who commanded his son never to be afraid, but to stand his ground, even if he be the last surviving adherent of his luminous teachings."[126]

Clearly manifest in these ideas is the radicals' deterministic view of the future of the State of Israel. In its antimessianism, Zionism represents an obstacle in the inevitable path of history, one standing in the way of the redemption. The rebellious Jewish state is doomed to destruction in the process. "It is clear beyond all shadow of a doubt that the buildings put up by the heretics and apostates in our Holy Land will all be burned to the ground by the Messiah, leaving not a trace behind," Teitelbaum wrote following the 1967 victory, "and in their place the Lord, may He be blessed, will raise up for us other buildings sanctified by supernal holiness; and then 'the nations that are left around you shall know that I the Lord have rebuilt the ravaged places' [Ezek. 36:36], and they will not be as they were [before]."[127] It is as if the prophecies and midrashim concerning the cataclysm to precede the redemption, the terrible birth pangs of the Messiah, all referred to the fate of Zionism.[128] The Jewish state was conceived and born in sin; there can thus be no gradual process of evolution, improvement, or purification in its case, only a complete uprooting, with the structure of the future to be erected on the ruins of the past.

Ironically, a sense of Jewish solidarity is often a prominent feature of such discussions. The Neturei Karta say, "May the state be destroyed without a single Jew getting hurt!"[129] The Lord will find ways of clearing a path for the Messiah without shedding Jewish blood. Thus Teitelbaum, predicting the downfall of the "heretical kingdom" as a necessary precondition for the redemption, is careful to add, "Divine mercy will be needed so that this kingdom is destroyed entirely by divine means and not by the other nations, because if the nations do it there will of course be a great danger to the Jewish people."[130]

Even after the Six-Day War, which he saw as a manifestation of the demonic, he wrote, "While the war was underway there was no choice but to pray in earnest for the Jewish people that they not be devoured by [the Gentiles] and not meet a horrible end, God forbid."[131] And apparently his concern was not confined to the fate of those few thousand Jews in the Holy Land whom he saw as the "remnant of Israel."

The same could not be said for the sovereign Jewish state, that Tower of Babel erected by the Zionists. For it, there could be no escape from the sentence of deterministic messianism.

3

"The Revealed End":
Messianic Religious Zionism

"A MESSIANIC REALITY"

> How is it that the movement for concrete redemption in our time, including
> the settlement and conquest of the Land [of Israel] and the abandonment and
> abolition of exilic existence, did not originate with the religious? How is it
> that some religious spokesmen even withheld their support for Zionism and
> the movement for redemption? . . . They failed to recognize that it was not
> that we mortals were forcing the End, but rather that the Master of the
> House, the Lord of the Universe, was forcing our hand; that it was not human
> voices that broke down the wall separating us from our land, but the voice of
> the living God calling upon us to "Go up!"[1]

This declaration, made by Rabbi Zvi Yehudah ha-Cohen Kook (1891–
1981), mentor of the "redemptionist" religious-Zionist camp during the
decades following the establishment of the State of Israel, sums up con-
cisely and eloquently the way this camp reacted to ultra-Orthodox theological criticism of Zionism. For the former, the Zionist undertaking did
not stem from a merely human initiative or breakthrough, from nationalistic arrogance or self-assertion. Rather, it sprang from a divine thrust toward redemption, a compelling higher call to which the people of Israel
responded with historic fidelity. Zionism, "the movement for concrete redemption in our time," is thus part of a new phase of Jewish history in
which the people are released from their age-old, enforced passivity and
freed entirely of their fear of the three oaths.[2] Zionism actively assaults "the
wall separating us from our land" and goes on to build on the strength of a   79

new religious imperative not heard in previous generations. "No, it is not we who are forcing the End," Kook would say to his disciples, "but the End that is forcing us!"[3]

It is true, the rabbi and his followers would say, that many God-fearing Jews have not heard the voice charging them with "the divine historic imperative of ending the Exile." They have not discerned the signs of the new era, with its urgent messianic tidings. It is also true that many Zionists, including some of the most devoted pioneers, have not seen fit to acknowledge the divine origin of the call. They are not aware of the religious meaning of their undertaking and at times even deny it vehemently. Yet on a deeper level, both groups, religious and secular alike, are moving in unison toward the fulfillment of a single, well-laid-out messianic purpose. In their subjectively different ways they all fit into one objective plan. Whether they are aware of it or not, it is Divine Providence that grips them,[4] guiding them inexorably toward the final redemption of Israel.

Kook, yeshivah dean, ideologue, and educator, wielded considerable public influence, far beyond the circle of his students and immediate disciples. In the period following the Six-Day War, he was even able to impose the stamp of his personality and outlook on social developments in Israel as a whole. His public statements provided the impetus for energetic, wide-ranging political activity. To this day, more than a decade after his death, his ideas remain a beacon for many in the Zionist yeshivot, and even more so for the leadership of Gush Emunim and the movement for the settlement of Jews in Judea and Samaria.

The nationalist ideology of Rabbi Kook and his followers views the history of Zionism as an inevitable and decidedly messianic process, leading to the realization of prophetic predictions: "the State of Israel as the fulfillment of the biblical vision of redemption."[5] Messianism is no longer to be seen as the antithesis of concrete reality. It is no longer merely a critique of what is, nor is it addressed only to the future. Rather, messianic redemption springs from present events; it is embodied and realized in them. "Our reality is one of *teshuvah* [return to God, repentance], and it is a messianic one,"[6] writes Kook. In other words, the traditional religious categories of holiness, redemption, and repentance have now assumed concrete form in the Zionist endeavor itself. They are given living, dynamic expression as part of the process of the return to Zion and the Jewish national revival. This is indeed "the true redemption, as revealed in the full realization of [Jewish] settlement of the land and the resurrection of the Jewish people here, in the ongoing ingathering of the exiles . . . It appears when we fully inherit the land and achieve complete sovereignty over it, when our public life is thoroughly infused with the holiness of its concreteness."7

To be sure, this is "messianism" without a messiah, a redemptive process that takes place in the absence of a living human redeemer. In these circles, as distinct from those of the present generation of Lubavitcher Hasidim (see below), immediate religious expectation does not center on a personal messiah. Without abandoning traditional beliefs, attention is focused in a new way on the realm of collective history. One seeks the signs of Divine Providence amidst contemporary events in the life of the nation. "It is this divine dynamic that is the messianic process," writes Rabbi Shlomo Aviner, rabbi of Beit-El and dean of the Ateret Kohanim Yeshivah in the Muslim quarter of Jerusalem. "The messianic process is a concrete, divine reality, the action upon history of a powerful redeemer [God], the Rock of Israel, who lives within history." He continues with undisguised irony:

> If someone whispers in your ear that he has "not seen the Messiah lately, either in the fields of the Golan or in the expanses of the Sinai" [territories seized by Israel in the Six-Day War—Trans.], he may be an honest man . . . But if he goes a step further and says, "Since I have not seen it, it does not exist," his words are words of falsehood and seduction. Say to him, "You may not have seen it, but others have" . . . We declare the absolute certainty of our imminent redemption . . . All the troubles, delays, and complications we have endured are merely momentary and cannot obscure this mighty overall trend, this Messiah, whose power has been concealed since ancient times in the treasure house of history and who is now being revealed in actuality.8

Clearly, the messiah referred to here is merely a metaphor for the messianic idea and the messianic age. A personal messiah will certainly come but, contrary to the common conception among the ultra-Orthodox, it is not he who will bring about the historic turn, nor will he, with his own hands, set in motion the redemptive process. On the contrary, this turn and this process will give birth to him. The Messiah is not involved in the *at-ḥalta de-ge'ulah*, the beginning of redemption; he is not responsible for the planting and growth of the fruit, but rather for its ripening. The concrete, historical Beginning we are witnessing today has not come about through a personal redeemer, but through our collective activity and the changes that have taken place in our character as a people.

In one sense this approach is not new, of course. Were there not Kabbalistic teachers who taught that messianic redemption was the collective responsibility of the fellowship or of the community as a whole?9 And had not even these mystics concluded centuries earlier that the Messiah would not bring about the process, but mark its culmination? "This is why the purification and refining were necessary, to set everything aright . . . and until all is set aright, the King Messiah cannot come" (Meir Ibn-Gabbai, sixteenth century).[10] True enough, yet we see here an interesting departure (along the lines of the new tack already taken by the Harbingers of Zionism). Unlike the traditional Kabbalistic sages, who saw redemption as hinging entirely on spiritual rectification and the fulfillment of a mystical, cosmic mission, this activist school gives precedence to perfecting this world and achieving historical, political fulfillment. For them, it is the Zionist undertaking, in all its concreteness, that embodies the needed collective rectification and truly reflects the Jewish people's response to the divine call. And it is Zionism that, in the last analysis, prepares the way for universal personal redemption as well. Thus Kook wrote, "The End is being revealed before our very eyes, and there can be no doubt or question that would detract from our joy and gratitude to the Redeemer of Israel . . . The End is here!"[11]

A DIVINE POLITY

The establishment of the State of Israel and the reclaiming of the Land of Israel thus stand at the very heart of a decisively messianic process. This being the case, the Jewish state can no longer be portrayed as a merely historical or social phenomenon; its very existence is fraught with religious meaning, and in the final analysis it appears to embody something quite metaphysical. "Zionism is a heavenly matter," Kook went so far as to say. "The State of Israel is a divine entity, our holy and exalted state!"[12] In other words, the tidings of the redemption of Israel, the consciousness of present messianic realization, have not only toppled "the wall separating us from our land"; they have eliminated at one stroke the formidable barrier between the theological and the political, the heavenly and the earthly.

Indeed, some thirty years prior to the founding of the state, Zvi Yehudah Kook's distinguished father, Rabbi Abraham Isaac Kook, the Chief Rabbi of Eretz Israel, already envisioned "our state, the State of Israel, the pedestal of God's throne in this world" (see the introduction). But what for the father had been merely a utopian hope was manifest to the son and his followers as a concrete reality. The apparently eschatological laurels bestowed by Rabbi Kook on the future messianic state—"an ideal state, whose only aim should be that the Lord be acknowledged as one and His name one, which is truly the highest happiness"[13]—were now to be bestowed upon a given political-historical entity, in the here and now. The latent holiness that had so long awaited its appointed hour[14] now burst forth into the full light of day, in all its authenticity, in the shape of the state of the redeemed people of Israel. To be sure, the Jewish state is to be judged, not just by its outward appearance, but by its "inner hidden essence." We are asked to strip away its outer shell and, with a spiritual eye, gaze into its metaphysical core. In the words of a eulogy of Zvi Yehudah Kook delivered by one of his principal disciples, Rabbi Hayyim Druckman, dean of the Or Etzion Yeshivah and former member of the Knesset: "He was one of the few in his generation—I dare say the only one—to grasp fully the messianic revelation the State of Israel represents, to see the light of the Messiah shining forth from the State of Israel . . . He was the only one who taught us how to embrace wholeheartedly the truth that this state, with all its problems, is a divine one."[15] The point was made even more strongly by Rabbi Eliezer Waldman, dean of the Kiryat Arba Yeshivah, likewise a former Knesset member, in response to a debate that raged in Israel following the Lebanon War: " 'Our state, the State of Israel, the pedestal of God's throne in this world'—this has, in fact, been the purpose of the Jewish state ever since it was founded. Its purpose is to reveal the unity between the most exalted divine values and their manifestation by Israel in the world."[16] Here we have the image of the Jewish state as an integral theopolitical whole, the very existence of which aims at the realization of a Jewish "City of God" here on earth. Borrowing for a moment the rhetoric of the sociologists of religion,[17] we may say that in this concept religious faith sanctifies the sociopolitical structure, transferring it to the realm of the absolute and thereby bestowing upon it a transcendent validity.

Inevitably, the concrete actions of the Jewish state too become hallowed. "The holiness of the divine service [*avodah*, literally, work], the service of the Temple, is extended to the work of the state as a whole, both practical and spiritual, both public and private," wrote Zvi Yehudah Kook.[18] By the same token, Israel's wars, too, come to be seen not merely in terms of national survival (in halakhic terms, "rescuing Israel from the enemy")[19] or reclaiming the ancestral land. They are portrayed in ethical and theological terms, as a mighty struggle to uproot evil and achieve universal rectification.

"From the perspective of faith we see the divine hand spread over us, and especially over our wars. It leads us to recognize the righteousness of our actions and our wars and their indispensability, not only for us but for all the nations!" Thus writes Rabbi Zvi Tau, a leading light of this camp in the last two decades. "The wars of Israel are essentially wars against war, for whoever rises up against Israel rises up against the light of God in the world, which is the supernal peace!"[20] A struggle that appears to be over particular national interests is in fact over universal human values. This conclusion is, in fact, a direct consequence of the peremptory identification of the political Israel and the theological one. From this point of view, the State of Israel's enemies are by definition enemies of the God of Israel, "the exaltation of Israel is the exaltation of heaven," military victory is tantamount to spiritual victory, and "the wars of Israel represent the steps of the Messiah, marching toward his own coronation."[21]

Rabbi Waldman fleshes out this idea:

> When the [Lebanon] war broke out, there were those who claimed we had not come to impose order on Lebanon but rather to save the Galilee. But we pointed out that it is Israel's task to bring order into the world. This statement incensed many learned Jews . . . but we must not recoil or shrink from this responsibility. It is our duty to establish an order of faith and holiness, an order such as is described in the verses, "My house shall be called a house of prayer for all peoples" [Isa. 56:7] and "The land shall be filled with devotion to the Lord" [Isa. 11:9], an order in the relations between man and God and between man and man, an order among nations, among countries. Who is going to bring order into the world? Those who submit to evil? The great powers, which are themselves suffused with wickedness or give in to it? The people of Israel is the only one which is prepared to bring order . . . The situation of crime and injustice . . . will continue until we make order.[22]

All distinctions between the spiritual and the military have been deliberately blurred here. The army of Israel, which is the army of the Lord, is called out of Zion to establish a *pax Judaica* in the Middle East and ultimately in the world as a whole, in preparation for the fulfillment of the vision of the End of Days. To be sure, this is an extreme expression of the kind of political messianism we are discussing. But it emerges from the heart of the camp and is not unrepresentative of trends present there. Rabbi Dov Lior, dean of the Kiryat Arba Yeshivah and a radical spokesman of these groups, said at the time that "the war [in Lebanon] has proven to the whole world that there is in the Middle East only one people militarily strong enough to be considered a real power . . . Rooting out the dens of iniquity [of the terrorists] is but a preliminary to the eventual rooting out of all evil in the world. The present situation proves that the State of Israel is the one power in the world with which all nations are compelled willy-nilly to reckon."[23]

Let us now cast a look back over the entire development. Jewish mysticism always understood "Israel" not only as a collection of individual men and women, but as an overarching idea. "The People of Israel" and "the Congregation of Israel" are anchored in a higher, metaphysical realm of being, and the whole is greater than the sum of the parts. Redemptionist Zionism, which drew amply upon this notion and added to it the modern, European element of the "national spirit," has now applied the concept directly to the State of Israel. The latter, the political embodiment of the Congregation of Israel, is perceived as "a stairway set on the ground, and its top reached to the sky" (Gen. 28:12). Earthly military exploits are also raised to a metaphysical plane and take on a universal, messianic meaning and validity.[24]

Note that in this instance religion is not lending its sanction to a conservative social structure but to an innovative one (i.e., Jewish political sovereignty), a structure that represents revolutionary change in the life of the people. "Messianism is the dynamism of the Torah,"[25] Zvi Yehudah Kook taught, and it is therefore messianism that makes it possible and, indeed, praiseworthy to sanctify the new.

NATIONAL REVIVAL AND THE RECONSTITUTION OF THE SANHEDRIN

In the preceding sections, I discussed some of the ideological assumptions underlying the radical-redemptionist interpretation of the history of Zionism and the State of Israel. Of course, we cannot detach these views from the actual social and political phenomena. Ideas shape historical events but are also responsive to them, in ways that are sometimes obvious, sometimes less so. However, our main concern here is with the ideas themselves, both theological and ideological: their development and impact on the course of events.

What were the principal sources of redemptionist Zionism? It will be recalled that by the middle of the nineteenth century there were rabbinical voices—those of the Harbingers of Zionism—calling in messianic terms for Jewish settlement in Palestine and giving concrete, worldly content to the need for collective repentance and rectification. But their vision had only limited influence at the time. In fact, as I stressed in the introduction, religious authorities such as "the Netziv" (Naftali Zvi Yehudah Berlin), who supported the Lovers of Zion in the 1880s, and even more so rabbis like Reines and Rabinowitz, who joined the leadership of the Zionist movement at the end of the century, sought to suppress the messianic hopes that were being pinned on the new movement. They attempted to draw a sharp distinction between the current practical need to settle in the Land of Israel and the religious redemption expected in the Time to Come. But with the passage of time—the beginnings of real Zionist achievement, the Balfour Declaration—overtly messianic sentiments were once again heard in religious Zionist circles. Thus the national undertaking came to draw upon traditional longings for messianic redemption.

It was only in the writings of Rabbi Abraham Kook (father of Rabbi Zvi Yehudah) in the first third of the twentieth century, however, that the redemptionist position was fully articulated, in a manner laden with historiosophic and mystical overtones. And as I have just illustrated, this view was further sharpened, intellectually and politically, in the ensuing generations, under the impact of the destruction of European Jewry, the establishment of the State of Israel, and the wars fought by Israel.

In fact, more than any of the other religious authorities considered in this work, it is Rabbi Abraham Kook who has been of interest to scholars of Jewish thought. Dozens of books and hundreds of articles have been devoted to his teachings in recent years, and, understandably, there does not appear to be any end in sight. We are thus excused from an overall consideration of Kook's thought. Nonetheless, we may well ask what was the point of departure for Kook's innovative, dialectical notions of national revival and messianic redemption? What was the inner problematic that gave rise to these ideas and accompanied them throughout? Finally, how are Rabbi Kook's ideas on the national question related to the larger body of his historiosophic and theological thought? These questions, which are of course vital to our inquiry, have not yet been fully dealt with, and so we shall consider them first.

We shall then return and ask, How do the ideas of the father Rabbi Abraham Kook relate to those of the son Rabbi Zvi Yehudah and the latter's disciples? How have these ideas become radicalized over the years, and at the same time, how have they affected the living social and political reality of the State of Israel?

I shall begin with the first signs of Rabbi Abraham Kook's Zionist aspirations. In 1898, when political Zionism was in its infancy, a young Latvian rabbi wrote a programmatic pamphlet on the question of Zionism and religion, or more precisely on the proper relation between the Jewish national revival and the laws of the Torah. The rabbi had been greatly impressed by the First Zionist Congress, which had just been held in Basel, where the intention of establishing a "homeland" for the Jewish people in Palestine had been proclaimed. But this writer, unlike the (anti-Zionist) "protesting rabbis," developed an original, bold approach to the new national undertaking in terms of its religious significance. On the one hand, he attempted to defend Zionism against its ultra-Orthodox critics, "to remove the fear of some of the leading sages and God-fearers that the Zionist movement will, in the spirit of reform, bring about schisms in our holy Torah."[26] On the other hand, he rejects outright the secular tendencies associated with Zionism, aiming "to purify Zionism of all the filth and mire smeared upon it by reckless writers."[27] Indeed, the high hopes the author has for the new Jewish national movement go far beyond the declared goals of the fathers of political Zionism themselves.

The author, then serving as rabbi of the small community of Boisk, is none other than Abraham Kook. The pamphlet is apparently his first work on the question of national revival, yet it has unfortunately been ignored by all Kook scholars. What is more, one of the essay's central features is a daring call for the reconstitution of the Great Sanhedrin (the supreme religious and judicial assembly of sages in ancient Palestine) and a renewal of the historic chain of rabbinic ordination. Yet the work has been overlooked even by those who, after the establishment of the state, fought for this very idea, chief among them being the leader of the Mizrachi movement, Rabbi Judah Leib Maimon. Faced with harsh criticism from various rabbinic quarters, they nevertheless failed to marshal Rabbi Kook's work to their defense.

In fact, it seems likely that the author himself, the young Kook, chose at first to keep the essay out of the public eye, which explains why it was first published more than twenty years after its composition.[28] Nevertheless, this forgotten pamphlet provides us with an interesting insight into the sources of Kook's later thinking on the national question, his mature redemptionist philosophy, which was clearly formulated only after his immigration to Palestine. The pamphlet also shows us the first signs of the inner problematic that was to characterize Kook's teachings for many years to come.

What distinguishes Kook's position at this time? First, unlike the well-known Zionist rabbis of the day, he continues to elaborate the dream of the Harbingers of Zionism, endowing the Zionist undertaking with a clearly messianic import. Needless to say, his essay takes an activist, worldly stance on the question of national revival: "Nothing in our faith, either in its larger principles or in its details, negates the idea that we can begin to shake off the dust of exile by our own efforts, through natural, historical processes . . . that we have a sacred duty to try to do so by whatever means are at our disposal." He rejects out of hand the commonly held traditional view that, in his words, "we cannot hope for the salvation of Israel except through palpable miracles, such as the coming of Elijah, upon which our own efforts have no bearing."[29] But the young Kook goes further, daring to speak openly of "the generation of the Messiah" and "the roots of the coming of the Messiah" as being embodied in the concrete historical process of the return to Zion. In his view, and in contrast to the common interpretation,[30] even the Talmudic concept of *hilkheta di-meshiha* (messianic law) refers, not to legislation wondrously ordained by a personality of a higher order, but simply to Halakhic legislation enacted collectively in the Land of Israel at the time of the Jewish return to Zion. For, as I have already emphasized, the Messiah is not to be understood as the driving force behind the historical process but as its outcome. "The term *meshiha* [Messiah] can also refer to the time when Israel returns to *bitzaron* [literally, stronghold; i.e., Jerusalem (according to Zech. 9:12)], since this return is the very root of the Coming of the Messiah, even though full redemption has not yet been attained. What is decisive is that this is the generation of the Messiah, who sets his seal upon the superiority and greatness of Israel. There is thus no contradiction between this Talmudic statement [concerning *hilkheta di-meshiha*; BT Sanhedrin 51b; Zevahim 45a] and the obligation to strive for the salvation of our people, just as Nehemiah and his followers strove for it in Second Temple times."[31] Furthermore, the young Kook expects Zionism to propel the nation, not only to political, but to spiritual revival as well. He charges it with the comprehensive task of bringing about radical change in the life of the Jewish people, of sparking a thoroughgoing renaissance—political, cultural, legal, spiritual—with untold consequences. Here, too, his views differ significantly from those of his Zionist rabbinical contemporaries who, as we have seen, sought to confine nationalistic activity, for the time being, to the pursuit of material and political goals.[32] Terrified that the new Zionist initiative would trespass into religiously sensitive realms, that it might usurp the spiritual role of Judaism itself, they tried to neutralize it from any involvement in Jewish religion or culture.

It is interesting to note how Kook rationalizes his comprehensive demands. On the one hand, as he could learn from the political philosophy of Maimonides,[33] political freedom for the nation is a necessary precondition for spiritual freedom and cultural efflorescence. Neither the elite of the Jewish people nor the rank and file can find the wellsprings of their spirit or their creative voice "as long as they are not planted in the land of our forefathers, led by rulers who spring from our own midst and are independent of outside control. Only then will our spirit soar."[34] Or, in the terms of the debate over the nature of Zionism that was going on when Kook's pamphlet was published, it is only the full realization of "political Zionism" that can prepare the ground for the realization of "spiritual Zionism."

Yet the reverse is also true: there cannot be a political rebirth without a parallel spiritual one to guide it. As Kook warns us in light of the development of the national idea in Europe, "When nationalism alone"—in the absence of spiritual or moral depth—"takes root among the people, it is as likely to debase and dehumanize their spirit as to elevate it." National reawakening in and of itself is perennially prone to rapid degeneration into a narrow, crude "patriotism" that tramples underfoot the divine image within Humankind. Kook apparently has in mind in particular the sharp decline of the French Revolution into various forms of tyranny, while still wrapped in the mantle of the "general will." To be sure, Kook writes, "our own nationalism is immune to such excesses, but only as long as it is guided by its true nature, which is the spirit of the Lord that is over us and that His prophet adjures us not to let depart from our mouths or the mouths of our offspring until the end of time."[35] It is only the religious spirit, he believes, that can protect the Jewish national revival from the malady of totalitarianism.

Above all these pronouncements hovers Kook's firm faith in the organic connection between the Congregation of Israel and the God of Israel, between the "national idea" and the "divine idea"—to draw upon concepts he develops in his later work. There can be no revival of the one without revival of the other.

Now Kook sees the hoped-for historical turnabout as beginning with frankly institutional measures. Just as the fathers of political Zionism saw the establishment of a Jewish state as the focus of a national revival, he sees the reestablishment of the Great Sanhedrin, once the supreme authority in the realm of the Oral Law, as the focus of a religious revival. He places utopian hopes in the supreme Jewish religious center that is to be established in Palestine, a center he sees as capable of healing the many spiritual ailments the people suffer because of their exile. First and foremost, this center can restore vitality and stature to the Torah and thereby overcome latter-day tendencies to religious watering-down and outright secularization. The Jerusalem Sanhedrin's aura of antiquity and the great dignity it will derive from the fact that it will bring together the most distinguished rabbinic personalities will, he believes, give the body the authority, enjoyed by the ancient sages: to legislate vigorously, mend breaches in the wall of religion, and teach a single Torah and code of laws to the entire people.

Judaism will thus be restored to its former glory as the focus of national identity. Thus in his pamphlet Kook writes:

> We who believe in the rebirth of our people . . . know that we shall yet be planted on our land. We shall then build and establish our way of life as befits a living people aspiring to freedom and justice . . . Our first duty will be to establish a religious center . . . and above all a Great Sanhedrin, from which Torah and instruction shall issue forth to all Israel, so as to restore the great pillar, that of the Oral Torah, to its rightful place . . . It is not too wondrous a thing nor is it far off that all the sages of Israel will [come together to] make decisions, when we have been planted on our land with all the appurtenances of statehood, and the great well-being that the restoration of rabbinical ordi-nation will bring the people shall be in evidence. [The Sanhedrin] will exam-ine each ruling and custom, acting in accordance with the Torah. And there is no doubt that even the freethinkers will admit that the people need a religious center . . . Now that the national genius is, with God's help, extending its scope; now that there is increasing recognition of and desire to take pride in the sancta of our people; and given the certainty that these will grow even more as the Zionist movement grows and prospers, God willing, we can be certain that respect for the Torah will increase among the people as a whole, and no one will even think of desecrating it in the slightest way.[36]

> Unless we are planted in our ancestral land and live an independent life ruled by our own, we cannot expect to see widespread knowledge of the Torah to-gether with a broadening of wisdom and fear of God. Only then shall our spirits be exalted and our hidden talents revealed in such great measure as befits the shepherds of Israel.[37]

That is, the restoration of a supreme Jewish religious authority, both legis-lative and judicial, was regarded by Rabbi Kook as a means of bringing about the renewal of the Jewish religious spirit as a source of inspiration and creativity. Such a development would seem to flow from the very na-ture of Judaism as a law-oriented religion.

Nevertheless, we can only wonder whether the author took into con-sideration the serious question of how power would be divided between the religious and the political authorities.[38] Did he intentionally ignore the re-bellious spirit of the secular Zionists, or had he perhaps not yet had an op-portunity to get to know this spirit and so believed in all innocence that the secularists would submit to religious authority and that "no one will even think of desecrating [the Torah] in the slightest way"?[39] Furthermore, was Kook not aware of the obstacles that would confront any attempt to bring all the great Torah sages together under a single institutional umbrella and a single halakhic regime?[40] Was this then a program or merely an apology for the Zionist movement and its religious-revivalist elements?

We do not have clear answers to these questions. In any case, it is clear that the pamphlet's utopian spirit relieved Kook of the need to tackle questions of the future head on, to devise Halakhic instrumentalities and detailed religious responses to the whole range of weighty issues that could be expected to arise when the Jewish people actually returned to its land and regained its political freedom. Kook explicitly declares that "we need not determine [in advance] the laws that will govern practice once our people is resurrected, for then the Sanhedrin will have to be reestablished, and it in turn will rule on all doubtful matters . . . It will examine every issue, every ruling and custom, and act in accordance with the Torah."[41] Rabbi Kook could thus speak definitively about the pattern of a solution, about the framework and its sources of authority, without taking any stand at all as to the concrete content.[42]

Kook eventually retracted his bold idea of reestablishing the Sanhedrin, but did so mainly for tactical reasons, related to the practical difficulties involved. "This is not the right time," he wrote in Palestine in 1910, in response to an inquiry from one of the rabbis. "No one will be willing to listen to this idea; we will be attacked for it from every quarter."[43] Kook spoke in a similar vein some twenty-five years later, in 1935; from a purely halakhic point of view, he said then as well, we could decide to reconstitute the Great Sanhedrin, but "I see no possibility of a meeting of minds of the sages of Israel in our generation, which is afflicted to an unprecedented degree with mutual criticism among the scholars." Consequently, we cannot undertake such an "exalted and holy thing without preparing the ground, both spiritually and practically . . . Still, the way remains open to us, if we proceed gradually."[44]

In fact, as the years went by, Kook ceased making public mention of his old, forgotten plan. But there is reason to think that when he founded the Palestine Chief Rabbinate in 1921 he saw it as a step toward the great messianic goal of reestablishing the Sanhedrin.[45] "In private," reports Rabbi Maimon, chief advocate of the idea after the establishment of the state, "his great dream was the reconstitution of the Sanhedrin in the Land of Israel as soon as circumstances were right."[46]

It is important to note that this dream had long been associated in Jewish thinking with messianic expectations. Maimonides, for example, teaches that the prophetic vision expressed in the verse "I will restore your magistrates as of old" (Isa. 1:26) is to be fulfilled "before the coming of the Messiah," and his teaching was later interpreted as a direct invitation to messianic activism in the form of the reinstitution of rabbinical ordination. The sages of sixteenth-century Safed, who thought redemption was imminent, even drew practical conclusions from Maimonides' words, while the Jerusalem sages, who advocated passivity on the messianic question, attacked them furiously.[47] The question has been in the air ever since, arising once again in our own time in connection with the national revival.[48] Thus the young Kook did not speak out in vain; he was aware of the real significance of his proposal and foresaw its consequences, however remote.[49] Here, as in other well-known instances, a hope for the future is presented as a hope for the recovery of the past. Israel is called upon to "renew its days as of old," to bring about a renaissance. But this call is based upon an idealization of the past, "restoration" as "utopia."

As I have pointed out, "the time when Israel returns to Jerusalem and its stronghold is the very root of the coming of the Messiah . . . who sets his seal upon the superiority and greatness of Israel." We may say, therefore, that in this forgotten pamphlet Kook laid the cornerstone for the whole history of redemptionist Zionism in Eretz Israel.

In sum, these are the main features of Kook's essay: activism on the messianic question; utopian Zionism; daring, global thinking, short on practical details and concrete solutions; great emphasis on the organic connection between Jewish nationalism and religious sentiment; and rejection a priori of the self-consciousness of the secular Zionists ("Israel lives by its faith"). As we shall see, Kook consistently espoused these views over a period of many years, and they would therefore, at a later stage, have a noticeable effect on radical religious Zionism as well.

On the other hand, the larger corpus of Kook's theological and historiosophical thinking was as yet undeveloped, and would reach maturity only after his immigration to Palestine. Thus he did not yet have at his disposal the full panoply of original dialectical concepts with which he would later grapple with the question of modern Jewish nationalism and with the hidden religious significance of the Jewish "rebellion" attributed to him by his contemporaries.

THE "BASEL DECREE"

Kook's essay on the reconstitution of the Sanhedrin was written under the deep impression of the First Zionist Congress in Basel. But it did not take him long to discover that his religious perspective on the new movement was very far from that of many of the movement's leaders and thinkers. He was soon forced to confront secular nationalism and its freethinking advocates head on.

Moreover, Kook eventually heard rumors that the first Zionist congresses had taken as their motto that "Zionism has nothing to do with religion." The alleged news naturally came as a heavy blow. This was not, as he saw it, merely a pragmatic attempt to sidestep the controversy raging over religion in the Jewish world, but rather a blatant move toward secularization and sacrilege, a deliberate severing of the "national idea" from the "divine idea," and hence from its own spiritual and historical roots. It is no wonder, then, that Kook's reaction to this "decree," which he attributes to the organized Zionist movement, is bitter and condemnatory to a degree unparalleled in the entire vast body of his work. Indeed, he attacks the "decree" with some of the strongest imagery in the lexicon of Jewish historical memory.

> The congresses' decree that "Zionism has nothing to do with religion" is harsher than the decrees of Pharaoh and Haman. It spreads the terrible, black wings of death over our tender, lovely, young national sentiment, by cutting it off from the source of its very life and the light of its splendor. The Basel decree . . . that makes religion a separate faction in Jewish life and disconnects it from Jewish nationalism—this abomination, this perverse statement, is the poison within [Zionism] that is destroying it and turning it into an empty vessel . . . filled with a spirit of destructiveness and strife.
>
> This foolish ordinance, the product of the alienation of its authors from Judaism—until this deposit of error is expunged from their hearts, Zionism will languish lifeless, incapable of protecting itself from rot and destruction, so that the worthless are bound to triumph; it shall putrefy and be covered with worms.[50]

In point of fact, the Zionist congresses at Basel never issued such a "perverse statement." Some two months before the first congress, Max Nordau, its vice president, did write a polemical article including the following: "Zionism has nothing to do with theology; and if a desire has been kindled in Jewish hearts to establish a new commonwealth in Zion, it is not the Torah or the Mishnah that inspire them but hard times."[51] But Herzl himself, in his political wisdom, carefully dissociated himself from Nordau's pronouncement, writing on the manuscript: "We must not drive the Zionist rabbis away. Let us not discourage them, even if we have no intention of handing them the leadership."[52] The "Basel Decree," then, was never issued, either at the First Zionist Congress or at those that followed. Yet while Rabbi Kook was mistaken about the details—he may have been misled by press reports of the congresses—he was not far wrong concerning the overall trend. This trend, which was indeed led by Herzl, sought to keep questions of religious belief and law separate from the question of national rebirth.[53] Organized Zionism was certainly far from heeding the rabbinic call that its aspiration to national political revival be linked to the traditional hope for national religious repentance. And for Kook, who saw Judaism as all-encompassing, this refusal indeed represented a serious rent in the fabric.

Thus, at this early stage in the development of his thought, and in the absence of the complex dialectical tools he would later employ in his encounter with the secular pioneers, Kook sometimes sounds like one of Jewish nationalism's severest critics. For example, he writes in 1902: "The inner difference between those who are faithful to the Torah and those who have abandoned it is greater than the difference between Israel and the nations. Though we differ from [the other nations] in our religion, we are nevertheless warned to love and respect them. But the wicked among our own people, who cast off the yoke of the Torah, we must hate and spurn."[54] Anyone familiar with Kook's later teaching, particularly his mystical doctrine of the inner power of the "uniqueness of Israel" and the objective stature of "the Assembly of Israel," cannot but be surprised by these sharp words.[55] Moreover, so uncompromising a stance in regard to Jewish identity, excluding the unobservant as it does from the circle of Jewish fellowship, could not but undermine any possibility of cooperation between religious and nonreligious in pursuit of Zionist ends. Yet this position has ample precedent in classical Jewish sources, which Kook uses in mounting his bare-knuckled challenge:

> If those who tear off the garment of religion and deny the Torah think they are still Jews, still within the fold of their people and related to it by a national tie, by national brotherhood and national longings . . . [I say,] absolutely not! Those who observe the Torah and the commandments do not and cannot recognize any national solidarity with those who have washed their hands of the soul of the people and the source of its very life, nor can bonds of race or homeland [provide a substitute].
>
> Jewish religious sentiment militates strongly in favor of excluding from the brotherhood of the nation all heretics and those who cast off the yoke of Torah and faith in a systematic and deliberate way. Be not led astray by the propitiating words of those weaklings, religious people, who fail to confront you with this bitter truth.[56]

Needless to say, such pronouncements were more characteristic of the Lithuanian ultra-Orthodox and German Orthodox of the day than they were of the religious Zionists. From the very beginning, one of the distinctive features of religious Zionism was its new attitude to Jewish peoplehood. In the incisive words of Ehud Luz, "The Assembly of Israel had [in the religious Zionists' view] ceased to be only a community of the 'observant' and now included those previously regarded by the ultra-Orthodox as 'heretics' or 'infidels,' whom it was obligatory to exclude from the Jewish people."[57] By contrast, Kook's statements at this stage of his ideational development seem to shunt aside all the given elements of national identity—historical, sentimental, existential, ethnic—in favor of religious commitment.[58] Even devotion to the return to Zion is not a sufficient basis, in his view, for "a national tie . . . national brotherhood and national longings."

To be sure, some of these strong statements should be seen as rhetorical, aimed at reproof and warning. Nevertheless, they reflect clearly the tension into which the writer was drawn in those early days, when his hopes for national and religious rebirth suddenly ran into the recalcitrant reality of a stubborn secularist insurrection, and he had not yet found the conceptual tools with which to confront and subdue it.[59]

The forum in which Kook chose to disseminate his ideological thinking at this time—the monthly journal *Ha-Peles* (The scale)—is also suggestive. The journal had been edited by one of the most virulent Orthodox opponents of the Zionist movement, Rabbi E. A. Rabinowich of Poltava. The latter had left the movement and turned against it when the Second Zionist Congress rejected his demand that a "rabbinical committee" be established to oversee the movement's cultural activities, and he used *Ha-Peles* as a platform for his struggle against Zionism. Indeed, others had already expressed surprise at Kook's involvement in the movement: "What is a *kohen* [descendant of the priestly caste] doing in the cemetery?"[60] Matters would eventually reach a stage where Kook's son, Zvi Yehudah, would voice the suspicion that his father's writings had been tampered with by the anti-Zionist editor.[61] The charge is implausible, for had it been true, the elder Kook would have had ample opportunity to protest, and he did not do so. Nevertheless, the fact that such a suspicion arose calls into question the usual harmonistic approach to Kook's thought, which attributes a unity to the whole body of his work, even though some of it was written when he was quite young and some in old age, some before his immigration to Palestine and some after, some for public consumption and some not. This approach overlooks many sources and ends up distorting or sugarcoating them.

We thus see that Rabbi Kook's attitude to the new Zionist movement before he left for Palestine was ambivalent.[62] He preached vigorously against secular nationalism, calling upon the movement to return to its true self and to its God.[63] He had not yet come to the view he was to hold later, namely, that the secular Zionist, and in particular the pioneer in the Land of Israel, represented authentic, positive values, albeit partial ones. These types had not yet come to represent for him a healthy antithesis to exilic Jewish existence, a daring ambition to achieve personal and national freedom, albeit going too far and overstepping the bounds of legitimacy. At this stage, he still saw the new heresy in traditional terms, as an expression of spiritual emptiness and venality. As he wrote then: "Heresy arises as a force for evil, particularly in our leaderless generation. It is out of neither wisdom nor wickedness, but rather empty-headedness and an insufficient desire to consider even what is self-evident." As long as the Zionist leaders cling to these views and "do not draw near in their deeds to the Torah and the commandments, do not glory in the faith of Israel or relate to the Lord God of Israel, this movement will cause much immorality. But we expect matters to be rectified . . . [for if not] the people will become discouraged, heaven forbid, and eventually it will be left without a leg to stand on."[64] There is no mention here of remedial positive value, no partial filling of a need or constructive intent. The spiritual wagon of secular Zionism is empty, to borrow the well-known metaphor coined a half-century later by "the Hazon Ish" (Rabbi Avraham Karelitz).

On the other hand, we must not assume that Kook's deep misgivings concerning Zionist secularism provoked in him parallel, Orthodox qualms about Zionist activism. Never, even at this juncture, did he repent his activist stance regarding national rebirth. "If we sincerely desire to prepare our people for redemption, for return from the land of its captivity and exile to the place where it originally dwelled, let us do it, and we shall succeed!" He continued to identify unreservedly with the Zionist initiative and its daring aspiration to work a historic change in Jewish life. In 1903, about a year before he himself left for the Land of Israel, Kook wrote: "Who can refrain from taking part? Who will not lend a hand? Who will oppose those laboring for the common good? . . . Who knows? Perhaps [it is] the secret of divine wisdom that decrees that the beginning of the growth of the salvation of Israel should come through our own efforts . . . If so, why should we not be the ones to merit this and to act?"[65] However, at this early stage in the development of Kook's thinking, he was not yet able to give a systematic answer to the grave, unprecedented question posed by the new Zionist reality: How are these Jews, who willfully violate the Torah of Israel yet fully devote themselves to the people of Israel, to be judged?[66]

MESSIAH BEN JOSEPH

In the foregoing sections we have examined Rabbi Kook's earliest teachings on the question of national rebirth, as reflected in his 1898 pamphlet on the reestablishment of the Sanhedrin and the more comprehensive essays published in *Ha-Peles* in 1901–3. I have dwelt at length on these neglected writings because they illuminate many of the basic questions with which Kook was confronted throughout his creative life and contain the seeds of many of the ideas about national redemption he was to develop in later years.

We have noted the chasm that opened between Kook's hopes for a thoroughgoing Jewish political and religious renaissance, on the one hand, and the Zionist "decree" which he saw as threatening to sever Jewish nationhood from its spiritual roots, on the other; between Kook's messianic call for the reconstitution of a Great Sanhedrin in Jerusalem as the capstone of renewed Jewish independence in the Land of Israel, and the inroads of secularism among the Zionist leadership and intelligentsia. This was a painful dilemma, for unlike most Zionist thinkers, Kook did not see the national reawakening only in terms of correcting the relationships between individuals or between individual and nation; he also saw it in terms of correcting the Jew's relationship to God and the world as a whole. Would healing on the sociopolitical level need to come at the expense of healing on the metaphysical one? Could there be a more dramatic example of a good end achieved by evil means?

When gaps of such magnitude arise between expectations and reality, and one does not simply try to smooth them over or deny them, diverse reactions can be expected.

One possible reaction is the abandonment of all religious expectations regarding the concrete, historical phenomenon. This is what E. A. Rabinowich, the editor of *Ha-Peles*, did when he turned against the Zionist movement. (The case of Rabbi Aaron Samuel Tamares, a thinker who abandoned Zionism when it failed to espouse his antipolitical, pacifist views, is similar.) Another possibility is to curtail expectations in the light of circumstances. This was done by many of the Mizrachi leaders, who supported the common enterprise as being limited to earthly political development. But neither of these approaches suited Rabbi Kook, with his comprehensive vision of rebirth, his messianic activism, and his passionate belief in the organic rootedness of the "national idea" in the "divine idea." He chose a different tack, to fight for radical change. And so it was not long before he entered the main arena, the struggle for the soul of the new Jewish community in Palestine.

This move was to have a great, creative impact on Rabbi Kook himself. It would lead to a thorough revision of his views concerning secular Zionists and the revolutionary new life emerging around them.

Rabbi Kook immigrated to Palestine in 1904. He was appointed rabbi of Jaffa and the new farming colonies, which in effect meant responsibility for the religious life of the whole settler population. In Kook's rabbinical circles such a step seemed surprising and unconventional, but it suited his personality and convictions. A few weeks after he arrived, Theodor Herzl died. As one might expect, Kook viewed Herzl with ambivalence: as the founder and hero of the Zionist movement, but also as the author of the "Basel Decree." It was in this spirit that he delivered a fascinating and instructive eulogy of Herzl.[67] The eulogy, given in Jaffa, so angered "certain [ultra-Orthodox] Jerusalemites" that "they heckled and reviled him for it and sought to prevent him from saying it," as the rabbi's son later testified.[68] But what of Kook himself? How did he manage to translate his attitude toward the departed leader into the artful combination of praise and criticism that it turned out to be?

His solution lay in classical Jewish messianic imagery, particularly in the legendary figure of Messiah ben Joseph.[69] In ancient tradition this is a figure fraught with tension and linked in a tragic way to the Davidic Messiah. The first messiah is associated in the sources with the final battle that is to take place on the eve of the age of redemption. Although he helps the people toward worldly salvation, he also embodies the inevitability of crisis and defeat, the suffering that is to accompany the "birth pangs of the Messiah" as redemption approaches. He is condemned to be slain in his battle and thereby pave the way for the utopian appearance of the final redeemer, Messiah ben David. In his eulogy, Kook makes ample use of this paradoxical motif of the doomed redeemer. On the one hand, he does not hesitate to speak of Herzl and, more generally, of "the Zionist vision in our day," in decidedly messianic terms: "the footsteps of the Messiah," "paving the way for the messianic generation," and the like. On the other hand, he carefully restricts the use of these expressions to "material" messianism, the sort associated with Messiah ben Joseph and therefore with crisis and reversal: "[Therefore] the [Zionist] leader fell victim to trouble and suffering." In short, this imagery does not refer to the ultimate end, but to a path full of setbacks that leads to it. "The quest for physical strength and the general appurtenances of national life are the preparations of Messiah ben Joseph, while the forces making for spirituality are those that prepare the way for Messiah ben David." Nevertheless, Kook continues, our people cannot achieve its exalted destiny, of raising aloft the name of the Lord by which it is called, without completing both sorts of preparation . . . The separation that obtained in exile made it appear as though the two were indeed distinct, and thus he who took up the fight for material improvement [in the life] of the people became, for our many sins, a foe of the Torah and the fulfillment of the commandments and all the holy ways that are unique to the Jewish people. [On the other hand], he who strove for Jewish [spiritual] uniqueness thereby made himself an enemy of material change. As a result, on the [nationalist] side there was a break [from traditional norms], while on the [religious] side there appeared weakness and discouragement. Now, in our time, like the footsteps of Messiah ben Joseph, comes the Zionist vision, which leans entirely toward the material side of things. Because its preparation is lacking [in the other dimension], the forces are not united . . . until [in the end] the [Zionist] leader fell victim to the reign of evil and sorrow . . . This man, whom we may consider to have been the harbinger of Messiah ben Joseph, in terms of his role in achieving the great aim of national rebirth in the general, material sense.

This emphasis on the material dimension of nationhood may darken [the vision] and prevent spiritual elevation . . . Yet the various forces will all end up submitting to the light of the Torah and the knowledge of God . . . for the basis of the preparation for the generation of the Messiah is in the use of cruder strengths together with the goodness and holiness with which Israel has been crowned.[70]

That is, Zionism heralds the Jewish people's worldly salvation, embodying "the stirring of the desire for a healthy material life that is felt by the whole nation." But this stirring and creative vitality carries with it a base, destructive element as well; it is borne aloft on clipped wings that let it slip to the ground, that "darken [the vision] and prevent spiritual elevation." The untimely death of the Zionist leader is thus a fitting symbol of the failure of this "clipping," of the tragic conclusion of the separation of the earthly and the heavenly, the sociopolitical and the religious, the vision of the "state of the Jews" and the laws of the Torah.

Thus in Kook's eulogy of Herzl we see the first blossoming of his later, more complex, dialectical views on the national question. In the imagery he uses here, healing and destruction are, in the best tradition of dialectical thinking, already bound together in a single entity. The selfsame phenomenon is a mixture of light and darkness. Herzl and his movement, "the footsteps of the Messiah," represent a positive, constructive turn in Jewish history, but they are an antithetical eruption, a severing and lopping off, as well, and for this reason they are doomed to forsake their independent course and be incorporated into a higher, more complete synthesis: "Thus Messiah, son of Joseph, is destined to be killed. When he is, everyone will recognize the distortion; for this generation has not been able to see the value of [mundane] achievement . . . while subordinating it to the loftier side of Jewish destiny, to the messianism of the house of David . . . [Then] all will understand that these forces are not really opposed and that everything should be brought together."[71] Kook thus rejects the accepted generalization that "following Herzl's death the idea took hold among religious Zionist leaders that he had been a great penitent and that had he not died young he would have found his way back to Jewish religion." The fact that "in his eulogy of Herzl Rabbi Kook awarded [him] the title 'Messiah, son of Joseph'" was seen as a clear illustration of this view, that "it was in the religious-Zionist camp that Herzl found his most loyal allies, allies who were prepared to follow him almost blindly."[72] But this was not true of Kook. On the contrary, his estimation of the Zionist leader was much more sophisticated and complex, both in the latter's lifetime and afterward, as demonstrated by his use of the imagery of the fallen redeemer.[73] Nor does Kook hesitate, ten years later, to demand that the Zionist movement broaden "the narrow circle of the late lamented Dr. Herzl's dream, despite all its beauty and strength."[74] Herzl the man, Kook writes to the Mizrachi delegates at the Eleventh Zionist Congress (1913), was able to set the Zionist "body" on its feet, but it has now become urgent to inject a soul into "this sculptured body."

> This soul cannot be injected into the [Zionist] movement as long as the forehead of the latter bears that mark of Cain, the [declaration that] "Zionism has nothing to do with religion" . . . This is a base imitation [of European culture], much more shameful than the fanciful imitation [implied by] the transfer of the place of the Temple to "Tel Aviv" [in Herzl's *Altneuland*], against which Ahad Ha-Am rightly raised such a storm.[75]
>
> The passing fancy that a despised people is in need of a secure refuge from its persecutors will not be sufficient to vitalize this earth-shaking movement; rather, it is that a holy people, unique among nations, the lion cub of Judah, is stirring from its long slumber, returning to its inheritance, to "the pride of Jacob whom He loved" [Ps. 47:5].[76]

There is no clearer or loftier formulation anywhere of the sharp rift, already evident at that time, between Herzlian Zionism, with its vision of the "state of the Jews," and messianic Zionism, with its vision of the "revealed

End." Rabbi Kook juxtaposes the two: an ordinary political movement versus an "earth-shaking" one; a mere quest for refuge versus a full-fledged return to "the pride of Jacob"; the Temple and Temple Mount as figments of literary imagination versus religious realities; "Tel Aviv" versus "the banner of Jerusalem"; Messiah ben Joseph versus Messiah ben David. . . . "Thus Messiah, son of Joseph, is destined to be killed . . . [Then] all will understand that these forces are not really opposed and that everything should be brought together." This, as we have seen, was Kook's eulogy of Herzl. "God breaks the vessels He uses," Herzl once said himself.[77]

HISTORICAL PROGRESS

I have shown above that, early in his intellectual development and in his public career, Kook had to confront the fact that "the preparation of the generation of the Messiah" in his own time would not grow out of a conciliatory return to religion but, to the contrary, out of a "spiritual insurrection." We have now seen how, in the eulogy of Herzl Kook gave shortly after his immigration to Palestine, he made his first attempt to conceptualize this development in theological terms, viewing the historical shock of the break with religion as but a phase in the process of messianic redemption.

But it was only later, as he came into contact with the freethinking pioneers in the Land of Israel, that Kook was to expand these ideas into a bold, fully fleshed-out historiosophy. The task he set for himself was to explain on religious grounds, not only the historical crisis that was taking place, but also the motivations of the antireligious rebels. While in his eulogy of Herzl he had confined the role of the revolution to the material plane, he now began to see its creative potential on the level of the spirit as well. In the end, he came to view the secularist pioneer as no less than an unwitting *ba'al teshuvah* (returnee to Judaism), with a central role to play in the process of salvation!

How did it happen that a rabbinical scholar in the Lithuanian mold, a Kabbalist, and (contrary to his usual image) a not particularly lenient legal authority, came to view the secular nationalist rebellion in the classical terms of traditional religious hopes? How did the Orthodox rabbi of Jaffa come to see the new settlers, whose watchword was "Let us arise and live without a messiah!" (Joseph Hayyim Brenner), as in fact paving the way for the Messiah's advent? Consider the fact that it was Kook who, early in his career, proclaimed that the Torah required "excluding from the brotherhood of the nation all heretics and those who cast off the yoke of the Torah and the faith in a systematic and deliberate way."[78] It was he who later taught that "the brazen ones of this generation, those who are wicked on principle, those who commit crimes out of spite and not out of pleasure, their noses in the air—these are the lights of Tohu!" (an allusion to a concept in Lurianic Kabbalah: the "lights of Tohu" were heavenly rays that shone downward with such force that they could not be contained by the "vessels" below and so shattered them). Indeed, Kook wrote, these renegades "choose destruction and cause destruction; the world is disrupted by them and they with it; but the source of their courage is in the bit of holiness [that remains in them]," and it is this that "gives them their vigor."[79] Of course, no stamp of approval for sin or rebellion is meant here, yet there is a new understanding for the motives of the sin and the meaning of the rebellion.

> As redemption approaches, brazenness increases. A storm gathers, breaches appear everywhere, audacity breeds audacity . . . These fiery spirits assert themselves, refusing to be bound by any limitation. The weak who inhabit the world of order, the moderate and well-mannered, are intimidated by them . . . But the strong know that this show of force comes to rectify the world, to invigorate the nation, humanity, and the world. It is only in the beginning that it appears in the form of chaos; ultimately it is to be taken away from the wicked and given to the righteous, valiant as lions they be . . . These storms will bring abundant rain; these dark clouds will be the vessels of great light.[80]

Rabbi Kook proceeds to explain the creative role of this bursting energy, this thirst for freedom. It represents, in his interpretation, the necessary beat of a dialectical historical rhythm. It belongs organically to a series of vibrant, antithetical thrusts that come together to achieve a greater "harmony" and *teshuvah* of a higher order. In other words, Kook tries to integrate the "breaches" and the "storms" into the messianic drama unfolding in the Land of Israel. Of course, these ideas have a respected Western philosophical tradition behind them, but they also grow directly out of Kook's own understanding of Jewish mysticism.

We cannot fully grasp these notions without taking into account Kook's particular devotion to the idea of progress. He never espoused the static view of man and his role in history, so common among halakhists and medieval Jewish philosophers: the idea that man's basic, existential situation is unchanging and that time is a neutral element in the spiritual and ethical life. Kook was even further from the regressive, conservative view of history, according to which there is a decline from one generation to the next. The passage of time was not for him inherently a matter of degeneration, in which the human image gradually diminishes as Eden and Sinai, the primordial ideals, recede into the past. The past, for him, does not swallow up the present or the future.

On the contrary, Kook was faithful all his life to the idea of ever-faster human progress, the gradual perfection of human nature, and the strengthening of the human determination to achieve eschatological fulfillment: "There is an essential, inherent good in the world, and it is increasingly being lifted up. It is to be found in human nature and the human will as well. In the past these were wilder than they are now, and in the future they will be more fully developed than they are now. As the human spirit develops, man's intellect and volition aspire more and more to the absolute good, which is the divine good."[81] For Kook the grounds for the optimistic view that history is drawing ever closer to redemption greatly outweigh the grounds for the pessimistic view that history represents a regression from the idyllic past. At least insofar as the nation and humanity as a whole are concerned, as opposed to specific individuals, there is a steady improvement.[82] The later generations are not to be seen merely as dwarfs perched on the shoulders of giants, but as standing tall in their own right. In this sense Kook can be seen as a typical figure of the nineteenth century, when the prospects for the human spirit, human achievement, and human freedom were thought to be constantly improving.

Thus we read in his *Orot ha-kodesh* (Lights of holiness): "The cleansing of the world through the passage of the generations and the higher realization of the Divine Presence in Israel in each age, as well as the gradual improvement of social relationships and the broadening of the sciences have greatly refined the human spirit, so that, although it is not yet entirely pure, a considerable part of its thinking and inherent desire are focused on the divine good. And the part that has already been purified inevitably gives way to liberality and anarchy."[83] (The term "anarchy" appears in the manuscript but was deleted by the editor.)[84] It is as if the prophetic prediction, "I will give you a new heart and put a new spirit into you" (Ezek. 36:26), referred, not to the End of Days, but to events within history itself. The idea of progress makes history as a whole a stage for messianic fulfillment, realization, and repair. Note too that Kook speaks of "the human spirit" in all its aspects. He does not distinguish between science and ethics, knowledge and values, the cognitive and the conative. The widening of human horizons leads inevitably to an expansion of human autonomy and spontaneous goodwill.[85] Thus the golden age of human freedom lies ahead of us and not behind.[86]

In fact, Kook sees historical progress in a broader, cosmic perspective. He connects it with the traditional Kabbalistic doctrine of the ongoing elevation of all being, the movement of all worlds and all creatures toward their exalted divine source. For him, the improvement of the human race, central as it may be, is but one instance of "the overall aim of nature, which is to refine all things until they reach the peak of perfection."[87] Kook wrote these words in 1901, and he continued to expand upon the idea in later years: "Everything flows onward, bestirs itself and aspires higher . . . reaching upward toward purity and exaltation . . . [This] mighty desire . . . is inherent in all of creation. It is this power that propels all existence . . . It is this that supplies the inner motive force for human culture, widespread among the different nations."[88] In other words, progress is rooted in an ontological principle. Humankind and the world, history and nature, are gradually driven toward their redemption by a single cosmic will. Kook regards even biological evolution as part of this great cosmic yearning for divine perfection.[89]

It was this metaphysics that made it possible for Kook to embrace the conquering spirit of modernity with its promise and its hope (as opposed to the postmodernist spirit, so laden with disappointment and fear). He gives a new interpretation to the classic Jewish mystical doctrine of the lifting up of the worlds,[90] injecting into this doctrine the modern European notion of historical progress.[91] And of course, the Jewish people is placed at the very heart of the process, as the leavening agent and as the bearer of universal destiny.

The idea of progress developed in modern European thought along two distinct paths.[92] One formulation, prevalent among eighteenth-century French thinkers (Turgot, Comte, et al.), tends to see history as a continuous, linear, almost one-dimensional march from the primitive to the sophisticated, without any significant stumbling or backtracking. In this view, it becomes the story of the continuous triumph of the human race. Setbacks are considered inessential, the accidental result of ignorance or the wickedness of tyrants, and are soon left behind. According to the other view, developed mainly in nineteenth-century Germany (Schelling, Hegel, et al.), crisis and reversal are inherent in the course of historical development. True being and true awareness can only arise out of a dialectic, both destructive and constructive, out of both elimination and creation of worlds. "Growing pains" are essential to human history, and it is only through them, through mutual negation and the resultant synthesis of opposites, that progress takes place.

Where does Rabbi Kook stand? If we carefully examine the change in his thinking over the years, in which he came to see the secular rebellion as itself part of the process of religious redemption, we find a movement from the one concept of progress to the other, from the "innocent" view that rules out destructive backtracking to the dialectical view that sees revolution as an integral part of the constructive march of events. Let us see how these concepts play themselves out in the context of Jewish history, of "the destiny of Israel."

In his earlier essays, Kook stresses unequivocally the need for measured progress, "according to the gradual pace established by '[He] who announced the generations from the start' [Isa. 41:4]," without breakthroughs or shortcuts. He repeatedly warns his readers against "forcing the hour," even in the intellectual sphere. "A push for rapid progress," he stresses, would lead to a social "shattering of the vessels," to "turmoil and confusion and reversal, [so that] the arrival of the good in the world would be delayed even further."93 Clearly, he does not yet envision a destructive clearing of the path, the audacious antithesis that constitutes the "footsteps of the Messiah."94 Only "a return to the mighty fortress of the Torah and the commandments, a return to the Lord, [can bring] a beginning of the healing of the national sickness that plagues our people," he writes at this time. "It was the abandonment of the covenant of the Lord that led to our exile, and it is the return to observance of His covenant that will restore us to our land,"95 he stresses again and again. For "[Zionism] cannot coexist with religious anarchy." Still living outside Palestine, Rabbi Kook looks forward to steady spiritual and material improvement without any rupture or violent uprooting.

In his later writings, following his immigration to Palestine, Kook gradually comes to see things rather differently.96 He does not relax his efforts to stem the flight from religion, but now, confronted with the pioneers' "shattering of the vessels," he comes to the daring historiosophical conclusion that "there are times when laws of the Torah must be overridden, but there is no one to show the legitimate way, and so the aim is accomplished by a bursting of bounds . . . When prophecy is blocked, rectification is achieved by a sustained breach, outwardly lamentable but inwardly a source of joy!"97

Rabbi Kook now increasingly stresses that "destruction for the sake of construction is itself a kind of construction,"98 and that "the travail of creation [entails] the destruction of entire worlds."99 Eliezer Goldman has recently pointed out the growing role of Kabbalistic ideas in the development of Kook's thought.100 This process is also evident in his early transition from a "simple" concept of progress to a complex, dialectical one. Here the imagery of the Lurianic Kabbalah—bursts of light, the shattering of vessels, rising sparks, the unification of opposites—acquires a dominant role.[101] I have shown how Kook anchors the modern notion of progress in the classical mystical notion of the elevation of all being toward its divine source. I now add that he joins the idea of progress, in its dialectical version, to the mystical drama of breakage and repair: "That which the Kabbalah conveyed through the myth of the destruction and reconstruction of worlds, Kook in his historiosophy expresses in terms of [human] destruction for the sake of construction, the building up of the sacred by the fresh efforts of secular, heretical forces."[102]

Gershom Scholem claimed that this concept of the "shattering of the vessels" was developed by the Kabbalists in response to the concrete historical experiences of the expulsion from Spain and of exile, which they transfigured into cosmic events. They saw Israel's dispersion among the nations as the reflection of a higher exile, that of all being, and as the symbol of the scattering of the divine sparks, which had fallen captive among the powers of impurity.[103] Other contemporary scholars dispute Scholem's view.[104] Be that as it may, Kook was clearly moving in the opposite direction to that attributed by Scholem to the mystics, bringing the cosmic notions of the Kabbalah down to earth and applying them directly to historical events. The myth of the shattering and restoration of the sparks became, in his mind, a symbol of actual events in the life of the nation and not the other way around.

To be sure, Kook gives the Lurianic ideas a distinct coloring of his own. In his optimistic view, the "shattering of the vessels" is not a cosmic catastrophe but, on the contrary, a positive manifestation, a vital step in the steady movement of all reality toward perfection: "Fragmentary being is crushed by an excess of goodness, by the life force itself; it is shattered by its own aspiration. But the good is not thereby deterred from its striving; it comes back after the break and begins to build anew, and the new construction arises very beautifully, inestimable in its worth."[105] Kook denies the existence of evil as an independent entity. As a result, he does not see the "shattering" as the complete negation of "repair," but rather as an integral part of the restorative process: "It is worth suffering all the pangs of the shattering and the ill effects of the destruction in order to bring forth these perfected worlds, containing such a richness of life that it [would seem to be] beyond their capacity to bear [and thus likely to lead to a bursting apart]."[106] The same is true of the historical "shattering" that takes place in the life of the nation, the "ill effects of the destruction" now accompanying the Zionist construction.

It is no wonder that in this dialectical perspective all the classical paradoxes of Jewish messianism are softened, the traditional dichotomies broken down and synthesized. For example, Kook writes as follows in a well-known article that appeared two years after his immigration to Palestine: "Ours is an amazing, astonishing generation, practically without parallel in all our history. It is a combination of opposites, a mixture of light and darkness, both degraded and exalted; utterly guilty and utterly innocent . . . Furthermore, 'Impertinence waxes, the son knows no shame before his father, the young humiliate the old' (M Sotah 9:7); but at the same time kindness, honesty, fairness, and mercy are on the rise, and the spirit of knowledge and idealism is ascendant."[107] What we have here is a new interpretation of the ancient texts, based on both experience and ideology. Let us briefly trace its two main elements. First, there appears in the Babylonian Talmud, mainly in the tractate Sanhedrin, a series of paradoxical sayings regarding the coming of the Messiah. Thus "the Son of David will come only in a generation that is either wholly innocent or wholly guilty" (BT Sanhedrin 98a). How does Kook understand this? He makes the wholly innocent and the wholly guilty generations into two aspects of a single historical phenomenon,[108] thereby apparently resolving the dichotomy between them. Consider the fact that ultra-Orthodox writers of his day, by contrast, seek to sharpen the original paradox as much as possible. They hold that messianic redemption is indeed close at hand, but precisely because the present generation is so completely debased that it can fall no lower, so that there is no way out for it but a miraculous, messianic one. Rabbi Kook transforms the paradox and incorporates it into a dialectical pattern.

Second, Kook makes interesting use here of a well-known Mishnaic passage (from the end of the tractate Sotah) concerning the character of the period that is to precede the coming of the Messiah (i.e., the "footsteps of the Messiah"). The picture is a harsh one: it is to be a time of growing brazenness, of mendacity and apostasy, of moral decline and fall, of retribution and physical destruction. Thus the expected transition from "the footsteps of the Messiah" to "the days of the Messiah" had been seen throughout the ages as revolutionary, a leap across a chasm separating opposites. How does Kook handle this paradox? For him, "the footsteps of the Messiah" and "the beginning of redemption" are no longer antithetical concepts, but two sides of one process, a process that is now visibly underway. "Brazenness" and "kindness" are mixed in a single historical phenomenon and nourish each other. Here, too, the ultra-Orthodox literature of the day presents a stark contrast, positing a deep gulf between the curses of "the

footsteps of the Messiah" and the blessings of "the days of the Messiah."
The messianic age is completely separate from the historical age and
springs out of its ruins (as I shall show in greater detail in the next chapter).
Kook, on the other hand, sees redemption growing out of the given historical reality; hence, what is called for is not a paradoxical process but a dialectical one.

With time, Kook's thinking moved further and further in this direction.

> The evil and brazenness of the footsteps of the Messiah that vex every heart
> are the gloomy steps leading to a rarefied, joyous existence.[109]

> For a new vineyard to be planted among the House of Israel in a way that
> allows Israel's essence to reemerge in the true light of prophecy, conventional
> values must also be erased by the brazenness of the footsteps of the Messiah.
> From [the latter] shall come a new light, radiant in its splendor, pure as the
> heavens.[110]

In other words, the transition from exile to redemption requires a radical
spiritual turn; many fundamental ideas must be uprooted and others
planted in their place, even though the present rooting out and supplanting
may seem excessive. Thus Rabbi Kook takes the original Jewish apocalypse, the dread "footsteps of the Messiah," and turns it into the birth
pangs of organic growth.

There are many ramifications of this idea throughout Kook's work. For
example, it is in this way that he interprets the deep rupture in the classical
religious worldview caused by scientific revolutions, from Copernicus to
Darwin to Einstein. These innovations, which appear to negate both the
notion of an absolute cosmic center and the centrality of the human race in
the cosmos, threaten to relativize and thus undermine traditional beliefs
and values. Yet for Kook these very revolutions also serve as new sources of
illumination, leading to an expanded view of the world and a higher religious consciousness. Out of the depths of the crisis created by the new
worldview will emerge a new, richer understanding of the boundless divine
creativity, "that skips no steps and leaves no gaps."[111] "Seen correctly, the
new beliefs about the nature of the universe are much more revealing of the
divine light, of its infinite grandeur and splendor, than was the limited cos-
mology of the early philosophers. The constricted view was better suited to
inducing deep faith [at the time] than the expanded perspective would have
been had it emerged [then]. But once human beings became more open to
the sacred, the great expanses had to be revealed, and only enormous bene-
fit can derive from this disclosure. 'In distress I called on the Lord; the Lord

answered me and brought me relief' [Ps. 118:5]."[112] Rabbi Kook tries to understand the social, cultural, and ideological upheavals of his day—nationalism, socialism, anticlericalism, among Jews and non-Jews alike—in a similar vein.[113] All these phenomena he sees as reactions, destructive as well as constructive, to the weaknesses of the old order. Later, even the Great War and its horrors seem to him merely as birth pangs, a cleansing, shaking up, and purification leading to rebirth, a final "shattering of the vessels" of the culture of the sword. (The war was not seen at the time as merely a "first" world war, of course, but rather as *the* world war, a final global struggle that would crush and root out all the old evils.) We stand here on the verge of paradox and apocalypse,[114] yet even here the very act of destruction is seen by Kook to be constructive: " 'The time of singing [*zamir*] has come,' the time of the cutting down [*zamir*] of the tyrants. The wicked are being destroyed and the world is refined; 'the song of the turtledove is heard in our land' [Song 2:12] . . . Atonement must come: a general clearing away of all present-day foundations of civilization, with their mendacity and falsehood, their evil pollution and poisonous venom. All culture that takes pride in the ring of its lies must be wiped out, to be replaced by a realm of transcendent holiness. The Light of Israel shall appear, and he shall establish a world made up of peoples informed by a new spirit."[115]

As we shall see, this very pattern is later to be taken up by Kook's son Zvi Yehudah in his attempt to interpret the Second World War and the destruction of European Jewry. Astonishingly enough, he explains even the horrors of the Holocaust as a kind of "heavenly surgery," a "deep, hidden, divine therapy aimed at purging [us] of the impurity of exile."[116] The Holocaust too is a kind of shattering, the destruction of a rotten culture (that of exile) for sake of national rebirth and the fulfillment of the vision of "the revealed End." This calamity, Zvi Yehudah Kook writes, is "the angry blow of the Lord's hand [aimed at] removing us from the nations and their worthless culture!"[117] We shall return to this matter below.

AN ASTONISHING GENERATION

In 1921 the Gurer Rebbe, Abraham Mordecai Alter, the leading figure of Polish Hasidism and of Agudat Israel, visited Palestine. Although the controversy raging in Orthodox circles surrounding the personality and writings of Rabbi Abraham Kook was then at its height, Alter was not deterred from visiting him and confronting him with current issues.[118] He did so on subsequent visits to Palestine as well and was unrelenting in his efforts to reconcile the warring camps. For the Jerusalem zealots, the very fact that he visited Kook was enough to condemn Alter to punishment. "He who smiles at the wicked angers God! Avraham [Kook] and Avraham [Alter] are to be treated alike!" screamed a poster that appeared in the streets of Jerusalem following one of these meetings. "It is not for nothing that the starling followed the raven; they are two of a kind [*min,* both guilty of] apostasy [*minut*]!"[119] Such opposition might have been expected from the fringes of the ultra-Orthodox camp, but how did the Rebbe of Gur, the spokesman of the ultra-Orthodox mainstream, himself feel? What impression did he have of his interlocutor? "The sage Rabbi Abraham Kook, may heaven preserve him, is a man of many accomplishments,"[120] Alter writes to his associates in Poland after their first meeting;[121]

> but his love of Zion is so excessive that he deems pure what is impure and treats it favorably [BT Eruvin 136] . . . and this is the source of the strange things he says in his writings. I argued with him at length, for "his intentions are desirable but not his actions,"[122] for he is supporting wrongdoers, as long as they persist in their rebellion and blasphemy. As for his claim that in this he is merely imitating God, citing the verse, "You lend a hand to wrongdoers,"[123] I say that "their hand is sent forth against the sanctuary"[124] and that, particularly in that case, "construction by mere boys is destruction" [BT Megillah 31b; Nedarim 40a] . . . His approach in regard to "the raising up of the divine sparks" is also a dangerous one; so long as they do not repent their iniquity, the "sparks" are insubstantial. Moreover, he is thereby endangering pure, innocent souls who might be tempted thereby to join forces with the wrongdoers. Our sages, may their memory be a blessing, therefore taught us, "O wise men, guard your words" [see M Avot 1:1]; and even concerning the wisest of men [Solomon] they said, "They sought to hide the Book of Ecclesiastes," even though later they said, "Solomon [the author of Ecclesiastes] spoke well."

This is a penetrating but measured criticism of Rabbi Kook's defense of the secular Zionists.[125] It also reflects the essence of Kook's challenge to the mainstream ultra-Orthodox of his day, "the strange things he says in his writings."

I shall present the matter one step at a time, proceeding from the least grave to the most. First, Kook distinguishes carefully between the subjective intentions of the individual acting in history and the objective results of his or her actions. One may play an effective role in a sequence of events, helping to move matters along and even struggling toward a certain end, without grasping the inner logic of the events, their true meaning or real consequences. The latter can turn out to be "bigger" than oneself, far removed from or even opposed to one's individual awareness. This is the convoluted path of what Kook calls "the irony of history" (and of what Hegel calls "the deceptiveness of reason"),[126] and it is impossible to understand the stance of the freethinking Zionists without it. The latter see their nationalistic enterprise as having a purely secular meaning and occasionally even take up the cudgels against religion and messianic hopes. But in the end they will prove to have been actors in a cosmic drama quite different from what they personally aimed for. Unwittingly, it is they who with their own hands are laying the earthly foundations of spiritual rebirth and religious redemption:

> The bricks can also be borne by those who do not divine [the religious meaning of the work]. They can even supervise the work. When the time comes, however, the hidden meaning will be revealed.[127]

> There are people who do not have the slightest idea what an important role they play in the scheme of Divine Providence. They are called but do not know who is calling them . . . But this terrible concealment will end with a great disclosure of lasting import.[128]

Kook thus interprets the work of the pioneers in extrahalakhic, meta-ethical terms. He imputes to it a long-range religious and historical significance in terms of its "objective" contribution to the messianic goal, quite apart from the immediate aims of the individual protagonists. The Gurer Rebbe, on the other hand, judges these same pioneers by their avowed intentions and concrete deeds, their values and willful violations of religious norms. He rejects entirely the messianic historiosophy of his interlocutor, warning that "construction by boys is destruction, even in the case of the Holy Temple!"[129] On this level of discourse, many of the secular settlers themselves would probably have felt more at ease with the fulminations of the Rebbe, who took their personalities and ideas at face value, than with the role unwittingly assigned to them by Rabbi Kook in the larger scheme of things. Consider the fact that the latter goes so far as to compare the pioneers to Herod the Great who, by a bitter irony, had the privilege of reconstructing the Second Temple.[130] He also compares them to Cyrus the Great, who fostered the original construction of the Second Temple without realizing the meaning of the project in the divine plan.[131] He compares them elsewhere to the Gentile workers described in 1 Kings 5:20, who took part in building the First Temple: "Just now, the outwardly visible aspects of the messianic construction are being executed by workers eminently fit for this task, as were the Sidonites, who knew how to hew wood from

Lebanon to build the Lord's house."[132] If the pioneers understood these similes, it seems unlikely they would have relished them.[133]

It is typical of all-embracing historiosophies, however, that they tend to view human beings as mere mortar and bricks in a larger, comprehensive process: "progress," "the march of enlightenment," "the workings of Divine Providence," and so forth. Such attempts are, by their very nature, less concerned with individuals' motivations than with the cumulative historical outcome of their actions. Did not Joseph, the first Hegelian historiosopher, already make this point? "You meant evil against me, but God meant it for good," he tells his brothers, explaining the meaning of his having been sold to the Ishmaelites and gone down to Egypt.

But this is only the first stage of Kook's analysis. In addition to having sought to understand the underlying, objective significance of the enterprise in Palestine, he goes on to probe the unconscious spiritual purpose of its heroes, the secular pioneers. "They themselves do not realize what they want," he writes. "The divine spirit informs their strivings in spite of them."[134] In the final analysis, therefore, Kook concludes that the builders themselves, "those who carry the bricks," are not entirely alienated from the foundations of what they are building; they are, in fact, connected with its true purpose. The whole enterprise of the modern return to Zion, the national rebirth, the pioneering, and the social revolution in fact constitute a veiled spiritual movement of return to the source, an unconscious process of *teshuvah*, repentance. "The very reawakening of the people's desire to go back to the land, to its essence and spirit and character, is motivated by the light of *teshuvah*."[135]

How so? Kook understands religious faith as an innate human tendency, not, as other religious thinkers claim, a matter of taming human nature. "It is the most natural thing for a human being to desire to cleave to the Lord," he writes.[136] If this is true of people in general, how much more so is it true of the Assembly of Israel. Kook takes the radical view that Israel is distinguished among the nations by an inherent religious quality. The chosen people draws its very life from an organic connection to the divine, a given, collective link that can never be severed. "It is established as a covenant for the Assembly of Israel," Kook writes, "that it will never be utterly defiled. The spirit of the Lord and the spirit of Israel are one!"[137] Thus, even if the voluntary choices made by individuals do not measure up to this hidden spiritual distinction, it is a mere fluke that does not detract from the essential character of the people. So Kook interprets the legacies of Judah Halevi, the Kabbalists, and the Hasidim.

It would appear that this level of involuntary spiritual distinction corresponds to that of the "objective" and "unconscious" that we have seen in previous dichotomies in Kook's thinking, while the level of "choice" corresponds to the "subjective" and "conscious." And "the [innate] distinction carries incomparably greater weight and is far holier than that which is a matter of choice!"[138] What we have, then, is a series of optimistic, deterministic assumptions about the given, objective nature of religious devotion, in human beings in general and in the people Israel in particular. Add to this the idea of historical progress, the messianic hope, and the belief in the spiritual bounties of the Land of Israel,[139] and one can only conclude that the modern Zionist awakening, too, springs from a holy source,[140] however hidden or unrecognized. The very fact that Israel is returning to its land, its language, and its collective form of life will ultimately prove to have been a return to its God.[141]

We thus see that, for Kook, the traditional concepts of faith, repentance, and holiness can all apply as well to activities never intended to be "for the sake of heaven" (i.e., for religious purposes)—indeed, to activities that may even have been designed to spurn religion. This is, of course, a bold expansion of the usual criteria of religiosity. Yet Kook goes even further, extending the concepts of Torah and religious meaning to include all endeavors aimed at truth, beauty, or goodness. Is there any pursuit of truth, ethical passion, or authentic creativity alien to the divine? Is there any quest for freedom that does not have a holy source?

> We need never lament the lack of mention of the divine in the achievement of social justice, for we know that the aspiration to justice, whatever form it may take, represents in itself the most radiant divine influence. [Consequently,] while [the protagonists] may believe that the good they accomplish is contrary to the Torah, it is in fact of its very essence![142]

Such ideas were no doubt abetted by the pantheistic elements in Kook's thinking, his tendency to see all reality as permeated with the divine. Given this tendency, even revolutionary aspirations could appear to him grounded in the "lights of holiness."[143]

These are the roots of Kook's radical view that the secular Zionist revolt is a corrective to exilic religious existence. They enable him to broaden traditional religious concepts and norms to encompass the temerity of the pioneers and the "growing pains," to make these integral parts of the messianic progression. To be sure, full redemption will require a change in awareness as well. The "natural" spirituality of the individual will have to rise to the surface and inform his or her voluntary choices on a conscious level. But during the dialectical process leading up to redemption, this change in individual subjectivity is not yet a necessity.

Obviously, this defense of the freethinkers was anathema to the ultra-Orthodox rabbis. Even the Gurer Rebbe attacks Kook for it. More precisely, Alter's critique is as follows: when Kook reads religious significance into secular activity and rebellion, he is really talking about the mystical effort to "raise up the divine sparks"[144] and rescue them from the captivity of the "husks"; but, the Rebbe warns, so long as the rebels do not repent their evil ways, "the sparks will be insubstantial, and pure, innocent souls will be endangered."[145] He rejects outright Kook's extension of the notions of holiness and repentance to include activities beyond the bounds of the Torah, calling for a simpler, traditional definition of what constitute good and evil deeds, unadulterated by mystical, ideological, or historiosophical thinking. In his sharp formulation, "[Kook] is supporting wrongdoers, as long as they persist in their rebellion and blasphemy . . . [and] 'their hand is sent forth against the sanctuary.'"[146] Unlike Kook, Rabbi Alter does not recognize a dialectic in which light and shadow, "sinners" and "penitents," are combined, but only heresy pure and simple, the breaking of the covenant and casting off of the yoke. Good deeds are not accomplished by means of evil ones, and the Holy Land cannot be built by profane deeds.

If such are the views of a Hasidic Rebbe, how much more likely are they to be expected from a Halakhist such as Rabbi Joseph Hayyim Sonnenfeld, chief rabbi of the Jerusalem Edah Haredit (see chapter 2): "[Kook's] way of thinking does not seem right to me . . . What have we to do with their 'inner distinctions'? God sees into the heart, but we mortals can only see what is out in plain view, can only rule according to law and precept . . . We must punish with utmost stringency those who violate religious law, and if the Holy One, blessed be He, has hidden considerations, He will do as He sees fit."[147] Against this background, Kook's boldness in judging the secularists by extra-Halakhic criteria becomes all the more salient.

(Indeed, there was a price to be paid for this boldness. Once the bonds of halakhic exclusivity are loosened, there inevitably arises the question of permissible limits. If these historiosophic criteria are to be used to justify those who desecrate the Sabbath and eat forbidden food, may they not be used to justify those who shed blood as well? What guarantee do we have that meta-ethical rationales will not, in the hands of others, be extended to deeds never dreamt of by their authors? For example, in 1984, when the "Jewish underground" was uncovered and charged with murder and conspiracy to blow up the Dome of the Rock,

Gush Emunim came to the group's defense,[148] citing a statement of Kook's already quoted above: "There are times when a law of the Torah must be overridden, but there is no one to show the legitimate way, and so the thing is accomplished by a bursting of bounds . . . outwardly lamentable but inwardly a source of joy"!)

In this instance as well, would not Zionist freethinkers be more likely to prefer the outright rejection by the ultra-Orthodox leader to the embrace of Rabbi Kook? "Zionism began among people who rebelled against the dominion of religious law, refused to live in accordance with it," wrote Amos Oz in a 1982 attack on the second generation of Kook's disciples. True, "you can adopt a patronizing, insulting interpretation in which the early pioneers thought they were acting from an idealistic world-view but were really no more than an instrument of God and that the holy sparks flew out of their secular, socialist 'shell' without their intending it. This is trampling the spiritual autonomy of others, and it has always made me feel insulted and bitter."[149] From time to time Israeli intellectuals, in their encounters with Kook's disciples, are heard to make such judgments about his defense of the secular Zionists. For example, both Professor Yirmiyahu Yovel and the writer Ehud Ben-Ezer have spoken in this vein.[150] Even Rabbi Aharon Lichtenstein, dean of the Alon Shevut Yeshivah, has stated publicly that Kook's defense is in effect based upon "falsification," on a forced misreading of the secularists' declared aims.[151]

Do Kook's personality and teachings (as opposed to those of his disciples) require this judgment?[152] I do not think so. For one thing, it overlooks the degree to which he himself internalized significant aspects of the pioneer ethos. How is one to draw the line between a patronizing portrayal of the spirit of another and an authentic identification with that spirit? May seeing the other in one's own image not result from internalization as well as from superimposition? A close reading of Kook's writings reveals that the "audacity" and "tempestuousness" of those around him were not at all alien to him, and that the quest for "freedom and openness," with its autonomous moral pathos, not only struck a responsive chord in him but, indeed, corresponded to a strong tendency in his own spirit. "The soul that does not roam free, seeking with all its heart the light of truth and goodness, will not suffer spiritual setbacks but will also not achieve or build anything of its own."[153] Moreover, "there is constructive holiness, and there is destructive holiness . . . Destructive holiness produces the great warriors, who bring blessing to the world; it is the quality of the strong-armed Moses, who broke the tablets."[154]

Kook undoubtedly yearned his entire life to bring all the "constructions" and "destructions" together in one great synthesis, in which the frictions and contradictions would be dissolved. Would it be unfair to see this merely as a desire to still his own inner turmoil? I, at least, do not detect in his writings the sense of harmony and reconciliation others see there, but rather, above all, a desire for harmony and a firm belief that conflict will one day be overcome. As he writes to himself: "How great is my inner battle. My soul is constantly struggling upward, seeking to rise above all lowliness, pettiness, and limitation . . . [But] suddenly a flood of [religious] duties appears, while I have not yet reached the level . . . of sensing the sweetness of all the [Halakhic] details . . . I am [thus] full of pain, and I look forward to salvation and light . . . to the dripping of the dew of life even from these narrow [legal] conduits, from which I shall suckle and be satisfied."[155] I therefore tend to agree with the writer Joseph Hayyim Brenner, the spiritual leader of the pioneers, in his portrayal of Kook as "a stormy, wave-battered, yearning" soul (1909),[156] rather than with many of Kook's current followers and critics. Would it not be fairer to Kook to apply his own method in our assessment of his character, drawing from it the hidden "sparks"?

In fact, the question of Kook's "openness" apparently needs to be understood from an entirely different angle. As we have learned from the recent work of Yossi Avneri and Michael Nehorai, Kook's Halakhic positions on a number of significant issues in the life of the Yishuv—Jews standing guard, certification of compliance with the dietary laws, women's suffrage, conversion, milking on the Sabbath—were stringent ones, not adopted later by mainstream religious Zionism.[157] Indeed, he found it difficult to apply to the pioneers, in practice, standards in any way different from those applied by his colleagues, the ultra-Orthodox rabbis. To mention one well-known example: in 1914 Rabbi Kook was asked to eulogize members of the Ha-Shomer militia who had been killed in the course of duty. He wrestled mightily with the Halakhic question of whether it would be proper to do so for people who had deliberately abandoned the ways of the Torah! When at last he was able to come up with formal grounds for leniency on this question,[158] he still judged them with terrifying harshness, according to their overt behavior and pronouncements rather than any presumed hidden motivations.[159] As a passionate philosopher of history, Kook could see the freethinking pioneers as unwitting penitents, but as a halakhic scholar, acting within history, he was fiercely opposed to their "crude, contemptible heresy"[160] and deliberate transgressions—certainly not "trampling" in the slightest on their "spiritual autonomy" or "falsifying" what they were about.

This should not surprise us. Historiosophy, particularly the messianic variety, tries by its very nature to transcend ideologies and specific actions. It is called upon to interpret and integrate them into an all-embracing framework. The same cannot be said of real life or real leadership, which require taking concrete stands and fighting concrete battles.

This tension is clearly discernible in the life of Rabbi Abraham Kook. On the one hand, on the level of historiosophic principle, he tries to rise above secularists and ultra-Orthodox alike. "There is a great war on, and each camp has good reason to fight and defend itself. The freethinkers are fighting for the good sparks of the [human] will in their desire to put an end to unnecessary bondage, which is purely negative" at the present stage of historical progress and human emancipation. Meanwhile, "those who are subjugated, who recognize the glory of the past, defend [the principle of] their own subjugation, seeking to ward off the destruction of the noble structure of the world by the evil elements still remaining in [human nature]." They want to prevent the premature loosening of all bonds and the disintegration that would follow. Each camp thus represents a fragmentary truth, "and people of spiritual stature must seek reconciliation between the combatants by showing each his proper sphere."161 As Benjamin Ish-Shalom puts it, "It is astonishing to see how Rabbi Kook describes and analyzes the two warring camps as if he stood above the fray."162 His is the perspective with which God Himself, as it were, looks down upon human actions. "[Rabbi Kook] thought he could turn harsh trumpet blasts into a symphony, putting each [protagonist] in his proper place, and thus follow zealously the Guide of History," writes Isaac Breuer, the profound Orthodox thinker, in his eulogy of Kook, mixing admiration and irony.163

On the other hand, on the level of everyday practice, Kook puts sublime dialectical syntheses aside and does not merely "seek reconciliation between the combatants." He himself plunges into the fray, as belligerent, plaintiff, and challenger, and not merely as one who "describes and analyzes": as a subject of history and not as "the Guide of History." "I declare openly that we are embarking on a war against [the transgressors]. It is, however, a war against our own brethren and not against [foreign] enemies," he said at a meeting in Jaffa held to protest public desecration of the Sabbath and the festivals by Jewish workers of the Second Aliyah.164 Nor does he ever desist from this particular struggle. On this second level, then, he is still immersed in conflict and antithesis. Indeed, the gap between these two points of view, that of messianic historiosophy and that of concrete history, would eventually emerge as the central problem in Kook's teachings.

A RECALCITRANT REALITY

Did Rabbi Kook bequeath his followers effective Halakhic or conceptual tools for bridging the gulf between messianic utopia and recalcitrant reality? On this point we run up against some of the most difficult, perhaps even tragic, themes of his legacy to the present age.

To begin with, Kook makes no allowance whatever for the possibility of an ongoing secular Jewish life. True, the moral and social pathos of the secular Zionists, as well as their authentic search for freedom, were granted a positive, dialectical role in the national rebirth, but there is no grappling on Kook's part with the stubborn persistence of secularism as such. How long can one go on justifying sinfulness as a necessary concomitant of the work of overcoming exilic existence? How to come to terms with a banal Jewish secularism, emptied of its original revolutionary fervor? Are Kibbutz Deganyah and Dizengoff Circle to be measured by the same yardstick? (Deganyah was the first of the kibbutzim; Dizengoff Circle is the heart of Tel Aviv's entertainment district.—Trans.)

Furthermore, Kook's doctrine assigns each of the competing points of view a well-defined historical role as a component of a larger dialectical whole. But what of Kook's doctrine itself? Can it too not be seen as a mere component in some larger historical scheme? As a historiosophy, it would, of course, be exempt from this question, pretending to be above all particular views and to gather them up into a redemptive, harmonistic whole. But as an ideology, it calls for action, for everyday involvement, and indeed, Kook's disciples are no less involved than he was himself in the very heart of passionate controversy. They are religious, even political, protagonists and not merely philosophical onlookers. So they are in danger of mistaking their own part for the whole, their subjective reality for the objective one, their own thesis for the synthesis. In other words, the heirs of Kook's original openness, his attempt to encompass all the competing viewpoints in a single harmonious whole, now run the risk of being closed in on themselves, imagining smugly that they alone represent true integration.[165] In the abstractness of a historiosophy there is room for a variety of stances, but concrete historical reality leaves room to choose only one, to the exclusion of all the others.[166] Avoiding this pitfall calls for nobility of spirit, struggle, and a rare capacity to listen. But, as Eliezer Schweid has put it, "such brilliant intuition is not one of those things that can be passed on."[167]

The two problems I have raised here are clearly interrelated: on the one hand, the stubborn persistence of secular Jewish life in Palestine for the last three or four generations; on the other, the difficulty of acknowledging the positive contribution made by other parties and competitive views. The incorrigibility of secular life reinforces the tendency of religious people to close themselves off spiritually and to deny the potential value of the secular "other."

But the juxtaposition of present-day Israeli reality with Rabbi Kook's vision of redemption raises other questions as well, both halakhic and political. Kook's messianic expectations freed him of the necessity to confront the question of what concrete, premessianic Jewish sovereignty would entail. Yet his disciples have been plunged into this reality and must somehow find their way in it.

It will be recalled that Kook's early pamphlet on the reconstitution of the Sanhedrin, the first of his writings on the national question, prefigures this problem. His utopianism there relieves him of the need to provide detailed Halakhic solutions to the many difficult questions that the modern return of the Jews to their homeland would entail. As the young rabbi writes in 1898: "We need not determine [in advance] the laws that will govern practice once our people is resurrected, for then the Sanhedrin will have to be reestablished, and it in turn will rule on all doubtful matters . . . It will examine every issue, every ruling and custom, and act in accordance with the Torah."[168] This hallmark of Kook's thinking persists down through the years. In fact, his utopianism is reinforced by the experience of actually living in the Land of Israel. Only now, the expectation that the Sanhedrin will be reconstituted is replaced by that of the renewal of prophecy. The prophetic illumination that is at hand will heal all the people's ills, he foresees, and provide a way out of the present halakhic straits. In short, Kook now begins to stress the charismatic model of leadership associated with First Temple times (the prophet) over the legal model of the Second Temple period (the Sanhedrin). He yearns with all his heart for such prophetic revelation. In a surprising and unusual passage, the daring opening sentences of which were deleted by the editor of *Orot ha-kodesh,* Kook speaks eloquently of this matter.

I listened and heard in the depths of my soul, in the stirrings of my heart, the voice of the Lord calling out. And I trembled greatly: have I sunk so low as to become a false prophet, to say that the Lord sent me, when His word was not revealed to me? I heard the voice of my soul in its yearning:[169] prophecies are blossoming and the sons of the prophets are awakening; the spirit of prophecy is at large in the land, seeking refuge, seeking champions filled with strength and holiness. They shall know how to speak; they shall proclaim the truth, telling how God's word was revealed to them; they shall not lie or flatter but faithfully express their spirit . . . And if the [Jewish religious] heritage, in its many forms, has not revealed its splendid beauty [to the present generation], a prophetic spirit shall come; it shall begin by clarifying what is in its heart, in clear language, and this clarity of language will have a shattering effect, giving strength to the downtrodden . . . The spirit of the Lord, which is upon Jacob, shall begin to fill his neglected offspring, and out of darkness and gloom the eyes of the blind shall see.[170]

Here we have rather clear testimony to a personal religious experience, as well as a vision of an imminent national spiritual revival. There is other evidence, too, of Kook's fervent desire for a renewal of prophecy as a guide for the revival of Jewish life in the Land of Israel.[171] However profound and sweeping the legacy he leaves his disciples, its utopian character does not encourage them to confront the reality of the modern revival of the Jewish people in concrete, halakhic terms, unless illumined by a prophetic, re-deeming transformation.

The same may be said of response in the political sphere. Rabbi Kook's vision seems to have been indifferent to the question of what political structure or government the new commonwealth would have. At a time when he himself was hard at work trying to organize the Flag of Jerusalem movement, he wrote his son: "As for me, my main concern is the spiritual content, grounded in holiness. It is clear to me that, no matter how matters develop on the governmental level, if the spirit is strong it can lead to the desired goals, for with the sublime manifestation of free, shining holiness we shall be able to illuminate all the paths of government."[172] One would be hard put to find in Kook's writing any real consideration of the political questions that might arise in a sovereign Jewish state in an unredeemed world. On the contrary, one gets the impression that for him the political restoration of Israel depends on a moral transformation of global proportions, that the Jewish return to history is conditional on the elimination of all the corruptions of worldly politics. "We left the political arena [and went into exile] under duress but also with a certain inner willingness, until that happy time when a polity could be governed without wickedness or barbarism. The delay has been necessary. We have been disgusted with the terrible iniquities of ruling during the evil age. Now the time has come, is very near, when the world will be refined and we shall be able to prepare ourselves [for our polity] . . . It is not for Jacob to engage in government as long as it entails bloodshed, as long as it requires a knack for wickedness."[173]

This conception is of course directly related to Kook's belief in human progress, in the elevation of human nature and will. Indeed, as Shalom Rosenberg has written, "It was possible during the [First] World War to believe that a new era was dawning . . . The old-new problem of religious thought in our time in this area has arisen from the fact that [such a transformation] did not take place and that reality continues to confront us with the problems of living in a world of contradictions."[174]

In fact, I have serious doubts whether in Kook's view a Jewish return to history and politics, in the world as we know it, is feasible. In other writings he stresses the need for a deep moral transformation, beginning among the Jews themselves, that would prepare them for a more exalted national existence. Without this, he fears, a premature resumption by them of "social life and political sovereignty will immediately bring out the anomy in their hearts, and the ancient corruptions will be revived."[175] But Kook is convinced that the required moral transformation is in fact at hand. Here is how he portrays public life in Palestine, as he experienced and imagined it. "[Regarding] the colonies in the Land of Israel, the thirty communities," he writes in 1907,

> let us examine their moral level in relation to that of the multitude of other peoples that dwell on their own land . . . The serious crimes so common among the multitude—robbery, theft, murder, and the like—are unknown, the integrity of the family is respected, doors can be left open at night without fear. Is this not an oasis of peace; is it not the tent of the upright? The community councils conduct public affairs, and it does not occur to anyone to suspect those ordinary people, preoccupied with life's concerns, of taking bribes or pursuing graft, not even a little . . . The pains of exile have spurred the achievement of cures, and the holiness of Israel has been restored. We are now entitled to take pride in our ability to ensure that, as the Jewish public [here] becomes better defined and its social life and institutions become better developed, its splendor and beauty, its culture and the caliber of its leadership, will be to the greater glory of God and man.[176]

No balanced view of Kook's ideas can ignore such passages, though for some reason they often are ignored. For it is only in light of them that one can understand Kook's expectation, his demand, that "once the Lord's people are established on their land in some definite way, they will turn their attention to the [geo]political realm, to purifying it of its dross, to cleansing the blood from its mouth and the abominations from between its teeth."[177] We have already seen what a utopian role Kook envisioned for the State of Israel, "the sole aim of which shall be that the Lord be acknowledged as one and His name one, which is truly the highest happiness."[178]

The real question, then, is how Kook's ideas will stand up to the obdurate reality of the State of Israel as it confronts these challenges: the unswerving secularism that resists any higher religious synthesis; the intense political and ideological strife that deprives the combatants of the calm and openness needed for historiosophic reflection; the pressing Halakhic issues, with "no one to show the way" and with the "blockage of prophecy" not yet over; and the return of the Jewish people to the political arena, to "social life and sovereignty" in a world with norms of its own, where pious, ordinary, and sinful people will have to live together in one framework.[179]

These challenges could be expected to sow the seeds of ideological tension and social polarization. It was also to be expected that, once Kook's doctrines acquired a substantial following, the latter would also be imbued with energy and an acute sense of mission, if not with practical solutions to immediate problems. Indeed, once his conception caught on, it would prompt religious Zionists to shed the traditional Mizrachi image of mere fellow-travelers of the Zionist movement and instead grasp the reins of history. For it would be they, and not the secularists, who understood the true, redemptive meaning of the national revival. Put differently, if the secularists represented the unconscious workings of the Jewish spirit, the religious Zionists, following Kook, would raise this spirit to the level of conscious choice. Consequently, they would no longer need merely to tag along but would be obliged to take the lead.

Once this happened, the younger generation would be able to free itself of the wishy-washy image of the three preceding generations, the image of "middlemen" between the freethinkers and the ultra-Orthodox, devoid of any distinct coloring of their own.[180] As distinct from the "thesis" of the ultra-Orthodox, drawn from the past, and the "antithesis" of the secularists, directed against the past, they, in their redemptive synthesis, would represent the future.

Of course, such a development could only come after Kook's abstruse doctrines underwent considerable popularization and social application. But it would be a vivid example of a theory that turns into a political force, a philosophy of history that wields real social and psychological power.

HISTORICAL NECESSITY

Rabbi Kook's teachings did not rapidly win large numbers of adherents in the religious-Zionist camp. Nor did the seeds of radicalization in his doctrine bear fruit until a full generation after his death in 1935. Though his ideas were always in the air and were enthusiastically quoted, few took the trouble to study them in depth or to construct a social or political program around them.[181]

Nevertheless, the central role played by these ideas in the wake of the 1967 Six-Day War did not emerge from a vacuum.[182] Kook's son Zvi Yehudah had labored for more than thirty years to lay the groundwork for this development, and the disciples he had gathered around him had been consciously preparing for it since the 1950s, as Gideon Aran has pointed out.[183] Zvi Yehudah Kook and his school carried the elder Kook's notion of redemption to its logical extreme. They also saw in the new reality of Israel the certain realization of his utopian vision. "The late Rabbi Zvi Yehudah's greatness lay in his translation of the broad, deep teachings of his father into the language of action. Though he himself was not a man of action, he was able to bring his father's exalted ideas into focus in such a way that when, at just the right moment, they encountered a public yearning to act, they turned into a powerful movement."[184] So writes one of Zvi Yehudah's leading disciples, Rabbi Ya'akov Ariel, now chief rabbi of Ramat Gan, on the tenth anniversary of his teacher's death. He continues:

> Turning great ideas into practical challenges involves a certain distillation. An exalted, abstract concept can contain opposing elements. In their openness and inclusiveness, the teachings of our master the Rabbi [Abraham Kook], of blessed memory, bring together all that is good and beautiful in the treasure house of Jewish thought throughout the generations, as well as the choicest of universal ideas. But when it comes to focussing these teachings on real life . . . one must frame, sharpen, expand them to a certain degree, and stress what is most important and needed . . . Thus, on the political level, if his father, our master, of blessed memory, was above parties and factions, loving all of them, Rabbi Zvi Yehudah, of blessed memory, had to take a clearer public stand . . . and intervene in key ideological matters.

Here we find an incisive attempt within the camp itself to trace the source of the transition from the thought of the father to the activity of the son. Naturally, the "translation . . . into the language of action" and focusing on central points which are described here take a heavy price.[185] They come at the expense of intellectual "depth and breadth," the dialectical quality of Kook's teachings, and the stormy vicissitudes of his personality. They require overcoming tensions and avoiding questions that Kook left open: the national versus the human, freedom versus authority, will and intellect, redemption and repentance, the earthly and the spiritual, the historical and the religious. Moreover, what was a messianic expectation now becomes a political program, holiness comes to be embodied in a given state structure, and historical progress is limited to the Israeli scene. Western science and philosophy also lose much of the importance attributed to them by Kook, and are no longer seen as necessary for the development of Jewish religious thought.

I will not dwell on these changes in detail, especially since they represent instances of a universal phenomenon, typical of encounters between ideas and social reality. Rather, I will continue to concentrate on the fascinating history of a single question, that of messianism and the Jewish state.

How, then, was Rabbi Kook's vision to be interpreted in the face of the rise of a sovereign Jewish state in the Land of Israel? How was this vision "translated into the language of action" by his heirs and turned into the moving force behind political radicalism? At the beginning of this chapter, I noted the boldness of Rabbi Zvi Yehudah Kook and his disciples in removing all the barriers between the theological and the political, in attributing a messianic quality to the existing State of Israel in all its symbols, activities, and struggles. I shall now return to this issue, this time in terms of the elder Kook's legacy, and attempt to clarify the strong connection between theology, historical experience, and political activity.

To begin with, among Zvi Yehudah Kook and his followers the elder Kook's optimistic expectation and messianic faith are turned into absolute certainty about the future. In their view, there can be no going back now that the redemption of the Jewish people has begun to unfold. We are caught up in an inexorable process, in which the beginning guarantees a positive outcome. True, we can hasten this process or delay it; we can join it or oppose it; we can remove obstacles from its path or, heaven forbid, obstruct the way that leads to the Lord's house. But these ups and downs are merely momentary digressions that have no bearing on the direction of the process or its ultimate result. The fate of the national rebirth and the building of the State of Israel have been sealed on high, for blessing and not for curse, for life and not for death. As Zvi Yehudah Kook writes: "The divine historical imperative, clearly revealed to us, to put an end to the Exile, cannot be changed or distorted, either by the wickedness and stubborn resistance of the nations or by our own mistakes and un-Jewish deviations. The brief delays all these can occasion do not have the power to reverse the movement, which proceeds onward and upward with utmost certainty."[186]

Many Jewish sources over the centuries, from the apocalyptic to the philosophical literature, promise that, unlike the first redemption (from Egypt), which was cut short, and the Second Commonwealth, which came to an end, "the third redemption will never cease" (*Midrash Tanhuma*).[187] "The first redemption was followed by suffering and subjugation, but the last redemption will not be followed by suffering or subjugation" (*Pesikta Rabbati*, 36).[188] Even in Maimonides' *Guide of the Perplexed* we read, "With regard to the permanence of the King, that is, the Messiah, and to Israel's kingdom not being destroyed after that, he [the prophet] says: 'Thy sun shall no more go down,' etc. [Isa. 60:20]."[189] All these statements are now understood to apply to our own time, to the "the revealed End" that is taking place before our very eyes "with utmost certainty." It is utterly clear, therefore, that the Zionist enterprise will bring about full redemption and full repentance.

Just after the State of Israel was established, Rabbi Zvi Yehudah Kook began to take a definitive stand on this question. Tirelessly, he stressed again and again the power of "historical necessity" and "cosmological determination" to guide the current national movement toward its destiny, "without wavering or vacillation." No doubt this determinism was intentional. Already at the time of the outbreak of the War of Independence in 1948, he declared:

> This special life necessity, following its one certain path with utmost fidelity . . . toward its well-established destination and its perfect, immutable realization—this life necessity is none other than the historical necessity and cosmic determination that come about through the grace of the divine covenant with the Eternal One of Israel, [a covenant] that shall never fail even if "the mountains may move and the hills be shaken" [Isa. 54:10] . . . that through all the vicissitudes of time continues to press onward, conquering and consolidating, with the aim of establishing the "one nation on earth" . . . It is this higher, inner life command that constitutes and clarifies the absolute certainty of the process of our return and recovery here, the building up of our people and our land, our culture and Torah, our military power and sovereignty . . . Here, at the site of our vitality, there appears this absolute imperative in all its forms, and without wavering or vacillation it establishes and marks off and blazes and illumines the one clear and certain path, the path of life and construction, the path of revival and redemption.[190]

Obviously, such deterministic language is not mere rhetoric. The aim is to dispel doubt and hesitation and nip in the bud all possibility of counterargument. What is more, the messianic significance of the modern return to Zion is not confined to the national plane, to the ingathering of the exiles and the recovery of sovereignty over the land; it is part of a cosmic process of universal redemption. Hence "historical necessity" is intertwined with "cosmic determination," and together they guarantee success. This is quite a new version of Kook's idea of progress.[191]

I believe this categorically messianic view of Zionist history bears the deep impress of the Holocaust, then a fresh experience. This may be a surprising claim. After all, hadn't the elder Kook's hope for redemption, so pegged to universal progress, been completely discredited by the Holocaust? Had he lived to see the genocide, could his optimism about human perfectibility have survived? Could his teachings have continued to attract followers after this great reversal? Would faith not have given way to fear?

Harold Fisch has written that "[Abraham Kook's] reading of Zionism and of the Jewish destiny in the modern era does not provide us with any means of comprehending the nature of the Nazi Holocaust which took place so soon after his death . . . One has the impression sometimes with Kook that evil need not be actively resisted because it has no true reality; it is simply shadow."[192] Yosef Ben-Shlomo makes a similar point: "What would Rabbi Kook have said about the destruction of the Jews in our generation? Could he have found a positive 'spark' even in this extreme manifestation of evil? The Rabbi recognized that there was evil in the world; he also knew about the beginnings of Nazism; but he could not have known where it would lead. His metaphysics would have obliged him to say that the principle of the good was operating here too, for otherwise he would have had to revise his entire doctrine from the ground up."[193]

There is considerable truth in these remarks. But historical development revealed another side to Kook's thinking. It was he, after all, who introduced the notions of crisis and reversal into the debate over the meaning of the events of the day, who spoke of a dialectical process of redemption, replete with contradictions—unlike his predecessors the Harbingers of Zionism, who saw the process as a smooth, organic one. (Kalischer, it will be recalled, saw even the emancipation of the western Jews as a sign of redemption.) Furthermore, as we have seen, Kook viewed the First World War in well-nigh apocalyptic terms. He interpreted this war as the destruction of an old world in order to build a new, messianic one, the uprooting of a civilization of falsehood in order to plant one of truth. Now, barely thirty years later, his son Zvi Yehudah carried these ideas to their logical limits, if not beyond, in explaining the demise of European Jewry.

Can the argument of destruction for the sake of construction really be applied to the hell of the Holocaust? Shall we really look for "a positive 'spark' even in this extreme manifestation of evil" (Ben-Shlomo)? Yes! says Zvi Yehudah Kook, as long as we do not persist in trying to justify what has happened in terms of the accepted categories of sin and punishment, guilt and expiation, but view it rather in terms of the special causalities of exile and redemption.

> The Jewish people has been brought here, severed from the depths of exile to come to the State of Israel. The blood of the six million represents a substantial excision from the body of the nation. Our whole people has undergone heavenly surgery at the hands of the destroyers, may their name be blotted out . . . God's people had clung so determinedly to the impurity of foreign lands that, when the End Time arrived, they had to be cut away, with a great shedding of blood . . . This cruel excision . . . reveals our real life, the rebirth of the nation and the land, the rebirth of the Torah and all that is holy . . . These historical, cosmological, divine facts must be seen as such. Seeing is more than understanding; it is encounter, encounter with the Master of the Universe.[194]

In other words, the destruction and suffering are not to be explained by classical causality, as the result of sin, but teleologically, as aiming toward redemption. Where the elder Kook explains the First World War as the uprooting of a debased gentile culture, the younger Kook explains the Holocaust as the rooting out of a debased Jewish culture, the culture of exile. The catastrophe was, in his words, "a deeply hidden, internal, divine act of purification, [to rid us] of the impurity [of exile] . . . a cruel divine surgery aimed at bringing [the Jews] to the Land of Israel against their will."[195]

From this perspective, only a deterministic, messianic interpretation of the State of Israel can confront the Holocaust and endow it with any religious "meaning." The calamity may have been profound, immeasurable, and unprecedented, but the redemption that followed was also unprecedented and final. However far the satanic destruction may have brought us down, the messianic salvation raised us up. (We see this dynamic in the ancient apocalyptic notions of Gog and Magog, the birth pangs of the Messiah, and "Let him come, but let me not see him in my lifetime" [BT Sanhedrin 98a]). No partial, merely historical explanation can achieve this symmetry between the destruction and the construction. Only an explanation that purports to be absolute, total, and final can balance the demonic loss and justify it.[196] And this in turn requires the elevation and sanctification of the State of Israel as "the pedestal of God's throne in this world."

I do not believe, therefore, that the success of this viewpoint in religious circles can be attributed only to the Six-Day War. This war, with the suspense that preceded it and the relief that followed, is known to have stirred up associations with the Holocaust—the feeling of "a nation that dwells alone," the fear of renewed antisemitism, and so forth—among the Israeli public.[197] Yet the new messianism had also been a direct if un-spoken reaction to the earlier mass murder, with its implicit threat to the principles of traditional religious faith.[198] How could we continue to live in a world in which the wicked Haman had triumphed, unless the Messiah were on his way?

It will be recalled that the extreme anti-Zionists gave their own religious "explanation" for the Holocaust: it had been a collective punishment for the collective sin of Zionism in forcing the End. By the same token, there were redemptionist Zionists, at the other end of the spectrum, who also saw the Holocaust as a collective punishment for a collective sin: ongoing Jewish unfaithfulness to the Land of Israel. (Rabbi Mordecai Atiyah was a leading advocate of this idea.)[199] Rabbi Zvi Yehudah Kook and his disciples, for their part, avoided this harsh position, but they too theologically related the Holocaust to the Jewish rejection of Zion. Kook writes, "When the End comes and Israel fails to recognize it, there comes a cruel divine operation that removes [the Jewish people] from its exile . . . because of the reality [expressed in the verse,] 'They rejected the desirable land [and put no faith in His promise]' [Ps. 106:24]."[200] In this way, the religious mind could now confront and "explain" the horrors of the Holocaust in terms of a necessary messianic sequence of events.

This deterministic view, promising unconditional redemption, was indeed quite attractive to Rabbi Zvi Yehudah's disciples.[201] As Rabbi Eliyahu Avihayil writes in 1982: "We are living at the end of history. The redemption of Israel no longer depends on Israel's deeds . . . Divine Providence no longer operates, as a rule, according to Israel's actions but according to a cosmic plan . . . None of the redemptive processes currently under way, processes from which there is no backtracking, are dependent upon us."[202] All is foreseen, then, but freedom of choice is not given (an ironic play on Avot 3:15—Trans.). The wheels of history turn according to an unconditional "cosmic plan" laid out in advance. Moreover, it is within man's power to know this plan—not only of its existence, but to know its contents and future course. The Jew need only study well the dramatic events transpiring, on the one hand, and the promises of the prophets, on the other, to grasp the whole. " 'How can you be so sure you understand the divine plan?' we are asked.[203] 'Isn't it presumptuous to think you can understand the divine reality?' True, we cannot know precisely what God has in store . . . but when things happen and God acts before our very eyes, one must be blind not to see what is going on. It is not presumption, but keeping one's eyes open" (Rabbi Eliezer Waldman, dean of the Kiryat Arba Yeshivah).[204] As for the predictions of the prophets,

Yes, we have communication [with God]. The Prophets of Israel [had] communication even with regard to the future, and they passed the secret of this communication on to us. (Rabbi Shlomo Aviner, dean of the Ateret Kohanim Yeshivah)[205]

With the help of God, it is being revealed directly to us, and there can no longer be any room for doubt, or grounds for holding back our joy and gratitude to the Redeemer of Israel. (Rabbi Zefaniah Drori, dean of the Kiryat Shmonah Yeshivah)[206]

A few years ago, I devoted an article to contemporary messianic determinism, both Zionist and anti-Zionist, tracing its sources and motives.[207] There were many responses, direct and indirect. I would now like to return to this issue and consider the questions it raises.

One may well ask, What is so remarkable about this religious determinism? Does not messianic faith imply it by its very nature? Doesn't the expectation of redemption always grasp history as a vector or arrow, the direction of which is set ahead of time by the Great Planner? The answer is that in this instance the believer makes definite claims about a specific, concrete, future course of events, about the destiny of this particular national movement and state, and not merely concerning something hoped for, the course and timetable of which are unknown. The believer foresees a positive outcome for a certain historical manifestation, and not just for humanity or a people in general. This is not just another version of the all-embracing idea of progress, but one that gives priority to a particular time and place in all their concreteness. "Our situation will lead us ineluctably to build the Third Temple," Rabbi Hayyim Druckman, dean of the Or Etzion Yeshivah, has stated. "There will be ups and downs, but there can be no reversing the process."[208] To be sure, Maimonides teaches that the course of events leading to the messianic age will be hidden from us, but "the question is, what if these things happen and you close your eyes, saying, 'There's nothing there; I don't see a thing'?"[209] This way of thinking was naturally given a dramatic boost by the outcome of the Six-Day War.

Another question that arises is how the belief in historical necessity is to be reconciled with the activism of people in the redemptionist camp? If one has faith in the inevitability of historical progress, why not sit and wait for it? Yet the history of modern-day European social and political movements demonstrates that such deterministic beliefs, religious and secular alike,[210] do not go hand in hand with passivity but rather, quite the contrary, serve to galvanize, to spur activism and overcome inhibition. Those who believe they know the future want to be the first to announce it. They want to appear as the avant-garde, leading the march to the drumbeat of history. They want to be a part of the flow and to help it toward its destined goal. Whatever their social or numerical weight, they see themselves as playing a central role in the unfolding of events.[211]

We should not therefore identify the belief in historical necessity with fatalism and passivity. Determinism means that the end result is foreseen, but it is precisely this foreknowledge that motivates the believer to intensified activity.[212] One who has deciphered the secret, redemptive direction of history has no fear of failure. One feels called upon to step into the breach, to take matters in hand, to press onward, to join the wave of the future.[213]

It is this mentality that characterizes the Jewish messianic activism that has emerged in our generation.

> What we want are believers, who, out of faith in God, arise to act . . . It is this faith that accompanies him from the moment he begins to act, that gives him the strength to intervene in historical and political events. The believer knows he has the Lord's blessing at every step of the way.[214]

> It's a pity it took a tragedy like the "Bus of Blood" on the Coastal Road [an Arab terrorist attack on an Israeli civilian bus] to get the government to take the correct and necessary steps, to come to its senses and remember its mandate and go into Lebanon. The war should have been declared out of an inner Jewish rhythm and not merely in response to the wickedness of the world and the other nations. It should have been a response to the End that is forcing us! (Hanan Porat)[215]

How does this modern activism relate to traditional Jewish messianism? I will suffice with one instructive example. The tractate Sanhedrin (98b) speaks of two alternatives that can catalyze redemption: Israel's merit, and the arrival of the appointed End Time. Citing Isaiah 60:22—"I the Lord will speed it in due time"—the Talmud says, "It is written, 'in due time,' yet it is also written, 'I . . . will speed it'! [What is meant is,] if they are worthy, 'I will speed it'; if they are not worthy, [it will come only] 'in due time.' "[216] Throughout the ages this passage was understood to mean that, if Israel repented, redemption would come sooner than the appointed time, but if not, it would only come at the appointed End of Days. But Israel would be redeemed in any event.

Interestingly, many who see "the revealed End" in the events of our day tend to interpret the former as having come "in due time" and not before, that is, not as a result of any particular spiritual merit on Israel's part. The greater the stress placed on the inevitability of redemption, the more one might have expected complacency and passivity. What role would remain for human initiative on the historical plane? Yet this has not been the case. As with secular messianisms, the very certainty that redemption is on the way has proven a goad to action. Had Israel merited it, redemption would have come suddenly, in a miraculous fashion ("I will speed it"). Since they have not merited it, redemption has come by natural means,[217] bit by bit, through worldly efforts and the building up of the Jew.[218] "The revealed End: its beginning is in human hands, its conclusion in the hands of God."[219]

There is a paradox here: the original revolutionary idea of religious Zionism that national rebirth would be brought about by natural means nevertheless comes to be understood in eschatological rather than historical terms. The Zionist undertaking, concrete and worldly as it is, is no longer seen as the return of the Jews to history, but rather as their march toward the End of Days.

Does this way of thinking broaden or constrict the scope of religious responsibility? Two different answers are possible. On the one hand, such messianic certainty enlarges the realm of "authentic" Jewish activity well beyond traditional limits, for by its lights the appropriate response to the needs of the hour can no longer be confined to the narrowly spiritual. One is now called upon to act on the plane of history in its totality. On the other hand, the notion of "the revealed End" also restricts the human role,[220] for it implies that we are only responsible for the beginning of the process (of return, settlement, and struggle), whereas its successful outcome will be guaranteed by Divine Providence.[221] "Its conclusion is in the hands of God." "The more we commit our bodies and souls to the divine undertaking, using all the natural means at our disposal, the more miracles we shall witness from on high, and these shall combine with our earthly collaboration, natural with supernatural, in a shining unity" (Shlomo Aviner).[222]

HISTORICAL NECESSITY AND POLITICAL RADICALISM

This messianic theology has had clear implications for politics, settlement activity, and military affairs. "The Master of the Universe has His own political agenda, according to which politics here below are conducted," Rabbi Zvi Yehudah Kook teaches. "Part of this redemption is the conquest and settlement of the land. This is dictated by divine politics, and no earthly politics can supersede it."[223] Rabbi Zvi Yehudah Kook goes so far as to identify the eternal Israel and its transcendent power explicitly with the political and military power of the State of Israel.

> The State of Israel is divine . . . Not only can/must there be no retreat from [a single] kilometer of the Land of Israel, God forbid, but on the contrary, we shall conquer and liberate more and more, as much in the spiritual [as in the physical] sense. "The Glory of Israel does not deceive or change His mind" [1 Sam. 15:29]. We are stronger than America, stronger than Russia. With all the troubles and delays [we suffer], our position in the world, the world of history, the cosmic world, is stronger and more secure in its timelessness than theirs. There are nations that know this, and there are nations of uncircumcised heart that do not know it, but they shall gradually come to know it! Heaven protect us from weakness and timidity . . . In our divine, world-encompassing undertaking, there is no room for retreat.[224]

As we can see, those scholars who have sought to detach hawkish politics from messianic theology have not fully understood the thinking of the circle of the Merkaz ha-Rav Yeshivah (that of Zvi Yehudah Kook) and the religious teachers. Although it is true that many Israelis, religious and otherwise, take hawkish positions without reference to messianic questions, in the case of the ideological leadership it is otherwise.

In fact, until the time of the return of the Sinai to Egypt, there were young rabbis in these circles who would promise, on theological grounds, a blessed future, not only to the national enterprise in general but to particular political programs. For example, several weeks after the Six-Day War a group of them met with religious members of the cabinet to encourage them in the upcoming struggle against territorial compromise. A spokesman of the group, Rabbi Ya'akov Filber (later, head of the Merkaz ha-Rav Junior Yeshivah), stated that "I believe with perfect faith that if the Holy One, blessed be He, gave us the land in a patently miraculous way, He will never take it away from us. 'The Holy One, blessed be He, does not perform miracles in vain.' It is not for the government of Israel to decide on the integrity of the Land of Israel." Why, then, he said, have I come here? "Not to give political guidance, but to give spiritual and educational guidance: "I have come to argue, not for the dignity of the Land of Israel, but for that of religion and the religious community . . . [For] how shall we answer our students when they see that the leaders of the religious party have disassociated themselves from the integrity of the land?"[225]

Filber later reiterated these sentiments even more sharply in writing: "Above and beyond what we do there is a divine power hovering over all and forcing us to advance, in accordance with the divine plan, toward full redemption . . . Since the liberation of the Land of Israel west of the Jordan [in 1967], not a day has passed without an attempt, either through diplomacy or military attrition, to turn the clock back . . . Not a single country, including . . . Israel, has affirmed that the whole of the Land of Israel must remain in [our] hands. Yet, miraculously, no conditions have been created to force Israel to withdraw, even a little, from the borders that came into being as a result of the Six-Day War."[226] This, then, was the fate of the elder Kook's idea of progress. In the 1970s, before they were confronted with the reality of withdrawal, quite a few other rabbis spoke in the same vein: "All the attempts of the Gentiles to arrest the process of our redemption are futile and will come to nought. All their plans, their idle talk of cutting away the inheritance of our forefathers, of chopping up our holy land, and of harming the Lord's people, are in vain. None of this will ever happen" (Aviner).[227] True, there were those among them who understood such statements simply as an expression of determination or as an educational ploy. "There is [ordinary] innocence, and there is creative innocence," Hanan Porat stated at a 1976 meeting of the executive committee of Gush Emunim. "We must educate ourselves to the fact that there is no such thing as withdrawal, any more than there are such things as ghosts."[228] But later, just before the 1982 evacuation, there were disciples of both schools who stood before the houses of the Israeli city of Yamit on the Sinai coast, who swore openly that God, the guardian of Israel, would forestall the evil decree and never permit any backtracking in the process of redemption. For these young people, this was the clear implication of what they had been taught.

"We proclaimed daily that there would be no withdrawal," Rabbi Ariel, dean of the Yamit Yeshivah, said later, taking stock for the group. "This slogan was a mistake from the point of view of both faith and education. No believing Jew should ever make such absolute pronouncements. 'All is foreseen, but freedom of choice is granted' . . . We should have adopted slogans that would educate people to faith, to an uncompromising will to act; never should we have instilled absolute belief in things that might never be realized."[229]

The ideology of messianic determinism thus grew gradually more extreme, from Rabbi Abraham Kook to his son, to the latter's disciples, to a new generation of youngsters. At the next stage, there were some on the fringes of the movement who went so far as to plot the destruction of the Muslim shrines on the Temple Mount. In one sense this was a political move, designed to sabotage the Camp David Accord. But in another sense it was a mystical attempt to cut off the forces of impurity, the "husk of Ishmael," from the source of their vitality on the holy mountain. For some, however, it was also an apocalyptic move to bring about a historic turn, to force the hand of the Master of the Universe by bringing on a catastrophe. By precipitating a great holy war against Israel, they would "oblige" the Redeemer of Israel to wage a great and terrible campaign on their behalf. By forcing the End below, they would activate the higher powers above.[230]

Was this a logical, organic outgrowth of Rabbi Zvi Yehudah's teachings? On the one hand, the deterministic element was certainly essential to this development (I alluded earlier to the use made of the elder Kook's approach to the crossing of halakhic bounds). Moreover, Rabbi Ya'akov Moshe Harlap, one of the elder Kook's leading disciples, explicitly predicated final salvation on a paradoxical worldwide outburst of hostility toward the Jewish people. "When the age of redemption dawns," he writes, "the other nations will regret having helped the Jews; they will turn into persecutors, paving the way for us to behold the light of redemption."[231] This notion found a ready response in the radical camp. Yet these elements by themselves were not enough to justify the violent plot. It was only in conjunction with other alien ideas that the notion came into play.

Indeed, some of the leading figures in the redemptionist camp were alarmed by the plot and rushed to condemn it as a perversion. "We are dealing here with a messianic sect seeking to bring about the Jewish people's redemption through force of arms," Rabbi Zvi Tau fulminated. "They have the blatantly idolatrous idea that by blowing up the mosques they will force the Master of the Universe to redeem Israel. This is the thinking of small-minded, superficial students of Kabbalah who, with all their limitations, are led by curiosity into the sacred precincts and cause great destruction."[232]

Since then, or, more accurately, since the evacuation of Yamit, there has been a marked tendency in this camp to moderate its political and even in its theological determinism.[233]

In conclusion, let us now return to our point of departure and ask what role Rabbi Abraham Kook played in the evolution of this ideology. In 1975 this question provoked a vigorous argument at Merkaz ha-Rav Yeshivah. The debate reached such a pitch that when one of the participants suggested reading the elder Kook differently from his son—that is, that for the former, the future of the state depended on the behavior of the Jewish people—Zvi Yehudah Kook dismissed him from his teaching post.[234] It was clear that the attempt to read into Rabbi Abraham Kook's teachings an element of warning—that the predictions and promises were conditional—had struck a sensitive cord, and that the group felt its basic convictions to be threatened.

In fact, the elder Kook's position on this question was complex. On the one hand, he was, as we have seen, a principled optimist who believed firmly in historical progress and the gradual elevation of humankind and the cosmos. This optimism was even stronger in regard to the revival of the Jewish people and the Land of Israel. There is no doubt that Kook saw Zionism as a human response to a divine call and that he confidently expected its success as such, looking forward to improvement and illumination rather than the opposite. The events of his day—the Balfour Declaration, the strengthening of the Yishuv, the devotion of the pioneers, and the like— encouraged him to grow "daily in the conviction of speedy salvation, light, and purity from on high."[235]

It is precisely here, however, that the other side of his thesis emerges: complete redemption would depend on a transformation of spirit and mind, not only on outward historical and political reconstruction. Redemption should also be reflected on the level of personal decision, where implicit *teshuvah* would be made explicit. The innate, "objective" distinctiveness of the Jewish people would not be sufficient. "Moral character always needs to be developed; it does not grow of its own accord."[236] In Rabbi Kook's view, both the ultra-Orthodox "thesis" and the secularist "antithesis" needed to be elevated in the conscious messianic synthesis. Could such a change be inevitable? Could it have been preordained? Did it not inherently turn upon human freedom of choice?

In the above-mentioned article, I cited a number of passages in Rabbi Kook's writing in which redemption is made dependent upon voluntary human response. Other such passages could be quoted.[237] Some have suggested an alternative interpretation,[238] but no one has thus far succeeded in proving, on the basis of Kook's own words, that individual freedom and personal spirit are crushed under the wheels of divine, historical determination. None of these commentators would impute to Kook a Christian bias, that while we act freely we are also assured that Grace will turn our hearts toward the Redeemer.[239] Nor has anyone proven that Kook's assessment of the future of the Zionist undertaking was unconditional, that for him its success was "not dependent upon our actions," or that he separated redemption from *teshuvah*. These ideas are a more recent development, in the wake of the experiences and achievements of Zionism.

Rabbi David Henshke, writing independently, has tellingly criticized the deterministic reading of the elder Kook: "Rabbi Kook's perfect faith that the revealed End was indeed at hand in no way contradicts the notion that we may, heaven forbid, miss the mark . . . We must act in full awareness of the mighty messianic potential of our era . . . There is, however, a fine line between appropriate faith and false confidence, between true reverence that knows how great is the gulf separating it from its Creator and the arrogant certainty that presumes to know the mind of the Most High . . . We must undergo the difficult test of educating to complexity. And we bear an exalted responsibility to see that the potential is realized."[240] Kook was a great believer in the power of faith. He meant to lead the people to its destiny by means of messianic observation and an optimistic long-range faith. "The whole people believes that, following the redemption now beginning before our very eyes, there will be no more exile, and this deep faith is itself the secret of [our] existence" (*Orot*, p. 77).

IDEA AND REALITY

Shortly after the Yom Kippur War, on the twenty-seventh anniversary of Israel's independence (1974), Rabbi Zvi Yehudah Kook preached to his jubilant students and the hundreds of guests gathered at the yeshivah for the holiday. The elderly rabbi pointed out to his listeners the greatness of the hour and the religious meaning of Jewish national restoration. "There are those who speak of 'the beginning of redemption' in our own time," he said, using the expression accepted by many religious Zionists. But "we must perceive clearly that we are already in the midst of redemption.[241] We are already in the throne room, not just in the antechamber. The 'beginning' took place more than a century ago, when Jewish settlement in the Land of Israel was renewed."[242] True, the society and the state are not yet run in full accord with the Torah. But we must learn to separate the wheat from the chaff, between the precious essence embodied in the very fact of Jewish sovereignty in the Land of Israel and the incidental flaws that have accumulated along its redemptive path. "The principal, overall thing is the state. It is inherently holy and without blemish. It is a supernal, heavenly realization of [the prayer] 'He restores His presence to Zion.' All the rest is details, trivia, [minor] problems and complications. These cannot detract at all from the holiness of the state. The intrinsic value of the state does not depend on whether it has a greater or smaller number of religious people. Naturally we look forward to the time when the whole nation will 'belong' to the Torah and the commandments, but the state is holy in any case!"[243]

The gap between utopian vision and historical reality is thus explained here by drawing a sharp distinction between "essence" and "existence," between the shining idea of the State of Israel and the passing shadows that have accrued to it. The "true" state is to be evaluated according to its inner, a priori, unconditional religious meaning—"its holiness"—not according to its temporary laws or the everyday behavior of its citizens. The State of

Israel was conceived and born in holiness, in a messianic mode, and therefore its pedestals cannot be shaken or found faulty. It is as if a utopia had already been given, outside time and space, so that it could not prove disappointing. As Rabbi Yitzhak Shilat later wrote: "Our teacher Rabbi Zvi Yehudah [Kook], of blessed memory, saw the achievement of actual Jewish sovereignty in the Land of Israel as a matter of divine command and inherent sanctity, not dependent on either the personalities of the state's leaders, the structure of its institutions, or this or that sin in the way it is run. These are all individual matters, whereas the holiness of the people and its sovereignty are common to all Israel and cannot be diminished by sin."[244]

It will be recalled that it was the elder Kook who distinguished between the subjective choices made by individual Jews and the objective distinction of the people as a whole. Though the visible decisions made by individuals might not measure up to the invisible national standard, this was only a temporary, incidental deviation that did not affect the overall trend. Now what Kook said about the nation, or more precisely the idea of the nation, was said by his son and the latter's disciples about the state and the idea of the state.

The elder Kook wrote: "The great love we bear for our nation should not blind us to its faults, yet however critically we examine it we still find it innocent. 'Every part of you is fair, my darling, there is no blemish in you' [Song 4:7]."[245] His followers later made a similarly essentialistic assessment of the State of Israel, as the political embodiment of the people Israel. As we have seen, they judged the Jewish state in terms of what it ought to be— "the pedestal of God's throne in this world"—and not what it actually was. True, the state's citizens were expected to narrow the gap between the ideal and the real, between essence and existence; yet all their individual actions, however sinful and deviant, could not change the innate character of this state, which was conceived as a metaphysical sanctum. The messianic ideal, in its perfection, thus protected the fragmentary historical reality from its critics, from both the left and the right. "Every part of you is fair, my darling."

What we have here is the inverse of the radical ultra-Orthodox ideology described in chapter 2. The Satmar Hasidim and the Neturei Karta also judge the Jewish state and predict its future (albeit negatively) in terms of the inherent theological meaning they attribute to its existence and essence, not in terms of the concrete behavior of its citizens. In their view, the state was conceived and born in impurity. Their opponents take the precisely opposite view, that it was conceived and born in holiness. According to the former, the original sin embodied in its very existence cannot be rectified; it is therefore condemned to destruction. The latter group, Kook's disciples, for their part, believe the special sanctity inherent in the very existence of the state cannot be destroyed or defiled; it is therefore destined for redemption.

Both camps, then, take a deterministic view of the future of the Zionist undertaking, for it is its essence that will decide its outcome, for good or ill.

We should not be surprised at this parallel between the two radical positions, for both of them take as their point of departure an uncompromising messianism.[246] Both reject out of hand any partial revival of the Jewish people that is not grounded in the promise of ultimate redemption or measured according to the standard of ultimate perfection. According to the former, anti-Zionist view, the present return to Zion and recovery of political sovereignty do not represent a partial recovery of wholeness. They betoken, not a flowering, but a severing and a fragmentation of the whole. But the second, Zionist view, also refuses to recognize any partial realization as valuable in and of itself.[247] Its value derives entirely from the seed of perfection it contains, a seed that is destined to grow organically and inexorably into a pristine, absolute entity. This camp, too, believes there can be no return but the final, messianic one; however, it maintains that that is what the present return in fact is. The partly realized historical entity (*athalta de-ge'ulah*) derives its standing from the fully realized metahistorical one, and is therefore called upon to tailor itself, here and now, to the latter's specifications. "The commandment of redemption is neither a myth nor an 'apocalypse' . . . We cannot be satisfied with any less than the dream of all the generations of the Exile: the establishment of the realm to which all of creation, since the beginning of time, has aspired. Only through the attainment of this perfection, in the light of God's countenance, will there be an end to our tears, our sighs, our social frictions."[248] This is the charge of Rabbi Moshe Zuriel, editor of *Otzrot ha-Reiyah* ("The Treasures of Rabbi Kook"). A similar view was expressed by Rabbi Eliezer Waldman at the time of the Lebanon War: "We are past the point where we can build up the people and the land by halfway measures . . . The Jewish people's task is to establish order in the [entire] world . . . We now aspire to an all-encompassing perfection and greatness."[249] This is, in fact, "the perfection that encompasses the State of Israel . . . the holy bounty" (Rabbi Moshe Levinger).[250]

We may thus distinguish three ideas that may be said to be shared by the enemies and supporters of Zionism, by the Satmar Hasidim and the disciples of Rabbi Kook: determinism, essentialism, and perfectionism. But, as we have seen, it is precisely these common conceptions, precisely the absolute messianic demand that they share, that lies at the root of their profound differences.

Nevertheless, there are certain highly charged situations in which the two opposing camps, and particularly the more extreme elements within them, may find themselves on the same side. In a paradoxical way, the metaphysical elevation of the State of Israel threatens to undermine the authority of the given, earthly state. The wider the gap between the ideal and the real, between the anticipated perfection and the actual implementation, the more questionable is the existing state (at least for the more extreme messianic Zionists). At a certain point, it is no longer this mere shadow of the messianic state that is authoritative, but only "the State of Israel, the pedestal of the Lord's earthly throne," as it looms in the believer's imagination in all its unconditional redemptive significance. It was in this spirit that Rabbi Yisrael Ariel, for example, former dean of the Yamit Yeshivah and one of the most militant of Zvi Yehudah Kook's followers, defended the Jewish underground that appeared in Judea and Samaria in 1985. He was full of deference for the ideal "state," but had none for its actual existing authorities.[251] Such statements are issued by other groups as well, particularly when the possibility of Israeli withdrawal from Judea and Samaria is discussed. "If the leaders of our country decide to separate us from the [full extent] of the State of Israel and set up an alternative state in the land of the Philistines [i.e., Israel within the 1949 cease-fire lines], we shall deny their right to use the name 'State of Israel' and go on maintaining the [true] Jewish state in the heart of the country, under the banner of the duty to gather in the exiles and settle the land . . . To the extent that the state shirks its obligations, it forfeits its right to exist to those who are prepared to fulfill them in its stead."[252] Thus writes Barukh Lior in *Nekudah*, the magazine of the Jewish settlements in Judea, Samaria, and the Gaza District (1985). In this view, therefore, the "full" State of Israel will negate and undermine the partial state. Needless to say, such sentiments have been expressed more frequently and more vocally since the 1993 Oslo agreement between Israel and the Palestinians.

It should be stressed, however, that these statements have been subjected to internal criticism. "The Land of Israel versus the State of Israel? A Haredi-nationalist state in the Judean diaspora?" asks Yo'el Bin-Nun.[253] Similarly, when the Council of Settlements in Judea, Samaria, and Gaza proclaimed that it would treat any Israeli government that gave up part of the Land of Israel "as an illegal government, just as General de Gaulle treated the Vichy government of Marshal Pétain that had betrayed the French people,"[254] angry voices were raised in protest from within the settlement movement. We shall, they said, "treat the Council . . . that commits this crime as an illegal, treasonous council and not recognize its decisions."[255] What these polemics clearly demonstrate is the potential for radicalism inherent in the idealistic view of the state. It is true that good citizens can be expected to rise up against the state if it arrogantly abuses its mandate and tramples on their basic values. But generally an effort is made to avoid such confrontations insofar as possible. But when the state is held up to absolute, metaphysical standards, they cannot so easily be put off, and an explosion becomes a distinct possibility.[256]

Moreover, if the State of Israel is expected to realize final, messianic goals, how long can it content itself with being a mere "beginning" and not press forward? If we have already reached the age of redemption, realization, and conquest, how much longer can the Temple Mount and the Holy of Holies remain in alien hands? The more that is expected of present reality, the greater will be the pressure to "ascend the mountain" and take those measures that will turn the tide of history. Will young people burning with the fire of redemption be content to go on waiting on the threshold of the inner sanctum at the same stage where their predecessors did? Will they agree to work, to take the lead, and to initiate all kinds of activities for the sake of the Land of Israel but, when it comes to the very heart of the land, beating on the heights of the holy mountain, sit idly by? (This is precisely the demand made of them by their teachers at Merkaz ha-Rav, who forbid going up to the Temple Mount.) Is it conceivable that "when it comes to the Land of Israel we are Zionists, but in regard to the Temple Mount we are like Satmar Hasidim?"[257] as a young firebrand once asked Tau. The strong desire to eliminate the mosques from the Temple Mount is thus a direct result of this tension,[258] and not all will be able to restrain themselves indefinitely.

Finally, just as there can be no Jewish return to the Land of Israel except a complete return, there can be no Jewish notion of peace except a perfect peace. Peace is no longer merely a contingent political concept, attainable in the course of history, but an ahistorical, utopian one, the peace of the End of Days prophesied by Isaiah and Micah. "True peace" must be based on utter harmony, love, and brotherhood, not just on a balance of forces that keeps conflicting interests in check. Hence, as Gideon Aran has pointed out, many of the younger Kook's disciples, the leadership of Gush Emunim, saw the peace agreement with Egypt as a betrayal, not only of the ideal of the integrity of the Land of Israel, but also of the integrity of the Jewish idea of peace. Rabbi Ya'akov Ariel, in a speech before the national council of B'nai Akiva in 1979, protested:

What is being done today is a mockery of the word peace. The true peace
for which we aim and to which we must educate [our people] is a peace
based on the unification of the human race around one Torah . . . [The
present] peace is not the peace of the Bible.[259] . . . It is not for this "peace"
that a Jew lifts his eyes in prayer. True peace entails a spiritual revolution
. . . The idea of peace includes the absolute dominion of the Lord. A peace
that lacks the element of a common faith and a single [shared] idea is not a
true peace or a stable one.[260]

Clearly, in this area as well, the elevation of an idea to utopian status prevents it from being realized, even partially, in the here and now. Once peace
is understood in exclusively messianic terms, political activity aimed at
achieving it is, in effect, neutralized. "Without the [messianic] repair of the
world there will be no peace" (Hanan Porat).[261] "Until both sides acknowledge the power of almighty God, as opposed to the imaginary earthly substitutes for Him, there will be no true peace" (Yo'el Bin-Nun).[262] Note: the
very criticism leveled at Zionism by its bitterest ultra-Orthodox critics,
that it was attempting to reclaim the land in an unredeemed world, in history, is now being leveled within the Zionist camp in relation to the question of peace. Peace has been put off until such time as it can be realized
fully, even if that means leaving the field of history to the forces of war.[263]
For messianic perfection knows no compromise: it is all or nothing.[264]

CONCLUSION

In the two generations since Rabbi Abraham Isaac Kook's death, his messianic hopes have come much closer to realization in the material than in the
spiritual realm. Independence, the enormous growth of the Yishuv, the recovery of dominion over the Land of Israel, success in making the land pro-
ductive, military power and victory—all these material achievements have
given encouragement to the belief in the revealed End. But the spiritual picture is rather different: a nonreligious majority that stubbornly refuses to
heed the Call and ground its national identity in faith,[265] and the failure of
the new generation to reach higher moral ground. In sum, the visible elements of salvation have become more visible, while the invisible ones have
become more deeply hidden.

How have these developments been received by Kook's followers?
Zionism's material successes have certainly strengthened their belief in an
imminent realization, within history, of prophetic messianic hopes. The
Six-Day War and the propagation of Jewish settlements throughout Judea

and Samaria dramatically reinforced this belief. "The approach of the sages of Israel throughout the generations [was] . . . to view Jewish history with open eyes, in light of the Torah, and with complete faith in the guiding hand of the Lord. It was only from this perspective that Rabbi Abba could say in the Talmud that we would recognize the End by two clear signs: the beginning of the ingathering of the exiles and the flowering of the Land of Israel. With God's help, these things are coming to pass before our very eyes, and there can no longer be any doubt or grounds for holding back our joy and gratitude to the Redeemer of Israel" (Rabbi Tzefaniah Drori).[266] On the spiritual level, however, matters are different. It has been hard to avoid a sense of perplexity and bafflement: how to explain the fact that a collective return to religious observance has not yet occurred? Why has faith not yet surfaced on the level of personal conscious affirmation, as expected?

Given these developments, it is no wonder that messianic tensions have centered mainly on the earthly realm, on the flourishing of the land, and on political sovereignty. The latter are confirmed by every act of conquest and settlement.[267] Moreover, the messianic ideology is compelled to loosen as much as possible the traditional dependence of national redemption on religious renewal. As Rabbi Zvi Yehudah Kook put it, "The great ingathering of the exiles is a revelation of the light of the Messiah, which does not depend on our *teshuvah* but on the divine decree that 'this people I formed for Myself' [Isa. 43:21]."[268] The historical redemption, then, is not a function of achieving a higher spiritual state[269] but is, rather, preordained.

As we have seen, there are some who even believe that the people's collective destiny is completely independent of its actions. "The process of redemption is imposed upon us, in spite of what we do." Others, while not going this far, have still translated traditional expectations of spiritual renewal into worldly terms. In fact, what they are trying to do is superimpose the original, optimistic vision on a recalcitrant reality, turning it willy-nilly into a reality of *teshuvah*: "return to the Jewish people, return to Jewish heroism, return to physical labor and the tilling of the soil, return to social justice" (Aviner).[270] The outward historical reality itself constitutes religious renewal. What cause is there for complaint?

The roots of these ideas are, of course, to be found in Rabbi Abraham Kook himself. But what he hoped for was a gradual convergence of the outward and the inward, an imminent merging of outward historical salvation with inward religious awakening. He firmly believed that when the secularists achieved their worldly goals—legitimate goals, in his view—they would quickly realize that what they had really wanted all along was something more, something higher, a return to the Jewish soul and the commandments. He thus foresaw a process of perfection taking place in both realms, matter and spirit, land and Torah. But the longer this parallel development has been delayed, the more evident the revealed End, the more obscure the traditional *teshuvah,* and the greater the gap between the two, the more Kook's followers have felt the need to deepen their a priori interpretation and impose it upon the actual course of events. One must soften the sharp edges of the recalcitrant reality so as to see in it the shining vision. The vision is no longer put forward as a normative model by which society is to be judged. Rather, it is now to serve as a protective enclosure, justifying and defending what exists. "Our reality is one of *teshuvah,* and it is a messianic reality." Now, a messianic reality is something no right-thinking person can criticize or resist. Indeed, what one must do is live by its lights and try to integrate into it, judging oneself and one's comrades, not by any short-term yardstick, but by the long-term one of the great vision of the future.

It is in this perspective that we must interpret the criticism leveled at certain Zionist rabbis who protested the deterioration of the Lebanon War and its cruel aftereffects in the refugee camps; criticism such as that of Rabbi Oded Walensky, of the Merkaz ha-Rav Yeshivah: "The people of Israel are not in need of a weak, half-hearted ethic or of truncated liberal-Orthodox-existentialist beliefs and opinions . . . The indecision and laxity, the lack of will to strive onward in our work of national reconstruction in our land that these cause, and the retreat from absolute conviction and the ability to overcome all the obstacles set up for us by our enemies that occurs under their influence—[all these] make them decidedly immoral in comparison with the higher moral goals that underlie our national revival in wholeness and unity in the land."[271] Is it any wonder that several years later, when the Palestinian-Arab uprising began, Rabbi Zalman Melamed, dean of the Beit-El Yeshivah, wrote an article suggesting that this development was but another organic phase in the inexorable unfolding of the redemption of Israel?[272]

Finally, we would do well to ask about the other level to which Rabbi Kook's vision of redemption relates, the universal one. As we have seen, he anticipates the perfection of human beings as such, the reordering of society and of the world as a whole. The redemption of Israel, as he sees it, is bound up with the correction of all humankind: "The [material] building up of the nation and the emergence of its spirit are all one thing, and this, in turn, is one with the building of the world. The blessing of Abraham for all the nations of the world shall begin to take effect openly and vigorously, and on this basis our work of building in the Land of Israel shall be renewed."[273] As we have seen, even the agonies of the First World War and the social revolutions accompanying it seemed to Kook to herald a human rebirth. And indeed, his hopes did find support in subsequent events, so that he did not need have to impose them upon an altogether hostile reality.[274] It seemed briefly, in the wake of the war, that the nations might actually turn their swords into plowshares. But such hopes were soon dashed by death-dealing new regimes and the debasement of the revolutions that had once seemed so promising. The "postmodern" world is a much less cheering place than the "modern" one was.

In face of this gap, the two paths of spiritual response we have just described lay open to Kook's disciples: to concentrate on the redemption of the people of Israel, putting aside the universal vision;[275] or to reinterpret the national revival itself as actually bringing about universal redemption. They have fully explored each of these modes of response.

It is perhaps to this dichotomy that one of the leading figures at Merkaz ha-Rav was referring when he distinguished between the elder Kook and the younger: the father's personality, he said, was carved out of "the soul of Being (*nishmat ha-havayah*)," while the son's was derived from "the soul of the nation." This imagery is apt for characterizing the transition that took place from the universal, even cosmic, dimension that permeated the elder Kook's writing to the particular, Jewish dimension so highlighted in the work of the younger Kook. Indeed, the latter often said that if his father's book *Orot ha-kodesh,* which deals with metaphysical being, was altogether holy, his book *Orot* (Lights), which deals with the revival of the Jewish people, was the "holy of holies." For "the holy things particular to Israel," Rabbi Zvi Yehudah Kook said, "are the holy of holies."[276]

4

Exile in the Holy Land:
The Dilemma of Haredi Jewry

The two opposing views discussed in the previous chapters attributed a distinctive, inherent religious significance to the Zionist movement and the State of Israel—for good or for evil. Both views also professed to foresee—each from its own point of view—the destiny of Zionism and the future of Israeli society. However, the majority of ultra-Orthodox Jews utterly reject both of these ideological stances and dismiss their judgments regarding these questions. From this Haredi point of view, the State of Israel is a religiously neutral entity, part of the secular realm still belonging to the age of exile. The state's conception and birth were neither holy nor profane; it represents neither a messianic awakening nor an antimessianic eruption. Rather, it should be judged like any other historical phenomenon: according to its concrete relationship to the Torah, and according to the attitude of its leaders and adherents to the precepts of the Halakhah. "There is no independent absolute value in the Torah except for the Holy One, blessed be He, and His service . . . " Even the Holy Land, with all its importance and virtues, is not an independent value like a "homeland" among the nations. "The value of the Yishuv framework and its institutions is measured only by the degree to which they bring the people of the Lord closer to the Torah, the commandments, and the faith" (Rabbi Shlomo Volbe).[1] Accordingly, the future of the Jewish state is not preordained or predetermined by God. The people is invited to choose its own path and, accordingly, its destiny. God's judgment remains suspended and conditional.

The present chapter is devoted to the understanding of this basic position, which is accepted today among various streams within the Haredi community. We shall first examine the declared fundamental assumptions, both theological and pragmatic, of its spokesmen. We shall then explore the intellectual dilemma inherent in this outlook, and the inner distress recently undergone by Haredi leadership—specifically in wake of the growing political power and momentum of their disciples.

THE CONSCIOUSNESS OF EXILE

The social group commonly known as Haredi Jewry is composed of many diverse factions, each of which differs significantly from the others: Hasidim as against Mitnaggedim; Lubavitcher Hasidim as against those of Belz; Agudat Israel as against the Jerusalem Edah Haredit—each loyal to its own path and its own rabbi (and one may include among these also the followers of the Shas party—the Sephardic Torah Observant).

The differences among the various sections of Haredi Jewry occur at a number of different levels. One may distinguish between the various camps on the basis of their attitude toward modern culture or, alternatively, on the basis of their approach toward the Jewish people as a whole (*kelal Yisrael*), or toward the Zionist enterprise, or toward the historical dimension, and so forth.[2] That is to say, the major dividing lines fall between moderate rejection of modernity, and a view of modernity as the devil incarnate; between a sense of responsibility for the Jewish people in its entirety, and a preference to seclude and isolate the truly faithful; between non-Zionism and anti-Zionism; between a theology that sees direct divine intervention reflected in the unfolding historical process, and a worldview of Halakhists for whom current historical events are almost totally devoid of religious significance; or, as stated earlier, between the world of the Hasidic Rebbe and that of the Lithuanian *rosh yeshivah*.

As a generic term, therefore, "Haredi Jewry" may be artificial and only valid from the perspective of the outside observer who sees surface manifestations, but not the underlying conflicts of philosophy and outlook.[3] This problem certainly presents itself when we consider the variety of Haredi attitudes toward the existence, laws, mores, and activities of the sovereign Jewish state in the current (i.e., premessianic) era. That issue stands at the center of a sharp conflict within the Haredi community, occasionally resulting in mutual rejection and boycott. In light of this fragmentation, we must begin with the question, What common characteristics do these groups, in fact, share?

From one crucial angle, it would appear that all Haredi groups share a common base. This becomes clear via the following formulation: Who is a Haredi? Whoever views and experiences life in the Jewish state in Eretz Israel as exile—the exile of Israel in the Holy Land. One pole of the Haredi camp, the radical anti-Zionist one (particularly Neturei Karta circles), states that it is in exile because of the existence of the State of Israel, owing to both its betrayal of the Messiah and secular nationality; the opposite pole, the accommodationist non-Zionist one, maintains that it is in exile despite the existence of the State of Israel, despite the physical rescue and "the beginning of the ingathering of the exiles" that has accompanied its birth and existence. In any event—exile.

Those who share this perception, in all its various shadings, deny the possibility of an interim historical situation that is neither exile nor redemption. They unequivocally reject the validity of such a hybrid and recognize no Halakhic or theoretical model appropriate to it. Any reality that is not totally messianic is, by very definition, total exile. For exile is not a geographic condition that can be overcome by *aliyah* and settlement alone. Neither is exile a political condition that can be corrected by the attainment of national sovereignty and independence. The concept "exile" is a theological, metaphysical one—the exile of the Shekhinah (Divine Presence)—that will expire only with the final setting right of humankind and the world.[4] This responsibility imposed by exile on the Jewish people focuses exclusively on religious-spiritual activity, not on mundane political activity. The concept "exile" represents, first and foremost, a reality that has not yet been redeemed from sin: "Because of our sins we were exiled from our land" and "Israel will be redeemed only by repentance."[5]

For example, the late Lubavitcher Rebbe, Rabbi Menachem Mendel Schneersohn (1902–94), explicitly stated:

> The period in which we are now living is not the beginning of the redemption, and the *aliyah* of many Jews to the Holy Land is not the ingathering of the exiles, but rather the possibility of rescuing many Jews *during the time of exile* . . . The false redemption does not allow the true redemption to be revealed, for those who think that they are already living in the redemption do not perform the [religious] actions required for the going forth from exile and the revealing of the true redemption; they cause the prolongation of the Exile, the exile of the individual, the exile of the community, the exile of all Israel, and the exile of the Shekhinah. (Emphasis in original)[6]

Similarly, his outstanding critic Rabbi Eliezer Menahem Schach, the leader of the Lithuanian *rashei yeshivot* in Israel, declared, "The Jewish people is still in exile, until the arrival of the redeemer, even when it is in Eretz Israel; this is neither redemption nor the beginning of the redemption."[7]

The common factor shared by these two opponents is clear: all historical reality, by the very fact of its gradual course—progressing "bit by bit, and by natural means"—is the reality of exile. Any existence that is not messianic, perfect and miraculous and from which the flavor of sin has not been removed, is the existence of exile. This holds true for the partial return to Zion and for Jewish political resurrection in our time as well.[8]

This perception of the present historical reality as exile is not limited solely to a theological awareness. It is also reflected in a psychological and existential stance toward the secular environment, in a sense of personal and communal alienation. The concept "exile" does not merely denote the opposite of the destined messianic redemption; it also denotes the lack of a home, the home of one's father and grandfather as well as the sense of estrangement from the external society, its lifestyles and culture, and from the secular government and its institutions. These are depicted in many instances as a society and government that have completely lost all Jewish identifying characteristics, with nothing to distinguish them from the Gentile environment in any country—in other words, "exile."

This consciousness is reinforced by the intermittently renewed sharp public conflicts with the secular society and its leaders. For example, in a public assembly held in 1986 to protest the arson resulting in the burning of holy books in a Tel Aviv yeshivah, Rabbi Pinhas Menahem Alter, then head of the Sefat Emet Yeshivah of Gur Hasidim and the present Gurer Rebbe, lamented, "This is the most difficult exile, exile under Jewish rule." This is "the most difficult exile," specifically because that which was supposed to be home seems strange and hostile and arouses in the mind of the speaker associations with persecutions of Jews by non-Jewish nations. Or, as Rabbi Binyamin Mendelson, the late rabbi of Moshav Komemiyyut stated, "Our sins have led to our being put in exile in the Holy Land, in the hands of the nonreligious."[9] These are not metaphysical statements on the question of messianic redemption, but rather expressions of an existential state of alienation, both personal and collective, reflected in the identification of secular Jewish authority with the Gentile ruler. As Israel Eichler, editor of *Ha-Mahaneh ha-Haredi* (the mouthpiece of Belzer Hasidism), protested against the celebrations of the thirty-eighth anniversary of the State of Israel: "You should refute the heretics and defiant ones who seek to uproot our holy Torah, saying to them: your rejoicing is our mourning and despair. To the innocent, unsophisticated ones among them, however, we are obligated to tell the story of our exile—the State of Israel within the Land of Israel. For this exile is the most difficult of all exiles; it is founded in that very declaration of he who declared the creation of the State."[10]

Here a certain distinction needs to be made. Exile, in its primary, theological, meaning—that is, the absence of redemption—is not necessarily meant to express an attitude of delegitimation and principled negation of the contemporary collective Jewish enterprise in Eretz Israel. Rather, it is meant to convey the idea that the Jewish state exists within history, not beyond it: not in the End of Days. Only a messianic reality could redeem and break through the category of exile. On the other hand, exile in the second sense—the absence of a home—reflects a distancing from, and rejection of, the secular reconstruction of the Holy Land, of Jewish nationalism that is not anchored in the Torah and its commandments. This life together with, and under the leadership of, transgressors is the life of the exiled, of the resident alien, of the cast aside, even beyond the fact of the Messiah's tarrying. Those speaking for Haredi Jewry recurrently use, in various contexts,[11] expressions and depictions that express this consciousness of a double exile in the Holy Land.[12]

There is nothing new about this phenomenon. As early as 1937, in his speech to the world convention (Kenesiyyah ha-Gedolah) of Agudat Israel in Marienbad, Rabbi Elhanan Bunem Wasserman envisioned the future Jewish state as the exile of Israel—exile in both senses. He stated that the observant Jew is deeply hurt when he hears talk of the "beginning of the redemption"; on the contrary, a Jewish state, should it arise and come into being according to the secular Zionist vision, would be nothing other than "the beginning of a new exile"—an unprecedented "exile amid the Jews," the "exile of the Yevsektsia."[13]

The horrors of the Holocaust, in which Rabbi Wasserman himself perished, somewhat blunted the style of the confrontation, but not its content or its message. In 1945, for example, after the destruction of European Jewry, Rabbi Moshe Blau, one of the outstanding leaders of Agudat Israel in Eretz Israel, issued a call to Haredi Jewry to mobilize for the rebuilding of the Diaspora from its ruins. The Haredim, he declared, must not be deceived by the Zionist call for the "liquidation of the exile"; the reconstruction of Eretz Israel and the reconstruction of the communities abroad were of equal importance.[14] In Eretz Israel the faithful Jew actually found him- or herself living in a triple exile: at the hands of the British, of the Arabs, and, especially, of Jews who had thrown off the yoke of the Torah. In Rabbi Blau's words,

At present we have three exiles in Eretz Israel: the exile of Edom, the exile of Ishmael, and the exile of the freethinkers. And Eretz Israel perhaps surpasses the foreign lands in this last exile, which at any rate does not exist, in this form, in any other place outside Eretz Israel. The word of the Lord, "And you

I will scatter among the nations" [Lev. 26:33] is ultimately valid, just as the promise, "He will bring you together again from all the peoples" [Deut. 30:3] is ultimately valid. As long as "He will bring you" has not been fulfilled—and anyone is whose heart a spark of true Judaism burns will not say that the government by the freethinkers in Eretz Israel conforms to "He will bring you"—then the validity of "And you I will scatter" obviously still exists . . . Haredi Jewry in Eretz Israel is unbearably oppressed, the heavy hand of the freethinkers has overpowered it since it has lost the support of the healthy, vibrant Jewry in the exile of Europe.[15]

It is ironic that the spokesman of Haredi Jewry apparently did not invent the image of the future Jewish state as the exile of Israel in Eretz Israel. Credit for this should be given to those nonreligious writers who, at the end of the nineteenth century, expressed their profound fear of the expected takeover by the rabbis of the free life of the people. Judah Leib Gordon, for example, launched an attack on settlement activity in Eretz Israel that was not part of, or accompanied by, a spiritual liberation from the ghetto—that is, by a cultural and ideological revolution. Gordon explained his opposition by his fear of the heavy hand of the *Shulḥan Arukh* (code of Jewish law) and of its rabbinical interpreters over the Jews. This, he believed, would prevent the true redemption of the people and was liable to turn life in Eretz Israel into a new exile. In his words, "I have felt this on my own body; the exile under Israel is more difficult for us than the exile under the nations of the world."[16]

A STATE IN THE SECULAR REALM

As stated in the first chapter, there have been three basic elements in the ultra-Orthodox opposition to Zionism. The Haredi polemic against the fledgling Zionist movement began with an opposition to the secular nature of the modern Jewish national revival, speedily moving on to challenge the very legitimacy of the collective historical effort for mass *aliyah* from the Exile—depicted as trespassing on the bounds of the promised messianic redemption. In addition, it was argued on pragmatic grounds that the Zionist idea was simply an illusion, lacking any basis in actual historical reality: "What is the difference between those who believe that the Messiah will come, humbly and riding on an ass, or on a light cloud, and the Zionists in our time, who believe that the kingdoms will assemble and will give them the land of Palestine with the agreement of the Sultan? Is there anything in this belief, even the smallest particle, about which we can say that it will come about in a natural way?"[17] To the contrary, it seemed that the messianic idea is the only realistic solution.[18]

The success and gradual fulfillment of Zionism, the Balfour Declaration, the strengthening of the Yishuv in Eretz Israel, and, finally, the establishment of the State of Israel and the *aliyah* of several million Jews (and, on the other hand, the terrible destruction of European Jewry who simply wished to dwell in tranquility)—all left their mark in the ideological sphere and generated profound changes in the conduct of the debate. The practical argument concerning Zionism was gradually set aside by the force of historical reality. The standing of the theological argument, which regarded Zionism as an undue hastening of the End, was greatly undermined, retaining its original validity only among the separatist camp of the Neturei Karta and the Satmar Hasidim. Only the argument concerning the nature of secular nationalism and the abandonment of the Torah has retained its force. Indeed, recent events have provided a broad arena for a renewed and intensified confrontation over this issue.

But a noticeable change has taken place in this sphere as well. A confrontation with an abstract idea, with a Jewish state that is merely a vision or dream of the future, is not the same as a real-life confrontation with an actual and concrete Jewish state. The aspiration for radical separation from an ideological movement (Zionism) and from individual Jews (the secularists) was markedly different from any present attempt to maintain one's distance from an entire society with its own political, judicial, and economic institutions. Therefore, a sharp distinction has developed between the separating theoretical sphere of principles and the unifying pragmatic sphere; between forbidden ideas and values, on the one hand, and permitted political institutions and organizational tools, on the other hand; between a priori assumptions and ex post facto adaptations.

To bring matters into focus: the prevalent position currently dominant among most of the Haredi circles in the State of Israel (in a variety of versions) recognizes the secular Jewish state de facto, but has not granted it de jure recognition.[19] Haredi representatives cooperate in a circumscribed and conditional manner with the institutions that are the outcome of the Zionist idea and the Zionist movement, but they deny the validity of the Zionist doctrine per se; that is, they reject the founding ideology of the national enterprise.[20] The State of Israel as a political entity and act of political organization by Jews is deemed to be devoid of religious significance, whether positive or negative; it is in itself a neutral phenomenon, existing within the secular realm; it is neither within the sphere of transgression nor of obligation, but rather within the voluntary sphere. The position of the outstanding scholar and leader of the previous generation, Rabbi Avraham Yeshayahu Karelitz (known as the Hazon Ish), was recently and reliably summed up: "The Hazon Ish did not view the state as the height of the darkness of exile, and certainly not as redemption, but rather as something merely technical and administrative; it therefore has no significance in principle, neither as a success nor as a disaster, and it has no connection with the redemption."[21]

This consistent distinction drawn between the constituent idea of an Israeli state and the political institution itself, between values and "technical and administrative" tools and instruments, is intended to avoid the need of taking any essential a priori—and certainly theological—position vis-à-vis the Jewish state in premessianic times. The distinction permits both a clearly pragmatic approach to the state and its enterprises, and life alongside the State of Israel and cooperation with its institutions, openly based on accommodation in practice—that is, on post factum acceptance of the given political reality. This life is supposed to be free of ideological commitment or identification, innocent of any normative decision and a priori recognition. "We stand before the fact that they established a state on a part of our Holy Land, and hence we do not have before us a Halakhic question of permitted or prohibited, for this question has already been resolved by those who do not ask [religious] questions. All that remains is for us to clarify our position and our attitude toward this reality with which they have presented us . . . And we have not found, either in the Torah or in the Talmud or in the later Halakhic authorities, any concepts or laws indicating when to recognize or not to recognize a state. This is nothing but a custom employed by Gentiles for propaganda purposes."[22] Thus Rabbi Avraham Weinfeld, one of the distinguished *mashgiḥim* and ethical preachers within the world of Lithuanian yeshivot. This is likewise the tradition conveyed in the name of the Klausenberger Rebbe, the late leader of the Sanz Hasidim.[23] Or, as the idea was formulated by other Haredi leaders—citizenship in the new state, as distinct from membership in a voluntary movement (e.g., the Zionist movement), is compulsory participation, a given reality that is imposed on the residents of the state, therefore lacking normative significance.[24] It takes place within the realm of facts, not within that of beliefs.

Accordingly, every assessment regarding the state and its actions (like every other mundane phenomenon) must be taken ad hoc according to the merits of the case: based upon its link with, and assistance to, the Torah and its students; and according to the attitude of the state's leaders to the demands of the Halakhah.[25] If the state, its institutions, and its budgets support Torah students and bring closer those distant from the tradition, then they are judged favorably. If they deny Torah Jews their due and cause those close to the tradition to abandon it, they are judged unfavorably. When the state rescues Jews and contributes to protecting the lives and well-being of Jews, wherever they are, the evaluation will be positive (i.e., the saving of life as a religious value). When it endangers the safety of Jews, the evaluation will be negative. This criterion is used to evaluate every collective Jewish enterprise in the lands of their dispersion and remains applicable to their activity in the exile of Israel in the Holy Land.[26] It follows that, when Haredi circles make their support of one government or another conditional on increased financial allocations to yeshivot and Torah institutions, for example, they are merely being faithful to their philosophy: Of what use is a Jewish state, of what use are public institutions and parliamentary committees, if not for the purpose of promoting Torah study in the Holy Land?

This position appears to be consistent, simple, and clear. In contradistinction to the two previous opposing approaches, it does not seem to need any complicated ideological structures or tortuous theological justifications. For example, when in the wake of the Six-Day War the Israel army reached Judea, the Western Wall, and the Temple Mount, they did not need to demonize the military victory and to explain it as a test with which God was trying the truly faithful (see chapter 2). On the other hand, in contradistinction to redemptionist religious Zionists, neither did they need to deal theologically with events that appeared to be a retreat in the process of redemption, such as the withdrawal from Sinai and the evacuation of the Yamit region. They were not pressed to explain it in a convoluted way as descent for the purpose of an eventual ascent or as a national will that had failed and not raised itself to the heights of the divine will (see chapter 3).[27] The prevalent Haredi outlook is spared the troubles besetting these two approaches, in that it neither pins its hopes on the downfall and failure of the state nor foresees with certainty the state's triumph and divine vindication. It consciously refrains from absolute theological and historiosophical claims regarding the Zionist state and its future.

Thus things appear on the surface. Later on, I shall discuss the internal dilemma confronting this outlook. At this point, however, it should be presented as it defines itself, within the terms of its declared axioms and self-awareness.

For example, in recent years Rabbi Eliezer Menahem Schach has used the above-mentioned midrashic oaths quite differently from the Neturei Karta and Satmar Hasidim. The oath not to rebel against the Gentiles, for example, provided him with a rational for warning the Israeli government against engaging in adventurist military actions or political acts that provoke the Gentile nations (e.g., the settlement of Judea and Samaria and the Lebanon War).[28] That is to say, these prohibitions have been placed in a pragmatic and practical context rather than in a theological one. So, too, the late Lubavitcher Rebbe and others consistently inveighed against trespassing into the realm of the destined miraculous redemption. Such statements, however, are no longer directed at the invalidation of the principle of Jewish political sovereignty per se, but against any conception that places the State of Israel within the frame of reference of redemption—that is, against those religious Zionists who seek to impart messianic significance to the State of Israel.[29] True, Rabbi Schach and Rabbi Schneersohn of Lubavitch would have conducted a bitter argument concerning the question of Jewish policy at the present time: Should Jews maintain a low profile vis-à-vis the Gentile world (Schach) or one of strength and pride (Schneersohn; see chapter 5). However, this would not be a theological argument concerning "the oaths" or "the revealed End," but rather a practical controversy concerning the appropriate Jewish policy in time of exile.

Indeed, some formulations of this position include direct criticism of the two messianic approaches to its right and left, portraying them as illegitimate deviations from the classical Jewish middle way. As Rabbi Binyamin Silber, one of the great scholars and leaders of Agudat Israel's Council of Torah Sages, declared:

> We are not among those who calculate the End, give it names, [for example,] the beginning of the redemption, the beginning of the Beginning . . . neither are we among those who say that at present there is no obligation of *aliyah*, and that even promotion of the settlement of Eretz Israel oversteps the vow not to return to the land collectively . . . Just as we have not contracted with the Lord of Israel to eliminate the Exile and to bring about the redemption, so, too, we have not entered into a contract to make specific efforts to remain in exile, and to be scattered and dispersed among the nations . . . Both versions [of the oath as interpreted by Rashi] that Israel will neither "hasten" nor "prolong" [the End] are, rhetorically speaking, true.[30] Any tendency toward either pole brings bad results; "We will follow the king's highway, turning off neither to the right nor to the left" [Num. 20:17].[31]

Other religious leaders would present this same approach as agnostic in principle to the messianic question, denying human beings any claim to knowledge concerning heavenly plans. For example, Rabbi Avraham

Weinfeld states: "There are those who view this as praiseworthy and as the beginning of the redemption, and there are those who see the entire existence of the state unfavorably, claiming that it is against the Torah, and the work of the devil . . . This [debate] has already gone beyond the bounds of the halakhah for which there are Torah sources; thus we feel our way as the blind in the dark, without any clear knowledge as to whether this is to be judged positively or negatively; therefore, we must admit that we do not comprehend the nature of this reality; in order to do so, we require prophecy and divine inspiration."[32] The pragmatic, nontheological position regarding the Jewish state is interpreted here as a manifestation of human humility before heaven—as against the messianic pretenses to break through behind the divine veil. "Both camps, those who affirm the vision of the revealed End as well as those who deny it, force themselves, as it were, into the secrets of the Almighty, as if the upper world were unfolded before them like a garment," writes Rabbi Joseph David Epstein. "But the heavenly voice has not yet emerged!"[33]

To summarize, the achievement of political independence in the Holy Land does not represent a transformation or a dramatic turning point in Jewish history. It demands neither new categories of thought nor a specific Halakhic confrontation. Even more so has it nothing to do with messianic hopes. "The world follows its usual path"—and in this world, one should adhere to the traditional practical guidelines regarding the age of exile.[34]

A NATION AMONG THE NATIONS?

The ultra-Orthodox approach discussed in this chapter vacillates in practice between two different poles.

Rabbi Yitzhak Ze'ev ("Velvl") ha-Levi Soloveichik of Brisk, who lived in Jerusalem, once heard a member of Neturei Karta curse the State of Israel, to which he responded, "This man is a Zionist." How so? "In Poland or in Russia would he thus curse the authorities? Would he act like this in America?" Since he acts differently here, then he must necessarily find a different essence in the Jewish state, a unique experience. "He must therefore be a Zionist."[35] Rabbi Hayyim Ozer Grodzinski, one of the leading Torah scholars of the pre-Holocaust generation, also seems to have intended this in his response to the view that a Jewish state would constitute a violation of the oath taken by Israel not to "rebel against the nations." If a Jewish state were indeed established, Rabbi Grodzinski said, it would also be a "nation" among the nations of the world, and the prohibition of rebelling against the nations of the world would apply to it as well![36]

These two statements express a complete value neutrality toward the meaning of the Jewish return into political history. The statements are not directed toward the nature of the Jewish state and its laws and mores, but rather toward its institutional, "technical and administrative" existence (noted earlier). Its existence, as such, has been emptied of any specific Jewish significance: a nation among the nations. As Rabbi Velvl's approach was later summed up by his nephew, Rabbi Joseph B. Soloveitchik: "No place was found for the state in his system of halakhic thought and in his scale of Halakhic values. He was incapable of translating the concept of secular political sovereignty into halakhic content and values."[37] Or as Rabbi Hayyim Ozer Grodzinski put it in 1937, "Even if such a state were to be founded, it would be, at best, a state whose rulers are Jews, and not a Jewish state."[38]

Such fine scholastic expressions are characteristic, in the main, of the Lithuanian yeshivah circles—both in terms of their tendency to neutralize contemporary history of all religious significance, and in terms of their fondness for sharp logical paradoxes. However, these statements also reflect a basic widespread intuition in broader Haredi circles. In essence, they reflect the consciousness of exile in its most pristine, most consistent, and most alienated form.

Reality, of course, is more complicated and complex, and often does not correspond to such precise formulations. For example, the Haredi community does not recite prayers for the welfare of the State of Israel, as is customary for every other state in which Jews live, despite the claim that Israel is a state like any other. (It refrains from doing so, for fear that it be interpreted as support of Zionism.) Does this not indicate that the State of Israel is, nonetheless, different from all other states?[39] In fact, the declaration of indifference toward the uniqueness of the new political-historical reality has been unsuccessful. Israel's specific nature as a Jewish state—and as a secular Jewish state—is not ignored, and the fine line separating the political-institutional and the ideological-normative realms is not easily maintained.

In any event, it is precisely this consciousness of exile that removes historical affairs and political realities from the dimension of religious values and of Jewish uniqueness that, paradoxically, enables Haredim to accept coexistence with the state. It also facilitates pragmatic political and economic cooperation with the authorities, just as Jews have always done throughout the centuries of their exile. In the words of Rabbi Meir Karelitz,

"In all the countries of the nations of the world, Jews would seek a *shtadlan* (intercessor) who would act on behalf of Haredi Jewry within government circles; therefore, if there is a possibility of including within the government of Israel a *shtadlan* who will be on guard for the affairs of Torah Jewry, then this must be done, unhesitatingly."[40] Or, as it was radically put by Rabbi Raphael Reuven Grozovsky, the head of the Council of Torah Sages in the United States during the last generation, "There are those who compare the present situation to that of Joseph [in Egypt!], of Mordecai, Daniel, and Nehemiah [in Persia!], of Rabbi Samuel Hanagid [in Granada!], of Abrabanel [in Portugal and Spain!], or of Obadiah [the prophet] in the court of [King] Ahab, and of many *shtadlanim* among Israel."[41] Thus the emissary of Haredi Jewry to the political institutions of the State of Israel is perceived as a *shtadlan*, in a long chain of *shtadlanim,* who acts within a "nation" among the nations. These spokesmen thereby seek to avoid coming to grips at the value level with the profound change that has taken place in the situation of the Jewish people, a change that has actually confronted them with an exceptional and unanticipated historical entity:[42] Jewish sovereignty in the Holy Land prior to the messianic era, led by transgressors.

This approach is not followed by all Haredi circles, nor is it applied under all circumstances. Other voices, which assess current events in light of a religious perspective and search for the hand of Divine Providence as revealed in historical occurrences, are also to be heard among such Hasidic circles as those of Gur and Lubavitch, and on occasion among mitnaggedic Torah scholars. These voices are heard mainly in times of dramatic historical events, such as the Balfour Declaration, the establishment of the state, and the Six-Day War. The most far-reaching statements were made during the first years of the state, by Rabbi Yitzhak Meir Levin, the political leader of Agudat Israel (and son-in-law of the Rebbe of Gur). Rabbi Levin, who served for over four years as a minister in the Israeli government, spoke publicly about the "State of Israel that was established with manifest miracles," the "wondrous vision of the beginning of the ingathering of the exiles," "the finger of God" as revealed in the establishment of the state, and "the hand of Divine Providence which directs the steps of the State of Israel" in its land.[43] Things went so far that, when Neturei Karta issued a broadside attacking him for these statements,[44] spokesmen for Agudat Israel saw fit to deny publicly that such expressions as "the finger of God" were in fact issued by their leader.[45] (But today, now that a collection of his speeches has been published, his public statements are available to all.)[46]

The sense of salvation and greatness of the hour was marked in statements made at the time by various Hasidic leaders.[47] Similarly, in 1949 dozens of rabbis from different circles signed a preelection announcement that included the expression "the first budding of the beginning of the redemption with the establishment of the State of Israel" (this was, of course, only a metaphor, not a manifestation of a messianic outlook).[48] But when the first excitement passed, expressions such as these faded and, in fact, almost completely vanished within Haredi circles. Nevertheless, more than thirty years later, the Lubavitcher Rebbe wrote about the "great and manifest miracles" that had taken place at that time[49] and (regarding the Six-Day War), about a "propitious hour," the "great rescue of millions of Jews in Eretz Israel," and similar expressions.[50] (I devote chapter 5 to the peculiar approach of contemporary Habad Hasidism.)

Clearly, these spokesmen had distanced themselves considerably from the traditional apprehension about a Jewish political renaissance during the time of the Exile, and did not feel the need to declare apathy and neutrality toward the historical dimension. But for this very reason their statements tend to emphasize another aspect of the traditional Haredi argument with Zionism, focusing on the secular nature of the state and society and on the acts of the transgressors who became the leaders of Israel—legislators and ministers. It is precisely the sense of salvation and the awareness of the uniqueness of these events for Jewish history that motivate the confrontation with secular institutions and individuals and that guide their attitude to the question of Torah observance in Israel. It cannot be ignored, because this, and only this, will decide the fate of Israel for good or ill. The Haredi way of thinking teaches that the active responsibility of the Jew is limited to the religious-spiritual sphere, whereas responsibility for the fate and the mundane prosperity of the Jewish people rests solely in divine hands. The theses of conventional historiography must therefore be reversed. It is not the secular Zionist who creates the opportunity, the greatness of the hour; on the contrary, his rejection of the yoke of the commandments and his violation of the covenant represent the danger of missing the hour appointed by heaven. He embodies the very antithesis of the opportunity, the challenge and, needless to say, the future redemption.

The late Lubavitcher Rebbe, for example, drew the following picture of the rebirth of the state, the hope and the missed opportunity:

> The Holy One, blessed be He, the source of good and mercy, who performs miracles and wonders and who changes all systems, is the one who created, by His inner intent, the causes that led to the miracles and *the great rescue of millions of Jews* in Eretz Israel, for during those years the time was pro-

pitious, and there was a will from above . . . After the Holy One, blessed be He, saw the suffering of His people Israel, that they were being slaughtered and massacred, heaven forbid, in horrible and awful persecutions, He gave them the opportunity *in the midst of exile* to conduct all their affairs according to their will, in an organized fashion, with their own institutions. Thus tens, hundreds, thousands, and tens of thousands of Jews came to a place of refuge in Eretz Israel . . . Indeed, if the people of Israel had captured the moment and acted properly, this would have been a wonderful opportunity for it to prove that it was already worthy of redemption. Instead the leaders argued whether to mention the name of God in the well-known Declaration [of Independence],[51] and whether to be dependent upon Moscow or upon Washington. But the essential thing they forgot and abandoned, because they had decided to be like all the nations in internal affairs and matters of law. They based the existence of the large community of Jews in the Holy Land on foundations that have nothing in common with the Torah of Israel. In several matters they even opposed the Torah of Israel, may the Lord save us. Thus, to our great sorrow, once again Israel did not succeed in rising above itself, to seize the opportunity and prove that redemption can indeed be revealed. (Emphasis in original)[52]

Israel's rebirth and development are thus the results of heavenly initiative and visitation. If earlier Lubavitcher Rebbes fiercely opposed the Zionist enterprise and predicted its inevitable failure,[53] historical success is here portrayed—after the fact—as divine confirmation of the legitimacy of collective Jewish action (as long as we realize that this takes place "in the midst of the time of exile"). Nevertheless, great and wondrous as the hour and events may be, they do not have the capacity to confer legitimacy on a secular national awakening, to a collective Jewish enterprise that entails transgression. Thus an acute tension is created, a profound gap between the revelation of the divine face as manifested in the mundane political success of the people, and the masking of the human face that is apparent in the religious-spiritual fall of the people. This gap is the cause of the missed opportunity—indeed, it is itself the missed opportunity.

Not surprisingly, the advocate of these views tended to intervene regularly in the general affairs of the state on a broad agenda of issues, ranging from religio-national identity (Who is a Jew?) to foreign affairs and security. The Lubavitcher Rebbe sought to influence the activities of all Jewry in a wide range of areas and did not limit his activity and confrontation to the specific affairs of the Haredi community. Clearly, this approach no longer sees Israel as a nation among all the nations, but rather as a unique Jewish reality; hence, we are not exempt from the obligation to struggle over its image, to guide it, and to redeem it from both spiritual and physical danger.

This pattern of Haredi response, which emphasizes the greatness of the hour and warns against the missed opportunity, at times spills over into the school of the Lithuanian yeshivot as well. It should be noted that a common sensitivity underlies their reaction to historical events as exemplified here: "When the British government published the well-known Balfour Declaration regarding Eretz Israel, the Hafetz Hayim [Rabbi Israel Meir ha-Kohen] viewed it as a form of divine intervention in favor of redemption, but said that he feared lest the nonreligious spoil it, heaven forbid. He used to say that on many occasions there had already been a propitious hour, but that the people of [previous] generations had spoiled it" (his son's testimony).[54] It was stated—even in the name of Rabbi Joseph Hayyim Sonnenfeld, the leader of the anti-Zionist Edah Haredit in Jerusalem— "Let us assume that rain had not fallen for two thousand years, and a small cloud was suddenly seen in the sky. Would not everyone become excited and say, 'Perhaps nevertheless, perhaps nevertheless.' And is not the British Mandate as least such a cloud?"[55] Again, twenty years later, when the British government presented the Peel Commission report for the partition of Palestine, Rabbi Yehudah Leib Tzerelsohn, president of the Kenesiyyah ha-Gedolah of Agudat Israel, found in it the hand of "Divine Providence, embodied in the order of the British government," adding his hope that the Torah scholars, not "our nonreligious brethren," would have the upper hand in the leadership of the future state, because "ultimately the truth, namely, the Torah, should win."[56] His expectation has not yet been fulfilled, as is clear from the statement later attributed to Rabbi Isaac Ze'ev Soloveichik of Brisk: "The agreement of the United Nations for the establishment of the state was a smile by Divine Providence, but its rulers spoiled it." Similar sentiments were also cited in the name of Rabbi Elijah Lopian, one of the leaders of the Musar movement.[57] Let it be clear: in all these examples, the religious consciousness concentrated, not without reason, on the political initiatives of non-Jews, albeit under divine direction, rather than on Jewish deed—that is, Zionist initiative. The references are all to international decisions in which the Gentiles suddenly treated the Jewish people generously, taking positive decisions with regard to its political rebirth and right to the Holy Land.[58] Such acts naturally aroused associations with the distant past such as the proclamation of Cyrus;[59] they were depicted as a significant change in the status quo that had characterized the relations between Israel and other nations throughout the generations ("It is known that Esau hates Jacob"),[60] and were thus to be viewed in a theological perspective. Moreover, the spheres of political and mundane activity were divinely entrusted to the Gentiles; hence, their actions and initiatives toward Israel were of particular significance. The people of Israel, on the other hand, were not entrusted with such historical initiative. Their responsibility was limited to the sphere of religious response, Torah study, prayer, and repentance. It was only the rise of secular Zionism that presumed to overturn this situation. In the words of Rabbi Elijah Dessler, a leading exponent of Musar philosophy a generation ago,

> The Lord, may He be blessed, has returned many Jews to Eretz Israel and they rule it. Those who have cast off the yoke of the Torah boast as if they brought this about by their own might, and the greater their arrogance the more will their insolence increase, and the more, God forbid, will their desire to introduce heresy increase. This is the last trial of the exile of the Shekhinah, the most difficult trial . . . Those who claim that we have done our share—we came to Eretz Israel, we fought over it, and we rule it—and the Holy One, blessed be He, will do His share, and that, as time passes, faith and piety will increase, are completely mistaken.[61] We must realize that they confuse that which is in the hands of the Lord and not in the realm of [human] choice—for "the Lord is a man of war" and His hands have performed all this—with that which is incumbent upon us to do and which is not in the hands of heaven— because "everything is in the hands of heaven except for the fear of heaven." Those who withstand, forcefully and with spiritual might, this difficult test of the false opinions of "my strength and power of my hands" . . . and who devote themselves to the inner service of Torah, prayer, and the fear of heaven, are the ones who shall merit the complete redemption by our righteous Messiah, speedily in our days.[62]

These two Haredi responses—the one of religious indifference to the political-historical dimension, and the other moved by the ways of Providence in current history—come together at this critical juncture. They share a common consciousness of exile that does not allow an effective place for mundane Jewish activity, for collective national initiative that shapes the course of history. The first response, confronted with Jewish political sovereignty in premessianic time, denied it any specific Jewish significance and portrayed it as a nation among other world nations. The other response rejected out of hand, as it were, any idea that the Jewish people were active in creating and shaping the mundane political sphere, and it attributed all this to the non-Jewish nations (and to the Creator). Both take the view that mundane political activity oversteps the bounds of the Torah into the secular world—in other words, that it is removed from the bounds of authentic Jewish activity. The Jewish people leaves "everything in the hands of heaven, except for the fear of heaven."

CHANGE IN POLITICS AND CONSCIOUSNESS

Over the years a number of influential Israeli secular writers have attempted to understand the deeper, historical sources of the present tensions among religion, nation, and state in Israel. They sought to uncover the roots of the conflict and to place it within the context of Jewish religious tradition and Jewish collective memory. For example, Gershon Weiler has argued that the Jewish religion, by its very nature, does not allow its adherents to accept the authority of Jewish political sovereignty because of its own fidelity to the concept of theocracy—the rule of heaven.[63] Or as A. B. Yehoshua, making interesting use of psychological symbolism, has claimed, the Jewish people found itself from the dawn of history in perpetual conflict between the religious and national forces. By choosing exile, Jews escape the need to make a decision between the rival forces and to take on the full burden of national, earthly responsibility.[64]

The perspective developed in the previous sections does not confirm these assumptions—at least not with regard to contemporary Haredi Jews. They simply evade the argument by resorting to the concept of exile in both its aspects—the metaphysical-theological and the social-existential. It is precisely the consciousness of exile that permits adaptation to the State of Israel and acceptance of its authority: "They shall not rebel against the nations"; "The law of the kingdom is the law" (*dina de-malkhuta dina*).[65] There is no need for a principled long-range solution to decide the questions of the source of the authority or the status and validity of human government. In current, premessianic time, a pragmatic, accommodationist solution is sufficient, as was customary for Jews under Gentile domination throughout the world. Such a solution may not satisfy the strict demands of the philosopher, who requires clarity and consistency, but it has served many generations of believers in exile efficiently. Similarly, with regard to the argument of A. B. Yehoshua, the Haredi community is indeed seeking to distance itself from comprehensive, political-historical responsibility— and it admittedly does so! But in order to do so, one need not go into geographic, physical exile. Exile in the Holy Land occurs in time and not in space. It permits passivity and spiritual introversion in Eretz Israel itself. According to this view, the historical present is no more than a corridor we need to pass through in order to arrive at the "hall." It was never more than a narrow bridge leading toward the messianic future. So long as we are still walking on the bridge itself, we may not become rooted in time and space, and we must not undertake all-inclusive historical responsibility.

An acute dilemma is revealed at this point as a direct result of the positive changes in the political power and standing of the Haredi circles in the State of Israel in the past decade. Such a worldview (or state of mind) is possible only from a position of weakness, from a social position on the margins of society. It is nurtured by, and constructed from, the self-consciousness of a minority on the defensive, of resident aliens in their own land—politically, economically, sociologically, and psychologically. In the past years, however, these groups have been propelled from the margins of the Israeli political arena into its center, to a position of decision-making authority and responsibility that had not been chosen initially by their leaders and that they now have difficulty in absorbing.

Certain developments in Israel—pertaining to coalition politics; demographic, electoral, and ethnic changes; and a loss of self-confidence on the part of the secular majority of society[66]—have suddenly provided Haredim with power and influence, both material and spiritual, to a degree far exceeding that required by, or appropriate to, a life based on a qualified acceptance of a strange and alien reality. These developments have increased their direct involvement[67] in questions of society and economy, land settlement and foreign policy, and peace and war to a degree that is inconsistent with their intellectual and psychological inclinations, based as these are on passive ex post facto adaptation and retreat and spiritual turning inward. On the other hand, once power and responsibility have been conferred, they are not easily waived or abandoned.

I shall illustrate this in one area, that of political involvement. In 1949, after Agudat Israel had joined the Israeli government (together with other religious parties within the framework of the United Religious Front), Rabbi Aaron Kotler, a leading *rosh yeshivah* in America, sharply censured its coalition participation at the Agudat Israel convention in the United States. It showed lack of fidelity to principles and was pragmatically unwise. At the same time, he praised the Marxist-oriented Mapam (of all parties) for not joining a government with whose basic principles it disagreed. The emissaries of Haredi Jewry, he insisted, had a much greater chance of reaching goals and attaining concessions from their natural place outside the government.

In response to this criticism, Rabbi Yitzhak Meir Levin, Agudah's representative in the Israeli government, wrote to New York providing a dramatic description of the scenario to be expected were it not for the influence and presence of religious cabinet ministers in government institutions. The railway would run on the Sabbath; the State of Israel would openly import nonkosher meat; yeshivah students would all be drafted into the army; the independent Haredi educational network (Ḥinukh Atzmaʿi) would be seriously impaired, and other religious needs would not be supplied.[68] The general tone of this response was that of a minority group, threatened and besieged by the secular majority, seeking to salvage what it could and to defend its soul and that of its children. This was further illustrated in an apologetic article published by Agudat Israel alongside Rabbi Levin's letter, expressing the Haredi situation and consciousness as follows: "It is essential for Haredi Jewry that its representatives sit in the government . . . Unfortunately, we do not possess the institutions around which we could unite and struggle against the tremendous torrents that inundate us from every side. We are weak; the strong instruments are in the hands of our opponents; separated and divided, we stand against storms that threaten to annihilate us, God forbid. Laws that will injure our innermost being will make our situation tragic and unbearable, and we must therefore maintain our guard and repulse the attacks against us from within the government."[69] Paradoxically, membership in the government was not presented here as an expression of strength, but rather as one of weakness. The cabinet minister does not seek power or national leadership; instead he is required to stand in the breach, to serve as a barrier against the attacks of the well-organized secular public. Thus the political involvement of Haredi Jews was not directed on the practical level toward the enactment of religious legislation, but rather toward preventing the passage of antireligious legislation.[70] Fears were even expressed that the *aliyah* of Haredim would be actively hampered by the responsible officials.[71]

An upheaval had taken place in Jewish history: those who had until recently constituted the overwhelming majority of the Jewish people had now become few in number and were called on to defend the very right of the minority to live its life according to its faith and its customs. In the words of the prolific and influential Haredi writer, Rabbi Moshe Sheinfeld,

> The first to be exiled in the State of Israel was the Shekhinah . . . the spirit of the Torah and its commandments were driven out from the courts, the schools, the Army, the sessions of the Knesset, the city streets, and the government ministries, into the remote corner of synagogues and study halls . . . *Thus we have come from the exile of the Shekhinah to the exile of the Torah observant in the State of Israel.* Years ago those throwing off the yoke of the Torah demanded from us an attitude of toleration and freedom of conscience

for themselves. Today we demand for ourselves the freedom to enjoy the Sabbath rest in our special neighborhoods, a right enjoyed by all the ghetto dwellers in the countries of the non-Jews. (Emphasis added)[72]

Agudat Israel left the government in 1952 over the specific issue of the drafting of young women into the Israeli Defense Forces (IDF); thereafter, it remained outside the cabinet as part of a general decision to refrain from overall ministerial responsibility for the actions and failings of the sovereign secular Jewish government.[73] The very policy that had previously been advocated by Rabbi Kotler was finally adopted by the Haredi leadership under the guidance of the Council of Torah Sages. It was no longer a patchwork solution of political participation as a reflection of weakness, but rather the demonstrative choice of a remote existence, of opposition in principle to the ruling majority. For the next twenty-five years, the Agudah followed the political pattern aptly described by Zalman Abramov:[74] The Neturei Karta attacks Agudat Israel for its participation in the Knesset, and Agudat Israel replies with an attack upon the National Religious Party for its membership in the government. Thus in 1965 Rabbi Schach criticized the political activity of the Mizrachi: "The state is not a state of halakhah, but rather a state of [secular] law. . . .And for this they compromise, and in this they participate and share responsibility. Where is this liable to lead?"[75]

Given recent changes, the very same criticism clearly applies to the representatives of Haredi Jewry, including those who accept the direct authority of Rabbi Schach. During the past fifteen years, Haredi members of Knesset have attained key positions prior to the formation of every coalition and, at the same time, benefited from the rising strength of a nationalist right that views them favorably. This has resulted in a new, clever, and effective pattern: participation in government in ministerial roles, no; support for the government coalition as a quid pro quo for achievements in the religious sphere, yes; chairmanship of key Knesset committees such as the Finance Committee and the Labor and Social Welfare Committee, yes; appointment as deputy minister, yes.

Thus the traditional policy is formally maintained, but involvement and power have, in fact, continued to increase. If one adds to this the formation of a new, ethnic-based party (Shas), which is close in spirit to Ashkenazi Haredi circles but not committed to their traditional anti-Zionist political position[76] and which, therefore, is ready to join the government in ministerial roles,[77] one can understand the strength of this new trend.

Moreover, these changes are not limited to the political realm; they are rooted in extensive cultural, demographic, and economic processes that have occurred in Israeli society, but it is political life that has exposed the latter to the public eye.

A THEOLOGICAL AND EXISTENTIAL DILEMMA

These developments currently pose a direct threat to one of the central concepts of Haredi self-consciousness in the State of Israel—that of exile. This holds true with regard to both aspects of exile mentioned earlier: alienation (the absence of home) and a downtrodden existence in the theological sense (the opposite of redemption).

As to the first, the nature of the dilemma troubling Haredi circles is clear, for example, from a complaint that appeared in 1984 in the Agudat Israel newspaper, *Ha-Modi'a:* "In the last seven years Haredi Jews have swarmed [!] through the Knesset building—from all points of view a negative phenomenon. We must examine whether we have not begun to think that this is our building."[78] In other words, a building that was intended, in the Haredi view, to be a focal point of exile, of *shtadlanut,* is suddenly beginning to resemble a home, and the sensation of being alien is likely to fade.[79] The writer specifically attributes the beginning of this phenomenon to the political upheaval of 1977 that brought the right-wing Likud to power, warning of the emergence of a broad gap between the ideological doctrine, on the one hand, and the new psychological reality, on the other—a reality that is gradually and imperceptibly being fashioned as a result of increasing political, social, and economic involvement. A comparison of current developments with Y. Gitlin's 1959 programmatic essay, "Torah Jewry and the State," further illustrates this point. He writes: "Abstaining totally from the acceptance of government services is a burden that the community cannot bear . . . Obviously, it is no tragedy to utilize the right to vote so as to elect representatives to government institutions who will defend to the hilt the rights of the Torah, and express a more public protest from the Knesset rostrum—*on condition, of course, that they do not take any step that entails bearing shared responsibility for the government of the state as a whole*" (emphasis added).[80]

As noted, the declared attitude of Haredi Jewry toward the State of Israel was initially one of de facto recognition and post factum participation, not de jure recognition and involvement in principle; pragmatic cooperation, not long-term ideological solutions. Emerging reality, it seems, is gradually undermining the validity of this position. The moment participation in institutions also entails the adoption of comprehensive national policies, taking positions with regard to long-term issues and undertakings, and engaging in decision making concerning the funding of secular-state educational and cultural institutions, one indeed draws closer to a more active and a priori acquiescence.

Paradoxically, this change is one of the major reasons for the present escalation of the public conflict between Haredim and secular Israelis. A consciousness of exile is by its very nature a moderating factor. The exilic Jew always knew how to come to terms with a given reality, to restrain him- and herself and to wait patiently until the storm had passed. Exile is a period of nonrealization, of deficiency and half and quarter solutions. In the words of Maimon the Dayan (the father of Maimonides), "While the stream destroys walls and sweeps away stones, the pliant object remains standing. Thus is the Exile . . . The Holy One, blessed be He, saves the pliant nation."[81] As this factor decreases, and the feeling of gradually striking roots and of achievement and fulfillment increases (even if it remains undeclared), the motive for confrontation grows. From this point on, the responsibility of the Haredi Jew is not restricted to what happens in certain enclaves in Jerusalem and B'nai Berak, but covers the larger "home," including secular neighborhoods such as Rehaviah in Jerusalem and north Tel Aviv. It is highly implausible that persons who find themselves in a pivotal position with regard to major national questions, such as the convening of an international peace conference (Rabbi Schach) or the development of the Lavi aircraft (the chairman of the Knesset Finance Committee, Abraham Shapira), will adopt a stance of passivity and resignation only with regard to religious issues.

This open confrontation reflects an additional inner tension. The increasing involvement described here is restricted to functional areas, to the political and economic realms of "this world," but is not expressed in cultural terms and does not profoundly touch the life of the Haredi individual. A profound gap still exists between Haredi society and the secular community (and even modern Orthodoxy) with regard to patterns of education, culture, and creativity. Moreover, various processes, such as the unprecedented growth of Torah study and of Haredi yeshivot, on the one hand, and a decrease in the Judaic education and links to tradition among broad sectors of secular society, on the other hand, only serve to deepen this gap. These factors are reinforced by late entry into the workforce, which results in the postponement of daily contact with the external environment, and a steady increase in exemptions from military service among Haredi youth, who are thus excluded from one of the most decisive socialization experiences of Israeli society. These and other factors clearly prevent the creation of a culture and mentality common to both the majority and the minority. They create difficulties for the construction of a shared language—not to speak of a common faith and lifestyle. Under such circumstances, public ferment becomes inevitable, creating conflicts and clashes for which Israeli society may be ill prepared.

The theological dilemma is even more profound. The basic assumption that permits the majority of Haredi Jewry—as distinct from Neturei Karta and Satmar Hasidim—to coexist alongside the State of Israel is a total and consistent separation between the longed-for future redemption, on the one hand, and Jewish political organization in current premessianic time, on the other. As the Lubavitcher Rebbe put it more than a decade ago: "Since there is such a large ingathering of Jews, they must have leadership (and not a kingdom, God forbid, because there will only be a kingdom upon the coming of the Messiah), so that there will be order, both in internal affairs and in their dealings with kings and ministers of other nations, as well as in matters of security, vehicles, etc., as is the natural way of things. However, it should be remembered that all this has no connection with the matter of redemption."[82]

Having come this far with the secular national community founded by the Zionists, however, the Haredim, who preferred to place themselves consciously and as a matter of principle in a remote corner of this community, now find themselves propelled into its center. Thus, willingly or unwillingly, they occupy a position of influence and decision-making responsibility.

Assuming that they were able to go beyond the constant struggle for religious legislation and succeeded in establishing in the Holy Land a state based entirely on Torah law, would this not also threaten to hasten the End? In other words, would not a Jewish people who had ingathered its exiles, returned to its land, freed itself of foreign oppression, enjoyed the fruits of the land, and repented and built its life according to the Torah, have to be regarded as reaching at least the outer edge of redemption? And having attained all this gradually and naturally by human action, would it not mean that they had "forcefully and collectively returned" and intruded into the sphere of authority of "the presumed Messiah" (in the words of Maimonides)?[83] In view of the fact that the Zionist enterprise was founded against the explicit wishes of the leading Torah scholars of previous generations and was characterized for many years by the abandonment of religion and the rejection of Jewish law, the theological dilemma is even sharper. Can the wicked bring about good things? Can the Holy Land be rebuilt in a profane manner?

It should be noted that traditionally Haredi circles, with Agudat Israel at their center, did not seek to engage in a comprehensive struggle for the establishment of a Torah state.[84] It was the moderate Mizrachi who made much of this slogan, declaring their aspiration to fashion the public and government character of the sovereign Jewish state according to halakhah. By contrast, Haredi demands either did not focus on this goal or simply refrained from promoting it,[85] and for good reason. At the conscious level this aspiration was, in fact, presented as unrealistic and unattainable, but it would seem that at a much deeper level it exposed the substantive dilemma confronting these circles.

The concept of a "Torah state" in the premessianic era blurs the boundaries between current historical reality and the vision of future redemption, between the actual and utopian. In short, it overextends in both practice and theory. In the current historic era, religious meaning is totally exhausted within the confines of the life of the individual and the community. The traditional organization of Haredi Jewry into separate communities and residential neighborhoods and the self-isolating school system therefore reflected a declared restriction of the bounds of direct responsibility, a conscious intent to concentrate on shaping the character of a specific group, one that lives entirely within the world of Torah and on which the spiritual welfare of the world depends.[86] Political activity was thus initially directed toward the defense of the rights and interests of Torah-observant Jewry, not toward the establishment of the Torah state.

It must be remembered that every mundane event during the time of exile is intrinsically transitory and random. The life of exile is "a life lived in deferment, in which nothing can be done definitively, nothing can be irrevocably accomplished . . . There is nothing concrete that can be accomplished by the unredeemed."[87] Recent developments threaten to undermine these basic assumptions; they threaten to blur the boundaries between, on the one hand, the domain of the individual and the sacred community—which live in historical time—and, on the other, the domain of the nation and the restoration of its kingdom—a matter for the messianic era.

BIRTH PANGS OF THE MESSIAH

Haredi leaders have traditionally made explicit use of those Jewish sources in which the future redemption is depicted as an apocalyptic phenomenon—a transition from one extreme (of darkness) to the other (of light), an upheaval that is not built on present reality, but that totally negates it.

Throughout Jewish literature, we find that manifestations of heresy and religious apostasy and of moral and social deterioration are taken as clear signs of the "birth pangs" of the Messiah and the redemption. For example, a well-known passage in the Mishnah (tractate Sotah) provides a long list of the calamities destined to befall society on the eve of the redemption. Some of these calamities are material—"Prices will rise . . . the Galilee will be destroyed . . . the Golan will be desolate"—but most are spiritual and moral, entailing a precipitous fall by the public and its leaders: "Insolence will increase . . . the kingdom will become heretical, and there will be none to [voice] rebuke. The study hall of scholars will be a place of licentiousness, the wisdom of the scribes will be despised, the truth will be absent, youth will put the elders to shame; a son will make light of his father, a daughter will rise against her mother, the countenance of the generation will be as the countenance of the dog, a son will not be ashamed before his father. And upon whom shall we rely? Upon our Father in heaven" (M Sotah 9:15).[88] It should come as no surprise that Haredi rabbis and writers referred to such extreme formulations in criticizing and explaining current events. The depictions of redemption breaking out from the depths of degradation, from the pits of spiritual and material disintegration, matched the consciousness and experience of these religious leaders, who longed for the final redemption but were deeply disturbed by the falling status of Torah in Israel, on the one hand, and the physical distress of the Jews, on the other.

This picture of religious transgression, alongside physical distress and persecutions, as the birth pangs of the Messiah, as the harbinger of the redemption, has been extremely popular in Haredi intellectual, homiletical, and polemical literature of the past few generations, down to the present. During the First World War, Rabbi Shmuel of Sochaczew wrote: "Before the light, the power of darkness grows. Similarly, during the birth pangs of the Messiah arrogance grows among the nations who curse and despise the Torah, as is manifested in these days . . . [as well as] in the hearts of the rebellious among our own people."[89] This depiction may indeed be found in the writings of various authorities, representing a broad range of opinions: Hasidim and Mitnaggedim, leaders of Agudat Israel and its Haredi critics, and others.

For some, the expression "the footsteps of the Messiah" serves mainly as a rhetorical device; for others, it provides an important linguistic and conceptual pattern that assists in dealing with contemporary events; whereas for others, it is charged with a concrete internal messianic ten-

sion—the actual anticipation of the drumbeats of the redemption spring-
ing forth from the depths of crisis. Some detailed works trace the signs and
manifestations of the "footsteps of the Messiah" in current historical reality. One important example is the extremely influential (and recently reprinted) essay by Rabbi Elhanan Bunem Wasserman, *Ikveta de-meshiha*
(The footsteps of the Messiah), written on the eve of the Holocaust.

> The period that we are now experiencing is a special period, particularly for
> the life of Israel. We are witnesses to phenomena that we could never have
> imagined . . . If we wish to understand the essence of the events in our lives,
> we must search for the verses and the teachings that pertain to the period of
> the footsteps of the Messiah . . . It is written in Daniel that the distress of
> those days shall exceed anything that has befallen Israel since it became a
> people, that is, it will exceed in scope even the distress of the destruction of
> the Temple . . . In Ezekiel it is prophesied that in the time of "the footsteps of
> the Messiah" they will proclaim the slogan, "Let us be as the other
> people" . . . All humanity is seized by a spasm of excitement. It seems that
> we are dwelling in a dense forest amid angry and predatory animals . . . Dur-
> ing the footsteps of the Messiah the rule of the Torah will be routed . . . [And,
> indeed, we see that] only national feeling is demanded of the Jew: the person
> who buys the [Zionist] shekel and who sings Hatikvah is exempt from all the
> commandments in the Torah. It is clear that this approach is considered to be
> idolatry according to the Torah . . . In our days, which are the footsteps of the
> Messiah, in which the heretics are the leaders of the generation, and do not
> permit Torah scholars to raise their heads, and wage open war upon the
> Torah . . . [there is] a terrible situation the likes of which we have not experi-
> enced since Israel became a people.[90]

In other words, the entire world is in ferment—all are at war with all,
Israel is persecuted to an unprecedented degree, religious transgression has
reached previously unknown depths. All these, however, prophesy the advent of a new world order and a new Jewish spiritual condition that does
not flow naturally from the present reality, but rather contradicts it and
completely uproots it. This is a paradoxical conception of redemption:
"the footsteps of the Messiah" and "the Messiah" do not lie side by side on
one continuum, but rather at two opposing points. The light will come and
drive out the darkness. In the words of the Hafetz Hayim, Rabbi Wasserman's mentor, "There is no doubt that our time is that of the footsteps of
the Messiah . . . the foundations and principles of our holy Torah have
been abandoned, God forbid . . . and reason dictates that the arrival of our

righteous Messiah will not be prolonged further, for we find ourselves on such a level that it is not possible to be worse and sink lower."[91] If Jews had deserved it, they would have been saved from the evil of "the footsteps of the Messiah"; since they have not, the redemption will come after a terrible fall, when Jewry is at its lowest ebb. "The King-Messiah must come speedily, for in a little while there will not be anyone for whom to come!"[92]

Such rhetoric and patterns of thinking are prevalent now as well. They provide a conceptual framework that facilitates the expression of sharp criticism against the secular Jewish state, its laws and mores, along with the anticipation of salvation. In the words of Rabbi Schach,

> All the signs that the sages transmitted to us in their holy spirit, at the end of tractate Sotah, of what will happen during the time of the footsteps of the Messiah . . . all have been fulfilled in the state and its laws, for does not the [Israeli] law of common-law marriage fall under what the sages said about "place of licentiousness"? And similarly, the law permitting abortions increases licentiousness, for shame has been removed. "A son is not ashamed before his father" and "a daughter is rising against her mother," and "those fearing sin are rejected" and "the truth is absent"—everything is done brazenly . . . and "the entire government has turned to heresy," afraid to mention the name of God.[93]

Israeli reality thus reveals new facets in the midrashic depictions of the "rising insolence" on the eve of the redemption and provides new interpretations of the horrors of "the footsteps of the Messiah."

Given these patterns of thought, is it at all possible to present a model of a legitimate Jewish state, in current historical time, that constitutes neither redemption, on the one hand, nor the most terrible birth pangs of redemption, on the other? Is it possible for there to be a proper Jewish sovereignty that avoids the birth pangs of the Messiah but is not their complete, antimessianic antithesis? Furthermore, if such an interim historical entity were possible, can it arise gradually—step by step, law by law, repentant Jew after repentant Jew—from within a reality that has been depicted for several generations as complete spiritual calamity, as the very insolence and abandonment of religion? Such an evolutionary approach, it seems, completely contradicts the presuppositions and apocalyptic expectations of a total upheaval, of a sudden change from one extreme to the other. In the words of Rabbi Wasserman in the 1930s, "Since the suffering of the Jewish state is liable to be the greatest suffering, we must hope that this will bring the redemption closer, just as it was in Egypt, when enslavement brought the End closer."[94] Or, as Rabbi Schach put it, " 'Let him come, but let me not be a witness to his coming' [BT Sanhedrin 98a] . . . a state of [secular] law and not a state of halakhah, i.e., a state with the laws of the idolaters and not a Torah state."[95]

On the other hand, after being pushed from the sidelines and propelled into the center of activity, is it still possible not to strive to reform and achieve gradual, step-by-step victories? These elements all join together to create the fundamental internal dilemma (just described) that stems from the danger of blurring the boundaries between goals appropriate for current history and the prophetic goals connected with the Last Days, which means the danger of hastening the End and trespassing against the realm of the Messiah.

DEVELOPMENTS WITHIN VARIOUS SCHOOLS

I have analyzed the anti-Zionist polemics of some leading Torah scholars at the inception of the Zionist movement (see chapter 1). I shall now conclude with a number of illustrations that compare the statements of early scholars with the views and attitudes of their contemporary followers, again focusing on the two main hasidic dynasties of Lubavitch and Gur, as well as on the Lithuanian yeshivot.

It will be recalled that in 1900 the Lubavitcher Rebbe, Shalom Dov Baer Schneersohn, ruled that even if the Zionists strictly followed God's commandments, the Torah-faithful Jew is forbidden to join them and to seek redemption by human efforts. His son and successor, Rabbi Joseph Isaac Schneersohn, reiterated the call "to separate from this congregation . . . which is striving to come up to Eretz Israel, contrary to the law of the Torah and contrary to the command and the prohibition of the Lord."[96] Neither did he spare Agudat Israel and its Hasidic leader, the Rebbe of Gur, who indeed separated from the Zionists and refrained from direct cooperation with them, but was actively engaged in the material development of Eretz Israel in "establishing a society for the settlement of Eretz Israel by building workshops and factories." Rabbi Joseph Isaac strongly opposed all secular activity and mundane labor in Eretz Israel. Past Torah leaders, according to his claim, "did not permit the defiling of the land by any form of material thing, stores, workshops, and factories!"[97]

On the other hand, his successor, the late Rabbi Menachem Mendel

Schneersohn, ruled the village of Kefar Ḥabad,[98] whose livelihood is based on "workshops and factories" and whose influence extends to many other material activities as well. Moreover, he granted explicit legitimacy to collective political and military Jewish organization in the Holy Land, "in matters of defense, vehicles, and horses," and his followers are deeply involved in many spheres in the state. (Part of this discrepancy was resolved by maintaining that the state exists "in the time of exile," thereby preventing a verbal contradiction with the statements of his predecessors, who opposed going out from the Exile by "material powers and stratagems.") Moreover, after the Six-Day War, the Rebbe publicly stated that the merit of those who participated in the war was even greater than that of those who studied Torah.[99]

No wonder that such constant involvement in the affairs of the State of Israel has attracted the criticism of the contemporary extreme Haredi anti-Zionist camp. It has bluntly censured the close contact maintained by the Lubavitch court with "heretical and inciting rulers . . . who have been seated as welcome guests at the head of the mass assemblies with the Rebbe, while royal honors are bestowed on them."[100] It appears that Ḥabad Hasidism has moved in practice (if not in theory) from its traditional approach, which demanded greater separation from the Zionist enterprise than did other Haredi circles, to one of maintaining more contact with the Zionists and their leaders than do other contemporary Haredi circles.

Essential differences, however, remain. The last Lubavitcher Rebbe also postponed the time of the ingathering of the exiles until after the longed-for appearance of the Messiah and the miraculous reconstruction of the Temple. In practice, he directed his followers to maintain each of the Jewish Diasporas until the actual messianic revelation.[101] In this he completely repudiates a central Zionist doctrine. Neither is the hawkish political stance characteristic of Ḥabad today identical ideologically with that of any Zionist party. That stance has been summed up by Rabbi Aharon Dov Halperin, editor of the journal *Kefar Ḥabad*, as "total opposition to Zionism and nationalism, coupled with a stringent prohibition against handing over a single inch of the territory that the Lord granted us."[102] Needless to say, the profound messianic tension in Ḥabad Hasidism (which I shall discuss extensively in the next chapter) is utterly detached from the State of Israel and its enterprises.[103] It focuses on the spiritual effort, the acts of self-sacrifice performed to draw the hearts of the Jews closer to their Father in heaven, and on the personality of the Rebbe, "the faithful shepherd, all of whose words are truth and righteousness."[104]

By way of contrast, from the very outset the leaders of Gur Hasidism did not oppose settlement or other forms of material activity in the Holy Land as constituting the hastening of the End. As early as the end of the previous century, the Rebbe, Rabbi Aryeh Leib Alter, regarded *aliyah* as blessed, even though he refrained from ruling officially in its favor.[105] His son and successor, Rabbi Abraham Mordecai, explicitly encouraged Haredi settlement in Eretz Israel, in theory and practice,[106] and went there himself in 1940, fleeing the Holocaust. He is also reported to have responded positively to the UN decision to establish the State of Israel.[107]

Notwithstanding these more positive attitudes toward settling the Land of Israel, the opposition of both Rebbes to the Zionist movement and to cooperation with secular settlers remained implacable. Rabbi Aryeh Leib Alter taught his followers that "Zionism . . . is apostasy and heresy, God protect us, and whoever adheres to it, is as if he adheres to idolatry." He also warned against any connection with the Zionists. "An upright Jew should not join together with the wicked" (1900)[108]—that is, the Zionists. His hesitation with regard to a formal positive ruling on the question of settlement was explained, inter alia, in terms of his apprehension about "the sects of wicked unbridled ones that have spread in Eretz Israel and in Jerusalem" (written in 1891).[109] His successor, Rabbi Abraham Mordecai, likewise continued to oppose the Zionist movement and was careful to lead Agudat Israel "without associating with the wicked and the different, even in the fulfillment of a commandment."[110] After his son-in-law and subordinate, Rabbi Yitzhak Meir Levin, returned to Poland in 1935 from a visit to Eretz Israel, he sharply attacked the Mizrachi movement, which stood by in the face of "the utter destruction that secular Zionism and antireligious nationalism is wreaking on the souls of Israel . . . and silently accepts the matter. It even views itself as a religious party while cooperating with the antireligious elements; instead of waging war against the antireligious who are destroying Judaism, they act with them in love and fraternity."[111]

Rabbi Levin later became the leader of Agudat Israel and its representative in the Israeli government; he was sharply attacked by separatist Haredi circles for his own cooperation with the secular Zionists. In any event, the two Rebbes who have led Gur Hasidism during the period of the state, Rabbi Yisrael Alter and Rabbi Simhah Bunem Alter, permitted and expanded such an involvement; under the leadership of the latter, the Haredi town of Emmanuel was established in Samaria, much to the displeasure of Rabbi Schach, at the time Alter's colleague in the leadership of the Council of Torah Sages, who saw this as an act of provocation against the non-Jews. The political representatives of Gur Hasidism in the Knesset have been totally immersed in parliamentary and economic activity, and can no longer be presented as "living in a remote corner."

Of course, the distinction between opposition to Zionism as a "doctrine" and actual participation in Israeli politics is maintained. A few years ago, Rabbi Pinhas Menahem Alter, then *rosh yeshivah* and now Rebbe of Gur Hasidism, protested, "Agudat Israel was created to confront the heretical movements, chiefly the Zionist movement . . . Because of certain circumstances, we have been forced to base our establishment upon their money, organizational instruments, and political patterns."[112] It is somewhat ironic that such statements were made at the very time that Rabbi Alter's loyal follower, Abraham Shapira, was serving as chairman of the Knesset Finance Committee and head of the Advisory Council of the Bank of Israel (and sometimes jocularly referred to as "the country's director-general").

Let us now turn to the circles of the Lithuanian yeshivot. As one might expect, the impression of inner historical transformations is less visible among these circles, which tend to play down the religious dimension of historical events in general. What has the Torah to do with change? Nevertheless, one who observes them and reads their words carefully will find that they too are caught on the horns of the dilemma discussed here.

From the very beginning of the Zionist awakening, their polemics focused to a greater degree on the rejection of religious observance by the Zionists and the secular nature of the national movement than on the theological question of the hastening of the End and the collective return (see chapter 1). To be sure, this fierce opposition has not yet abated. There is little to distinguish the approach of Rabbi Hayyim Soloveichik of Brisk at the birth of Zionism from that of Rabbi Velvl Soloveichik after the establishment of the state,[113] just as the criticism leveled then against the Zionists by the Hafetz Hayim and Rabbi Elhanan Wasserman is once more extensively cited today, buttressing the attacks made by Rabbi Schach and his circle. As Rabbi Schach quipped, "When I am asked by the heavenly court why I did not identify with the Zionist idea, I will unhesitatingly place the blame for this on the Hafetz Hayim and the other leading scholars who preceded me, and they will already know what answer to give."[114] That is, neither the Holocaust nor the creation of the state require any new categories of thought: there is nothing new under the sun. To the contrary, manifestations of identification or temporary enthusiasm, such as raising the Israeli flag on the roof of the Ponevezh Yeshivah on Israel Independence Day (as was the practice of Rabbi Kahaneman, who preceded Rabbi

Schach as head of the yeshivah) or other such phenomena that appeared in the wake of the Six-Day War, have since ceased.

The fact that Lithuanian circles did not undergo serious change (as in the case of Ḥabad Hasidism) or a softening (as in the case of Gur Hasidism) highlights the gap between their ideological opposition to Zionism and their blunt criticism of Israeli society, on the one hand, and their holding of key political positions and participation in fateful national decisions, on the other. Apart from that of Neturei Karta, the most extreme rejection of Zionism appears in the newspaper of the Lithuanian circles, *Yated Ne'e-man:* "We do not protest against the antireligious acts of party X . . . We demonstrate against the entire Zionist enterprise in Eretz Israel. The leading Torah scholars already warned, at the birth of Zionism, that whoever thinks that the Zionist goal is the establishment of a state, errs. Their goal is the uprooting of religion."[115] Concrete events and transient political change should not have any effect on this ideological opposition in principle. As Rabbi Aaron Yeshaya Rotter commented, following the political upheaval in 1977 that brought Agudat Israel into the government coalition: "No change at all has taken place in this state due to the new government; it remains the same state that declared that the House of Israel would be as all the nations, heaven help us. All the laws enacted in the Knesset are laws drafted by those who perform the most serious transgressions, and we declare that we have no portion or inheritance in them."[116]

On the other hand, in past years it would appear that no other spiritual leader in Israel has wielded greater influence on issues concerning the coalition and the government than Rabbi Schach. During the Eleventh Knesset (1984–88), two Israeli political parties fell under the range of his direct authority: Agudat Israel and Shas. To be sure, Rabbi Schach takes care to formulate his positions within the context of axioms characteristic of the period of exile. Gentile nations initiate and are active within the mundane political sphere; Jews react and respond and do not rebel against them, although they do not trust them. Thus Israel should agree in principle to a territorial withdrawal and refrain from establishing settlements in Judea and Samaria, which would constitute rebellion against the nations of the world; but an independent Israeli initiative for an international peace conference is opposed, because one can neither trust the nations who will attend the conference nor the promises given by Arab leaders. The development of the Lavi combat aircraft had to be halted as it was against the wishes of the United States, and the State of Israel must not rebel against America.[117] Thus, according to Rabbi Schach, "the Jewish people is still in exile until the coming of the Redeemer . . . and we are commanded not to provoke the nations of the world . . . [even though] this Gentile today shows you a smiling face for political gain, but in truth acts deceitfully."[118] In other contexts, the secular Jewish politician is the one who is portrayed in the traditional role of the Gentile ruler, whereas the truly faithful Jew responds after the fact, passively and conditionally.

"Our participation in the state and its institutions is performed due to the pressures of the time and the force of circumstance, similar to our behavior under foreign regimes outside of the land. It may be defined as stealing into the camp of the enemy," declared recently Rabbi Nathan Ze'ev Grossman, the editor of *Yated Ne'eman*. He went on to protest in harsh and alienated terms: "We consider the secular government as an alien and hostile regime. Just as Jews in the lands of exile have sent their representatives to the foreign parliaments, and no one has interpreted it as an act of recognition or sympathy for the foreign government, we too do not mean to express any kind of identification with the Knesset and the institutions of the ruling state by electing representatives to them . . . One who, during the course of two thousand years of exile, has been accustomed to participate in ruling bodies, while feeling contempt for them in his heart, and to conduct negotiations with his enemies, does not see any connection between these two spheres."[119]

Need one reiterate that these statements were issued by one who at the time (1991) was an explicit spokesman for one of the ruling parties in Israel? True, they represent an apologetic response to the attacks of the radicals against his party's political involvement. It is precisely for that reason, however, that these statements reflect the sharpness of the dilemma discussed here—the inner gap between exiles who walk on the side of the road and rulers who march on the high road.

Indeed, even the spiritual leader himself, Rabbi Schach, is not freed of this problem in principle. Let us close with his words, which illuminate the dilemma and add to it a new, peculiar dimension.

We see a terrible and frightening sight. A collective revolt against the kingdom of heaven . . . There is a tremendous difference between an individual who sins in matters concerning himself, and a mass community that has organized to live systematically a life of sin and iniquity. This is especially serious when there exists a Hebrew government in Eretz Israel . . . We are talking about free Jews, in our own state, the State of Israel, with our own president, with a government and an army, everything our own product— and who is it that prevents our holy Sabbath being observed here? It is a state of [secular] law, and not a state of the halakhah, and in this regard things are worse here than abroad, as there everyone who transgresses commits an individual sin, while here sinning is legalized. According to our conviction and faith, those who presume to maintain the state are those who endanger it, and despite what is written in the Torah, "So let not the land spew you out for defiling it" [Lev. 18:28]; they enacted laws to permit the most severe [transgressions], such as bloodshed, as in the Abortion Law, and so forth.[120]

In one key respect, the style of this rebuke is reminiscent of the most extreme Haredi opponents of the State of Israel: "a collective revolt against the kingdom of heaven." But in another respect, there are clear expressions of affinity and direct involvement, "our own state, our own president," that could not have appeared in the writings of Schach's predecessors. Rebuke and affinity are not the neutrality of remoteness;[121] no longer is Israel portrayed as a nation among the other nations.

In essence, these statements accord profound religious significance to the change that has taken place in the condition of the Jewish people in the period of the state—and they claim it specifically as a result of the precedence of Torah and halakhic criteria in judging the individual, the entire community, and the country. The sin of the community is more than that of the individual.[122] It represents open opposition to heaven and a violation of the obligation of mutual guarantees. Thus, from the moment that an independent Jewish collective, a community of "free Jews" has arisen, religious responsibilities entailing great obligation and risk have been imposed on it. Moreover, sins committed outside Eretz Israel are not those committed in Eretz Israel; life in the Holy Land demands a higher spiritual and religious commitment, especially as the land rejects transgressors and spews them out to a place of exile.

In our generation these demands have joined together in the existence of a Jewish collective in the Holy Land. Consequently, the significance of the deeds and the severity of their punishment is multiplied. This conception may be seen as the reverse image of classical, moderate religious Zionism, which also emphasizes the redoubled religious challenge confronting the Jewish people on its return to its land and political independence but which finds in this a glimmering of hope, an opportunity for national or religious rebirth. Rabbi Schach and the members of his circle, by way of contrast, do not recognize manmade rebirth and do not psychologically identify with the endeavor; they focus not on the opportunities but on the risk, on the severity of the law. They do, however, underline the depth of the responsibility and mutual accountability that are imposed as a result of historical developments. It is this sense of collective obligation that leads them to struggle, admonish, and protest.

Hypothetically, what would happen if one day they were to succeed and the nation heeded their call, grounding its collective life in the Holy Land on the Torah and its commandments? Would this not be a case of achieving a sanctified aim through impure means, a salvation originating in a collective revolt against the kingdom of heaven? Or would this perhaps fulfill the expectations of those religious Zionists who, from the outset, found an opportunity and a glimmer of hope in the historical process? Would it not be a hastening of the End? Is this not a struggle that it is forbidden to win—where victory is its very defeat?

The question remains. Does Haredi Jewry possess a conceptual framework, a theoretical model of a legitimate Jewish state in historical, premessianic time, a state that renders unnecessary the birth pangs of the Messiah but that is not the Messiah?

5

The Lubavitch Hasidic Movement:
Between Conservatism and Messianism

Late in 1812, after the armies of Napoleon Bonaparte had invaded the kingdom of Russia, Rabbi Shneur Zalman of Lyady—the founder and formulator of the teachings of Ḥabad Hasidism—prayed for the welfare of the Russian empire and for the victory of Czar Alexander I. The "Alter Rebbe" likewise expressed a paradoxical vision concerning the anticipated results of this war for Russian Jewry. As he wrote in one of his letters, "I was shown [from heaven] that, if Bonaparte would be victorious, the Jews would prosper and enjoy a more dignified position, but their hearts would become distant from their Father in heaven." On the other hand, "If our master Alexander were victorious, even though the Jews would be poorer and their status inferior, in their hearts they will be united and bound to their Father in heaven."[1] In other words, the material benefits and civic privileges the Jews would be likely to enjoy under French rule were opposed to their best religious and spiritual interest. It would therefore be better for them were they to remain under the harsh yoke of the czar.[2]

One can give numerous examples from later Jewish reality in Western Europe, and particularly in the contemporary United States, confirming the observation of the rabbi of Lyady and justifying his fears concerning the potential results of Jewish political emancipation and economic prosperity. Yet, interestingly enough, Ḥabad Hasidism itself has been astonishingly successful in the modern world. It has harnessed this very situation to its own spiritual and institutional purposes in a manner unprecedented in its previous history. In fact, the contemporary center of Lubavitch Hasidism in the United States sends emissaries to all corners of the globe, and in particular has provided religious guidance and facilities to Jews in countries of oppression and persecution. More so than any other ultra-Orthodox group, Ḥabad Hasidism has learned how to utilize the advantages of a prosperous society and the tools of modern technology for the dissemination of its teachings. True, it is not the largest Hasidic court in contemporary Jewry, but it surpasses others both in its actual social presence and activity and in its impact upon the outside world, both Jewish and non-Jewish. It explicitly recognized the positive nature of the contemporary sociopolitical condition of the Jews within the American democracy, which it considers "a kingdom of kindness." Moreover, recently, in an utterly unprecedented move, the Rebbe (now deceased) and his disciples even assumed direct responsibility for the ethical state of the non-Jewish population in America, calling upon them to fulfill the "seven Noachide commandments"—namely, those religious obligations imposed upon every human being, according to Jewish tradition—thereby preparing themselves to greet the imminent advent of the messianic redemption: that is, the ultimate personal spiritual ascent and the final universal harmony.

Yet another paradox: in 1904 the fifth master of the Ḥabad dynasty, Rabbi Shalom Dov Baer Schneersohn, "the Maharshab," articulated a harsh vision, this time directed against a worldly political enterprise of the Jews themselves, namely, the recently arisen Zionist movement. As explained in chapter 1, Rabbi Shalom Dov Baer anticipated the inevitable failure of the new Jewish national pretension to take an activist, historical initiative: "The Zionists will never succeed in gathering themselves together [in the Holy Land] by their own power. All their forces and many stratagems and strivings will be to no avail against the will of God."[3] This time, the actual historical development did not match the forecast of the Rebbe.[4] Yet interestingly enough, Ḥabad Hasidism itself displays great vitality and energetic involvement within the contemporary State of Israel—the fruit of this selfsame Zionist enterprise. Their direct impress can be seen in many and varied walks of life: from broad educational activity to intensive political agitation, ending with communal settlement.

In Israel, as in the United States, young Hasidim periodically engage in public campaigns of religious influence and propaganda, beginning in the streets of the great cities and ending in remote villages and army bases. They address the individual Jew, appealing to him or her to perform, on the spot, one of the commandments of the Torah (even if it merely be the recitation of *Shema Yisrael*), thereby renewing direct personal connection with the Almighty. Simultaneously, they appeal to the broader community by means of the mass media, both printed and electronic, as well as through advertisements and enormous billboards crying out, "Prepare for the imminent coming of the Messiah!" They likewise distribute leaflets, newsletters, pamphlets, and books in enormous quantities, unparalleled in the rival ideological streams. Moreover, they manifest energetic involvement in the political life of the State of Israel. In 1988 their intense activity had a decisive role in the surprising success in the Knesset elections of the ultra-Orthodox Agudat Israel party, which doubled or tripled its electoral strength, while in 1990 its representatives played a central part in determining the fate of the parliamentary coalition and of the new government of the State of Israel.

The outstanding feature of the contemporary Ḥabad movement is hence its fervent, dynamic activism, which constantly seeks new stimuli and new peaks. Shortly after the establishment of the state, Ḥabad Hasidism abandoned its traditional fear of secular activity and mundane labor in the Holy Land to establish a rural settlement, Kefar Ḥabad, as a physical base for its spiritual enterprise. From that time on, the Ḥabad movement has established many centers throughout the land, from Kiryat Malakhi in the south to Safed in the north. Moreover, in a seemingly paradoxical sense, despite their full commitment to their traditional non-Zionist stance, contemporary Ḥabad Hasidim repeatedly call upon the government of Israel to adopt a clear-cut hawkish policy, to oppose any territorial concessions, and to manifest a firm Jewish stance toward the nations of the world. They likewise do not refrain from initiating "religious legislation" in the secular legislature, Israel's Knesset.

In other words, in Israel no less than in the United States, Ḥabad Hasidim display an astonishing dynamism and ability to adjust. Modern reality, and Jewish existence within that reality, provides Ḥabad with a far-reaching and fruitful framework for the dissemination of its message—notwithstanding the fact that Ḥabad Hasidism openly rejects many of the values and trends characterizing this very reality. To put it another way: on the one hand, Ḥabad Hasidism adheres to a consistent, radically conservative posture regarding matters of faith and religious norms: it clearly rejects such concepts as liberalism, pluralism, and universal human equality; it condemns any trace of modern epistemological skepticism; and it openly advocates fundamentalist positions on questions relating to religion and science. On the other hand, more than any other trend in contemporary Haredi Jewry, it displays a dynamic and activist attitude, approaching reality as a field of movement and change, consciously expanding the boundaries of its religious involvement. Should one therefore conclude that Ḥabad's treatment of modern reality is purely instrumental and manipulative? Is the movement to be interpreted exclusively by way of analogy to parallel phenomena of religious radicalism in the Western world? Finally, and perhaps of greatest interest in the context of this paper: What is the relationship between the traditional theological and ideological patterns of Ḥabad Hasidism since its inception more than two hundred years ago, and its present modes of thought and activity? Is the secret of the movement's success and its ability to adjust itself to the present situation rooted entirely in the sociological realm—in its organization and structure, and in the personal charisma of its spiritual leader? Or is it perhaps anchored as well in immanent theological elements, on the one hand, and in a later ideological evolution, on the other, which together paved the way for its present conquests?

I will begin with some manifestations of continuity within Ḥabad—that is, those traditional theological patterns that have shaped its concrete encounter with the modern situation and its present social expansion. I will thereafter discuss certain ideological changes found in contemporary Ḥabad: first and foremost, its acute and unprecedented messianic fervor. I will then conclude with an attempt at a cautious look into the future.

SACRED AND PROFANE IN THE MODERN REALITY

Since its earliest beginnings, Ḥabad thought has rejected any sharp dichotomy between sacred and profane, spirit and matter, God and the world. On the deepest level, everything that exists is a direct revelation of the infinite divine essence, which penetrates to every being and encompasses all reality. The divine immanence brings into existence and gives life to all; it is present everywhere in equal measure, down to the lowliest and most corporeal manifestations. Rabbi Shneur Zalman of Lyady and his disciples carried these ideas further than other Hasidic trends and eventually developed a far-reaching acosmic conception: not only does all of reality reside ontologically within the divine Being, but, in truth, God Himself is the only true reality. It is only the deceptive consciousness of humans and their sensory illusions that fool him into believing in the existence of a cosmic reality apart from the divine source.[5]

Consequently, the highest goal of religious life was reinterpreted in this spirit: the service of God is intended to reveal the immanent Divine Presence and to realize it in every action and thought, in every place and time, thereby bringing humankind into close contact with the divine root of reality. Hence, all of being was conceived as an arena for the service of God, inviting human intervention and involvement: man is called upon to discover divinity even on the lowest levels of reality, to "draw" godliness into the concrete particulars, and to expand the realm of religious activity into every domain of life. Parallel to this, any sacred use by man of one of the components of physical reality—be it mineral, vegetable, or sentient being—elevates that being to its sublime source within the divine realm. Consequently, no realm of human life or activity is bereft of a direct religious challenge.

Loyal to this conception, the latest Lubavitcher Rebbe, Rabbi Menachem Mendel Schneersohn (1902–94), insisted that some of the regular Torah lessons be set specifically on weekdays, and not only on Sabbaths and festivals; similarly, he tended to play down the exclusive unique religious significance of the synagogue, as opposed to other locations, as even the latter are filled with sanctity and invite man to enter the divine realm. It is against this background that one must understand the Rebbe's recurrent call to the Jews of the Diaspora to "create a Land of Israel here!"[6]—a call that evoked severe criticism from some radical Zionist rabbis.[7] The dimensions of "holiness of time" and "holiness of space" are, as it were, themselves removed from time and space: the Jew is called upon to encounter God and to realize the heights of religious tension in every situation and under all conditions. Note: one line of thought in traditional Jewish eschatology indeed assures Israel that, in the future, it will enjoy "an eternal Sabbath" (sanctity of time) just as the Land of Israel will in the future "spread out over all the lands" (sanctity of place).[8] The Ḥabad Hasid is thus called upon to anticipate this state of being in present reality; to "taste" (in their language)[9] in the here and now the ultimate future redemption.

It therefore should not surprise us that Rabbi Schneersohn's demand to broaden the scope of religious involvement and to sanctify the mundane is applied today to the new realms and horizons opened to modern people. In particular, one should not ignore the new scientific or technological discoveries without exploring their inner religious significance. For example, in 1980 the Satmar Hasidim severely attacked the Ḥabad Hasidim for using the radio to broadcast lessons on the *Tanya* (the basic book of Ḥabad Hasidism). The former criticized the very idea of utilizing such an abominable vehicle—"an act of Satan"—which usually disseminates a message of heresy, for sacred things. They thereby expressed, in effect, their characteristic demonization of modernity. Interestingly, the Lubavitcher Rebbe, who publicly supported the broadcasting of these lessons, did not stop with an instrumental argument, describing radio as a neutral tool without any value significance. On the contrary, he claimed that the radio waves are themselves "a tremendous power implanted by the Creator within nature so that, by means of an appropriate instrument, the voice of the speaker may be heard from one corner of the world to the other—at the very moment of speech. In radio, there is reflected a sublime spiritual matter."[10] Moreover, the Rebbe did not even refrain from using, in this context, a form of expression usually reserved (in religious language) for the divine realm: "radio [waves], which transcend any measurement and any limitation of time and space in our world!"[11]

Other forces and manifestations of modern reality elicit a "new midrash" of this type—a monistic interpretation of reality that anchors the profane in the sacred, the corporeal in the spiritual, the finite in the infinite. The implication seems to be that, "if there are fools who exploit these things for purposes other than that of sanctity, the Holy One, blessed be He, will not allow a good thing to go to waste by their doings."[12] Ironically, then, what makes it possible for Ḥabad Hasidim to utilize the fruit of modernity and to "uplift" it is precisely their a priori negation of one of the salient features of the modern consciousness, namely, the acknowledgment of the existence of a neutral saeculum.[13] Even were one to argue that the above is only an ad hoc theory, propagated for utilitarian, pragmatic purposes, it is nevertheless elicited by traditional Ḥabad patterns of thought.

The reader is similarly astonished by the dualistic attitude taken toward the accomplishments of modern science. On the one hand, the Lubavitcher Rebbe preaches a stubbornly and consistently fundamentalist view regarding the relationship between the literal meaning of the biblical text and scientific conceptions. Whenever any contradiction is to be found, the scriptural passage should be read in its clear, literal fashion.[14]

Thus the world was created 5,756 years ago; if fossil research suggests otherwise, or if calculations of the period of time required for light rays to have arrived at the earth from remote galaxies seems to indicate otherwise, one must assume that God originally "created fossils in their present state," and that, "just as the stars were created, so were [simultaneously] the rays of light."[15] (A similar argument was raised at the end of the nineteenth century in the Christian polemic against Darwinism.)[16] Similarly, as is implied by the literal meaning of Scripture, the sun revolves around the earth: the theory of relativity and the principle of equivalency assist one to reject any contradictory categorical scientific statements out of hand.[17] In like fashion the phenomenon of spontaneous generation of living things does exist (as stated in the Talmud),[18] and experimental zoology cannot prove otherwise; and so on . . . Indeed, the doctrine of evolution "is liable to lead astray the imagination of uncritical people, to the point that they perceive it as a 'scientific' explanation of the mysteries of creation." Yet it is in fact without any real scientific basis: "The six days of creation are days, in the literal sense . . . each one of the species was created separately, *by itself*, not evolving from one another" (emphasis in original).[19] Any exegetical attempt to read the relevant verses differently is dismissed out of hand as mere apologetics, created by ignoramuses who understand neither the limitations of scientific research nor its conditional and hypothetical nature.[20] The Rebbe has indeed made efficient use of his own academic, scientific education in order to develop these arguments in detail.

On the other hand, modern science gradually and confidently brings humankind closer to a recognition of cosmic monism and of the organic unity of reality. The inner connection drawn by physical science between matter and energy; the discovery of the centrality of psychosomatic interconnections in the human realm; the development of a model representing the orbital motion of electrons in the microcosmos, parallel to the orbital motion of heavenly bodies in the macrocosm—all these innovative concepts are leading human consciousness toward the unified One. In the final analysis, the recognition of cosmic monism gradually elevates humankind to an awareness of acosmic monotheism, as "one cannot speak of the mutual influence of two existing things, when the only real Being is God, and the entire Creation is included in His unity." Scientific reflection can thus raise one up to the secret of mystical contemplation.

The following reply exemplifies this point. It was given by the Lubavitcher Rebbe to a group of Orthodox Jewish scientists, concerning the "mutual influence between Torah and secular sciences."

> The very [dualistic] concept of monotheism cannot tolerate that of "mutual influence." He, may He be blessed, is present in all places and in every thing, and there is thus nothing that is not included in His Being . . . Consequently, all of the true sciences are included within and stem from the Torah of God, while those "sciences" that are based upon falsehood are not sciences at all . . . An inner relationship exists among electronics, acoustics, physics, and mathematics. Einstein's great accomplishment was manifested in his success in finding the inner connection between energy and matter. Any separation between different branches of knowledge is thus inconceivable; acoustics, mathematics, philosophy, and religion all belong to one and the same unity.[21]

Eventually, the "primary importance" of the sciences is revealed to us only "when man 'knows how to use them for the service of God and His Torah'

[*Tanya,* chap. 8] . . . This corporeal world, like the higher spiritual worlds, receives its vitality from the Torah; therefore, it ought to be exploited entirely for the purpose of profound understanding of the Torah. It is very dangerous and harmful to see the Torah—as is done by a certain professor in Jerusalem—as something separate from the world and distinct from everyday life . . . This is an attempt to denigrate the Torah and to distort its meaning."[22] This "certain professor in Jerusalem" is doubtless the late Yeshayahu Leibowitz, the most radical and profound spokesman for the approach that sets a sharp division between the realms of religion and science;[23] the Rebbe of Lubavitch thus knew well whence to direct his criticism. To use the language of sociology of religion,[24] one may characterize the approach of Ḥabad as one of religious expansionism, as opposed to that of compartmentalization, on the one hand, or complete rejection of modernity, on the other.

ḤABAD, THE JEWISH PEOPLE, AND THE OTHER NATIONS

Let us now turn to the question of the religious-social mission of Ḥabad Hasidim and the relation of this movement to the Jewish people, and toward humankind in general.

Were one to ask an articulate Ḥabad Hasid about the number of adherents to his movement, he would probably answer, "Prima facie, all of the Jewish people are Ḥabad Hasidim." Unlike other ultra-Orthodox groups, which are primarily turned inward, seeking to build a loyal and well-defined bastion of Torah, the Ḥabad group is turned largely outward, assuming responsibility for the collective soul of Israel and seeking to teach its path to the broad Jewish community. It sends its young emissaries on remote missions, "to the most distant ends, beyond which nothing could be farther 'outside'" (from both the geographical and spiritual viewpoints):[25] from the central bus station in Tel Aviv, to the Berkeley university campus, to far-flung Jewish communities in the Soviet Union and Morocco. Moreover, deviating from generally accepted norms, the Ḥabad teacher does not refrain from expounding to his listeners mystical doctrines concerning the very essence of the Godhead, and will publicly reveal the secrets of Kabbalah and Hasidism. He thereby removes many of the traditional barriers distinguishing between the exoteric and the esoteric, on more than one occasion bringing upon himself the wrath of religious leaders who adhere to other schools.

These features already characterized Ḥabad Hasidism in its earliest days. In his own day Rabbi Shneur Zalman of Lyady was the only Hasidic teacher to formulate his doctrine of Hasidism in a systematic work, the *Tanya;* in this work, he expounded Hasidic doctrines regarding the Godhead, the human soul, and the service of God in accordance with a logical conceptual system, thereby making them available to a broader public. At the time, the revelation of these secrets, through their publication in book form, aroused severe controversy.[26] As might be expected, his critics advocated the limitation of mystical contemplation to a select elite, and sought to guide the broad public to a simple faith and fear of God. However, Rabbi Shneur Zalman remained adamant in his position: "it is impossible to be God-fearing without contemplation."[27] The "Alter Rebbe" also devoted himself wholeheartedly to organizational activity, establishing new Hasidic centers. The social situation created as a result of this activity was described at the time by one of his critics, Rabbi Asher of Stolin: "There are thousands upon thousands, almost an entire country, who only speak in secrets of Torah and in allusions."[28] This portrait is of course drawn in exaggerated language, but even according to Ḥabad tradition, there were many who opposed the rabbi of Lyady's declaration that "it is my definite opinion that one ought to teach the path to the many,"[29] and were unable to tolerate this new order, which "sought out and revealed such an intense [spiritual] light to young people."[30]

These old traditions of Ḥabad reappeared in each generation, shaping the consciousness of the rebbes and their disciples—with regard to both the question of organizational activism and the dissemination of mystical secrets. As the previous Rebbe, Joseph Isaac Schneersohn, wrote (concerning organizational matters): "We may [safely] assume that propagating is not without fruit"; "organization and the dissemination of its ideas have always occupied an important place in the Hasidic camp."[31] Or, as the late Rebbe stated not long ago: "One ought not to think that, because some people are on the 'outside,' on a lower level, one therefore ought to teach them only in accordance with their lower degree. [One should not think that] the more 'elevated' matters of Hasidism, because they are so 'precious,' are irrelevant for those who are on the 'outside' . . . [On the contrary,] we emphasize that study of the doctrines of Hasidism must be performed by spreading forth—disseminating them widely, to the very farthest place, without any contraction or limitations."[32] The Hasid is called upon to adhere to the ways of godliness—to disseminate and to "spread his fount outward," without limit. All are invited to share in the mystical secrets, without which true service of God is inconceivable.[33]

Indeed, today the spiritual and social mission imposed upon Ḥabad Hasidim is stressed with full urgency. This is, in fact, a threefold mission:

first, toward those observant Jews outside of the Ḥabad camp; second, toward those Jews who are removed from religious observance of Torah and mitzvot; and third, toward the other nations. Let us examine these areas one by one.

Already in its earliest days, Hasidism taught that the authentic religious leader enjoys an inward, essential connection with the members of his flock, and his soul encompasses the souls of all his Hasidim and unites them. According to some doctrines, the soul of the *Tzaddik* is connected in its root to the souls of the entire Congregation of Israel, wherever they may be. It is "composed" of all of them together, and therefore embodies the inner spiritual structure of the whole people. The *Tzaddik* thus serves as an intermediary between the individual Jew and his God, as "the influx of the Creator, blessed be He, is very great. It is thus impossible to receive His influx save by means of an intermediary."[34]

Contemporary Ḥabad Hasidism preserves the original, radical formulation of this view. Thus the late Rebbe was accustomed to speak of the "universal soul" of his teacher and predecessor,[35] while his own disciples spoke and wrote about him in even more superlative terms. For example, in an issue of the newsletter *Kefar Ḥabad* from 1983, we read that the substantive connection of every Jew to the rebbe is "an existing fact that does not require the confirmation [of the individual], a fact stemming from the very place of the soul [of each person] as a small fragment of the Jewish soul organism, which the rebbe—the brain—oversees." The denial of this inner connection by any Jew is "tantamount to denial of his very belonging to the Jewish people—heaven forbid!"[36] By definition this view recognizes neither the existence of non-Hasidic trends within Judaism (Mitnaggedim), nor that of the numerous other Hasidic courts and rebbes: there are only those who are actual and conscious Ḥabad Hasidim, and those who are potential, unaware Ḥabad Hasidim. Both groups are objectively anchored in the same "universal soul." Thus Rabbi Halperin, editor of *Kefar Ḥabad*, writing on the occasion of the Rebbe's eightieth birthday (1982): "It is incumbent upon us to light the torch of faith in the Moses of our generation[37] . . . Specifically, during this era and in these days, it is obligatory to emphasize that faith in the Rebbe and connection to the Prince of the Generation is not merely one more detail of divine service, however important a detail it may be. Faith in the leader of the generation is the primary and necessary condition for removing the entire Jewish people from the voracious mire, and to redeem them eternally . . . For this reason, we should not, under any circumstances, respond with kid gloves to expressions of opposition to our father and shepherd."[38] In other words, there is only one authentic Judaism[39] and one "Moses of this generation," and Ḥabad Hasidim are the emissaries and disseminators of this truth. This, then, is their first mission.

As for the second mission, it follows from the above that the adherents of Habad entirely reject the concept of a "secular Jew." Just as they reject the very separation between the sacred and the profane, they deny the distinction between a Jew who is "religious" and sanctified and one who is "secularized." Jewish religious identity is a matter of essence and substance: a given, objective fact. It is not based upon ethnic, cultural, mental, or historical factors, nor even upon the actual relationship of the individual to Torah and to halakhah (Jewish law), but is rather a result of the divine nature of the Jewish soul. Thus when Rabbi Eliezer Schach—an opponent of Ḥabad—recently challenged secularists and kibbutz members within Israel with the provocative question, "In what way are you Jewish?" the Lubavitcher Rebbe cried out in protest, affirming the solid Jewish identity of each and every Jew, both far and near. The power of inner, objective Jewish merit is far greater than that of external, voluntary will; potential being, even if unconscious, is stronger than conscious actuality. The basic religious and social mission of Ḥabad is thus intended to elevate the conscious choice of the individual to the level of his inner Jewish chosenness, that is, to actualize his inner given holiness.[40] In order to accomplish this aim, one must go out into the streets to persuade the Jew to place tefillin on his arm and to say *Shema Yisrael:* one does not sit passively, waiting for a spontaneous, conscious decision of the individual Jew, but one seeks him or her out, to restore Jews to their own nature and roots (even if only by performing a mitzvah on a one-time basis). Thus the Rebbe has taught that "the importance of a Jew does not stem from his own self, but from his attachment to and union with the Holy One, blessed be He. He is not an independent being; rather, all of his existence is the existence of the Holy One, blessed be He!"[41]

Again, this monistic view, which considers all of Israel as one objective unity, clearly rejects any possibility of intra-Jewish religious pluralism. It similarly erects an ontological barrier between Jews and non-Jews, interpreting the singularity of the Jewish people as a metaphysical, innate trait of chosenness.

It is precisely against this background that we confront the third mission of the contemporary Ḥabad Hasid, that directed exclusively toward the Gentiles. The chosen are not exempt from responsibility. On the contrary, in recent years, the Rebbe has increasingly come to emphasize that the encounter with the non-Jew also entails a religious challenge of the first order. His remarks concerning this subject reveal an attentiveness and sensitivity to new developments in the social and political condition of the Jews in the West.

It is well known that Jewish religion is a particularistic one: it does not seek out members of other peoples in order to convert them to Judaism. Non-Jews may fulfill their obligation to the Creator by performing a limited number of religious and ethical demands (including, first and foremost, the prohibitions against idolatry, bloodshed, and sexual license), and by establishing an appropriate social and legal order. Withal, in those times and places where Jews enjoy political power,[42] the halakhah requires that one impose the fulfillment of these universalistic obligations upon the non-Jews. Indeed, the Lubavitcher Rebbe openly demanded that his followers transform every encounter with the non-Jew, whether it be political or commercial, into an arena of persuasion by which their interlocutor would be brought closer to the observance of the "Noachide commandments." In his words, the present situation of the Jew grants him or her social and political opportunities that were unavailable to the persecuted ancestors, inviting Jews to expand the domain of their direct religious responsibility to include other peoples and faiths![43] Ḥabad Hasidim even elicited a positive declaration from President Reagan concerning the subject of the Noachide commandments, which they interpreted as additional confirmation that the time was ripe to take upon themselves this universalistic responsibility.

The Rebbe went even further in this demand: he claimed that the Jewish people is called upon to prepare humankind for the forthcoming redemption. Every Jew should guide his non-Jewish neighbor to be prepared to meet a world of peace, brotherhood, and universal faith. The Jew is called upon to convince the non-Jew to act right now in a way "similar to the [anticipated] perfection in [messianic] times."[44] From here on in, the prophetic vision of the End of Days must serve the Jew as a guiding norm in his or her educational encounter with the non-Jew. This directive clearly goes far beyond the original boundaries of the "seven Noachide commandments," transcending the limits of their minimal demands within the historical realm into the utopian realm.

To the best of my knowledge, these concepts have no precedent in Jewish history. They attract our attention in several respects: they reflect a clear consciousness of the new historical transformation—a consciousness not at all common in the ultra-Orthodox world; they illustrate the powerful messianic tension to be observed in contemporary Ḥabad Hasidism (see below); and they bear a certain measure of similarity to certain trends on the contemporary American scene. It is likewise interesting to note that the Lubavitcher Rebbe, unlike the overwhelming majority of Jewish religious leadership in the United States (including Orthodox leadership), supported the introduction of a "moment of silent meditation" in the American public schools. The other leaders feared this innovation because of the breakdown it represented in the wall of separation between church and state (which would presumably be against the Jewish interest),[45] and because of the potential alienating implication of this custom upon Jewish pupils. The Rebbe, on the other hand, gave greater weight to the universal religious interest, as he understood it, wishing that every non-Jewish child confront, each morning, his or her Creator.

ACUTE MESSIANISM

I have thus far discussed the role played by traditional patterns of thought in shaping the present path of Ḥabad Hasidism, both in terms of the broadening of the scope of religious involvement ("every path," "every place") and that of social expansion and conquest ("every person"). Let us now turn, by way of contrast, to manifestations of social and ideological change.

By far the most important change in the ethos and style of contemporary Ḥabad, in contrast with earlier generations, is the placing of messianic concerns at the focus of religious consciousness and religious life. In this respect there has been a definite transformation: at the beginning of its path, Ḥabad Hasidism advocated an approach of silence and the suppression of questions of collective historical messianic redemption, whereas today it is marked by clear expressions of concrete, acute messianic tension, unparalleled in latter-day Judaism. Moreover, the absolute certainty of the imminent coming of the Messiah has now become the supreme and decisive test of Jewish faith. Let us trace the various stages of this evolution.

Generally speaking, the founders of Hasidism addressed themselves very little to the messianic question, neutralizing *ab initio* any concrete messianic tension.[46] Hasidism treated any discussion of redemption in the social sphere, both national and universal, as marginal, concentrating most of its attention upon the personal salvation of the individual—that is, upon the mystical *tikkun* (correction) of the inner spiritual exile, here and now. Hasidism of course remained loyal to the traditional Jewish utopian vision, but it was not this vision that served as the impetus for the Hasidic religious revival or prompted it to shed new light upon the service of God.

The tendency toward suppression of messianism is clearly reflected in the writings of the first teachers of the Ḥabad school. Like their counterparts, they preferred to concern themselves with the inner redemption of the individual rather than with the external, historical redemption of the community.[47] At the same time, they stressed the constant Divine Presence which sustains the world, rather than the transcendent, singular messianic breakthrough anticipated in the future. The reader is thus hard put, in the writings of the first four leaders of Ḥabad, to find any serious attempt to clarify the question of collective redemption.

This silence was partially broken at the beginning of the twentieth century by the fifth leader of Ḥabad, Rabbi Shalom Dov Baer Schneersohn, who addressed himself to a number of theoretical questions concerning messianic redemption. It is easy to identify the immediate cause for his open engagement with messianism: the Zionist national awakening. Rabbi Shalom Dov Baer perceived Zionism as a pretentious attempt to force the End and to realize explicitly messianic goals (first and foremost, the ingathering of exiles) by human means; he therefore declared total war against it. This struggle required him to pose an alternative model of authentic—heavenly, miraculous, and spiritual—messianism against the deceptive Zionist ambition. He attempted to provide the ideological underpinnings for the traditional approach, which requires the Jewish people to practice complete historical and political passivity until the coming of the divine redemption.[48] Needless to say, the Jew is called upon to engage in intensive spiritual activity—and in particular, to spread the teachings of Hasidism—so as to bring nigh the redemption. However, "we must not heed their [i.e., the Zionists'] call to achieve redemption through our own powers, for we are not permitted to hasten the End even by reciting too many prayers [*sic*], much less so by corporeal stratagems—that is, to set out from exile by force."[49] Ḥabad was hence called upon to clarify the fundaments of the traditional belief in a national messianic redemption.

Only forty years later, the next, third stage in the development of the messianic approach within the Ḥabad movement emerged: that of acute messianic tension. Such a tension was clearly manifested during the period of the Holocaust, when the previous Rebbe, Joseph Isaac Schneersohn, cried out in public for an "immediate redemption!" This may be seen as a classical example of catastrophic messianism: the leader led his flock during a period of indescribable suffering, and experienced one exile after another. He witnessed the pogroms against the Jews of Russia at the beginning of the century, the Communist Revolution, and the civil war; he was imprisoned, was released, fled to Latvia and Poland, and, at the outbreak of the Second World War, was saved by his disciples and settled upon the alien soil of the United States. It is not surprising, therefore, that he should have clearly seen the destruction of European Jewry as the height of the birth pangs of the Messiah: "The troubles of Israel have now reached the most terrible degree; the people of Israel have undergone the birth pangs of the Messiah . . . Therefore, the days of the redemption shall come immediately. This is the only true answer to the destruction of the world and to the anguish of the Jews . . . Be ready for redemption soon, shortly, in our day! . . . The righteous redeemer is already at our window, and the time to prepare ourselves to receive his face is now very short!"[50] The late Rebbe thereby found his own way of endowing the Holocaust with a religious meaning: not as a punishment for the sins of the past, as has been claimed by a number of ultra-Orthodox leaders, but as the collapse of the present world order in anticipation of future redemption.

Rabbi Joseph Isaac came out with manifestos in the newspapers in three different languages, publicly heralding the approaching redemption as "a matter of fact" and "nearer than near." Needless to say, this declaration served him as an opportunity to call upon the people to return to God fully and wholeheartedly, and thereby to merit receiving the face of the Redeemer: nothing is left for Israel but to "polish up the buttons of the royal garments," and thereafter, "Immediate Repentance! Immediate Redemption!"

But it was under the leadership of the most recent Rebbe, Rabbi Menachem Mendel Schneersohn, that this messianic tension reached its utmost heights. Under his leadership, it grew from year to year, indeed, from week to week. From now on, every act and every sermon, every "campaign" and every call, was accompanied by clear messianic indications. The Rebbe repeatedly told his Hasidim that the Redeemer would appear to them—with his full glory and miracles, literally, tomorrow, today, now! "The King Messiah can come immediately, 'in a twinkling of an eye' . . . And he certainly will come immediately. And as this is so, then clearly the King Messiah is already present in the world . . . Moreover, he is present as a 'great man (a *gadol*)—' . . . a king from the house of David who meditates upon the Torah and performs its commandments, like David his ancestor' [Maimonides, *Mishneh Torah,* Melakhim 11:4]. Therefore, in our generation, there must be an extra emphasis upon everything connected with the faith in the coming of Messiah and the anticipation of his coming—a faith and anticipation that penetrate all of a person's reality, all the faculties of his soul."[51] There was a definite tendency here to create an acute anticipation (perhaps in the belief that consciousness will shape reality?) of receiving the messianic revelation.[52] There was likewise an appeal for spiritual intensity, for constant religious agitation: there is so much that can be accomplished and so little left to be done! "It is within the grasp of each of us to act so that the redemption will come quickly, not just tomorrow or after some time, but today, literally. . . .At this very moment one opens one's eyes and sees our righteous Messiah among us, in this very synagogue and in this very Study House, flesh and blood, soul and body."[53] Note: this concrete, personal appearance of the Messiah is meant to bring about a total transformation—both historical and cosmic-metaphysical—"a new creation," the resurrection of the dead and the restoration of the world in the kingdom of the Almighty. Who would not lend hand and heart so as to hasten this? However, unlike the messianic hope of Rabbi Menachem Mendel's predecessor, which sprang from a sense of crisis and catastrophe, the recent messianic tension was specifically connected with a feeling of well-being and optimism, of success and fulfillment. The birth pangs of Messiah and their terrible travails have passed and are no more: "Trouble shall not rise up a second time" (Nahum 1:9).

For example, the Rebbe assured the Jews of South Africa that no harm would come to them, instructing them to remain in their place until the imminent ingathering of exiles by the King Messiah. In the very same spirit, on the eve of the Gulf War the Rebbe issued a call against the distribution of gas masks in the State of Israel. He promised his loyal disciples that God would protect and shelter the inhabitants of the Holy Land; indeed, many of his followers refused to accept the gas masks that were distributed by the Israeli Army to all residents. The Rebbe likewise called upon his Hasidim to visit Israel, despite the approaching war, and at the same time forbade its inhabitants to leave it. "It is obvious," he said during those difficult days, "that after the Holocaust distress shall not rise up a second time—neither hide nor hair of it, heaven forbid! To the contrary, there will be only goodness and mercy, goodness that will be revealed to all the children of Israel, wherever they are. I stress—goodness that is sensed and manifest!"[54]

Similarly, the above-mentioned campaign to persuade non-Jews to fulfill the universal Noachide commandments and to prepare themselves for redemption was based on the claim that the present situation of the Jews in the United States—"a kingdom of kindness"—presents them with new possibilities, unavailable to their persecuted ancestors in Asia or Europe. Most recently, the fall of the Communist empire, the disintegration of the Soviet Union, and the cessation of the armaments race between the superpowers constitute an explicit messianic sign, bringing the nations of the world away from atheistic heresy and closer to the observance of the

Noachide commandments, while advancing the entire world to meet the fulfillment of the prophetic vision of peace—"they shall beat their swords into plowshares." Moreover, unlike his predecessor, Rabbi Joseph Isaac, who made redemption solely dependent upon repentance, the late Rebbe anticipated unconditional redemption. This, then, is the nature of the fourth, optimistic stage in the messianic development within the Ḥabad movement.

This type of messianism, which has flourished under conditions of prosperity, with a feeling of success and conquest, must seek crest after crest, one climax after another. Otherwise, it would not sustain the ever-rising religious tension or renew the fervor of redemption. The previous, catastrophic type of messianism was supported by the very fact of distress and actual suffering; it did not require any other incentive. A messianism of prosperity, however, constantly requires new stimuli and ever-growing audacity; it is not designed for patience or for protracted waiting, and certainly does not leave room for a "descent for the sake of ascent," for a downfall or crisis. As I shall argue, this has been in fact the recent story of the Ḥabad movement.

At the end of the 1980s, and even more so at the beginning of the 1990s, Ḥabad Hasidim began to publish announcements in newspapers and on billboards openly proclaiming the imminent coming of the Messiah. They also published any number of pamphlets and newsletters concerning the subject of the redemption. In his public sermons and talks, the Rebbe himself repeatedly aroused this acute tension, intentionally placing the element of concrete messianic expectation in the focus of the religious consciousness of his Hasidim. At the end of Passover 5751 (April 1991), the Rebbe aroused a particular emotional storm, placing upon the shoulders of his followers, of every man and woman, the direct responsibility for the coming of the Messiah. To the astonishment of his Hasidim, he declared that he himself had exhausted all his efforts, all of his spiritual powers, and that the final push was solely dependent upon each individual and community. "Were you to pray and cry out in truth, then certainly, certainly, Messiah would already have come!" On Shabbat Pinhas 5751 (6 July 1991), the Rebbe aroused an even greater emotional frenzy when "he spoke of the coming of Messiah in sharp and clear terms, such as had never been heard before"—to quote the Ḥabad Hasidim themselves.[55] He said: "Certainly, without any doubt or shadow of a doubt, the time of redemption has already come. We have already seen concrete miracles witnessing that this is *the year in which King Messiah shall be revealed*, leading to *the hour that the King Messiah comes* . . . and to the proclamation that 'hark! . . . there he [i.e., the King Messiah] comes' [Song 2:8]—*he has already come!* That is, we already stand upon the threshold of the days of Messiah, at the beginning of the redemption, and immediately [there shall be] its continuation and completion" (emphasis in original).[56] But since then, even such declarations have become almost a matter of routine.

Moreover, from the perspective of many individuals within Ḥabad, the concrete messianic tension was focused upon the personality of the Rebbe himself. He was spoken of in terms that the Jewish tradition had reserved for the Messiah alone; there are some people who took this to such extremes that they have even brought upon themselves the wrath of the Rebbe.[57] However, all of them regarded him as the most worthy "candidate" for the title, a kind of potential Messiah. Indeed, has not the Rebbe himself said—thus they whispered privately—that "the King Messiah is already present in the world"? Moreover, is he not present as a *gadol* (a great man)?[58] Nevertheless, the Rebbe himself took pains to base his own authority and the source of his inspiration upon his predecessor, Rabbi Joseph Isaac; it was to him, and to him alone, that he ascribed the title "Prince of Our Generation." Likewise, the Rebbe publicly expressed his displeasure when he realized that several of his Hasidim were gazing at him during prayer, rather than concentrating their hearts entirely upon their Father in heaven. This notwithstanding, however, the messianic dynamic has a power of its own and a logic of its own.[59]

In fact, the "Ḥabad youth league" in Israel did not hesitate to publish recently a statement declaring that "there exists a prophet in our generation!" These statements are not intended only as hyperbole or metaphor, but make conscious use of the formal halakhic categories defining prophecy in the Jewish tradition: "The Lubavitcher Rebbe prophesied all the great events to take place in this generation." In a pamphlet distributed in synagogues throughout Israel, the Hasidim wrote: "The Rebbe manifests clear signs of prophesy. One of the signs of a prophet, according to Maimonides, is that 'he predicts future events to occur in the world, and his words are vindicated' [*Mishneh Torah*, Yesodei ha-Torah 10:1–5]. When one witnesses such a phenomenon, it is incumbent upon every Jew to observe the commandment, 'him you shall heed' [Deut. 18:15], and, as Maimonides continues, 'it is forbidden to suspect him, to question his prophecy . . . or to test him too much.' Consequently, we are certainly obligated to believe the central prophecy of the Rebbe—namely, that we are literally on the threshold of redemption, and that immediately, on the spot, 'this one comes'!"[60]

We have thus found in the contemporary Ḥabad movement a collective messianic agitation utterly unlike anything that preceded it; indeed, it would seem that its like has not been seen in Jewish history since the seventeenth century. Needless to say, the Hasid, unlike the outsider, would deny any deviation from the traditional path of Ḥabad. The earlier rebbes, he would claim, who knew themselves and their generation to be remote from the time of redemption, deliberately refrained from arousing messianic tension. "A long time yet before the time of redemption," Rabbi Shneur Zalman of Lyady said, "the messianic outcry is not yet heard."[61] But this was not the case of the previous Rebbe, who felt upon his flesh the very birth pangs of Messiah, or even more so with regard to the most recent Rebbe who, with his spiritual vision, perceived the rapid approach of the Messiah himself. They have been obliged "to cry out" and agitate every Jewish heart.

To express it in mystical language: in his day, Rabbi Shneur Zalman of Lyady taught that "the Redeemer will come only after the completion of all the *beirurim* [the spiritual-cosmic process of 'selection' and 'correction' by returning the divine 'sparks' to their source]."[62] His early heirs expressed themselves in like spirit. For example, "Hence the Exile continues, for all the *beirurim* are not yet completed," wrote the third Rebbe of Ḥabad, the Zemaḥ Zedek, "and when the *beirur* is complete, then the Messiah shall come."[63] On the other hand, the fifth Rebbe, Rabbi Shalom Dov Baer, already said that "now is the most final *beirur!*" and thus "ours is the generation of Messiah."[64] His son, Rabbi Joseph Isaac, already saw with his eyes the completion of the process of "selection" and "correction," and thus publicly declared that "nothing is left but to polish up the buttons [of the royal garments]." Finally, the late Rebbe explicitly said: "The service of the *beirurim* has been completed!"—that is, "All those [mystical] services needed to be performed in the time of the Exile have already been finished." In other words, the spiritual mission incumbent upon the Jewish people during the Exile has been completed and realized. If so, what possible reason can remain for the continuation of the Exile? And if it no longer has any reason, is not the path paved for the complete redemption? "Thus," the Rebbe said, "one may give thanks, and bless the birth and revelation of the Messiah, *Sheheḥeyanu*—'who has kept us alive and sustained us and brought us *to this day*'" (emphasis in original).[65] In sum, what the outside observer perceives as historical and ideological transformations within Ḥabad are seen by the believer as cosmic and metaphysical ones, taking place in reality. The former are no more than the appropriate religious response to the latter.[66]

In chapter 4 I noted that the recent messianic excitement within the

Habad movement is entirely detached from the State of Israel and its enterprises, and is clearly to be distinguished from religious-Zionist messianism; that, despite the fact that the contemporary Habad movement has moved considerably away from the actual militant struggle of its earlier years against the Jewish political and national revival, even today it continues to reject the Zionist ethos as such; and, finally, that the radically hawkish political stance that the Rebbe demanded of the Israel government, prohibiting any territorial withdrawal in favor of the Arabs, stemmed from different motivations, both halakhic and military, than that of messianic religious Zionists. I must now add that, on a deeper level, this political radicalism is directly connected with its acute messianic consciousness, which is, by its very nature, one of constant advance and conquest, not of retreat and withdrawal. It does not guide the believer toward compromise, but toward striving for wholeness and perfection, in both the temporal and the spiritual realm. The Rebbe likewise called upon the Jews to liberate themselves once and for all from the lowly stature traditionally characterizing the relationship of the Jew to other nations. It strives to establish a new and resolute stance in its place. The reality of exile has shrunk and enslaved the Jewish soul, say the contemporary Lubavitchers; therefore, on the eve of redemption, one needs to be freed of the exile mentality and to develop a new, proud and erect stature.

On the face of it, these remarks reflect an interesting parallel to the classical Zionist idea of "negation of the Exile"—and that in its most extreme form. In the case of Habad, however, only the miraculous Redeemer can in practice bring Israel out of exile; the Jews are commanded only to prepare their hearts. It is interesting to note that the newly erect stature vis-à-vis any non-Jew who tries to transgress against Jewish property is not limited to the Land of Israel. It is demanded as much in the Crown Heights neighborhood of Brooklyn (where the Rebbe forbade his followers to move out of their neighborhood, whose peaceful character seemed to be threatened by the intrusion of non-Jewish population) as it is in Gaza and Jericho.[67] The principle is one and the same—although, of course, in the Holy Land the validity of this principle is even greater, and based on additional religious arguments.

Here the circle has been closed in an ironic manner. The recent messianic swell in Habad Hasidism, which is self-sustaining and constantly searching for new heights, eventually brought many of the Hasidim to the conclusion that they must take the initiative of giving the messianic cart a final push by "helping" and encouraging the Rebbe to reveal himself as Messiah—that is, to actualize his potential messiahhood, by means of his "coronation" by the public. Initially, cautious hints and restrained articulations were thrown into the air. But, as it became clearer that the Rebbe, unlike his earlier practice, did not protest, some people became more daring. Thus, during the winter of 1991, they began to distribute petitions among Jewish communities, asking the people, in thousands and tens of thousands, to declare in writing that they took upon themselves the kingship of "his holiness, the Rebbe, long may he live, the King Messiah." A group of Habad women even publicly turned to the Rebbe, insisting that he no longer conceal his messianic mission—"that he be revealed to all eyes as the King Messiah, and immediately take us out of exile!"[68] The traditional activism of Habad Hasidim, which now reached a stage of hyperactivism, was thus turned toward the Rebbe himself—that is, toward the Messiah himself as it were. Is it surprising that their severe opponents in the ultra-Orthodox camp, the Lithuanian Mitnaggedim, now hurled against them one of the severest possible charges—that they were engaged in false messianism of the Zionist type, which sought to bring redemption by human efforts?

There is a great irony in the fact that Habad Hasidism, which at the turn of the century turned toward a theoretical examination of the messianic question as a negative response to Zionism, is now conceived by its opponents as a new and distorted manifestation of Zionist activism. Thus an official statement published by the circles of the Mitnaggedim declared that "this is a clear denial of the kingdom of heaven . . . They have turned the Messiah, the desire of all Israel in all the generations, from the act of the Holy One, blessed be He, to an act of man." This is, in quintessence, "the Zionist outlook, which succeeded in penetrating also to Jews who observe mitzvot: their idea that it is within the power of human beings to take themselves out of exile and to achieve redemption."[69]

Needless to say, the objective observer can distinguish quite clearly between the historical activism of Zionism, which took place entirely within the earthly political plane, and the messianic activism of Habad, which is located entirely in the religious-spiritual plane. However, one cannot deny that even this latter messianic activism reveals the profound process of transformation that has taken place within Lubavitch. As mentioned, the fifth rebbe, Rabbi Shalom Dov Baer Schneersohn, explicitly wrote in 1899: "We must not heed them [i.e., the Zionists] in their call to achieve redemption through our own powers, for we are not permitted allowed to hasten the End even by reciting too many prayers concerning this!" Thus Habad's opponents, cleverly basing their claim on the words of earlier Habad Rebbes, argue that the contemporary activity and mind-set of their Hasidic rivals revolves precisely around this type of "too many prayers" and "hastening the End."

In light of all that has been said, and especially in light of my claim that, since the seventeenth century, there has been no precedent in Jewish history to the present messianic agitation in Ḥabad, is this new phenomenon to be portrayed as a replay in smaller scale of the Sabbatean messianic hysteria that swept over the Jewish communities in 1666?

My answer to this question is negative. First of all, Ḥabad messianism has in no way been connected with any violation of the bounds of Jewish religious law, and has thus far not revealed any sign of religious antinomianism. On the contrary, the laws and norms of the Torah themselves constitute the laws and norms of the redemption; the messianic process is completely subject to the halakhic criteria and guidelines set down by Maimonides in the final section of his *Mishneh Torah*. Moreover, this messianic arousal was not accompanied by any significant change in the concrete way of life, political or economic. The Hasidim "succeed" in drawing a sharp distinction between their mystical consciousness and messianic fervor, on the one hand, and their pragmatic realism and practical shrewdness in everyday life, on the other. As opposed to other historical precedents, they did not pack their belongings to greet the anticipated *aliyah'* to the Land of Israel, nor did anyone sell his house or cease his professional activity. *Olam ke-minhago noheg*—"the world goes on as always."

For example, at the beginning of 1992 the Rebbe demanded that the government of Israel stand firm against any international pressure and refuse to grant autonomy to the Palestinian inhabitants of the West Bank and the Gaza Strip. In his words, political or civil autonomy would be likely to bring about, over the course of years, the establishment of an independent, hostile Palestinian state. The naive listener might well ask, What have we to do with gradual historical processes and long-range political considerations? Have we not just said that "this is the year in which the King Messiah shall be revealed" with wonders and miracles, that "immediately, Messiah comes," to redeem us from history and its travails? As we have learned from other religious phenomena, however, only a clear distinction between the two realms, that of mystical religious consciousness and that of practical, pragmatic life, enables the believer to continue functioning within the real world. Indeed, it is this that distinguishes the Ḥabad Hasid from visionary dreamers and moonstruck eccentrics. The believer prays to God to heal his child, but immediately thereafter goes to an expert physician. In contemporary Ḥabad Hasidism, too, the faith is firmly messianic, but politics continues to be conducted in the world as it is, and so on in all the other areas of everyday life: work, trade, family, medicine, and so forth. The messianic future, as close as it may be, does not intrude upon the present nor threaten to upset it. True, present-day Ḥabad Hasidism walks at the edge of the precipice, yet its mainstream has thus far avoided the danger of falling into the abyss. The more urgent question, of course, has always been the extent to which it would be possible for it to maintain this radical tension, to draw upon constantly renewed stores of energy, and to continue to ascend from height to height, without reaching a crisis.

SPIRITUAL AND CORPOREAL HELP

Finally, let me make some brief remarks concerning an additional pattern of change manifest today in the life of Ḥabad Hasidim, as against original Ḥabad ideology, namely, the all-inclusive, total role of the rebbe in shaping the concrete life and destiny of his Hasidim.

Rabbi Shneur Zalman of Lyady differed from the majority of contemporaneous Hasidic teachers in limiting the role of the Hasidic *Tzaddik* to one of spiritual guidance, to molding the spiritual personality of the Jew. The *Tzaddik* should not be expected to perform miracles or to aid his disciples in worldly matters; it is his task to direct their paths in the service of God and toward closeness to Him (*devekut*). Thus Rabbi Shneur Zalman responded sharply to the request of his followers to advise them in worldly matters: "Has there ever been in the past, or have you seen such a custom in any of the books of the earlier or later sages of Israel, that one ask [his rabbi] for counsel regarding corporeal matters? . . . save to [ask of] the true prophets, as there were before in Israel."[70] Contemporary scholars are divided as to whether the rabbi of Lyady actually adhered to this theoretical principle—that is, whether he in fact turned away all of the appeals of his suffering followers.[71] However, they all share the opinion that, unlike other Hasidic leaders, he made a tremendous effort to halt the expectations of his Hasidim of the Rebbe's involvement in their concrete, material life. As the "Alter Rebbe" himself had learned from one of his own teachers, Rabbi Menahem Mendel of Vitebsk: "The help of the bodies is beyond our power."[72]

A further erosion in this matter would seem to have taken place under the leadership of his successors. Yet Ḥabad traditions concerning Rabbi Shneur Zalman and his concept of religious leadership were faithful to the original, historical facts. For example, an important treatise composed during the last generation (perhaps by Rabbi Joseph Isaac himself?) repeatedly reports that the rabbi of Lyady refused to respond to the majority of requests concerning material needs, and even ordered, "to make it known and to publicize, that everybody who seeks advice in corporeal matters . . . will not be answered."[73]

However, the present social expansion of Ḥabad Hasidism, combined with the charismatic position of the Rebbe, further deepened the gap between the traditional, theoretical position and reality. The dependence of the Hasidim upon their Rebbe regarding matters of livelihood and healing, business and matchmaking, society and politics, knows no limits, to the extent that a loyal Hasid will make no significant decision without asking the blessing of the Rebbe. Moreover, Hasidic oral tradition removes Rabbi Shneur Zalman's remarks from their literal context. It is impossible, they say, to separate the physical and spiritual well-being of the Hasid, to separate "earthly matters" and "heavenly matters." In any event, they emphasize, the Rabbi of Lyady qualified his remarks by implying that one may ask corporeal advice of those who are "true prophets . . . as there were before in Israel" (according to an oral communication from Rabbi Tuviah Blau).[74]

CONCLUSION

I began the discussion with the question whether the success of Ḥabad Hasidism and the place it has carved for itself in our generation, both in the United States and in Israel, is rooted purely in sociological factors—its organization, its structure, and its charismatic leader—or whether it is also based upon immanent conceptual elements, inherent in the traditional ideology and theology of this movement. I now conclude by formulating a dual answer to this question.

On the one hand, the typical Ḥabad tendency to broaden the scope of religious involvement as far as possible, to include all those realms and horizons opened to modern people, is deeply rooted in its traditional theological apprehension. It is this very apprehension that has enabled Ḥabad, even today, to adjust itself to and conquer the realm of the "secular." We have also seen that the typical activism, the "mission," and the social dynamism of contemporary Ḥabad Hasidism are similarly rooted in its classical ideological elements. In other words, in terms of both aspects—"every place" and "every person"—the encounter between the new and the old has been a story of success and fecundation.

On the other hand, facing modern reality—the confrontation with the historical activism of Zionism, and even more so the encounter with a situation of freedom and prosperity—served as a radicalizing factor, shaping

Habad Hasidism's messianic sensibility, which led it from one peak to another to the threshold of crisis. Habad Hasidism, which germinated and developed over the course of generations under conditions of hardship and oppression, eventually reached a state of intoxication once the surrounding environment became favorable. Similarly, the total personal dependency upon the Rebbe and his guidance, developed over the course of more than forty years, contributed in no small measure to this messianic development. The ninety-year-old Rebbe was childless, and never openly prepared his own successor. Thus the inescapable threat of the end was gradually transformed and redeemed in their consciousness into the long-awaited, ineluctable End.

In 1992, when the elderly Rebbe was suddenly stricken by a severe illness, the Hasidim were forced to halt and to tarry, in the absence of the flowing and fermenting prophetic voice—an unaccustomed, confusing wait for which they had never been prepared. They were now forced, for the first time, to stand up to a crisis and make personal and collective decisions by themselves, a heavy yoke from which they have been exempt for decades. A group of Habad rabbis in North America, who were no longer able to sit idly by or to restrain themselves, published a "clear rabbinic ruling" declaring the messiahhood of the Lubavitcher Rebbe! They anointed him as "a king of the Davidic dynasty," and concluded that "there ought to be applied to the Rebbe the divine oath that 'his light shall never be extinguished,' and that he shall live eternally—a life of the soul within the body" (14 April 1992)! This was in fact a prayer, a crying out, a rejection of the apparent state of affairs; an "activist" attempt to recreate the historical and metaphysical reality in a time of travail. Other Habad rabbis expressed their explicit opposition to this act, and presumably not only for theological reasons: they realized that such a radical move would be likely to exacerbate the crisis—to deepen the fixation upon the charismatic figure of the present leader—and thereby place obstacles in the way of the future renewal of the movement.

With the Rebbe's death in July 1994, requiring this Hasidic group to exist without a messianic revelation and without the living presence of the charismatic *Tzaddik,* I imagine that it will be able to sustain the first two patterns described above, the models of ideological continuity (i.e., "every place" and "every person"). By contrast, the latter two patterns—the acute, concrete messianism and intense personal dependence—are likely to loss their force and even to be revealed as a subversive factor: it is unlikely that a charismatic heir of the stature of Rabbi Menachem Mendel Schneersohn will emerge in the foreseeable future. True, there are spiritual and institutional interests of the highest order which will assure the continuity of the movement in one fashion or another. It is difficult to believe, however, that it will sustain its present powers of mass attraction or its present social impact. If it can no longer breathe the air of the peaks, it is doomed to exist on a different scope and with a different social coloration.

Is it not possible that the fears of the founding father, Rabbi Shneur Zalman of Lyady, were justified regarding the far-reaching consequences for his community of emancipation, prosperity, and conquest?

Afterword

The Zionist national revolution confronted traditional Jewry with a unique, unforeseen historical situation: a Jewish political sovereignty in the heart of the Holy Land prior to messianic times, under the leadership of nonpracticing, rebellious Jews. Moreover, Zionism ultimately began the process of returning the dispersed exiles, yet within a context far removed from the traditional theological concepts of exile and messiah, covenant and promise, reward and punishment, sin and atonement. It is no surprise, then, that traditionalist Jews have hardly related to these transformations with equanimity; they catalyzed an intense ideological ferment, and led to the creation of a series of new interpretations of classical Jewish sources. In fact, they refocused divisive issues and refashioned conflicting camps of thought.

In this work, I set out to investigate the nature of this ideational creativity as reflected among the radical religious schools in contemporary Jewry: ranging from the stream that abhors and detests the new national enterprise, through that which sanctifies the Zionist project and elevates it to metaphysical heights; from the ultra-Orthodox approach, which displays indifference toward historic events, voiding them of all potential significance, to the Hasidic viewpoint, which forces history, investing its religious hopes and fervor within actual events.

Hence, the structure of this book does not necessarily correspond to current political or ethnic divisions in Israel. Rather, I have divided the chapters according to the ideological and theological debates within contemporary Orthodoxy.

Naturally, there are instances in which the ideological and political divisions are effectively identical. For example, "messianic religious Zionism," the subject of the third chapter, more or less guides the current path of the National Religious Party in Israel. Similarly, "Haredi Jewry," the subject of the fourth chapter, constitutes the decisive majority of Agudat Israel (the United Torah Front). Nonetheless, such a clear convergence of the theoretical and political divisions does not exist in other important groupings. For example, the Habad movement, the subject of the fifth chapter, has deliberately refrained in most years from associating itself with one particular political party. On the other hand, a party like Shas is not committed to any of the clear-cut ideologies discussed above: its young leadership has been greatly influenced by the Haredi Lithuanian yeshivah heads, while its spiritual leader, Rabbi Obadiah Yosef (formerly chief rabbi of Israel) takes a rather independent, ad hoc position, based on his personal understanding of the needs of the hour; finally, although many of the Shas electorate fluctuate to the Israeli political "right," their present representatives are bound by social, traditional, and ethnic ties rather than by a common political outlook.

In the present work, I have focused primarily on radical religious positions. Of course, we must not ignore the existence of other, more moderate religious viewpoints, which find expression even now within mainstream Orthodox Jewry. These approaches manifest themselves primarily in certain ideological groups within religious Zionism, as well as in certain rabbinic circles among Oriental Jewry. These groups, however, are rightly the subject of their own work, one that would not center specifically upon the question of Zionism and messianism.

Let me suffice with two brief comments on this matter. First, none of the religious outlooks discussed in this book acknowledge an intermediate historical model—a concrete mode of Jewish being that is neither exile nor redemption. They all maintain a dichotimistic approach (Galut or redemption), thereby rejecting entirely the more complex option of a partial Jewish revival within history that continuously hovers between the two extremes. By contrast, the alternative, moderate approaches seek religious significance specifically within the realm of historical, premessianic realization, precisely because of what such a realization opens up and invites, demands and promises. The advocates of this viewpoint see the present return to Zion as taking place in an "opportune moment," as a halakhic challenge based precisely on this maverick condition—that is, no longer "exile" but not yet "redemption." Hence, this group's model for the modern return to Israel, of the present "Third Commonwealth" (in Hebrew *bayit*, "home" or "house"), is that of the First Commonwealth—and even more so that of the Second Commonwealth—rather than the absolute messianic one. These two historical models were always portrayed by the collective Jewish memory as legitimate and desirable, even if not whole and total.

In other words, in this, as opposed to the ultra-Orthodox paradigm, the new national awakening has cured the psychological, existential element of exile by building a Jewish homeland. By the same token, however, unlike the Zionist-messianic outlook, Zionism has not yet cured the metaphysical, theological element of exile. It has brought about a national revival, but not religious redemption. On the contrary, the supporters of this stance would claim Jews have always distinguished themselves from Christians precisely in that they taught their sons and daughters to find positive religious meaning even in a premessianic world; to search it out even in a historical reality that has not yet been saved. Of course, they will say, the partial achievement can eventually lead to the perfect one, step by step. But this does not detract from the innate value of the part in itself. Historical time is not to be judged only from the perspective of eschatological time.

Second, the moderate stance places the concept of covenant in the focus of its religious awareness. How so? The biblical covenant between the God of Israel and the people of Israel is, by its very nature, a conditional one. It is based on a "two-sided" obligation, one of mutual responsibility and mutual commitment. The very idea of the covenant negates religious determinism; it is inconsistent with the concept of a predestined fate or a predetermined future. The covenant contains neither an unlimited guarantee to the people nor an evil, unconditional decree. Therefore, as opposed to the radical outlooks, which foresee an inevitable destiny for Zionism and the State of Israel—whether for good or for ill—the present outlooks emphasize the uncertainty of the future, and the human freedom to influence and alter events. It is true, its advocates would say, that the prophetic promise for redemption is absolute, but its definite realization in a specific society or a given generation is conditional and contingent.

Furthermore, as opposed to the prevalent ultra-Orthodox approach, the covenant was not made between God and righteous individuals or God and pious communities alone, but rather between God and the entire people of Israel, as is—"from woodchopper to waterdrawer" [Deut. 29:10]. Moreover, the covenant covers the entire spectrum of the Jewish community, in its real existence, from the saints to the ignorant. Therefore, according to this alternative stance, the present revival of the Jewish people enables the reestablishment of the covenant community. It is indeed intended for its the community's perfection, even though it is not a guarantee thereof, until the End of Days.

THE IMPACT OF THE THREE OATHS
IN JEWISH HISTORY

THE IDEA AND ITS IMPACT

"The People of Israel is scattered in every land . . . At the time that God shall remember our exile and lift up the horn of His Messiah, each one will say: 'I will lead the Jews and I will gather them [in their land]' . . . Were it not that we fear that the End has not yet come, we would gather together. But we cannot do so until the time of the song-bird is come and the voice of the turtledove is heard [in the land], until the harbingers declare, 'May God be great.'"[1] This early document cited in the *Travels* of Benjamin of Tudela reflects the tensions generated by the question of the redemption and the Land of Israel among twelfth-century German Jews[2]—"mourners of Zion and mourners of Jerusalem."[3] These Jews, like many others before and since, are depicted here as vacillating between two opposing poles—the anticipation of imminent redemption, and the traditional fear of forcing the End prematurely. For them, the Land of Israel and collective *aliyah* are explicitly messianic categories, an expression of their deepest religious longing, whose realization within history is forbidden, "until the time of the song-bird is come." It is noteworthy that these "mourners of Zion" are portrayed as speaking in all innocence and that their words do not represent an explicit ideological or theological position. Hence, the power that informs these words: "Were it not that we fear that the End has not yet come, we would gather together."

As explained in chapter 1, the fear of mass *aliyah* to the Land of Israel was inherent in the oaths taken by the people of Israel—according to the Talmud and the midrashic literature—to accept the yoke of exile, as well as in the primeval myth regarding the children of Ephraim who went up from Egypt prematurely and fell by the sword.

> What are these three oaths? One, that Israel not ascend the wall;[4] one, that the Holy One, blessed be He, adjured Israel not to rebel against the nations of the world; and one, that the Holy One, blessed be He, adjured the idolaters not to oppress Israel overly much. (BT Ketubbot 111a)

> "For God said, 'The people may have a change of heart when they see war'" [Exod. 13:17]. This is the war of the children of Ephraim . . . because they forced the End, and transgressed the oath. (Mekhilta de-Rabbi Yishma'el)[5]

> Rabbi Helbo said: There are four oaths here: that they not rebel against the kingdoms; that they not force the End; that they not reveal their mystery to the nations of the world; and that they not ascend as a wall from the Exile. Rabbi Onya said: These four oaths correspond to the four generations which forced the End and failed . . . [The children of Ephraim] gathered together and went to war, and many of them died. Why? Because they did not believe in God and did not trust His salvation, because they transgressed the End and the oath, "lest you awaken or excite my love." (Songs Rab. 2:7)

These ideas assumed different garbs in the midrashim and the Aramaic Targumim to the Bible.[6] We do not know for certain the exact background that elicited these early warnings against collective activism and premature historical breach. Our present concern, however, is with a different question: What impact would this concept have upon Jewish sources and Jewish history? Was its imprint clear across the generations, from the Middle Ages into the modern period? Why has its influence grown in recent times?

Virtually all the students of religion and Zionism who have pondered these questions are in agreement. In their view, the concrete impact of the three oaths, both in literature and upon the religious consciousness, has never been decisive; rather, these have always been treated as aggadic and nonbinding. Moreover, according to this view, throughout Jewish history the oaths never served as a direct barrier to *aliyah*. Their critical use, which was to emerge in the modern period, was almost exclusively the innovation of Western European proponents of Emancipation and of Eastern European Orthodox opponents of Zionism.

I shall note here the words of only two important scholars. In 1979 Professor Mordecai Breuer wrote:

Traditional Jewish thought understood the three oaths as landmarks for the people in exile, not as proscriptions addressed against those who wished to go up to Zion. Hence, the oaths did not contradict the ascent of Jews to the Land of Israel, even in large and organized groups, so long as the Jewish dispersion remained in their exiles . . . We have not found the three oaths explicitly cited as an ongoing halakhah . . . Even with the organization of large and cohesive groups of immigrants, from the *aliyah* of R. Judah the Hasid, who came up [to the Land of Israel] at the head of a thousand Jews in 1700, through to the *aliyah* of Hasidim and disciples of the Gaon of Vilna—the question of the three oaths did not arise as a practical halakhic one.[7]

Ehud Luz, in his book *Parallels Meet* (1985), summarized this question in a similar spirit: "It is in any case clear that in and of itself it could not provide a foundation for a halakhic prohibition . . . Most of the pro-Emancipation Orthodox thinkers in Western Europe relied on this midrash to support their claim that no tangible efforts should be made to bring on the redemption before the days of the Messiah . . . By contrast, it hardly appears in Eastern Europe before the advent of Herzlian Zionism."[8]

I had also tended to support this view. However, a survey of the sources, from both the Middle Ages and the modern period, has led me to reconsider this question. Close examination reveals that the wall placed by the oaths between the people and its land was far higher than the historians suggest. It was a wall that sprang up over the generations, resting on two foundations.

First, the three oaths definitely served to create a certain distance and dissociation from the land. They were repeatedly invoked, on various occasions, to deter possible mass *aliyah*. This was certainly the case when the attempt to emigrate to the land was also connected with messianic fervor. It is true that this warning was more often voiced in the twentieth century than in the nineteenth, and in the nineteenth century more often than in the eighteenth; and in the modern period generally more than in the Middle Ages. As I observed in chapter 1, during those long centuries in which neither the Land of Israel nor "ascending the wall" from exile were concrete social options, the very fear of transgressing these oaths was repressed by the nation. By contrast, when *aliyah* was perceived as a substantive possibility, and people stirred themselves to attempt the move, the warning was voiced anew. In a paradoxical manner, the appearance of the oaths serves as a kind of seismograph, measuring, as it were, the impact of the land upon the life of the communities.

Second, the three oaths were cited by those Jewish sages who sought to develop a comprehensive metaphysical understanding of exilic existence. They were interwoven within those theoretical approaches that attributed deep theological meaning to Jewish life in the Diaspora, endowing it with profound symbolic and mystical content. Of course, the two different uses of the oaths were mutually supportive.

In the following sections, I attempt to elucidate these two elements and explore their foundation. To this end, I selected specific sources that integrate the oaths in their context and treat them with reverence. Neglected by historical research, these sources now require renewed proof of their accumulated weight over time.[9]

FIRST IMPRINTS

The oaths first appear (after midrashic literature) in Hebrew poetical literature (*piyyut*). Already in the sixth century CE, Simeon ben Megas ha-Kohen referred to them in one of his *piyyutim:*

> From always and from antiquity
> You who examine innards
> With two oaths
> You adjured the lion cubs
> Saying: one, that they not force the future End
> and one, not to rebel against the four kingdoms.[10]

More than four hundred years later, Rabbi Samuel ben Rabbi Hoshaya, one of the outstanding geonic leaders of Palestine, composed a verse in the same spirit.

> I gave an oath to my multitudes not to rebel against the Wild One
> [Ishmael] and Edom
> Be silent, till the time that I make them as Sodom . . .
> I made you an oath, my careful ones, lest you rebel
> Await the End of Days and do not tremble.[11]

These *piyyutim,* urging the people to accept the yoke of exile, offer no thematic innovations nor any particular historical context beyond the substance of the early midrashim.

During the entire period of the Muslim conquest (634–1099), *aliyah* was rare and of extremely limited scope. Scholars differ as to whether this should be attributed primarily to objective conditions—the economic distress and physical danger in Palestine during this period—or whether it was also connected with a certain rabbinic recoil regarding *aliyah* in pre-messianic times.[12] In any event, it is clear that *aliyah* was not then perceived as religious-normative behavior binding on the individual, and certainly not as a practical social option. This is particularly striking in comparison with the repeated calls by the Karaite sages, who admonished their flock to immigrate to the Land of Israel. In 900 CE the Karaite Daniel al-Qumisi severely condemned the ideology of passivity toward the land: "The scoundrels among the people of Israel say to one another: 'We need not go up to Jerusalem until we are ingathered by He who has thrust us out.' These are the words of the fools who provoked God's anger."[13] Al-Qumisi was perhaps protesting against a prevalent rabbinic approach of his time. Even if his remarks were directed solely toward the Karaites, the absence of a parallel call for *aliyah* by rabbinic leadership appears to be no accident.[14]

In other words, one should expect to hear the warning voice of the oaths precisely when *aliyah* out of the Exile "as a wall" was a concrete possibility, and should not look for recognizable traces of the oaths in the contemporary literature.

Likewise, during the twelfth century, although a number of well-known rabbinic sages made pilgrimages to the Land of Israel, individual *aliyah* had not yet become an established form of behavior, let alone collective immigration and settlement. As mentioned above, a document attributing to German Jews an explicit fear of forcing the End by gathering in Zion is quoted in Rabbi Benjamin of Tudela's *Travels*. True, the source and date of this document are not entirely clear, nor is it certain that it was in fact written by Rabbi Benjamin himself. Still, this document clearly exemplifies the reluctance regarding any attempt to actuate the messianic era within history.

Maimonides was probably the first rabbinic figure to adduce the oath as a warning against an actual social upheaval, in his admonition not to follow the imagined messiah who was then agitating the Jews of Yemen. Fearful of the political consequences and persecutions that might befall this community owing to the messianic turmoil, Maimonides tried to dissuade them from this path by every possible means. He wrote the following in the *Epistle to Yemen* (1172):

> Solomon of blessed memory, inspired by the Holy Spirit, foresaw that the prolonged duration of the Exile would incite some of our people to seek to terminate it before the appointed time, and as a consequence they would perish or meet with disaster. Therefore he admonished them and adjured them in metaphorical language to desist, as we read: "I adjure you, O maidens of

Jerusalem, by gazelles or hinds of the field, do not wake or rouse love until it please" [Song 2:7]. Now, brethren and friends, abide by the oath, and stir not up love until it pleases. And may God, Who created the world with the attribute of mercy, grant us to behold the ingathering of the exiles to the portion of His inheritance.[15]

However, we cannot ascribe decisive importance to the appearance of this idea in the *Epistle to Yemen,* as in it Maimonides drew upon every means at his disposal, even if purely rhetorical, to rescue a Jewish community.[16] There are grounds for suspecting that it was only because of these circumstances that he related in this manner to the oath in question. Not only is no trace of the oaths found in Maimonides' Halakhic works, but he had little truck with the interpretation of the Song of Songs as a historical allegory of the relationship between God and the people of Israel, which underlies the midrash of the oaths (as may be seen both in his great halakhic work and in his philosophic writing).[17] It would therefore seem that Maimonides' reference to the oaths bore more of a political, contingent character than a Halakhic or theological character.

AWE AND FEAR

The thirteenth century saw an important change in the relation of Diaspora Jews to the Land of Israel. *Aliyah* gradually became a common pattern of behavior among the sages, particularly in Western lands.[18] Already at the beginning of the century, groups of Jews, primarily from the French schools of the Tosaphists, settled in Jerusalem and elsewhere in the Land of Israel.[19] These immigrations, it has recently become clear, had a well-defined, strictly religious motivation: the longing to fulfill the commandments that were conditional on residence in the land, and thereby to attain religious perfection. In other words, because the Land of Israel enables one to live a richer and fuller religious life, allowing for broader Torah observance, the immigrant rabbis performed a pious deed and subjected themselves to a multitude of religious precepts applicable only in the land. Their *aliyah* was prompted neither by a messianic agitation nor by a mystical longing for the Holy; it was, rather, a concrete, normative entry through the halakhic gates of the Land of Israel.

During this same period, however, one of the major figures of Ashkenazic pietism or Hasidism, Eliezer ben Moshe of Würzburg (a nephew of Judah he-Hasid), issued one of the strongest warnings against *aliyah* in the history of Jewish literature. As he saw it, any attempt to break through and ascend to the land prior to messianic times would involve a metaphysical danger and a gross profanation of the land's sanctity. The Land of Israel was likened by him to Mount Sinai as it was at the very moment of divine revelation—forbidden to approach or touch. Anyone who dared to break through put his very soul in danger! In Eliezer's words,

> "You shall limit the people round about" [Exod. 19:12]: around Jerusalem and around the Land of Israel. "Beware of going up the mountain"—for He has adjured Israel not to force the End and not go up to the land prematurely.
>
> "Into the mountain"—this is the Land of Israel and the Temple Mount; "nor touch its edge"—that they not approach the mount to build the Temple there before its time. Another explanation: "nor touch its edge"—that they neither postpone the End nor force it. And this is: "to touch its edge (ka-tzehu)"—the End (ketz).
>
> "Whoever touches the mountain shall surely die": whoever hastens to go up to the Land of Israel shall surely die. "No hand shall touch it, for he shall be stoned": whoever hastens [to go there] shall not live—whoever goes up before the End—for while the Exile persists they shall not go free. "And when the horn sounds long, they shall ascend the mountain"—when shall the people of Israel leave the Exile to ascend to the Land of Israel? When the horn shall be blown long [at the time of redemption].[20]

The way to the Land of Israel was thus blocked by an iron wall. The Exile represents the reality of history; the land, the utopia of the End of Days. Any attempt to remove the barriers separating them would be self-destructive: "Whoever hastens shall not live!" The author not only lent compelling, binding power to the oath not to force the messianic realization; he also heightened the traditional religious reluctance to approach the holy precinct, casting the whole Land of Israel as a religious object, a transcendent and awesome entity.

As Israel Ta-Shma has already observed,[21] one may presume that these extreme statements were not uttered in a void; they addressed a specific situation, that is, the concrete drive toward *aliyah* that had been renewed in the nearby schools of northern France. In fact, the very opposition to *aliyah* of a leading Ashkenazic Hasid is hardly surprising. He presumably received the idea from his predecessors, one of whom even wrote that whoever went to the Land of Israel at the present time would not only not expiate his sins but, on the contrary, he "further multiplies his transgression" by "neglecting his marital obligations to multiply, the study of Torah, and prayer."[22] Not until our own time, however, do we again encounter an admonition as fierce as that of Rabbi Eliezer of Würzburg. In any event, this episode manifests two polarized approaches toward the Land of Israel: one by the French sages who were drawn to the land by bonds of mitzvot and halakhah, and the other by German pietists, who turned away from the land because of their messianic conceptions and their religious fear of breaching the Holy.

THE ALIENATION OF THE SHEKHINAH

Only a few years later, Rabbi Ezra, leader of the Kabbalist circle in Gerona, issued an appeal to the people to make their peace with the yoke of exile. "At this time," he wrote, "the people of Israel are already exempted from the obligation of [living in] the Land of Israel. When they suffer exile for the love of the Holy One, blessed be He, and undergo affliction and subjugation, this serves as an altar of expiation for them; as it is said: 'For Your sake . . . we are slain all day long' [Ps. 44:23]."[23] Thus the concrete Land of Israel is not needed or required until the era of the Messiah; on the contrary, whoever goes there may be seen as forsaking the Shekhinah, which now dwells with the dispersed people of Israel.[24] A similar line was taken by Rabbi Azriel, the disciple of Rabbi Ezra (and apparently also his son-in-law).[25] He too set aside the Land of Israel during the premessianic period, asserting that the Shekhinah no longer dwelt there: "Wherever the people of Israel went into exile, sanctity dwells among them; therefore [the Holy One says], 'I will not come to the city' which has been joined together, to the lower Jerusalem, until the time of the End, when Israel will return there; and [only then] the Shekhinah will return together with them . . . During the time of the Exile, however, because 'the Holy One [is] in your midst,' He will not come to the city [Hosea 11:9]."[26]

The idea of the exile of the Shekhinah illuminated the three oaths in a unique mystical light. The lower, historical exile reflects the metaphysical, supernal exile—the separation of the Shekhinah from its higher, divine source; the oaths disinclined the Jewish people to rebel against their exile while the Shekhinah had not been delivered from its supernal exile. In the language of Rabbi Ezra: " 'I have adjured thee': these are the words of the Shekhinah in the time of exile; adjuring Israel not to force the End and not to arouse love until there comes the time of favor . . . [At the present time, however], the Shekhinah is far from its place."[27] As noted by Haviva Pedaya,[28] the particular notion of the three oaths may have been connected by Rabbi Ezra with specific Kabbalistic ideas regarding the concept of oath as such. According to this idea, the power of an oath forces itself upon the Godhead itself. God, too, is bound by the vow until the End of Days. In any event, it is clear that these oaths of passivity dovetailed with Ezra's mystical approach. Even at the time of redemption, he believed, the people of Israel will uphold their vow and not rebel against the nations of the world: "Thereafter Israel, the scattered ones who are dispersed among the nations, will place upon themselves one head, that is, Messiah son of David who was with them in exile, and will go up to the Land of Israel by the permission of the kings of the nations and with their help!" That is to say, the Third Temple, like the second one, will also be built only with the consent of the Gentiles.[29]

Is it mere chance that the best-known immigrant to the land in the thirteenth century, Rabbi Moses Nahmanides, emerged from this same circle of mystics in Gerona, but profoundly disagreed with them as to the mystical status of the Land of Israel? Nahmanides took a diametrically opposed position on all the above questions. In contrast to the view exempting contemporary Jews from the obligation of living in the Land of Israel, Nahmanides was the first to formally establish the act of dwelling in the land as "a positive commandment incumbent upon any individual in every generation, even in the time of exile."[30] In contrast to Rabbi Ezra's insistence that even in the messianic age the people of Israel will settle their land with the permission of other nations, Nahmanides insisted that "we not leave it [the land] in the hands of other nations, in any generation."[31] Moreover, as opposed to the view distancing the Shekhinah from the land until the messianic End, Nahmanides ascribed a supreme, exclusive significance to the religious life in the Holy Land. In fact, he denied any independent, inherent value to observing the commandments in the lands of exile.[32] No one before him had gone so far in placing the Land of Israel at the very center of Jewish teaching—not only in the age of the Messiah, but in present historical time.[33]

Does this ideological polarization—between the passive position of Ezra and Azriel, who would defer *aliyah* to the messianic era, and the activist stance of Nahmanides—indicate the existence of a dialogue and confrontation over this subject among the Gerona Kabbalists? It is not impossible. Apparently, the young Nahmanides learned Kabbalah from the elderly Ezra, while the latter used a work by the youthful Nahmanides.[34] By the time that Rabbi Ezra, in his last years, had set down his thoughts regarding the oaths and the permission of the nations, Nahmanides was already in his forties. Of course, we do not know the formative wellspring of Nahmanides' doctrine of the Land of Israel. Nevertheless, we may presume that the passive posture adopted by Ezra and Azriel on this question was not divorced from the living presence of the land in the consciousness of others, nor from the growing tendency toward *aliyah* in their own generation.

"THAT THEY NOT GO UP EN MASSE"[35]

Beginning with the fourteenth century, our assumption that a dialectical relationship existed between the references to oaths and the phenomena of *aliyah* is no longer based on circumstantial evidence alone. It has a clear basis in fact. Indeed, during this period the edict of the oaths, which had originated in midrash and in Jewish thought, found its way directly into halakhic literature too. Apparently, only after Nahmanides' ruling that made dwelling in the land an obligatory precept for future generations, and only when this ruling became widely known, was there a counterreaction, in which the three oaths were powerfully reinvoked and even worked into the realm of halakhic discussion.

Interestingly, this reaction is first apparent in the writings of those very sages who felt drawn to the Land of Israel, but considered themselves obligated by the oaths to qualify their positive attitude toward *aliyah*. They therefore distinguished clearly between the piously motivated move of an individual to the land, which was blessed, and a collective break out of exile, which was forbidden.

Thus Estori ha-Parhi, an aficionado of the Land of Israel and a researcher of its antiquities, although citing a Talmudic saying praising those who dwell in the land, yet hedged it with restrictions and denied any Jewish longing to acquire political control there in the present age: "[We read] in the Jerusalem Talmud, Shekalim (3:4): 'It was taught in the name of Rabbi Meir: Whoever dwells permanently in the Land of Israel and speaks the Holy Tongue, etc., is assured his share in the World to Come.' However, they may not go up in order to conquer until the End comes, as is stated at the end of tractate Ketubbot: '"Lest you arouse and awaken [the love]" . . . they should not ascend the wall.'"[36]

This restriction was formulated in the Land of Israel itself at the beginning of the fourteenth century. Indeed, its author saw fit to characterize his own personal *aliyah* in the same spirit: "[God,] who knows every secret, knows that our [only] intention is to become sanctified by the holiness of the soil of Israel. We go there in awe [*eimah*], not to ascend the wall [*homah*]!"[37] Estori ha-Parhi may have been responding here directly to contemporary opposition to *aliyah*.

At the end of the century we find similar restrictions in a halakhic responsum written in North Africa by Isaac bar Sheshet, "Ribash." This sage, a refugee of the persecutions of 1391 in Spain, ruled on the question of *aliyah* in accordance with Nahmanides: "Aliyah to the Land of Israel is a mitzvah." Surely, this dictum reflected the situation of Spanish Jewry following the pogroms, which inspired the move to the land. At the same time, the writer warned against any attempt to make a mass break from the Exile: "The prophet said to the people—'Build houses . . . ' [Jer. 29:5]— addressing himself to those living in the Exile decreed upon them . . . Now, too, one of the three oaths the Holy One, blessed be He, made Israel take is not to ascend the wall."[38]

Similarly, Solomon ben Simeon Duran, "the Rashbash," of Algiers, a son of refugees from those same pogroms, was asked a concrete halakhic question pertaining to *aliyah*. He responded in like spirit, taking great care to eliminate any possible messianic connotation accruing to *aliyah:* "It is incumbent upon every individual to go up to live [in the Land of Israel]." He wrote: "However, this is not an all-inclusive commandment for all of Israel in their exile, but is withheld from the collectivity[39] . . . For it is one of the oaths which the Holy One, blessed be He, has adjured Israel, that they not hasten the End, and not go up in the wall. Consider what happened to the children of Ephraim when they forced the End prematurely."[40]

Just as the opponents of *aliyah* made the Land of Israel a strictly messianic category, the proponents of *aliyah* attempted to dissociate the land from any messianic context. To go to the land, the latter said, is in fact an ongoing, binding commandment, but those who obey it are expected to be doubly careful to observe the high barriers separating the age of exile from that of redemption. They may not go up "in order to conquer" (Estori ha-Parḥi); they may not "ascend the wall" against the will of the ruling peoples (Ribash); and they may not go up collectively—"the entire people" (the Rashbash).[41]

During the second half of the fifteenth century, there was a mass movement in Castile; men, women, and children traveled by sea to the Land of Israel. This type of awakening, unprecedented for generations, was probably connected with messianic fervor[42] and, as might be expected, aroused anger and suspicion among other contemporary Jews. The heads of the Jewish community in Saragossa were severely critical, emphasizing in a letter to their Castilian counterparts the dangers involved in a mass voyage to the Holy Land. In this protest it is difficult to separate theological considerations from pragmatic apprehensions of the Gentiles' reaction to such a move. In any event, this mass migration to the Land of Israel was openly denounced as an attempt to force the End and to meddle with messianic redemption. As the Castilians protested in their letter,

People of small value and great number have set out for the Land of Israel . . .
We do not know what gave rise to this great foolishness . . . And if one will
say: is it not well known and renowned from days of old that the people have
always gone from every corner to the Land of Israel? [We answer:] This is
true, but they have done it only in small numbers each time, and with ade-
quate privilegia from the rulers of the lands; never has such a great crowd
been reported to go there together . . . Therefore, our learned brothers and
leaders, we beseech you: Let all those making this move turn back, let every
person return home in peace, and not hasten the End as the children of
Ephraim did, heaven forbid . . . [We pray that] our eyes shall see the Lord
returning to Zion . . . and all of the people of Israel shall [follow] and ascend
there to see the presence of the Lord our God in His chosen house.[43]

Again, the invocation of the oaths thrusts before us the way in which
aliyah became an actual religious question in different eras and in different
places. Their articulation in literature may reveal, paradoxically, the immediate presence of the Land of Israel in Jewish consciousness and its concrete
impact upon the life of the communities. Although the three oaths were
generally on the margins of Jewish discourse, from time to time they were
drawn inside to build a high barrier between the people and the land.

Two questions remain to be dealt with in this context: First, was the
edict of the oaths in fact limited to the Jewish collectivity only, to mass
aliyah, or did it sometimes stand in the way of individual Jews too?[44] As we
have seen, already in the thirteenth century one can find some rabbinical
reservations concerning *aliyah* as such—whether by individuals or by a
group—rendering it an explicitly messianic category. The sixteenth century saw an additional, Halakhic (!) attempt in this direction, based explicitly on the old message of the oaths. The author was Rabbi Joseph de Leon,
a Spanish immigrant in Italy. In his Halakhic work, *Megillat Esther* (on
Maimonides' *Sefer ha-mitzvot*), de Leon sought to exempt even individual
Jews from the call of the land.

The commandment to inherit the Land and dwell therein is not observed save
in the days of Moses, Joshua and David, and so long as the people of Israel
have not been exiled from their land. After they were exiled, however, this
commandment is not binding upon subsequent generations until the advent
of the Messiah. On the contrary, we are commanded, according to the end of
tractate Ketubbot, not to rebel against the nations by conquering the land
. . . not to ascend the wall. As for Nahmanides' statement that the Sages conceived the conquest of the land to be an obligatory war, this statement refers
to a future time, when we shall not be subjugated to the nations. But with

regard to his [Nahmanides'] statement that the Sage engaged in hyperbole in praising the act of dwelling in the land, this refers specifically to the time when the Temple stands; now, however, there is no commandment to live there.[45]

The question of the Exile and the land is not discussed here in terms of place, but of time; not with regard to geographical space, but to historical reality—both political and religious. In the absence of Jewish political sovereignty and without the Temple, the Land of Israel is, so to speak, beggared. It loses its power to bind and attract contemporary Jews. De Leon in this reinterpreted Nahmanides' ruling, which made dwelling in the land a positive commandment binding upon all generations. Even if one does not read his comments as a response to an immediate, concrete question of *aliyah,* one does find in them a principled Halakhic attempt to cope with the claims of the land.

Second, was the prohibition against "going up en masse" always connected with the apprehension of provoking the Gentiles and of rebelling against world kingdoms? Not necessarily. For example, Rabbi Samuel Yaffe, Ashkenazic rabbi of the community of Constantinople at the end of the sixteenth century, stated that, even if the ruling nations themselves would consent to the ingathering of the Jewish exiles en masse, this would still not free the people from the constraint of the oaths. As Yaffe wrote in his commentary to the Song of Songs: " 'They should not ascend the wall' until they are redeemed by the Messiah . . . It seems to me that this prohibition applies even with the permission of the [Gentile] kingdoms. As God has scattered us to the corners of the world, we have no right to be gathered together 'as a wall' to the Land of Israel until God by His Messiah shall gather us . . . 'they shall not force the end' to be redeemed with strong hand."[46] Yaffe clearly ruled out any possibility of a Jewish return to Zion by natural means, without a prophetic, miraculous revelation. Neither the political-historical reality nor the reaction of the Gentile nations are theologically relevant. We shall see later how Rabbi Jonathan Eybeschütz further elaborated and refined this idea.

EXILE AND ITS MEANING

Many of the examples cited in the previous section reflected the predominant moods among Spanish Jewry and its refugees during a period of decline and displacement. Yet in the wake of the expulsion from Spain and Portugal, which threatened to undermine even the Jewish exilic existence, a growing tendency emerged among Jewish thinkers to reflect upon Jewish history and destiny and to seek its metaphysical meaning. No wonder, then, that in this context, too, the three oaths found their organic place.

I will begin with a radical expression of this tendency. A major sixteenth-century Kabbalist in Safed, Rabbi Abraham Galante, adduced a striking myth concerning the Portuguese *conversos* and their stubborn allegiance to the oaths. The passage in question appears in Galante's mystical commentary to the Ethics of the Fathers, *Zekhut Avot*.[47] However, the printed version of this passage is confused and marred by lacunae (due to censorship?) and does not reflect its original force. I shall therefore cite the authentic text, as it has survived in manuscript form (Paris, MS.866).

Galante offered a Kabbalistic interpretation to the words of the Mishnah: "Love work and hate rulership, and do not make yourself known to the authorities."

> The Shekhinah was called "work" (*melakhah*) because now, in the secret of exile, it is sentenced to labor, to gives its overflow to the "external ones" [the evil forces] and to the seventy [heavenly] princes [of the Gentiles]. Lilith is called "rulership" (*rabbanut*), because she is now in rule. Go and see how many circuses and theaters are yet standing, while the lodging place of our God lies in waste. [Nevertheless,] the whole struggle [with the powers of evil] is to be performed by prayer and petition only, that is, to take place between you and your Creator alone. But "do not make yourself known to the authorities" (*rashut*), that is, do not take oaths against the [ruling] nations—do not rebel or wage war against them. [Indeed,] such a desire rose up in the hearts of the Jews of Portugal, who were all forced to convert. Realizing that they were twice as numerous as the Gentiles [around them], so they desired to lift up their heads, to kill [their persecutors] and seize the kingship. However, there was an elder one there who inquired concerning this, by means of the Tetragrammaton, and he was answered [from heaven]: "Lest you arouse and awaken the love [prematurely] . . . " As our rabbis interpreted it: "The Holy One, blessed be He, adjured three oaths to Israel, one, that they should not rebel against Him [*sic*]."

In other words, the *converso* Jews, both by virtue of their numbers and their magical power, should have been able to overcome their persecutors and "seize the kingship." During the time of exile, however, the political rule of the nations is paralleled by the metaphysical rule of evil. It is the edict of the Almighty, then, that during this era "kingship" (in both senses) would be in bondage to these foreign powers. Hence, any attempt to break through by physical strength or by magical power, thereby upsetting the political and cosmic order of exile, is tantamount to open rebellion against the Godhead. The *conversos* therefore took upon themselves not to attempt such a breach and to remain loyal to the oath even at the price of submission and apostasy!

A sweeping metaphysical and mythic burden is thus conferred on the oaths, well beyond their original mundane confines. They not only represent the passive acceptance of the historical exile and political subjugation of the people; they also imply a reconciliation with the cosmic exile and metaphysical captivity of the Shekhinah (see *Sefer ha-Zohar* 2:9a). In fact, Galante presented a striking antithesis to the famous story of Joseph de la Reina. In contrast to de la Reina's unseemly attempt to trap Satan by magical means and to bring about redemption prematurely,[48] the Portuguese *conversos* overcame such a temptation. They accepted exile and subjugation, upholding the divine oath. Thus the proscription of the oaths is directed simultaneously against both physical and mystical activity. It carries even greater force than forced religious conversion.

We turn now to a more central intellectual development of the sixteenth century, one that would have a profound impact upon later generations. This was the doctrine of exile, developed by Judah Löw, "the Maharal," of Prague, and the special role it ascribes to the decree of the oaths. The Maharal considered the phenomenon of exile less from the point of view of Jewish subjugation (like Galante) than from that of Jewish alienation.[49] Of course, exile is a historical situation of a nation that has been driven from its organic home and banished into an estranged existence among the Gentiles. At a deeper level, however, the nation's historical exile represents its metaphysical, existential estrangement from the very nature of the temporal world. Israel, the chosen people, has transcended the given, unredeemed order of reality. It belongs to a different order, which has not yet coalesced; and is consequently fated to experience the present time in an unnatural, exilic existence. The people of Israel is out of place and time—in every place and time—"for the portion of Jacob is the portion of the world to come . . . The people of Israel are persecuted, oppressed, and harassed in this world, because this world is not worthy of them; hence, they confront opposition in this world."[50]

Exile is indeed a divine decree. But it does not so much stem from Israel's sin and punishment as reflect their innate essence. The Exile is indeed an anomaly,[51] yet in an unredeemed world this anomaly itself is the norm for the chosen people. As might be expected, the three oaths dovetail with this idea: they decree that the people of Israel will continue to experience an alien existence; they call upon them to deviate from the natural order of space and time. At the same time, they produce a kind of "balanced" status quo between Israel and the nations. Israel will be submissive and not rebel, while the nations will allow the Jews to exist under their rule and will not oppress them to excess. The oaths, then, bring into being a unique social and cosmic order.

> Exile represents a change in the order of the world. Such a change of order is difficult to sustain: there is always a desire to negate it—that is, to gather together out of exile and ascend the wall . . . God, therefore, decreed that Israel are not to rebel against the nations by leaving their rule . . . and that the nations not subjugate Israel overly much, for otherwise the Exile could not exist . . . He decreed that they not ascend the wall and ingather the exiles . . . that they not force the End [even] by means of prayer and petition[52] . . . He adjured them by the heavens and earth: just as the latter keep the [cosmic] law ordained by God with no alteration, thus Israel will keep that which God, may He be blessed, has decreed upon them in their exile.[53]

In sum, the three oaths reflect the metahistorical nature of the Jewish people. Indeed, the Maharal took the oaths to an extreme: he demanded that persecuted Jews should sacrifice their life rather than uproot the Exile: "Even if [the Gentiles] wish to kill them with harsh tortures, Israel should not leave exile and not alter this order!"[54]

The Maharal's central position in the history of Jewish thought led scholars and ideologues of the last generation—Zionists and anti-Zionists alike—to reinterpret his words according to their own contemporary conceptions. Some, such as Rabbi Menachem Mendel Kasher, sought to minimize the force of the oaths.[55] According to this interpretation, the Maharal understood the oaths as a supernal decree imposed upon historical reality, rather than as a normative demand placed upon the human race. The oaths were intended to define the objective situation in the time of exile, rather than to place restrictions upon the Jewish people. Such a reading of the Maharal is, however, incompatible with the overall context of his ideas. The Maharal dealt explicitly with both demands upon man and the divine decree on reality. As he wrote in *Be'er ha-golah*: "The sages warned us to accept the dominion of the nations . . . this proscription not to rebel against the nations' kingdom is so harsh, to the point that [if we break it] our flesh may be stripped away, heaven forbid, like that of gazelles or hinds of the field [who fall prey] . . . Israel must not negate God's decree by force, but rather they should pray for the return of the kingship of Israel."[56]

On the other hand, some interpretations of the Maharal take the opposite view, exaggerating the oath's prohibitions. According to the late Satmar Rebbe Yoel Teitelbaum, the Maharal stated, paradoxically, that even if the foreign nations should force the people of Israel to return to their land, they are commanded to resist such a "decree" with great devotion and treat it as though it were "an edict of conversion."[57] They are to prefer death to leaving the Exile! Against this claim, however, it seems clear that the Maharal is referring to the threat of death and "difficult tortures" stemming from the very conditions of life in exile, rather than from expulsion from the Exile. Even so, his words are as hard as diamonds: "If Israel abandon the divine decree of exile, it will be their destruction in exile . . . [Even so] their blood has been spilt like water . . . [Even so] they endured cruel and harsh suffering . . . even if [the nations] should wish to kill them with tortures, they may not leave [exile]."[58]

Rabbi Isaiah Horowitz (Shelah), too, a great seventeenth-century sage who settled in the Land of Israel, tended to emphasize the metaphysical significance of the Exile in connection with the oath's decree. According to him, too, the mundane exile symbolizes the supernal exile; hence, one ought to be reconciled to its yoke: "During the period of exile, in which our great sins have engendered a separation within the supernal worlds, we must suffer, as stated in the Midrash, 'I have adjured you' not to rebel. To the contrary, we are commanded to be submissive."[59] Horowitz, it should be emphasized, attached great importance to individual *aliyah* to the land of exile, "so that one might sanctify himself and fulfill the mitzvot that are [applied] there."[60] However, this act of individual ascent occurs entirely in the age of exile, of national political passivity. It does not bring release in any way from the prohibitions dictated by the historical, premessianic realm. As Rabbi Horowitz wrote elsewhere: "All of the [biblical] battles of Jacob with Esau allude to the [national] future . . . Thus do we behave in our own generation, too, toward the children of Esau: our power is in our mouths only, that we may pray to God, may He be blessed, in times of trouble; but war, that is, fighting the nations [by the sword], does not pertain to us. Rather, we make 'war' by the efforts of our community emissaries, who are obligated to show their faces to kings and princes, to speak on behalf of Israel with all their strength . . . This is the pillar of exile . . . until our righteous Messiah comes."[61]

Here is a clear echo of the fourteenth-century teachings of Rabbi Bahya ben Asher, who wrote: "We should follow in the footsteps of our forefathers, that is, prepare ourselves to approach the children of Esau with gifts, and with humble language, and with prayer to God, may He be blessed. It is impossible for us to meet them in war, as it is said, 'I have adjured you, O daughters of Jerusalem' not to provoke war with the nations."[62] This aspect of the oaths, prohibiting the people of Israel from waging war during the time of exile, would resurface more strongly in later generations, beginning with the modern Hibbat Zion movement.[63] Horowitz understood exile less as a punishment than as a moment in the ongoing dialectic process of the sanctification of the nation. Exile is a necessary descent, for the purpose of ascent: "It is all for our good, that we may become refined in the furnace of the nations . . . the light will come from the very darkness . . . the curse itself will be turned into a blessing . . . for destruction is the cause of true construction."[64] In sum, during this age the Land of Israel would sanctify the righteous individuals, while exile would purify the nation as a whole.

LANDMARKS IN THE MODERN PERIOD

We found the three oaths resonating during the Middle Ages in two main, interconnected contexts: in relation to the practical question of *aliyah*, and in relation to the theological question of Jewish existence in exile. In the modern period, the notion of the oaths arose in the same contexts. Indeed, they were invoked with particular frequency following the failure of the Sabbatean movement. I shall note several high points in the later development of the idea.

The most interesting treatment of the midrash of the oaths, following Horowitz, appears in the writings of the two great rivals—Jacob Emden and Jonathan Eybeschütz, both sages eloquent in the praises of the Land of Israel.

Beginning with the second half of the seventeenth century, several large groups of European Jews attempted to settle in the Land of Israel. The most important of these, led by Rabbi Judah he-Hasid, came to the Land of Israel in 1700.[65] The group was driven by messianic fervor, and its members were even suspected of harboring Sabbatean tendencies. Rabbi Jacob Emden, for one, who relentlessly persecuted every remnant of the Sabbatean movement, was severely critical of the group: "There has sprung up a new sect of pietists in Poland, the fellowship of Judah he-Hasid, whose whole enterprise is built upon the fallen, vain foundation of Sabbatai Zvi, may the name of evildoers rot . . . They did bizarre things; they promised to bring the Messiah in a short time and went up as a wall[66] to the Land of Israel!"[67] Emden himself was enthusiastic about *aliyah*. However, he imputed false messianic tendencies to this group, and accused them therefore of forcing the End and going up "as a wall."

Indeed, Emden ascribed considerable importance to the edict of the oaths, as a tocsin against false messianism. He even devoted a special prayer to it: "Master of the Universe, be Thou for us a God of salvation from the Exile; for You have adjured us with four oaths lest we ourselves do anything to force the End, but only await [Your] salvation."[68] In fact, this strong-minded sage viewed the entire Sabbatean movement as a catastrophic transgression of the oaths. Emden perceived Sabbateanism as a demonic breach—an antimessianic messianism, as it were—that stood as an obstacle to Israel's true redemption, causing the people to miss the hour of supreme grace (the same thing would be said years later by the Satmar Hasidim and the Neturei Karta concerning the Zionist movement). In Emden's words, "One must know that in truth this event [of Sabbateanism] did not happen in a natural way . . . No doubt there was then a fortunate moment; redemption and salvation were imminent, had they not forced the End and violated the oaths . . . The spirit of falsehood was permitted to mislead Israel and to confuse the world.[69] [Shabbatei Zevi] forced the hour; therefore the hour forced him and was turned to evil."[70]

Likewise Rabbi Moses Hagiz, Emden's stalwart colleague in the struggle against the vestiges of Sabbateanism, warned sharply about the punishment for forcing the End: "For at that time [the period of Shabbatei Zevi] the plague began. Nearly all the people of Israel were exposed to the danger . . . and they were on the brink of death, heaven forbid, to be judged as rebels and violators of the oath that the Holy One, blessed be He, imposed upon Israel, while they are in exile among Edom [Christianity] and Ishmael [Islam]."[71] Clearly, then, in that period the edict of the oaths played a role similar to the one designated for it in Maimonides' *Epistle to Yemen*. It was to stand in the breach against any false messianic agitation.

This is not the case in *Ahavat Yehonatan* by Rabbi Jonathan Eybeschütz which contains a strong warning not against messianism but against *aliyah* en masse from the Exile.[72] Eybeschütz's doctrine of exile is a recondite, complex one, which I have discussed at length elsewhere.[73] Suffice it to note that Eybeschütz conferred a definitive, radical interpretation on the edict of the oaths, as only few sages—both before and after him—have done. As he put it,

The congregation of Israel shouted out their vow—"Lest you arouse and awaken the love"—against the ingathering of Israel. For even if the whole people of Israel is prepared to go to Jerusalem, and even if all the nations consent, nevertheless, it is absolutely forbidden to go there. Because the End is unknown and perhaps this is the wrong time. [Indeed,] tomorrow or the next day they might sin, and will yet again need to go into exile, heaven forbid, and the latter [exile] will be harsher than the former. Therefore the Congregation of Israel beseeched—"until it shall please"—that is to say: until the time comes when the entire world shall be filled with knowledge [of the Lord].[74]

The emphatic assertion that even the hypothetical support of the ruling nations to the ingathering of the exiles would not release Israel from the oaths is of particular interest. As we saw, Rabbi Samuel Yaffe wrote in a similar vein at the end of the sixteenth century. But Eybeschütz went further, applying this assertion even to those who returned to the Land in biblical times from Babylonia to build the Second Jewish Commonwealth.[75] According to him, the call of the prophet Zechariah (4:6)—"not by might, nor by power, but by my spirit"—was directed against the aspiration of these newcomers "to ingather the entire exile by force" before the messianic days.[76] That is to say, not even the declaration of Cyrus the Great overruled the prohibition on the people of Israel not to go up to the land from the Exile en masse. Historical and political reality makes no difference to the basic theological norm. On the contrary, the latter remains valid in all nonmessianic times, precluding collective *aliyah:* "The Holy One, blessed be He, adjured the congregation of Israel not to go up before their time."[77]

The notion of the oaths was later invoked frequently in Hasidic literature.[78] The founders of Hasidism, who neutralized the social-historical element of messianism in everyday religious life, referred to this notion both to warn of rebellion against the Exile by means of political activity, and against forcing the End through spiritual-mystical efforts. On the one hand, Rabbi Ya'akov Yosef of Polonnoye (before 1780) taught the doctrine of political passivity: "The Holy One, blessed be He, adjured Israel neither to rebel against the nations nor leave the Exile until the Last Days."[79] On the other hand, Rabbi Elimelech of Lyzhansk (1786) warned his followers not to overdo their mystical outbursts: "One should not exert oneself to exhaust them [the powers of impurity] completely and thereby cause the immediate coming of the Messiah, for our sages said: It is forbidden to force the End."[80] Warnings of this kind were repeated in dozens of homilies of Hasidic masters, from the Hozeh of Lublin (Rabbi Ya'akov Yosef) and his disciples in the early nineteenth century,[81] until the latter-day Hasidic opponents of Zionism. There is no room here to discuss the numerous Hasidic sources that invoked, over generations, the midrash of the oaths and the edict of Jewish passivity.[82]

Concurrently, the notion of the oaths played a leading role among the Orthodox seekers of emancipation in Western Europe. It provided them religious grounds for opposing collective *aliyah* as well as any other political-historical initiative during the time of exile. As mentioned in chapter 1, Moses Mendelssohn already declared that the Talmudic sages prohibited taking "the smallest step in the direction of forcing a return and a restoration of our nation." At the beginning of the nineteenth century, the rabbi of the community of Emden, Abraham Lebenstamm, wrote in a similar vein. In his words, even if "we are capable of going up to Jerusalem by force of arms . . . we are not permitted to take any initiative, so as not to violate the divine oaths."[83] This theme was emphasized more firmly by Rabbi Samson Raphael Hirsch, the leader of German neo-Orthodoxy. Hirsch, indeed, injected a clear antipolitical slant into the oath "that they not ascend the wall," glossing it to mean "that the children of Israel shall never seek to reestablish their nation by themselves" (this in 1837!).[84] We find echoes of this approach in later generations as well.[85]

The message of the three oaths was also articulated in that period on the fringes of the well-known *aliyah* of the Perushim, associated with the school of Rabbi Elijah, the Gaon of Vilna. "Our sages indeed praise dwelling in the Land of Israel," wrote Zvi Hirsch Lehren in Amsterdam. "But until our Father in heaven shall wish to redeem us, all buildings [in the land] are vanity and emptiness." Lehren repeatedly called upon the dwellers in the Land of Israel to behave even there in accordance with the edict of exile, in both the political and religious spheres. As for the political, "We are servants of the ruling kingdom. It does not become us, therefore, to be lifted above them 'until it please.'" As for the religious realm, one indeed ought to pray for the return of the Shekhinah from its exile, but "one should not make a commotion about this . . . they should not multiply supplications to hasten the End."[86]

As Aryeh Morgenstern has shown, other sages in the Diaspora who opposed the activity of the Perushim also drew on the rhetoric of the oaths. Rabbi Solomon Berliner, rabbi of the Ashkenazic community in London, who protested against the peculiar contacts of the Perushim with members of the London Missionary Society, used the language of the oaths against them.[87] Around the same time, Rabbi Moshe Teitelbaum, a leading Hasidic rabbi in Hungary (author of *Yismah Moshe*), expressed himself even more forthrightly. Teitelbaum explicitly blamed the act of *aliyah* for the Safed earthquake of 1837 and for other ill events in the land: "[All these] should teach us that it is the will of God, may He be blessed, that we not go up to the Land of Israel by our own power, but wait until our righteous Messiah leads us there."[88] Similar warnings were also voiced elsewhere at that time.

Moreover, the Perushim themselves took the edict of the oaths very seriously. Consequently, they made an attempt to invalidate the edict with respect to their own time and their specific action.[89] Ironically, perhaps, it was Rabbi Israel of Shklov, head of the Perushim in Safed, who gave a firm, halakhically binding status to the oath "not to ascend the wall." In his *Pe'at ha-shulḥan*, which deals entirely with the laws concerning the Land of Israel, Shklov wrote: "Dwelling in the Land of Israel is equivalent to obeying the entire Torah. Yet it is not an all-inclusive commandment incumbent upon the entire people of Israel. In the time of exile it is incumbent upon each individual only." The author stated explicitly that he qualified the commandment to dwell in the land in order to explain the edict "not to ascend the wall," for were it incumbent upon all Israel, then they would all be obligated to go up collectively.[90] In fact, a similar position had already been expressed by the Rashbash in the fifteenth century (see above). Yet only now, in the nineteenth century, was that position included ab initio in an authoritative Halakhic codex.

But let there be no mistake: even in earlier generations, the edict of the oaths was never absent from halakhic discussions. For example, in his novellas on the Talmud, Rabbi Samuel Idels, "the Maharsha," took pains to delimit the permission granted to "every Jewish individual to ascend to the Land of Israel," on the condition that "they not go up together by force to build the walls of Jerusalem."[91] By the early eighteenth century, another distinguished scholar, Rabbi Joshua Heshel Falk (*Penei Yehoshua*) also added his voice, claiming explicitly that the oaths "also apply at the present time."[92] It bears stressing, however, that the three oaths typically reside in the ideological and theological realm, not within the formal halakhic one.[93] Even when the prohibition did enter Halakhic literature, it reflected the religious consciousness, or even the religious anxiety, more than it did strictly legal considerations. Hence, the question I have raised in this chapter is not whether the edicts of the oaths were "explicitly cited as an ongoing halakhah." My concern is with their real impact upon Jewish life and literature, including Halakhic literature.

CONCLUSION

In light of all the above, it is not surprising that the deep-seated reluctance to rebel against the Exile or to force the End reemerged with renewed force in reaction to the appearance of the modern movement of Hibbat Zion, and even more strongly to the Zionist enterprise and the establishment of the

State of Israel. At its sharpest, of course, we find this reluctance in the ultra-Orthodox polemics against the national movement. But it is equally apparent in the consistent grappling with the notion of the oaths in the writings of the Orthodox supporters of the project of settling the land: from the "Harbingers of Zionism" and the "Lovers of Zion" of the nineteenth century, down to later, contemporary authors (as shown in several chapters of this book).[94] To quote Rabbi Simhah ha-Kohen of Dvinsk, "Many rabbis did not support [the settlement enterprise]; even those who sympathized with it in their hearts and wished to reach fruition kept their peace, lest the enthusiasts would overdo, and because of their fear of the three oaths that the daughters of Jerusalem were adjured. Now, however, Providence has caused an order to be issued at the gathering of the enlightened countries at San Remo that the Land of Israel shall be for the people of Israel. Thus the fear of the oaths has gone . . . It is therefore incumbent upon every person to help in the utmost of his ability to fulfill the commandment [of settling the land]."[95]

Indeed, the three oaths have not been at the crux of Jewish history, contrary to the claim of the radical religious opponents of Zionism. They were understood primarily as a theological guideline rather than as a formal halakhic proscription. Some sages went even further and downplayed the compelling force of the oaths. Rabbi Hayyim Vital, for example, restricted the edict to a particular time frame: "The oath is valid for one thousand years only."[96] On the other hand, Rabbi Phinehas ha-Levi Horowitz (author of Sefer ha-hafla'ah) confined it to a specific place: the people was warned not to ascend the wall from Babylonia, in particular, "so as not to forsake the [special] holiness residing there."[97] Moreover, from the words of the Gaon of Vilna one might conclude that the oath prohibited only a particular, clearly defined act: "They have been adjured not to go out by themselves to build the Temple, the supernal rose, until the advent of the Messiah."[98] The most extreme position was taken by Rabbi Moses Hagiz, who protested against "the opinion of several fools, whom I have heard saying that every city and each country in which Israel dwell is today holy soil like the cities of Israel and Judah . . . and supporting their ranting by quoting our sages about the three oaths Israel was adjured by God."[99] Paradoxically, though, this trenchant protest, from an eighteenth-century seeker of Zion, is itself a clear indication of how deeply rooted the oaths were in the consciousness of other contemporary Jews, and hence the barrier they represented to their potential aliyah.[100]

Indeed, even today the traditional fear against rising up from exile as a wall is not confined solely to extreme, outspoken religious groups. It flows in other channels as well, some of them hidden, making its impact upon several religious trends. Thus any attempt, scholarly or ideological, to ignore it or to describe it as a recently created phenomenon, *ex nihilo,* will miss one of the deepest roots of the tense interaction between the Jewish religion and the modern enterprise of Jewish national renewal.

NOTES

INTRODUCTION

1. Moses Sofer, *Torat Moshe* (Pressburg, 1879), 1:36. See also idem, *Derashot* (Klausenburg, 1919), 2:355. On Sofer's quietist approach to personal life, see Jacob Katz, "Toward a Biography of the Hatam Sofer" (in Hebrew), in *Meḥkarim be Kab-balah uve-toldot he-datot mugashim le-Gershom Scholem* (Jerusalem, 1968), p. 135.

2. Gershom Scholem, *Devarim be-go* (Tel Aviv, 1975), p. 190; idem, "Messia-nism: A Never-Ending Quest," in *On the Possibility of Jewish Mysticism in Our Time and Other Essays* (Philadelphia, 1996).

3. Gershom Scholem, "Reflections on Our Language," in *On the Possibility of Jewish Mysticism.*

4. Throughout, the English for the biblical passages is taken from *Tanakh: The Holy Scriptures* published by the Jewish Publication Society of America (Phila-delphia, 1985).

5. Elyakum Shlomo Shapira, *Or la-yesharim* (Warsaw, 1900), pp. 56–57 (em-phasis added).

6. The Hebrew of the short passage quoted here is interwoven with phrases taken from the following biblical passages of reproof and lament (in order of ap-pearance): Deut. 31:27, Isa. 6:10, Jer. 9:2 (Ps. 20:6), Lam. 1:22, Esther 8:6.

7. As noted by Zvi Yaron, *The Philosophy of Rabbi Kook* (Jerusalem, 1991), pp. 273, 366 n. 63, Kook refrained from using the terms "Jew" and "the Jewish people," preferring "Israel" and "the Israelite nation." However, Yaron surmised that Kook was the first to use the phrase "the State of Israel." See also Geulah Bat-Yehuda, "The Vision of the State among Early Religious Zionists" (in Hebrew), *Shragai* 3 (1989): 25.

8. Abraham Isaac Kook, *Orot ha-kodesh* (Jerusalem, 1964), 3:194; idem, *Orot* (Jerusalem, 1963), p. 160 (emphasis added).

9. BT Sanhedrin 38b; Hagigah 14a. See Yitzhak Shilat, "To Return to the Royal Road" (in Hebrew), *Nekudah* 89 (1985): 14.

10. Kook might have had before him the following sources: 1 Chron. 29:23— "Solomon successfully took over the throne of the Lord as king"—and BT San-

hedrin 20b—"The term 'throne' always refers to a king, as it is written, 'Solomon took over,' etc." In any event, Israeli politics is theology. Cf. Alistair Kee, ed., *The Scope of Political Theology* (London, 1978); Siegfried Wiedenhofer, *Politische Theologie* (Stuttgart and Berlin, 1976); G. Brady, "Définition de la Cité de Dieu," *Année Théologique Augustinienne* 12 (1952): 113–29.

11. Ze'ev Scharf, *Sheloshah yamim* (Tel Aviv, 1959), pp. 101–3.

12. Historians of modern Europe have demonstrated how Christian concepts and symbols that had been secularized, serving in "neutral" political and social contexts, thereafter served to lend religious meaning to these very political or social concepts. Jacob Katz has mentioned this phenomenon as a factor hindering the identification of Jews with the European state and its culture. See Wilhelm Kamlah, *Utopie, Eschatologie, Geschichtstheologie* (Mannheim, 1969), pp. 5–70; Jacob Katz, *Jews and Freemasons in Europe, 1739–1772* (Cambridge, Mass., 1970); idem, "Religion as Uniting and Dividing Force in Modern Jewish History," in J. Katz, ed., *The Role of Religion in Modern History* (Cambridge, Mass., 1975), pp. 2–3.

13. The sources for these terms will be elucidated throughout the course of this book.

CHAPTER ONE

1. See Alexander Altmann, *Moses Mendelssohn: A Biographical Essay* (Philadelphia, 1973), pp. 424–26; Berth Strauss and Bruno Strauss, "Wer ist der 'Mann von Stande'?" in B. Schindler, ed., *Occident and Orient* (London, 1936), pp. 518–25.

2. Moses Mendelssohn, *Gesammelte Schriften*, ed. G. B. Mendelssohn (Leipzig, 1843–45), 5:493–94.

3. Moses Mendelssohn, "Remarks concerning Michaelis' Response to Dohem," in P. R. Mendes-Flohr and J. Reinharz, eds., *The Jew in the Modern World* (New York, 1980), p. 43. But see also Ran Sigad, "Moses Mendelssohn: Judaism, Divine Politics, and the State of Israel" (in Hebrew), *Da'at* 7 (1981): 93–103.

4. Benedict de Spinoza, *Theologico-Political Treatise*, ed. R. H. M. Elwes (New York, 1955), pp. 101–2. See also Shlomo Pines, *Bein maḥshevet Yisrael le-maḥshevet ha-amim* (Jerusalem, 1977), pp. 277–305; idem, "Moses Mendelssohn's Comments regarding His Attitude to Maimonides and Spinoza" (in Hebrew), *Mehkerei Yerushalayim be-Mahshevet Yisrael* 2 (1983): 151–52; J. Yerushalmi, "Spinoza on the Existence of the Jewish People," *Proceedings of the Israel Academy of Sciences and Humanities* 10, no. 6 (1983); Leo Strauss, *Spinoza's Critique of Religion* (New York, 1965), pp. 20–21; Arnold Eisen, *Galut* (Bloomington, Ind., 1986), pp. 61–65.

5. Hermann Cohen described these remarks of Spinoza as "demonic irony." See Hermann Cohen, "Spinoza über Staat und Religion, Judentum und Christentum," in *Jüdische Schriften* (Berlin, 1924), 3:333. See also Eliezer Schweid, *Ha-Yehudi ha-boded veha-yahadut* (Tel Aviv, 1976), p. 136. Spinoza saw a Jewish revival as possible, but not as desirable. These remarks of his had considerable influence over Zionist thinkers; according to Klausner, they exercised a decisive influence upon Judah Leib Pinsker and the writing of his *Autoemancipation*. See Joseph Klausner, *Mi-aplaton ad Spinoza* (Jerusalem, 1955), p. 295; B. Z. Dinur, *Be-mifneh ha-dorot* (Jerusalem, 1972), pp. 252–53.

6. Pines, *Bein maḥshevet Yisrael le-maḥshevet ha-amim*, p. 303; Yirmiyahu

Yovel, *Spinoza and Other Heretics,* vol. 1 (Princeton, 1989); Ze'evi Levi, *Spinoza u-musag ha-yahadut* (Tel Aviv, 1972), pp. 28–29.

7. Yosef Salmon, *Dat ve-Tzionut* (Jerusalem, 1990), pp. 20, 150.

8. S. Z. Landau and Joseph Rabinowitz, eds., *Or la-yesharim* (Warsaw, 1900), p. 55. See also his letter against the Mizrachi convention of 1904, *Tel Talpiyot,* p. 187.

9. David Vital, *The Origins of Zionism* (Oxford, 1970), 1:336.

10. Mendel Piakarz, *Ḥasidut Polin* (Jerusalem, 1990); Yitzhak Alfasi, *Ha-Ḥasidut ve-shivat Tzion* (Tel Aviv, 1986).

11. Schneersohn's letter, in Landau and Rabinowitz, *Or la-yesharim,* pp. 57–61; Shalom Dov Baer Schneersohn, *Ha-ketav veha-mikhtav* (New York, 1917); idem, *Kuntres u-ma'ayan mi-beit ha-shem* (New York, 1943), pp. 46–51; idem, *Iggerot kodesh* (New York, 1982), vol. 1, secs. 122, 130; vol. 2, secs. 336, 459, 490. For additional sources, see Yosef Salmon, "The Stance toward Zionism of Ultra-Orthodox Society in Russia and Poland" (in Hebrew), *Eshel Be'er Sheva* 1 (1976): 393–400. See below, chapter 3.

12. On the prohibition against excessive prayers for the End of Days, see Rashi on BT Ketubbot 111b. Moses Sofer wrote, "But to pray for [the End of Days] every day is an obligation" (*Eleh divrei ha-berit* [Altona, Germany, 1819], p. 42). On the general prohibition against "forcing the End," see below.

13. Schneersohn's letter, p. 57.

14. S. D. B. Schneersohn, *Iggerot kodesh,* vol. 1, secs. 222, 292.

15. S. D. B. Schneersohn, in Landau and Rabinowitz, *Or la-yesharim,* p. 658.

16. S. D. B. Schneersohn, *Iggerot kodesh,* sec. 122.

17. See Maimon ha-Dayan, *Iggeret neḥamah* (Jerusalem, 1945), pp. 43–44. Rabbi Maimon used here an image that is as old as Greek tragedy. See Sophocles, *Antigone,* lines 696–99. This approach to the life of the Galut is widespread in Hasidic literature. See, for example, Elimelech of Lyzhansk, *No'am Elimelekh* (Lvov, 1849), *Va-Yishlaḥ.*

18. See Mekhilta: Bo 7; Judah Löw ben Bezalel of Prague, *Netzaḥ Yisrael* (Jerusalem, 1971), chaps. 47, p. 187.

19. S. D. B. Schneersohn's letter, p. 58. Schneersohn borrows expressions from Midrash Tehillim 36:10, which seeks to deflect religious attention from the personal Messiah to God Himself. See also E. E. Urbach, *The Sages: Their Concepts and Beliefs* (Jerusalem, 1979), pp. 690–91.

20. Schneersohn, *Iggerot kodesh,* vol. 1, secs. 130, 309–10. For the sources of this idea, see, for example, Rashi on BT Sukkah 41a. See also A. Aptovitzer, "The Heavenly Temple according to Aggadah" (in Hebrew), *Tarbiz* 2 (1931): 137–53, 257–87; E. E. Urbach, "Earthly Jerusalem and Heavenly Jerusalem" (in Hebrew), in *Yerushalayim le-doroteha* (Jerusalem, 1969), pp. 156–71.

21. S. D. B. Schneersohn, *Iggerot kodesh,* secs. 130, 309–10.

22. Yitzhak Ya'akov Rabinowitz, *Divrei binah* (Lublin, 1913), p. 27a.

23. A. B. Steinberg, *Da'at ha-rabbanim* (Warsaw, 1902), p. 39.

24. Many sources concerning this question are found in Piakarz's book on Polish Hasidism (*Hasidut Polin*).

25. Ehud Luz, *Parallels Meet: Religion and Nationalism in the Early Zionist Movement, 1882–1904* (Philadelphia, 1988), p. 216.

26. Maimonides, *Epistle to Yemen,* in A. Halkin and D. Hartman, *Crisis and Leadership: Epistles of Maimonides* (Philadelphia, 1985), p. 130.

27. Yeraḥmiel Yeshaya Minzberg, in *Daʿat ha-rabbanim,* pp. 20–23. The influence of the remarks of the Lubavitcher Rebbe is clearly visible here: faith in the utopian redemption pushes aside any possible "restorative" model of redemption; the messianic argument against Zionism stands on its own weight, and is affected neither by pragmatic considerations nor by the external political situation.

28. This radical position is not required by the classical sources. See the appendix.

29. Gershom Scholem, *The Messianic Idea in Judaism and Other Essays on Jewish Spirituality* (New York, 1971), pp. 1–48; E. E. Urbach, *Sages,* pp. 585–623; Yehuda Even-Shmuel, *Midreshei geʾulah* (Jerusalem and Tel Aviv, 1954); A. Z. Escoly, *Ha-tenuah ha-meshiḥit be-Yisrael* (Jerusalem, 1987); R. J. Z. Werblowsky, "Messianism in Jewish History," in H. H. Ben Sasson and S. Ettinger, eds., *Jewish Society through the Ages* (New York, 1969), pp. 30–45. Two relatively recent collections of articles on the subject are *Ha-raʿayon ha-meshiḥi be-Yisrael*(Jerusalem, 1982); Zvi Baras, ed., *Meshiḥiyut ve-eskhatologiah* (Jerusalem, 1984). For a detailed survey of research in this area, see Moshe Idel's introduction to Escoly's work cited here.

30. Hilkhot Melakhim 11:3, 12:1. See my article "'To the Utmost of Human Capacity': Maimonides on the Days of the Messiah," in J. L. Kraemer, ed., *Perspectives on Maimonides: Philosophical and Historical Studies* (Oxford, 1991), pp. 221–56.

31. Abrabanel disagreed explicitly with Maimonides: "[Maimonides] held that in the messianic age nothing in the natural order would change . . . and this is very surprising, since the prophets are unanimous in testifying and saying that in the messianic age the Lord will do great things for His people, and His kindnesses and mighty wonders [shall be] outside the natural order" (*Yeshuot meshiḥo* [Königsberg, 1861], p. 27). See Leo Strauss, *Isaac Abravanel: Six Lectures* (Cambridge, 1937), p. 109; Yizhak Baer, *Meḥkarim u-masot be-toldot am Yisrael* (Jerusalem, 1986), 2:381–97; Shaul Regev, "Messianism and Astrology in the Thought of Isaac Abrabanel" (in Hebrew), *Asufot* 1 (1987): 169–97; Aviezer Ravitzky, "Kings and Laws in Late Medieval Jewish Thought," in L. Landman, ed., *Scholars and Scholarship* (New York, 1990), pp. 88–89. On a Kabbalistic controversy with Abrabanel, see Yeshayahu Tishbi, *Meshiḥiyut be-dor gerush Sefarad u-Portugal* (Jerusalem, 1985), pp. 136–49.

32. Judah Löw, *Netzaḥ Yisrael,* chap. 28, p. 137; chap. 34, p. 156. See Benyamin Gross, *Netzaḥ Yisrael* (Jerusalem and Tel Aviv, 1974), pp. 173–235; Rivka Schatz, "Existence and Eschatology in the Teachings of the Maharal," *Immanuel* 14 (1982): 86–97; 15 (1982/83): 62–72.

33. Cant. R. 6:16; and see JT Berakhot 1:1; Yoma 3:2; *Midrash Shoḥer Tov* 18:51.

34. This question was discussed recently in a lecture by David Berger at the Tenth World Congress of Jewish Studies, Jerusalem, 1989.

35. Eliezer Rivlin, *Ha-Tzaddik Rabbi Yosef Zundel mi-Salant ve-rabotav* (Jerusalem, 1937), p. 18; Yisrael Bartal, "Messianic Expectations and Their Place in Historical Reality" (in Hebrew), *Cathedra* 31 (1984): 167.

36. Mekhilta: *Be-Shallaḥ,* beginning; BT Sanhedrin 92b; Targ. Ps.-Jon. to Exod. 13:17; Ps. 78:9.

37. The sources for the rest of the section are cited in the notes for the appendix.

38. Gershom Scholem, "The Neutralization of the Messianic Element in Early Hasidism," in *Messianic Idea in Judaism,* pp. 176–202; Rivka Schatz, *Hasidism as Mysticism* (Princeton and Jerusalem, 1993), pp. 326–39; Mendel Piakarz, "The Messianic Idea in the Formative Years of Hasidism" (in Hebrew), in *Ha-ra'ayon ha-meshiḥi be-Yisrael,* pp. 237–53. See also Isaiah Tishby, "The Messianic Idea and Messianic Tendencies in Early Hasidism" (in Hebrew), *Zion* 32 (1967): 1–45.

39. Moshe Halamish, "The Theoretical Doctrine of Rabbi Shneur Zalman of Lyady" (in Hebrew), doctoral dissertation, Hebrew University, Jerusalem, 1976; Yoram Jacobson, "Rabbi Shneur Zalman of Lyady's Theory of Creation" (in Hebrew), *Eshel Be'er Sheva* 1 (1976): 307–68; Rachel Elior, *Torat ha-elohut ba-dor ha-sheni shel Ḥasidut Ḥabad* (Jerusalem, 1982), pp. 25–60; idem, "HaBaD: The Contemplative Ascent to God," in A. Green, ed., *Jewish Spirituality,* World Spirituality, 14 (New York, 1987), 2:157–205; Louis Jacobs, *Seeker of Unity* (New York, 1966).

40. Jacob Katz, *Leumiyut Yehudit* (Jerusalem, 1983), pp. 263–365; Shlomo Avineri, *The Making of Modern Zionism: The Intellectual Origins of the Jewish State* (New York, 1981). For our purposes, Kalischer and Alkalai may be discussed together. For some distinctions between them, see Katz, *Leumiyut Yehudit,* pp. 329–31.

41. Aryeh Morgenstern, *Meshiḥiyut ve-yishuv Eretz Yisrael* (Jerusalem, 1985); idem, *Ge'ulah be-derekh ha-teva* (Elkana, 1989); Menahem Mendel Kasher, *Ha-tekufah ha-gedolah* (Jerusalem, 1967), pp. 411–539. The subject is a matter of disagreement among scholars. See Yisrael Bartal, "Messianic Expectations"; idem, "Messianism and Historiography" (in Hebrew), *Zion* 52 (1982): 117–30; Mordecai Eliav, *Eretz Yisrael ve-yishuvah ba-me'ah ha-tesha-esre* (Jerusalem, 1978), p. 85.

42. Judah Alkalai, *Kitvei ha-Rav Yehuda Alkalai* (hereafter *Alkalai*), ed. Yitzhak Werfel (Jerusalem, 1944), p. 529. See Katz, *Leumiyut Yehudit,* pp. 332, 337.

43. Zevi Hirsch Kalischer, *Ha-ketavim ha-Tzioni'im shel ha-Rav Zvi Kalischer* (hereafter *Kalischer*), ed. Y. Klausner (Jerusalem, 1947), p. 258.

44. G. Kretsel, *Rabbi Yehuda Alkalai—Rabbi Zvi Hirsch Kalischer* (Jerusalem, 1943), p. 88.

45. *Kalischer,* p. 38. See also *Alkalai,* p. 600; Rabbi Elijah Guttmacher, in A. J. Slutzki, ed., *Shivat Tzion,* pt. 2 (Warsaw, 1892), p. 40; Rabbi M. L. Malbim, in Nathan Friedlander, *Kol tzofayikh* (Hamburg, 1868), reprinted in H. Merhavya, ed., *Kolot korim le-Tzion* (Jerusalem, 1981), p. 123.

46. See n. 33 above.

47. Shalom Dov Volpe, ed., *Da'at Torah be-inyanei ha-matzav be-eretz ha-kodesh* (Kiryat Gat, 1982).

48. Kretsel, *Alkalai—Kalischer,* p. 88.

49. A. J. Slutzki, ed., *Shivat Tzion,* pt. 2 (Warsaw, 1900), p. 54. According to Rabbi Hazan, "only a few lazy Ashkenazim" opposed the activities of Kalischer's Society for the Settlement of the Land of Israel. See *Kalischer,* p. 232.

50. *Alkalai,* p. 244. See BT Ketubbot 110a.

51. Katz, *Leumiyut Yehudit,* pp. 311, 318.

52. Luz, *Parallels Meet,* pp. 43–44.

53. J. Liver, "The Doctrine of the Two Messiahs," *Harvard Theological Review* 52 (1959): 149–85; Joseph Heinemann, *Aggadot ve-toldotehen* (Jerusalem, 1974), pp. 131 ff.

54. *Alkalai,* pp. 219–22; Katz, *Leumiyut Yehudit,* p. 317. Alkalai's exegetical daring is notable when one considers the fate to which the tradition consigned the Messiah son of Joseph: war and death for the redemption of Israel. See the study by Yehudah Liebes, "Jonah son of Amittai as Messiah ben Joseph" (in Hebrew), *Mehkerei Yerushalayim be-Mahshevet Yisrael* 3 (1984): 269–311, especially pp. 303–6; idem, "The Messiah of the Zohar: On R. Simeon bar Yohai as a Messianic Figure," in *Studies in the Zohar* (Albany, 1993), pp. 63–65.

55. *Kalischer,* p. 37. For a similar change in traditional terminology, see *Kalischer,* p. 118.

56. Jody Myers, "Attitudes towards the Resumption of Sacrificial Worship in the Nineteenth Century," *Modern Judaism* 7 (1987): 35–43.

57. *Kalischer,* p. 49; see also *Alkalai,* pp. 250–53.

58. In contrast to the injunction not to "ascend the wall [*ba-homah*]," Alkalai cited an opposite midrashic proscription: "Had Israel ascended like a wall [*ka-homah*] from Babylonia, the Temple would not have been destroyed a second time" (Cant. R. 8:11; BT Yoma 9b). See *Kitvei ha-Rav Yehuda Alkalai* (Jerusalem, 1975), p. 240. In other words, Jewish existence finds itself in a constant tension between two dangers—on the one hand hastening the End, and on the other missing the hour. Sensitive balance is required to properly decipher the supernal call issued in every generation. Along this line, as against the traditional oath, "not to force [*she-lo yidhaku*] the End," Rabbi Nathan Friedland invoked an alternative reading found in the sources: "that they not push away [*yirhaku*] the hour" (*Kitvei ha-Rav Nathan Friedland* [Jerusalem, 1980], pp. 388, 391, 400, 412). Again, the Jewish norm depends upon a correct balance between activity and passivity—proper listening to the signs of the time—"not to anticipate and not to delay." Of course, at this time the people heard the latter call.

59. *Kitvei ha-Rav Yehuda Alkalai,* pp. 201, 288.

60. Ibid., pp. 202, 240, 302.

61. *Kalischer,* p. 204.

62. *Kitvei ha-Rav Yehuda Alkalai,* p. 240; *Kalischer,* p. 98.

63. *Kalischer,* p. 97.

64. Such as David Hazan, in A. J. Slutzki, *Shivat Tzion,* pt. 2, p. 53; *Kitvei ha-Rav Natan Friedland,* pp. 112, 136, 240, 348, 388, 391, 400, 412.

65. Rabbinic letters from 1891 praising the settlement of the land are published in the collection *Shivat Tzion,* pt. 1. The confrontation with the issue of the "oaths" was reiterated in these letters. For example, Samuel Mohilewer (p. 9); A. M. Lapidot (p. 35); Binyamin Diamant (p. 41); Z. V. Palongian (p. 51); Yosef Yaffe (p. 74); Shmuel Feinberg (p. 84); and see Yitzhak Nissenboim, *Alei heled* (Jerusalem, 1969), p. 160.

66. Yosef Salmon, "Religious Zionism and Its Opponents" (in Hebrew), *Zemanim* (Tammuz 1984): 54–65; Luz, *Parallels Meet,* pp. 47–48.

67. The Agudat Israel journal, *Kol Yisrael* 9 (1927), published a letter from

Rabbi Meir Simhah ha-Kohen of Dvinsk in which he too seeks to distinguish between positive efforts to settle the Land of Israel and the audacity of claiming to be
on "the path toward redemption" and "the end of exile."

68. Naftali Zevi Judah Berlin, *Mara de-ara Yisrael* (Jerusalem, 1974), pp. 15–
16. Berlin's letter from 1891 was first published in this book. The letter (and its
photocopy) seems authentic. I wish to thank Professor Jacob Katz for his confirmation concerning this subject, and Dr. Meir Bar-Ilan for checking the accuracy of the
manuscript. To be sure, Berlin himself speaks elsewhere of a "beginning of redemption" in the settling of the Land of Israel (Salmon, "Religious Zionism and Its Opponents" 54–65, but here he stops short of the presumption of presenting a
systematic doctrine foreseeing the stages of redemption. He also warns against the
severe response Jewish messianic propaganda is likely to elicit from the Gentiles.

69. Isaac Jacob Reines, "Orhot Yisrael," *Beit ha-midrash* 1 (1888): 60–70;
Geulah Bat-Yehudah, *Ish ha-meorot* (Jerusalem, 1985), pp. 50–51.

70. Isaac Jacob Reines, *Sha'arei orah ve-Simhah* (Vilna, 1899), pp. 8, 11–12;
idem, "Galut u-ge'ulah," in *Sefer ha-arakhim* (New York, 1926), p. 21; idem, "Or
Amim," in *Shenei ha-meorot* (Piotrkow, 1913), pt. 1, p. 53.

71. I. J. Reines, *Sefer ha-arakhim*, pp. 75, 284; idem, *Shenei ha-meorot*, pp. 54–
56; Bat-Yehudah, *Ish ha-meorot*, pp. 74, 78; M. T. Nehorai, "On the Essence of
Religious Zionism" (in Hebrew), *Bi-shevilei ha-tehiyah* 3 (1989): 29.

72. I. J. Reines, *Sha'arei orah ve-Simhah*, pp. 12–13; cf. Eliezer Don-Yihya, "Ideology and Policy in Religious Zionism" (in Hebrew), *Ha-Tzionut* 8 (1983): 108.

73. *Ha-Melitz* 78 (1900); *Sefer ha-Tzionut ha-datit* (Jerusalem, 1977), pt. 1,
p. 339.

74. Isaac Jacob Reines, *Or hadash al Tzion* (Vilna, 1902), pp. 30, 48–49, 53, 89,
111, 126–28, 138; Eliezer Schweid, "The Beginnings of National-Zionist Theology: On the Teaching of Rabbi I. J. Reines" (in Hebrew), in *Mehkarim be-Kabbalah
be-filosofiah yehudit . . .* , Tishby Festschrift (Jerusalem, 1986), pp. 689–720.
Some authors erroneously assume that the absence of the messianic element in Reines's characterizations of Zionism implies an absence of any religious element. But
the aforementioned sources show that, far from claiming that "Zionism has nothing to do with religion," Reines maintains that "anyone who connects the Zionist
idea with atheism is to be suspected of blasphemy." See J. L. ha-Cohen Maimon,
Yisrael, Torah, Tzion (Jerusalem, 1989), p. 355.

75. S. Y. Rabinowitz, *Ha-dat veha-leumiyut* (Warsaw, 1900), p. 127; idem,
"Hashkafa le-tova," *Ha-Melitz* 156 (1899); Shmuel Almog, *Zionism and History;
The Rise of a New Jewish Consciousness* (New York and Jerusalem, 1987), p. 63.

76. Yosef Salmon, "The Confrontation between Haredim and Maskilim in the
Hovevei Zion Movement" (in Hebrew), *Ha-Tzionut* 1 (1978): 43–77; idem, "The
Struggle over Orthodox Public Opinion in Eastern Europe" (in Hebrew), in E.
Etkes and Y. Salmon, eds., *Perakim be-toldot ha-hevrah ha-Yehudit*, J. Katz Fest-
schrift (Jerusalem, 1980), pp. 330–68.

77. I. J. Reines, *Or hadash al Tzion*, pp. 14, 111–12, 138–39, 141; Schweid,
"Beginnings of National-Zionist Theology," pp. 711, 720; Don-Yihya, "Ideology
and Policy," pp. 108–16; David Vital, *Zionism: The Formative Years* (Oxford,
1982), pp. 215–24; Joseph Wanefsky, *Rabbi Isaac Jacob Reines: His Life and
Thought* (New York, 1970).

78. Geulah Bat-Yehudah, "Mizrachi and the Question of 'Culture'" (in Hebrew), in *Sefer Shragai* (Jerusalem, 1982), pp. 66–86.

79. Israel Kolat, "Zionism and Messianism" (in Hebrew), in Baras, *Meshiḥiyut ve-eskhatologiah*, pp. 419–24; Shmuel Almog, "Messianism as a Challenge to Zionism" (in Hebrew), in Baras, *Meshiḥiyut ve-eskhatologiah*, pp. 433–36. On messianic tendencies in Zionism generally, see Anita Shapira, "Zionism and Political Messianism" (in Hebrew), in *Temurot ba-historyah ha-Yehudit he-ḥadashah* (Jerusalem, 1989), pp. 149–58; Eliezer Schweid, "Jewish Messianism: Metamorphoses of an Idea," *Jerusalem Quarterly* 36 (1985): 63–78. See also Menahem Brinker, "Brenner's Jewishness" (in Hebrew), *Proceedings of the Israel Academy of Arts and Sciences* 7, no. 8 (1987): 211–28.

80. Joseph Hayyim Brenner, *Ha-poʿel ha-tzaʿir* (Jaffa, 1910).

81. Eliezer Ben-Yehudah, *Yisrael le-artzo ve-lileshono* (Jerusalem, 1929), pt. 1, p. 221; Almog, *Zionism and History,* pp. 58–59.

82. As we have seen, the Zionist rabbis openly criticized "preachers or sermonizers who, while preaching about Zion, might also speak of redemption and the coming of the Messiah." That is, they opposed popularization of the ideas of the Harbingers. Nevertheless, one may note a certain continuity between them and their predecessors. Both schools wished to clear the way for concrete, collective, voluntary action and to free the present from the yoke of passive messianism. Both sides arrived at this via a clear distinction between the historical process and the utopian, messianic goal. However, while Kalischer and Alkalai and their associates made a change in the traditional conception of the Messiah, seeing the historical process as an organic stage in the emergence of redemption, Reines and Rabinowitz and their colleagues clung to the traditional passive view of the Messiah's coming. Hence, the latter group had to separate the historical process completely from the sphere of redemption. In short, they all took an activistic position, "in the spirit of the times" (*Alkalai*), but disagreed concerning the theological question of the nature of redemption and how it was to come about.

83. Charles S. Liebman, *Deceptive Images* (New Brunswick, N.J., and Oxford, 1988), pp. 43–60; idem, "Judaism and the Chaos of Modernity," in J. Neusner, ed., *Take Judaism for Example: Toward the Comparison of Religions* (Chicago, 1983), pp. 143–64; Peter Berger, *The Heretical Imperative* (New York, 1979); P. E. Smith, *Religion and Political Development* (Boston, 1970).

84. Charles S. Liebman and Eliezer Don-Yihya, *Civil Religion in Israel* (Berkeley and Los Angeles, 1983), p. 193.

85. Salmon, "Religious Zionism and Its Opponents," p. 65; Luz, *Parallels Meet,* p. 57; Schweid, "Beginnings of National-Zionist Theology," p. 720.

CHAPTER TWO

1. Baruch Kurzweil, *Masot al Sippurei Agnon* (Jerusalem and Tel Aviv, 1963), pp. 86–94.

2. The Agnon family home in Hamburg burned down in 1924, destroying Agnon's library and manuscripts. He emigrated to the Land of Israel that same year. On the theme of the disaster of fire in a sinful land, see Hillel Barzel, *Bein Agnon le-Kafka* (Ramat Gan, 1973), pp. 44, 112, 301; Agnon, *Ad henah*, p. 141. On the

motif of the house and its biographical background, see Dov Sadan, *Al Shai Agnon* (Tel Aviv, 1967), pp. 105–21.

3. See Moshe Goldstein, ed., *Tikkun olam* (Munkács, 1933), sec. 97, p. 151.

4. The source of this interpretation is to be found in Azariah da Fano, "Hakor din," *Asarah ma'amarot*, 2. 7.

5. Goldstein, *Tikkun olam*, p. 32. See also Hayyim Eleazar Shapira, *Tzava'ah* (Arad, 1937), p. 3; idem, *Hamishah ma'amarot* (Bergsas, 1922), p. 170.

6. Goldstein, *Tikkun olam*, pp. 34–35.

7. Ibid., p. 32. See the correspondence with the Gurer Rebbe, pp. 7–17; and see also Hayyim Eleazar Shapira, *Divrei Torah*, vol. 5, sec. 82.

8. Goldstein, *Tikkun olam*, p. 34, and see p. 146; H. E. Shapira, *Divrei Torah*, vol. 6, sec. 82. The first general convention of the Agudah (1923) and the Gurer Rebbe's visit to Eretz Israel prepared the ground for Haredi agricultural settlement. See also Shapira's remarks about the Gurer Rebbe: "How can I keep silent when I see . . . that he has written there [that it is praiseworthy] to engage in labor and material pursuits in all the trades in Eretz Israel, which is the Zionist way of building the land by human means and contrary to what we have learned [in the holy books]" (*Tikkun olam*, p. 18). See Shapira's speech in Jerusalem (1930), published in Moshe Goldstein, *Sefer mas'ot Yerushalayim* (Munkács, 1931), p. 105.

9. Goldstein, *Tikkun olam*, p. 32. The text was probably undergoing partial editing.

10. Ibid., p. 36. See Rivka Schatz, "The Confrontation of Haredi Literature with Zionism" (in Hebrew), *Nativ* 5 (1989): 48–52. Interestingly enough, in the late 1880s, Rabbi Isaac Jacob Reines, founder of the Mizrachi movement, was already trying to prevent such a conflict of interests. As Reines says, "I saw fit to warn members of the 'Hovevei Zion' group, which supports the settlements in the land, not to neglect—God forbid—the need to contribute to the traditional charities, which distribute money to the old religious community in Palestine. It would be a terrible sin to touch these funds, for we must not deprive food from thousands of our brothers." See Moshe Reines, *Netzah Yisrael* (Cracow, 1890), p. 49.

11. Goldstein, *Tikkun olam*, p. 34. See also Hayyim Eleazar Shapira, *Sha'ar Yissakhar* (Jerusalem, 1968), p. 376; idem, *Kutres yemot ha-mashiah* (Jerusalem, 1970), p. 69.

12. Goldstein, *Tikkun olam*, pp. 6, 34–35. Shapira attacked the Agudah on countless occasions. See, for example, Hayyim Eleazar Shapira, *Divrei ha-iggeret* (Jerusalem, 1932); idem, *Divrei Hayyim ve-shalom* (Munkács, 1940), p. 221; idem, *Sha'ar Yissakhar* 1:123, 125, 2:375, 385, 394, 457; idem, *Hayyim ve-shalom* 1:1, 3, 43, 63, 104, 2:24, 36, 40, 47, 64, 83, 99; idem, *Divrei Torah*, vol. 4 (Munkács, 1930), sec. 17; vol. 9 (Munkács, 1936), sec. 82; idem, *Divrei kodesh* (Jerusalem, 1934), pp. 4–5; idem, *Kuntres yemot ha-mashiah*, p. 69. The Lubavitcher Rebbe, like many other rabbis in Galicia, also opposed Agudat Israel in those days. See Itzhak Alfasi, *Ha-Hasidut ve-shivat Tzion* (Tel Aviv, 1986), pp. 86–89; Mendel Piakarz, *Hasidut Polin* (Jerusalem, 1990), pp. 25–31, 115.

13. B. R. Wilson, *Religious Sects* (New York and Toronto, 1970); idem, "An Analysis of Sect Development," in *Patterns of Sectarianism* (London, 1967), pp. 244–86. Shapira and his followers were the most militant of the ultra-Orthodox. The Lubavitcher school, who held similar views (see below), refrained from

such extreme and strident polemics. At this time their circle included the martyred Rabbi Issahar Shlomo Teichtol, one of whose letters appears in Goldstein, *Tikkun olam*, sec. 80 ("No human action or deed can help in the slightest to cause the horn of Zion and Jerusalem to be raised to the point where the Lord looks down from on high and pours over us a heavenly spirit of purity"). During the Holocaust, in which Rabbi Teichtol perished, he wrote a book, *Em ha-banim semehah* (Budapest, 1943), that reflects a change of heart.

14. See Goldstein, *Tikkun olam*, p. 38; Berish Weinberger, ed., *Iggerot Shapirin* (Brooklyn, 1983), p. 286; Hayyim Eleazar Shapira, *Kuntres divrei kodesh* (Munkács, 1934), p. 13.

15. See also the open letter signed by Hayyim Eleazar Shapira, Joel Moshe Teitelbaum, and others in the 1925 tract *Shimu devar ha-shem*, published in *Ha-kol kol Ya'akov* (Jerusalem, 1980), p. 2; the 1924 tract against the Zionists by Teitelbaum and others, published in Abraham Fuchs, *Ha-admor mi-Satmar* (Jerusalem, 1980), p. 228; Teitelbaum's 1927 broadside against Zionism, published in *Divrei Yo'el* (Brooklyn, 1980), vol. 1, secs. 62–63; and the latter's responsum condemning Agudat Israel, in the tract *Shomer emunim* (Budapest, 1939). The fact that Teitelbaum's views were nurtured in radical circles that even then had broken away from the ultra-Orthodox mainstream contradicts the thesis—put forth, for example, in A. L. Nadler, "Piety and Politics," *Judaism* 31 (1982): 135–52—that his position was in line with then-current ultra-Orthodox rabbinical opinion. On Teitelbaum's biography, see Fuchs, *Ha-admor mi-Satmar*; Aaron Rosmarin, *Der Satmarer Rebbe* (New York, 1967); I. Z. Rubin, *Satmar: An Island in the City* (Chicago, 1972), pp. 34–40.

16. "Yishuv Eretz Yisrael," in Yo'el Moshe Teitelbaum, *Va-Yo'el Moshe* (Jerusalem, 1978), sec. 149; see also sec. 68.

17. Hayyim Eleazar Shapira, *Hayyim ve-shalom* 2:99; idem, *Divrei Torah*, vol. 1 (Bratislava, 1922), sec. 113; vol. 9, sec. 27; idem, *Hamishah ma'amarot*, p. 94; idem, *Olat tamid* (Bratislava, 1922) p. 6; idem, *Sha'ar Yissakhar* 1:120, 2:375; idem, *Kuntres divrei kodesh*, p. 3; Itzhak Adler, ed., *Seder shanah ha-Aharonah* (Munkács, 1937), 1:8.

18. Meir Ben-Baruch of Rothenberg, *She'elot u-teshuvot Maharam* (Berlin, 1891), pp. 14–15; see Hayyim Eleazar Shapira, *Minhat Eleazar* (Bratislava, 1922; reprinted, B'nai Berak, 1968), vol. 5, sec. 16; idem, *Hayyim ve-shalom* 2:61; idem, *Divrei Torah*, vol. 4, sec. 17; vol. 9, secs. 10, 28; Weinberger, *Iggerot Shapirin*, p. 271. Shapira cites Rabbi Meir, who adds, "But whoever goes for the sake of heaven and lives there in holiness and purity shall enjoy unlimited reward, provided he can make a living there." See also E. E. Urbach, *Al Tzionut ve-yahadut: Iyyunim u-masot* (Jerusalem, 1985), p. 151; Elhanan Reiner, "Aliyah and Pilgrimage to the Land of Israel, 1517–1909" (in Hebrew), doctoral dissertation, Hebrew University, Jerusalem, 1988, pp. 100–108. For additional sources, see Eliezer Azkari, *Sefer Haredim* (Venice, 1871), pp. 57–60; Nahmanides, "Sermon for Rosh Ha-shanah" (in Hebrew), in H. D. Chavell, ed., *Kitvei ha-Ramban* (Jerusalem, 1964), p. 250.

19. H. E. Shapira, *Minhat Eleazar*, vol. 5, sec. 16; Goldstein, *Tikkun olam*, p. 134; I. Adler, *Seder shanah ha-Aharonah* 5:79–80; H. E. Shapira, *Sha'ar Yissakhar* 1:239. See below, on the demonology of the land of Israel.

20. Compare H. E. Shapira, *Olat tamid*, p. 7: "Settling the Land of Israel in this period of exile means worshipping in the Holy Land, not engaging in mundane follies, such as agricultural work, industry, artisanship, or socialist labor."

21. Hayyim Eleazar Shapira, *Sha'ar Yissakhar* 2:373; idem, *Ketzat rishumei devarim ve-immerot tehorot*, vol. 1 (Jerusalem, 1931).

22. The Lubavitcher Rebbe, Joseph Isaac Schneersohn, adopted a similar stance in those days. He, too, castigated those who "contaminate the land with all types of material things, stores, workshops, and factories." See Goldstein, *Tikkun olam*, p. 51.

23. Hayyim Eleazar Shapira, *Ḥayyim ve-shalom* 1:42, 70, 77–78, 2:25, 36–37, 41–42, 59, 68, 75; idem, *Ḥamishah ma'amarot*, p. 91; idem, *Sha'ar Yissakhar* 1:244, 291, 2:376; idem, *Divrei Torah*, vol. 4, secs. 8, 11–12; idem, *Ma'amar milei de-hespeda* (Bratislava, 1922), p. 8; idem, *Kuntres yemot ha-mashiaḥ* (Jerusalem, 1970), pp. 14–47.

24. H. E. Shapira, *Ḥayyim ve-shalom* 1:41, 71, 2:58, 88, 98–99; idem, *Sha'ar Yissakhar* 2:375; idem, *Divrei Torah*, vol. 6, sec. 16; vol. 9, sec. 82; idem, *Minḥat Eleazar*, vol. 5, sec. 16; idem, *Kuntres divrei kodesh*, p. 4.

25. H. E. Shapira, *Kuntres divrei kodesh*, p. 6.

26. Jonathan Eybeschütz, *Ahavat Yehonatan* (Warsaw, 1872), p. 74a. See also H. E. Shapira, *Ḥayyim ve-shalom* 2:55; idem, *Minḥat Eleazar*, vol. 5, sec 16; idem, *Divrei ha-iggeret*, p. 5; Weinberger, *Iggerot Shapirin*, p. 272; Goldstein, *Tikkun olam*, p. 136. For a discussion of Rabbi Eybeschütz's words, see Samuel ha-Cohen Weingarten, *Hishba'ti etkhem* (Jerusalem, 1966), pp. 11–12; Aviezer Ravitzky, "'Set Yourselves Landmarks'" (in Hebrew), in *Al da'at ha-makom* (Jerusalem, 1991), pp. 64–69.

27. H. E. Shapira, *Ḥayyim ve-shalom* 1:1, 2:37, 71; idem, *Divrei Torah*, vol. 4, sec. 22; Goldstein, *Tikkun olam*, p. 3; sec. 85, p. 147; and see H. E. Shapira, *Minḥat Eleazar*, vol. 3, secs. 46, 77.

28. H. E. Shapira, *Minḥat Eleazar*, vol. 5, sec. 16; Goldstein, *Tikkun olam*, p. 184. Note the disagreement with Rabbi Avraham of Sochaczew, the author of *Avnei nezer*. In Shapira's view the commandment to settle the land applied to all Jews only during the first Jewish conquest—in the era of Joshua—and therefore Maimonides did not include this obligation in his list of commandments. See also Hayyim Eleazar Shapira, *Ḥayyim ve-shalom* 2:37, 84; idem, *Divrei Torah*, vol. 4, sec. 17; idem, *Ma'amar adon kol* (Munkács, 1936), p. 14.

29. According to Shapira, the commandments that apply specifically to the Land of Israel are, by definition, contingent upon full redemption! See *Ḥayyim ve-shalom* 2:43, 95, 105–6.

30. See Rudolph Otto, *The Idea of the Holy* (Oxford, 1969), pp. 120–40.

31. See Mircea Eliade, *Patterns in Comparative Religion* (New York, 1972), p. 384.

32. This conception is commonplace in Kabbalistic literature. See, for example, Nahmanides' *Commentary on the Torah*, Lev. 18:25; idem, "Sermon for Rosh Hashanah," p. 250; *Sefer ha-Zohar* 1:108b, 3:209a. See also Berakhah Sack, "Land and Land of Israel in the Zohar" (in Hebrew), *Meḥkerei Yerushalayim be-Maḥshevet Yisrael* 8 (1989): 246–48; Tanhuma: Re'eh 88; BT Ta'anit 10a.

33. Hayyim Eleazar Shapira, *Ma'amar zikhron tzaddikim* (Munkács, 1925), p. 7. Compare idem, *Ḥayyim ve-shalom* 1:24.

34. See Haviva Pedaya, "Land of Spirit and Land of Reality" (in Hebrew), in A.

Ravitzky and M. Halamish, eds., *Eretz Yisrael ba-maḥshevet ha-Yehudit be-yemei ha-beinayim* (Jerusalem, 1991), pp. 233–89; Mordecai Pechter, "The Land of Israel in the Homiletic and Ethical Literature of Sixteenth-Century Safed" (in Hebrew), in the same volume, pp. 290–319.

35. I. Adler, *Seder shanah ha-Aḥaronah* 5:80. See H. E. Shapira, *Divrei Torah*, vol. 4, secs. 22, 30; idem, *Ḥamishah ma'amarot*, p. 94. On the Evil Urge's extra powers in the Holy Land, see Yeḥezkel Rabinowitz of Radomsk, *Knesset Yeḥezkel* (Bunden, 1913), p. 52; Piakarz, *Ḥasidut Polin*, p. 72.

36. H. E. Shapira, *Divrei Torah*, vol. 6, sec. 25. The question of the evil forces' control of Eretz Israel is discussed at length in Kabbalistic literature. See, for example, *Sefer ha-Zohar* 1:75b, 2:141a, 3:25b; Moshe Halamish, "On the Valuation of the Land of Israel in Kabbalistic Literature" (in Hebrew), in Ravitsky and Halamish, *Eretz Yisrael ba-maḥshevet ha-Yehudit*, pp. 215–32; Yoram Jacobson, "Rabbi Mordecai Dato's Doctrine of Redemption" (in Hebrew), doctoral dissertation, Hebrew University, Jerusalem, 1982, p. 431.

37. I. Adler, *Seder ha-shanah ha-Aḥaronah* 5:80, and see p. 73; H. E. Shapira, *Ḥayyim ve-shalom* 1:13; idem, *Sha'ar Yissakhar* 2:377. Abraham symbolizes the Divine attribute of *Ḥesed,* which guards the Land of Israel against the forces of defilement. See Menahem Recannati, *Perush al ha-Torah* (Lvov, 1930), *Lekh Lekha,* p. 21d.

38. H. E. Shapira, *Divrei Torah*, vol. 6, sec. 25; Goldstein, *Tikkun olam,* sec. 97, pp. 153–54. Shapira incorporated within his sermon quotations from Azariah da Fano's *Asarah ma'amarot* and from Ya'akov Shealtiel Ninio's *Emet le-Ya'akov* (Livorno, 1853), p. 100. For da Fano's passive ideology and his objection to emigration, see Shalom Rosenberg, "Exile and Redemption in Jewish Thought in the Sixteenth Century: Contending Conceptions," in B. D. Cooperman, ed., *Jewish Thought in the Sixteenth Century* (Cambridge, Mass., 1983), pp. 419–21.

39. I. Adler, *Seder shanah ha-Aḥaronah* 5:80. See also H. E. Shapira, *Ketzat rishumei devarim ve-immerot teḥorot,* p. 2.

40. H. E. Shapira, *Divrei Torah*, vol. 6, sec. 25; Weinberger, *Iggerot Shapirin,* pp. 236–38; Goldstein, *Tikkun olam,* pp. 147, 152. See also H. E. Shapira, *Ḥayyim ve-shalom* 1:7, 53, 2:56, 104; idem, *Divrei Torah,* vol. 4, sec. 65; Moshe Goldstein, *Mas'ot Yerushalayim* (Munkács, 1931), pp. 134, 238–40, 247.

41. Weinberger, *Iggerot Shapirin,* p. 237.

42. I. Adler, *Seder shanah ha-Aḥaronah* 5:80.

43. H. E. Shapira, *Divrei Torah,* vol. 5, sec. 24. See also idem, *Ḥayyim ve-shalom* 2:88, 89.

44. I hope to deal elsewhere with the fear of the Land of Israel in Jewish literature, and to distinguish this motif from the attempts to neutralize and spiritualize the land.

45. Teitelbaum, "Yishuv Eretz Yisrael," secs. 149, 68.

46. For a sociological perspective on this subject, see Menachem Friedman, *Ḥevrah ve-dat* (Jerusalem, 1978). On zealotry, see Friedman, *Ḥevrah ve-dat,* pp. 19–22; Yehoshua Kaniel, *Hemshekh u-temurah* (Jerusalem, 1982), pp. 190–210; Netanel Katzburg, "The Spiritual Polemic in the Jewish World and in the Yishuv in Jerusalem during the Nineteenth Century" (in Hebrew), in *Yerushalayim: Mi-shivat Tzion ad le-yetzi'ah min ha-ḥomot* (Jerusalem, 1980), pp. 168–

72; Menachem Friedman, "Religious Zealotry in Israeli Society," in *On Ethnic and Religious Diversity in Israel* (Ramat Gan, 1975), pp. 99–111; Charles S. Liebman, "Extremism as a Religious Norm" *Journal of the Scientific Study of Religion* 20 (1983): 75 ff. On changes in the Jerusalem Jewish community, see Shmuel Ravitzky, "On the History of the Jewish Yishuv in Jerusalem" (in Hebrew), *Ma'asaf Yavneh* 1 (1939): 154–72; O. Schmelz, "The Development of the Jewish Population of Jerusalem during the Past Hundred Years," *Jewish Journal of Sociology* 2 (1960): 57–73. On typical defenses against secularization and change, see Eric Vogelin, *The New Science of Politics* (Chicago, 1952), p. 122.

47. M. Friedman, *Ḥevrah ve-dat*, pp. 134–35, 141, 345. In a handbill issued in the fall of 1933, the city's ultra-Orthodox people were asked to sign a manifesto in support of Teitelbaum (Fuchs, *Ha-admor mi-Satmar*, p. 154).

48. In recent years, since the Satmarer Rebbe's death, disputes have erupted within these circles.

49. The language is that of Moshe Goldstein, a Munkaczer Hasid, in his *Ma'amar ḥayut esh* (Munkács, 1931). A Jerusalem handbill (1933) condemning the excitement in Agudat Israel over the Balfour Declaration bears the stamp of Margolis's thinking. And indeed, in *Tikkun olam*, edited by the same Goldstein, these words are attributed to "God-fearing people, the leaders of the zealots in the cause of the Lord of Hosts and His Torah" (p. 85).

50. See Yehudah Liebes, "The Ultra-Orthodox Congregation in Jerusalem and the Judean Desert Sect" (in Hebrew), *Meḥkerei Yerushalayim be-Maḥshevet Yisrael* 1 (1982): 137–52.

51. See Weinberger, *Iggerot Shapirin*, p. 264; Goldstein, *Mas'aot Yerushalayim*, pp. 27–31, 319; Yeshayahu Margolis, *Amudei arazim* (Jerusalem, 1932), pp. 30, 53, 64. Margolis also wrote a commentary on *Be'er la-hai roi*, by Rabbi Ze'ev Hirsch Shapira of Munkács, the father of Hayyim Eleazar Shapira. For a discussion of Margolis's relation to Shapira, see Weinberger, *Iggerot Shapirin*, pp. 234, 238, 262–64.

52. See also the reproduction of a letter from Teitelbaum to Margolis included in *Sefer midot Rashbi* (Meron, 1979).

53. See Joel Teitelbaum, *Divrei Yo'el*, vol. 1, sec. 88. The discussion there of the question of the elections was afterward expanded into the main body of Teitelbaum's *Va-Yo'el Moshe*. See the introduction to the 1978 Jerusalem edition, vol. 2; and *Mishmeret Ḥomatenu* 11, no. 41 (1959): 323.

54. See the beginning of Margolis's *Biur ha-shir "Bar Yohai"* (Meron, 1974).

55. Margolis, *Amudei arazim*, pp. 38–47.

56. Ibid., pp. 31, 35. Dozens of pages are devoted to demonstrating the halakhic and Kabbalistic importance of the various details of dress customary in the author's circle. See also Yeshayahu Margolis, *Ashrei ha-ish* (Jerusalem, 1925), p. 71. Compare with the words of the rabbi of Ringnow, quoted by H. E. Shapira in *Kuntres yemot ha-mashiaḥ*, p. 70.

57. Yeshayahu Margolis, *Kumi ori* (Jerusalem, 1925), p. 24, cited in M. Friedman, *Ḥevrah ve-dat*, p. 135; Yeshayahu Margolis, *Kumi roni* (Jerusalem, 1925), p. 44; idem, *Ashrei ha-ish*, p. 34.

58. Margolis, *Ashrei ha-ish*, p. 10. The author also suggests classical sources for these ideas.

59. Ibid., pp. 61–64. Numerous examples are found throughout the book, for example, pp. 5, 24, 32, 69, 75. See also Margolis, *Kumi roni,* pp. 44–45 and elsewhere.

60. Margolis, *Ashrei ha-ish,* p. 65.

61. Ibid., pp. 23–25.

62. Compare with H. E. Shapira's remarks in *Ḥayyim ve-shalom* 2:26; idem, *Divrei Torah,* vol. 9, sec. 10; idem, *Kuntres yemot ha-mashiah,* p. 43.

63. Margolis, *Kumi roni,* p. 39.

64. Margolis, *Ashrei ha-ish,* p. 25; idem, *Ma'amarei Rabbi Eleazar,* p. 22.

65. Yehudah Liebes, "The Messiah of the Zohar: On R. Simeon bar Yohai as a Messianic Figure," in *Studies in the Zohar* (Albany, 1993), p. 143. See also idem, "The Messianism of Rabbi Jacob Emden and His Relation to Sabbateanism" (in Hebrew), *Tarbitz* 49 (1980): 125.

66. Margolis, *Amudei arazim,* p. 6. The question of messianism and Zionism is treated at length in idem, *Kumi roni,* pp. 38–41; idem, *Ashrei ha-ish,* pp. 41–50; and throughout *Kumi ori.*

67. Margolis, *Ashrei ha-ish,* p. 56 (the book lambasts Rabbi Kook); Margolis, *Amudei arazim,* p. 5. See Liebes, "Ultra-Orthodox Congregation," p. 148; Rivka Schatz, "The Beginnings of the Campaign against Rav Kook" (in Hebrew), *Molad,* n.s., 6, no. 29 (1974): 251–62.

68. See Abraham Isaac Kook, *Hazon ha-ge'ulah* (New York, 1974), p. 195.

69. See I. Gruenwald, *Li-felagot Yisrael be-Hungariyah* (New York, 1929); Michael Silver, "The Sources of the Split in Hungarian Jewry" (in Hebrew), doctoral dissertation, Hebrew University, Jerusalem, 1985; Moshe Samet, "The Beginnings of Orthodoxy," *Modern Judaism* 8 (1988): 258–63; Netanel Katzburg, "The Jewish Congress in Hungary," in R. L. Braham, ed., *Hungarian Jewish Studies* (New York, 1969), 2:1–35.

70. Rabbi Solomon Eliezer Alfandari, a halakhic and Kabbalistic sage, taught in Turkey, Safed, and Jerusalem. Margolis was influenced by him (Margolis, *Ashrei ha-ish,* pp. 14, 35, 38; idem, *Amudei arazim,* pp. 37, 68), received his imprimatur for the book *Kumi roni* (most of his books were written after Alfandari's death), and tried to publish some of his halakhic responsa (*Mas'ot Yerushalayim,* p. 321). He complained that "strangers have trespassed upon [Alfandari's] patrimony, plundering his holy writings and the treasures of his teachings" (*Amudei arazim,* p. 53). On Alfandari, see A. Ben-Ya'akov, "Rabbi Shlomo Eliezer Alfandari" (in Hebrew), *Hed ha-Mizrah* 4, no. 6 (1945): 7; Pinhas Grayevsky, *Mi-Ginzei Yerushalayim* 19 (1931); Meir Benayahu, introduction to Raphael Bitran, *Middot tovot* (Jerusalem, 1988); Goldstein, *Ma'amar hayut esh.* See also Yitzhak Nissim, ed., *She'elot u-teshuvot Maharsha* (Jerusalem, 1932), pt. 1; D. Y. Weiss, ed., *She'elot u-teshuvot Saba Kadisha* (Jerusalem, 1973–74). On the nature of the Weiss edition, see Benayahu's introduction to *Middot tovot.*

71. Goldstein, *Mas'ot Yerushalayim,* p. 308. See the remarks attributed to Alfandari criticizing rabbis who "flatter the wicked" (p. 302) and praising the Munkaczer Rebbe for knowing how to "tell the House of Jacob its iniquities" (p. 313). See also his letter concerning the Chief Rabbinate (p. 308): "Rav Kook, may God preserve and protect him, must disavow the things he has written in his pamphlets, things which are not in accordance with the Torah, for this is the cause

of the bitterness against him on the part of the God-fearing, because it is against our holy Torah, as I have shown clearly in a pamphlet especially devoted to this subject." (However harsh his criticism, Alfandari's style is far more moderate than that of Margolis's calumnies.) See also his responsum concerning prayer in the company of sinners: "Now, in these latter days, we are not dealing with Jewish transgressors [in general], but with emissaries and witnesses [of the Evil Urge], and [the latter] seek only to overwhelm the God-fearing, using tokens of purity that make it [appear to be] the will of God." There can be little doubt that the objects of this attack are the religious Zionists, an observation relevant to Joseph Tubi, "The Roots of the Attitude of Oriental Jewry to the Zionist Movement" (in Hebrew), in *Temurot ba-historyah ha-Yehudit ha-hadashah* (Jerusalem, 1988), pp. 169–92, especially pp. 189–92.

72. See Weinberger, *Iggerot Shapirin*, p. 264; Goldstein, *Mas'ot Yerushalayim*, pp. 27–31; Solomon Eliezer Alfandari, "Teshuvah me-ahavah," in H. Y. D. Azulai, *Ein zokher* (Jerusalem, 1962).

73. Weinberger, *Iggerot Shapirin*, p. 262; and see Goldstein, *Mas'ot Yerusha-layim*, p. 20.

74. Goldstein, *Mas'ot Yerushalayim*, p. 121. Shapira's "Jerusalem journeys" of the year 1930, described in the book of this title, revolved around the charismatic personality of Alfandari. It was on the basis of the latter's explicit invitation and blessing that he made the trip, and he described his meeting with Alfandari as the journey's high point (Goldstein, *Mas'ot Yerushalayim*, p. 20). See also p. 24, on Alfandari as the leading saint of his generation. Haim Be'er has portrayed the episode in literary form in *Et ha-zamir* (Tel Aviv, 1987), pp. 200–25.

75. Goldstein, *Mas'ot Yerushalayim*, p. 121.

76. Ibid.

77. Ibid., p. 240.

78. H. E. Shapira, *Kuntres yemot ha-mashiah*, p. 33. Shapira goes on to say that Rabbi Menahem Mendel recovered immediately upon returning home.

79. Shapira later compared the thirteen days he spent in the Land of Israel to the thirteen years that—according to tradition—Rabbi Simeon bar Yohai spent in a cave (Goldstein, *Tikkun olam*, p. 152). He also cited halakhic reasons for his decision to leave the Land of Israel before the festival of Shavuot, "and also for secret reasons I did not remain in Israel during the festival" (Goldstein, *Mas'ot Yerusha-layim*, p. 365).

80. *Mas'ot Yerushalayim*, p. 358.

81. Ibid.

82. See Pinhas Miller, *Olamo shel abba* (Jerusalem, 1984), p. 228.

83. On contemporary Satmar Hasidism, see S. Poll, *The Hasidic Community of Williamsburg* (New York, 1962); Rubin, *Satmar;* Harry Gresh and Sam Miller, "Satmar in Brooklyn: A Zealot Community," *Commentary* 28 (1959): 389–99.

84. For appreciations of Teitelbaum and examples of his influence, see, for example, Raphael Reuven Grozovsky (onetime head of the Council of Torah Sages in the United States), *Ba'ayot ha-zeman* (B'nai Berak, 1960), p. 36; Binyamin Mendelssohn (rabbi of Komemiyyut), *Kuntres iggerot ha-RaB* (Komemiyyut, 1973), pp. 42–43; Moshe Sheinfeld, *Niv ha-moreh* (Tishri 5735 [1974]; *Hash-kafatenu* (B'nai Berak, 1978), pt. 1 (unpaginated); and *Kuntres mesit u-meidiah*

published by the Braslaver Hasidim (Jerusalem, 1987), p. 9. See also the eulogy by Rabbi Eliezer Menahem Schach in *Mikhtavim u-ma'amarim* (B'nai Berak, 1980), and eulogies and articles about Teitelbaum in *Sheki'at ha-ḥamah* (New York, 1980). More reserved assessments and outright attacks are even more numerous. See, for example, the Agudat Israel pamphlet *Lehasir masveh* (Jerusalem, 1951); S. Zalman Abramov, *Perpetual Dilemma* (Rutherford, N.J., 1976), p. 157.

85. See Lam. Rab., *Petiḥta* 2 (Buber ed., p. 2). As early as the turn of the century, the Jerusalem extremists were referred to tauntingly as Neturei Karta; see *Ha-Tzevi* 7 (1887); *Ha-Or* 11 (1893); Kaniel, *Hemshekh u-temurah*, p. 192. On the other hand, the Agudat Israel leader Rabbi Elhanan Bunem Wasserman also used this Talmudic passage to criticize the Zionists; see *Kovetz ma'amarim* (Tel Aviv, 1963), p. 130. See also the essay on the settlement of Eretz Israel in Teitelbaum, *Va-Yo'el Moshe*, sec. 125.

86. Amram Blau, *Torat Rabbi Amram* (Jerusalem, 1977), p. 20. See his remarks at the outbreak of the War of Independence (p. 17): "Their defamation and conniving against our holy Torah have placed the whole Jewish population in mortal danger, one percent against ninety-nine, plunging the surviving remnant of the people of Israel in the Holy Land into a war against powerful forces both within and without . . . We shall not be drawn into exposing ourselves, our wives, and our children to them, heaven forfend, to die for the sake of the Zionist idolatry. It is inconceivable that wicked, unbelieving, ignorant, utterly irresponsible heretics should come along and drag the entire population, several hundred thousand Jews, like sheep to the slaughter, God forbid, because of their false, insane ideas, and that the entire population, like an innocent dove, should allow them to lead it away to be killed, God forbid." On this question, see Yo'el Teitelbaum, *Al ha-ge'ulah ve-al ha-temurah* (Brooklyn, 1967), p. 85; idem, *Divrei Yo'el* (Brooklyn, 1980), p. 87.

87. See Teitelbaum, "Essay on the Three Oaths," in *Va-Yo'el Moshe*, secs. 10–25, 45, 75–78; idem, essay on the settlement of Eretz Israel, in *Va-Yo'el Moshe*, sec. 109; A. Y. Epstein, "Divrei Hesped," in *Sheki'at ha-ḥamah*, p. 196; Yerahmiel Domb, *Kuntres et nisayon* (Jerusalem, 1972), pp. 4–11; idem, *Kuntres al ha-nissim* (Jerusalem, 1957), pp. 44, 52; idem, *Lo nitzahon* (London, n.d.), pp. 7–8; idem, *The Transformation: The Case of the Neturei Karta* (London, 1958), pp. 1–14. See Uriel Tal, "Jewish Self-Understanding and the Land and the State of Israel," *Union Theological Quarterly* 26, no. 4 (1971): 57.

88. Teitelbaum, "Essay on the Three Oaths," sec. 76.

89. Domb, *Kuntres et nisayon*, preface.

90. See E. E. Urbach, *Al Tzionut ve-yahadut*, p. 352; Norman Lamm, "The Ideology of the Neturei Karta according to the Satmar Version," *Tradition* 13 (1971): 39–53.

91. Teitelbaum, "Essay on the Three Oaths," sec. 81; see also sec. 78: "The oath not to try to win their own redemption is much more severe than the adjuration made at the giving of the Torah!" For Maimonides' view, see secs. 31–36, 78, 80–81. Teitelbaum follows the version of the story given in the Babylonian Talmud, according to which Bar Kokhba was killed by Jewish sages, whereas Maimonides takes the view of the Palestinian Talmud, that it was the Romans who killed him ("Essay on the Three Oaths," secs. 39, 52). See also A. Ravitzky, "'To the Utmost of Human Capacity': Maimonides on the Days of the Messiah," in J. L. Kraemer, ed.,

Perspectives on Maimonides: Philosophical and Historical Studies (Oxford, 1991), pp. 221–30.

92. Teitelbaum, "Essay on the Three Oaths," sec. 81. Teitelbaum bases himself here on Rabbi Judah Löw, "the Maharal," of Prague. See also Menahem Mendel Kasher's critique in *Ha-tekufah ha-gedolah* (Jerusalem, 1967), pp. 272–81; Rivka Schatz, "Existence and Eschatology in the Teachings of the Maharal," *Immanuel* 14 (1982): 90–91; A. D. Kulka, "The Historical Background of the National Doctrine of the Maharal of Prague" (in Hebrew), *Zion* 50 (1985): 282.

93. Teitelbaum, preface to *Va-Yo'el Moshe*, p. 6.

94. Teitelbaum, "Essay on the Three Oaths, sec. 139. See preface to *Va-Yo'el Moshe*, p. 6.

95. See Irving Greenberg, "The Third Great Cycle of Jewish History," in *Perspectives* (New York, l981), pp. 14–42; idem, "Cloud of Smoke, Pillar of Fire," in E. Fleischer, ed., *Auschwitz: Beginning of a New Era* (New York, 1977), pp. 5–77; Irving Greenberg, "Voluntary Covenant," in *Perspectives* (New York, 1982), pp. 1–36. See also André Neher, *The Exile of the Word* (Philadelphia, 1981).

96. Among recent publications, see Emil Fackenheim, *To Mend the World* (New York, 1982), p. 10; idem, "Holocaust," in A. A. Cohen and P. Mendes-Flohr, eds., *Contemporary Jewish Religious Thought* (New York, 1987), pp. 399–408; Michael Wyschograd, "Faith and the Holocaust," *Judaism* 20 (1971): 286–94; Jacob Neusner, *Stranger at Home* (Chicago, 1981), pp. 65–81.

97. Teitelbaum, preface to *Va-Yo'el Moshe*, pp. 5–7.

98. As early as 1940 (!), the Neturei Karta published a proclamation pinning responsibility for the Nazi persecution of the Jews on Zionism. Such accusations multiplied after the Holocaust. "Everything is to be blamed," wrote one polemicist, "on the heretical, rebellious, seductive, and corrupting Zionist leadership, which held sway over the congregation of Israel and [induced it] to rebel against the [true] King, the King of the Universe, and His rule over the Holy Land and the holy city of Jerusalem" (*Ha-Ḥomah*, Shevat 5706 [1946]). The adjurations too were invoked in this context as early as the 1940s. For example, see Amram Blau, "On the Idol of Nationalism" (in Hebrew), in *Om ani homah* (Jerusalem, 1949), pp. 50–52; Yitzhak Ashkenazi, "'Do Not Rebel against the Nations'" (in Hebrew), in *Om ani homah*, p. 164.

99. See Amos Funkenstein, "Passivity as the Sin of Galut Jewry" (in Hebrew), in *Tadmit u-te'udah historit* (Tel Aviv, 1991), pp. 232–42.

100. There were rabbis sympathetic to Zionism who interpreted the text to opposite effect: the oaths, they said, are interrelated; now that the Gentiles have violated theirs, we are exempt from ours. In this view, the Diaspora survives because of a balance between Jewish passivity and the restraint of the Gentiles, however much the latter may subjugate and persecute the Jews. Another argument has it that the consent of the Gentiles in recent times (Balfour, the United Nations) has relieved the Jews of the fear of violating their oath not to rebel against alien rule. See also the critique of Teitelbaum in Abraham Weiss, *Ha-Maḥaneh ha-Ḥaredi* (organ of the Belzer Hasidim), 4 Elul 5748 (1988), among others.

101. "The Neturei Karta of Haredi Jewry" (in Hebrew), in *Lehasir masveh*, p. 3.

102. See Elyakum Schlesinger, "Hesped," in *Sheki'at ha-hamah*, p. 171. See also Epstein, "Divrei Hesped," p. 196; Teitelbaum, *Divrei Yo'el* 1:85, 108, 125; A. Blau,

Torat Rabbi Amram, sec. 6; A. Z. Partigol (the Skolener Rebbe), open letter to the Council of Torah Sages, published in the pamphlet *Shim'u devar ha-shem,* in *Ha-kol kol Ya'akov* (Jerusalem, 1964), pp. 30–34.

103. As explained earlier, such spiritual forebears of today's radicals as Hayyim Eleazar Shapira were already battling the Agudists of their own day. But it is not surprising that present-day radicals should place emphasis on the recent deviation of Agudat Israel from the teachings of its own forebears.

104. Eliahu Porush, "The Wood and the Iron of the Pharisee State" (in Hebrew), in A. Blau, *Torat Rabbi Amram,* p. 26.

105. A. Blau, *Torat Rabbi Amram,* sec. 6.

106. Yerahmiel Domb, *Ha-Ḥomah* 25 (1975): 94–95; idem, *Kuntres et nisayon,* p. 4 (emphasis in original). See also the supplement to *Mishmeret ḥomatenu* (Jerusalem, 1966).

107. Teitelbaum, preface to *Va-Yo'el Moshe,* p. 7.

108. Ibid., p. 13.

109. Teitelbaum, "Essay on the Three Oaths," secs. 77, 85. See the declaration of the Hitahdut ha-Rabbanim of the United States and Canada (an organization of Satmar rabbis) in *Shim'u devar ha-shem,* p. 37. A similar position had been taken earlier (1948) in a Neturei Karta handbill entitled *"Lifkoah einayim."*

110. *Lehasir masveh,* p. 12; Domb, *Kuntres et nisayon,* p. 142.

111. Domb, *Transformation,* p. 288.

112. Shimon Israel Posen, *Torat elokim* (Brooklyn, 1966), vol. 1, letter 19. On the author, see Abraham Fuchs, *Yeshivot Hungariyah bi-gedulatan uve-hurbanan* (Jerusalem, 1987), pp. 183–87.

113. Teitelbaum, *Divrei Yo'el* 1:113.

114. Yeshayahu Binyamin Holzer, *Yelamed da'at* (New York, 1984), p. 500; a proclamation by a group of rabbis, in the volume *Milḥamot ha-shem* (Brooklyn, 1983), p. 110; A. Blau, *Torat Rabbi Amram,* sec. 3.

115. Holzer, *Yelamed da'at,* p. 15. The book in its entirety is a polemic against the Lubavitcher Hasidic movement and its efforts to attract people to religion.

116. Paradoxically, a parallel demonological explanation for the Zionist success has been expressed recently by Muslim writers. See Hillel Fradkin, "The Roots of Islamic Fundamentalism," in R. Kozodoy et al., eds., *Vision Confronts Reality* (London and Toronto, 1988), p. 258: "What else but the fact that demons are free in the world—or even Satan himself—could explain the present success of the Jewish people . . . This view has found some expression in the statements of Khomeini, among others"!

117. Eulogy of the Satmarer Rebbe, published by Yeshivat Torah Veyirah (1979); Hayyim Katzenellenbogen, in *Sheki'at ha-ḥamah,* p. 194.

118. L. Festinger, *A Theory of Cognitive Dissonance* (Stanford, 1957); idem, *When Prophecy Fails* (Minneapolis, 1956). Chapter 3 will deal with an analogous phenomenon manifested among the "redemptionist" Zionists in the wake of Israel's withdrawal from Sinai and its evacuation of the settlements there.

119. See Katzenellenbogen, in *Sheki'at ha-ḥamah,* p. 194.

120. Teitelbaum, *Al ha-ge'ulah,* pp. 7–9. See the remarks of Richard Niebuhr, on people who could have been expected to be "terribly unsure" but turned out in fact to be "doubly sure," in Willard B. Gatewood, Jr., *Controversy in the Twenties:*

Fundamentalism, Modernism, & Evolution (Nashville, Tenn., 1969), p. 46. See Janet O'Dea, "Gush Emunim: Roots and Ambiguities," *Forum* 25 (1976): 47.

121. Teitelbaum, *Al ha-ge'ulah,* 20.

122. Y. L. Frank and M. Weiss, eds., preface to A. Blau, *Torat Rabbi Amram.*

123. Emanuel Sivan, *Kana'ei ha-Islam* (Tel Aviv, 1986), pp. 92–124.

124. Domb, *Kuntres al ha-nissim,* pp. 51–52.

125. Domb, *Lo nitzahon,* p. 12; idem, *Kuntres et nisayon,* p. 254; I. M. Dushinsky, *Der Id* (1980), issue for Parashat Emor.

126. Yo'el Moshe Teitelbaum, *Ḥiddushei Torah* (Brooklyn, 1960), chapter on the Torah portion *Va-Yishlah,* mentioned in the pamphlet *Dibrot kodesh,* included in *Ha-kol kol Ya'akov,* p. 14; idem, "Essay on the Three Oaths," secs. 158, 175; Domb, *Transformation,* pp. 68, 115, 120.

127. Teitelbaum, *Al ha-ge'ulah,* p. 133. For extreme deterministic formulations, see Domb, *Transformation,* pp. 126, 142, 148, quoted in my article "The Anticipated and the Permission Given" (in Hebrew), in A. Hareven, ed., *Yisrael likrat ha-me'ah ha-esrim ve-ahat* (Jerusalem, 1984), p. 140.

128. A handbill published by the rabbinical court of the Edah Haredit, chaired by Rabbi Y. Y. Weiss, on the eve of Independence Day 1980, states, "Dread the day of judgment and the day of reproof, for bitter and grievous will be the upshot of this great breach of faith and this rebellion against the rule of heaven, God forbid."

129. *Der Id,* 9 Iyyar 5744 (1984), cited in a lecture by Menahem Friedman. See also his remarks in an interview by N. Golan in *Ha-Tzofeh,* 26 Tishri 5749 (1989).

130. Teitelbaum, *Va-Yo'el Moshe,* p. 8.

131. Teitelbaum, *Al ha-ge'ulah,* p. 13.

CHAPTER THREE

1. Yosef Bramson, ed., *Ba-ma'arakhah ha-tzibburit,* ed. Y. Bramson (Jerusalem, 1986), pp. 24–25.

2. Furthermore, there are those who reinterpret the wording of the oaths in an attempt to find therein an activist call to *aliyah!* See Mordecai Attia, *Sod ha-shevu'ah* (Jerusalem, 1965), pp. 22–24; Mordecai-Gimpel Jaffe, "We Shall Raise the Banner in the Name of Our God" (in Hebrew), in E. I. Slutzki, ed., *Shivat Zion,* pt. 2 (Warsaw, 1900), p. 15; Yitzhak Nissenboim, *Masoret ve-herut* (Warsaw, 1939), p. 121.

3. Yosef Bramson, *Yemot olam: Ha-ketz ha-dohek* (Jerusalem, 1980), p. 7; and see Bernard M. Casper, "Reshit Zemichat Geulatenu" (in English), in S. Spero, ed., *Religious Zionism* (Jerusalem, 1989), p. 71; Shaul Y. I. Taub of Modzitz, *Imrei Shaul* (Tel Aviv, 1980), p. 187.

4. Zvi Yehudah Kook, *Le-netivot Yisrael* (Jerusalem, 1967), 1:56.

5. Ibid., p. 188.

6. Zvi Yehudah Kook, "Clarifications" (in Hebrew), *Amudim* 369 (1976): 380.

7. Z. Y. Kook, *Le-netivot Yisrael* 1:193–94.

8. Shlomo Aviner, *Am ke-lavi* (Jerusalem, 1983), 2:192–94; Uriel Tal, *Mithos u-tevunah be-yahadut yamenu* (Tel Aviv, 1987), p. 102.

9. The idea had already originated in *Sefer ha-Zohar.* See Yehudah Liebes, "The Messiah of the Zohar: On R. Simeon bar Yohai as a Messianic Figure," in *Studies in*

the Zohar (Albany, 1993), pp. 1–84. On the approach of Lurianic Kabbalah, see Gershom Scholem, "The Messianic Idea in Kabbalism," in *The Messianic Idea in Judaism and Other Essays* (New York, 1971), pp. 43–48; idem, *Sabbatai Sevi: The Mystical Messiah, 1626–1676* (Princeton, 1973), pp. 44–66; Isaiah Tishby, *Torat ha-ra veha-kelipah be-Kabbalat ha-Ar"i* (Jerusalem, 1965), p. 143. But see also Ronit Meroz, "Redemption in the Doctrine of Rabbi Isaac Luria" (in Hebrew), doctoral dissertation, Hebrew University, Jerusalem, 1982, pp. 255–360; Yehudah Liebes, " 'Trein urzilin de-ayalta' " (in Hebrew), in *Kabbalat ha-Ar'i*, a special issue of *Meḥkerei Yerushalayim be-Maḥshevet Yisrael* (10 [1992]), pp. 113–69.

10. Meir Ibn-Gabbai, *Avodat ha-kodesh* (Venice, 1566), "Ḥelek ha-Avodah," p. 37. In his own way, Rabbi Isaac Abrabanel also made the redemption dependent on the merit of the people, and not necessarily on the Messiah and his merit. See the introduction to his *Yeshuot meshiḥo* (Königsberg, 1861); and see Rivka Schatz, "Facets of the Political-Messianic Awakening following the Expulsion from Spain" (in Hebrew), *Da'at* 11 (1983): 60–61.

11. *Ha-Tzofeh*, 26 January 1975, quoted in Gideon Aran, "From Religious Zionism to a Zionist Religion: The Roots of Gush Emunim and Its Culture" (in Hebrew), doctoral dissertation, Hebrew University, Jerusalem, 1987, p. 445 (hereafter cited as "Religious Zionism"). See Abraham Isaac Kook, *Iggerot ha-Reiyah* (Jerusalem, 1962), 1:177; idem, *Orot* (Jerusalem, 1963), p. 73: "Now the End has already awoken, the third coming has begun."

12. Zvi Yehudah Kook, *Le-hilkhot tzibbur* (Jerusalem, 1987), pp. 244, 246; and see idem, *Le-netivot Yisrael* 2:157–58; interview with Kook in the periodical *Eretz-Yisrael*, Kislev 5735 (1974/75).

13. A. I. Kook, *Orot*, p. 160; and see the introduction above. On the issue of identification with the concrete State of Israel, see *Ma'or* 1 (1984): 35.

14. See Charles S. Liebman and Eliezer Don-Yehiya, *Civil Religion in Israel* (Berkeley and Los Angeles, 1983), p. 198; Eliezer Don-Yehiya, "Jewish Messianism, Religious Zionism, and Israeli Politics: The Impact and Origin of Gush Emunim," *Middle Eastern Studies* 23 (April 1987): 226. See also Isaiah Berlin, *Four Essays on Liberty* (Oxford, 1969), pp. 112, 132.

15. Hayyim Druckman, "Our Teacher" (in Hebrew), in *Rabbenu ztz"l* (Jerusalem, 1982), p. 47. He states there: "One may also understand Rav Zvi Yehuda's unique attitude toward the IDF in terms of that selfsame relationship to the state. As his late father put it: 'The armies of Israel are the Armies of God.' [Rav Zvi Yehudah] carried things to the extent that he saw even in the tanks of the IDF, its cannons and planes, objects of mitzvah and of holiness, as they served the commandment of settling the Land of Israel." Note: the remarks cited here from Rabbi Abraham Isaac Kook were made some thirty years before the creation of the state, and referred to the community and people of Israel (*Orot*, p. 24), but are now applied specifically to the ranks of the fighters.

16. Eliezer Waldman, "To Conquer the Mountain" (in Hebrew), *Nekudah* 55 (1983): 20.

17. Peter L. Berger, *The Sacred Canopy: Elements of a Sociological Theory of Religion* (New York, 1967), pp. 44–47; Alistair Kee, ed., *The Scope of Political Theology* (London, 1978).

18. See Z. Y. Kook, *Le-netivot Yisrael* 1:183; S. Aviner, *Am ke-lavi* 2:154.

19. This is Maimonides' wording in *Mishneh Torah*, Melakhim 8:1.

20. Zvi Tau, *Sihot be-et milhamah*, ed. Y. Haikin (Jerusalem, 1983), p. 42.

21. Ibid.

22. Eliezer Waldman, "To Conquer the Mountain," 23; idem, *Al da'at ha-zeman veha-makom* (Kiryat Arba, 1983), pp. 96–97.

23. These remarks were made during the Lebanon War and were published in the internal organ of the yeshivah in Kiryat Arba. Rabbi Lior also ruled that it is incumbent upon all generations to conquer all of the land, from the Brook of Egypt to the Mountain of Beirut, and that to do so one is required to endanger oneself in war (*mizvat milhamah*). See the interview with him in *Nekudah* 48 (1983).

24. See Z. Y. Kook, *Le-netivot Yisrael* 2:157–58. And see the interview in *Ma'ariv*, 14 Nisan 5723 (1963): "Every Jew who comes to the Land of Israel, every tree that is planted in the soil of Israel, every soldier added to the army of Israel, constitutes another spiritual stage, literally; another stage in the process of redemption, like the glorification and increase of Torah through adding yeshivot."

25. See Yitzhak Shilat, "Empty Messianism and False Messianism" (in Hebrew), *Nekudah* 76 (1984): 16–17.

26. Abraham Isaac Kook, "On Zionism" (in Hebrew), in *Ha-Devir*, vols. 7–9 (Jerusalem, 1920), p. 28; cf. Moshe Y. Zuriel, ed., *Orot ha-Reiyah* (Sha'alabim, 1989), 2:928.

27. Abraham Isaac Kook, *Orot*, vols. 10–12, p. 38.

28. We have only a portion of the original tractate.

29. A. I. Kook, "On Zionism," p. 29.

30. See, for example, Rashi's commentary and Meir Halevi Abulafia, *Yad Ramah*, on BT Sanhedrin 51a. Rabbi Kook did not hide the fact that his interpretation differed from the conventional one.

31. A. I. Kook, "On Zionism," p. 30.

32. As stated in chapter 1, even Rabbi Reines and his colleagues hoped that the return to Zion would bring in its wake a spiritual awakening and religious repentance. But this hope was clearly separated from the circumscribed operative realm of their Zionist activity.

33. Maimonides, *Guide of the Perplexed* 2:36, 40, 3:27. See also Aviezer Ravitzky, *Al da'at ha-makom* (Jerusalem, 1991), p. 76.

34. A. I. Kook, *Ha-Devir*, vols. 10–12, p. 36.

35. Ibid., p. 35. Compare Kook's remarks in "Israel's Destiny and Its Nationhood" (in Hebrew), *Ha-Peles* (1901): 227.

36. A. I. Kook, "On Zionism," pp. 28, 33.

37. A. I. Kook, *Ha-Devir*, vols. 10–12, p. 36.

38. But see BT Sanhedrin 18b–19a; Keritot 5b; Maimonides, *Mishneh Torah*, Sanhedrin 2:5.

39. Throughout Rabbi Kook's tractate is interwoven the faith and hope that "now that the national pride is continually expanding, we need not fear those who find it easy to change the explicit rules of the Torah" ("On Zionism," p. 30). Likewise, "Those who fear the Lord and heed His word are not a party within the people, but are the nation itself" (p. 38). Herzl made a similar claim regarding the status of Zionism within the nation.

40. See Jacob Katz, *Leumiyut Yehudit* (Jerusalem, 1983), pp. 181–90. Indeed,

according to the nation's historical memory, in the days of the High Court in Jerusalem "there was not much controversy in Israel" (BT Sanhedrin 88b) and the views of the different sages "were close to one another" (Maimonides, *Mishneh Torah, Mamrim* 1:4; idem, introduction to his *Commentary on the Mishnah*). It would seem that Rabbi Kook expected a substantive change of this type to take place through the very establishment of the Sanhedrin.

41. The utopian hope regarding a general national-religious improvement to take place upon the reinstitution of the Sanhedrin reminds one of Alkalai's hopes regarding the messianic power of "the authorized assembly" that will emerge from among the sages of Israel (see above, chapter 1), or even of the hopes attached by Joseppe Mazini in his day to the future "assembly of humanity." In all these visions, the gathering together of collective human inspiration will heal the problems of the people or of humankind. See Hans Kohn, *Prophets and Peoples* (New York, 1946); Jacob Talmon, *Ha-meshihiyut ha-medinit: Ha-shelav ha-romantit* (Tel Aviv, 1965), pp. 212–13.

42. A. I. Kook, "On Zionism," p. 30.

43. A. I. Kook, *Iggerot ha-Reiyah* 1:341. But in 1903 Rabbi Kook still made the national revival conditional upon the renewal of the Sanhedrin. See on this "Brooks in the Negev" (in Hebrew), *Ha-Peles* (1903): 719.

44. Zvi Makovski, *Ve-ashiva shoftayikh* (Tel Aviv, 1938), pp. 36–38; Zuriel, *Otzrot ha-Reiyah*, p. 151. See also A. I. Kook, *Iggerot ha-Reiyah* 4:80.

45. See Abraham Isaac Kook, *Ma'amrei ha-Reiyah* (Jerusalem, 1984), p. 457; Zvi Yaron, *Mishnato shel ha-Rav Kook* (Jerusalem, 1974), p. 269 n. 64.

46. Judah Leib Maimon, *Hiddush ha-Sanhedrin be-medinatenu ha-mehudeshet* (Jerusalem, 1951), p. 57; see also p. 54.

47. See Jacob Katz, *Halakhah ve-Kabbalah* (Jerusalem, 1984), pp. 213–36. On the hopes of Rabbi Israel Shklov for the renewal of the Sanhedrin, see Aryeh Morgenstern, *Ge'ulah be-derekh ha-teva* (Elkanah, Israel, 1989), pp. 61–78.

48. See the sources used by Katz, *Halakhah ve-Kabbalah*, p. 214 n. 5; Judah Leib Maimon, "On the History of the Idea of Renewing the Sanhedrin in Judaism" (in Hebrew), *Ha-Tzofeh*, 7 December 1951; Geulah Bat-Yehudah, "The Vision of the State among Early Religious Zionists" (in Hebrew), *Shragai* 3 (1989): 24.

49. Rabbi Kook mentions the "storm of controversy" that arose in Safed at the time concerning the renewal of *semikhah* (with the authority of ancient rabbinical ordination). While refraining from taking an explicit position regarding this polemic, it is quite evident toward which side his view tended: "What great happiness will come to the nations by means of the restoration of ordination according to the view of R. Jacob Berab of Safed."

50. Abraham Isaac Kook, "Brooks in the Negev," pp. 77, 71–76. See also idem, *Iggerot ha-Reiyah* 2:134, 164, 208; idem, *Hazon ha-ge'ulah* (New York, 1974), pp. 186–88, 194.

51. Max Nordau, "Ein Templersreit," *Die Welt* (Vienna), 11 June 1897; Shmuel Almog, *Tzionut ve-historya* (Jerusalem, 1982), p. 69. Over the course of time, Rabbi Kook was to draw a sharp distinction between Herzl and Nordau: "the latter is the abomination of my soul and of the soul of everyone who has a spark of Judaism" (*Iggerot ha-Reiyah* 2:294).

52. Herzl declared at the first congress that Zionism "is not intended to impinge

upon the religious consciousness of any stream in Judaism." At subsequent congresses he repeatedly declared that "Zionism does not do anything against religion." He thereby sought to bypass the polemic concerning this question. See Alex Bein, *Herzl* (Jerusalem, 1977), pp. 185, 193, 213; Y. H. Farbstein, "The Haredim and the First Congress" (in Hebrew), in L. Yaffeh, ed., *Sefer ha-Kongress* (Jerusalem, 1950), pp. 191–92; Joseph Adler, "Religion and Herzl: Fact and Fable," *Herzl Year Book* 4 (1965), pp. 271–303.

53. Abraham Isaac Kook, "Etzot me-raḥok," *Ha-Peles* (1902): 532; and see idem, *Musar avikha* (Jerusalem, 1971), 94–96; idem, *Iggerot ha-Reiyah* 1:99.

54. Of course, one needs to examine the specific context of each individual statement. See, for example, Abraham Isaac Kook, *Orot*, pp. 74, 84, 155–56.; idem, *Arpelei tohar*, ed. Y. Shilat (Jerusalem, 1983), 11–12; idem, *Iggerot ha-Reiyah* 1:70–71, 3:205; idem, *Ma'amrei ha-Reiyah*, pp. 452–54; Yoel Bin-Nun, "Nationalism, Humanity, and Knesset Israel," in [B. Ish-Shalom, ed.], *The World of Rav Kook's Thought* (New York, 1991), pp. 207–54.

55. Abraham Isaac Kook, "Afikim Banegev," in [B. Ish-Shalom, ed.], *The World of Rav Kook's Thought*, pp. 78–79; and see idem, "Etzot me-rahok," pp. 531–32.

56. Ehud Luz, *Parallels Meet* (Philadelphia, 1988), p. 61.

57. To use the later concepts of Rabbi Joseph Baer Soloveichik ("Kol dodi dofek," in *Ish ha-emuna* [Jerusalem, 1972], pp. 86–106), we may say that these declarations pushed aside the "covenant of fate" in favor of the "covenant of faith." They are also somewhat reminiscent of Rabbi Isaac Breuer's concept of "the people of the Torah" (see, e.g., his *Moriah* [Jerusalem, 1945], pp. 61–63). On the difference between the teaching of Breuer and that of Rabbi Kook, see Mordecai Breuer, "Nation and State in the Teaching of Isaac Breuer" (in Hebrew), in R. Horwitz, ed., *Yitzhak Breuer: Iyyunim be-mishnato* (Ramat Gan, 1988), pp. 163–73.

58. In fact, over the years Rabbi Kook never ceased to reflect upon this problem. See, for example, his harsh remarks in "Fallen on Our High Places" (in Hebrew), in *Ma'amrei ha-Reiyah*, pp. 910–93; *Hazon ha-ge'ulah*, pp. 235–36; *Iggerot ha-Reiyah* 1:264: "The refuse that is from the side of the mixed multitude who come from Russia, the worst of whom, it is impossible that they should have any hold in the Land of Israel."

59. See Zvi Yehudah Kook, "To Clarify Basic Things in Their Simplicity" (in Hebrew), *Amudim* 360 (1976): 40. Rabbi Abraham Kook and Rabbi E. A. Rabinowich had family connections: the father-in-law of the former, Rabbi A. D. Rabinowitz-Teomim, "the Aderet," was the uncle of the latter.

60. Ibid. See Zvi Yehudah Kook, *Or le-netivati* (Jerusalem, 1989), p. 281.

61. On other important issues in Rabbi Kook's early thought, see Eliezer Goldman, "Secular Zionism, the Destiny of Israel, and the Purpose of the Torah" (in Hebrew), *Da'at* 11 (1983): 103–26.

62. The expressions of warning and conditioning that appear in Rabbi Kook's writing during this period are too numerous to count. For example, "All this hardship . . . all this terrible decline that is likely to be brought upon the head of our nation by virtue of this [Zionist] movement unless it adjusts itself to our national nature and spirit . . . Only if we inscribe upon the banner of Zionism the name of the Lord God of Israel and the return to His Torah, then it will be uplifted and ascend" ("Brooks in the Negev," p. 79).

63. A. I. Kook, "Israel's Destiny," p. 47.

64. A. I. Kook, "Brooks in the Negev," p. 72.

65. Lionel Kochan, *Jews, Idols, and Messiahs* (Oxford, 1990), p. 189.

66. See Abraham Isaac Kook, "The Eulogy in Jerusalem" (in Hebrew), in *Ma'amrei ha-Reiyah*, pp. 94–99. For a summary of the article, see Zvi Yaron, *The Philosophy of Rabbi Kook* (Jerusalem, 1991), pp. 243–44. See M. Z. Neriyah, ed., *Ginzei ha-Reiyah* (Jerusalem, 1984), p. 16.

67. Zvi Yehudah Kook, *Le-sheloshah be-Elul* (Jerusalem, 1938), pp. 14–15. The official ultra-Orthodox leadership in Jerusalem did not oppose the eulogy. See Yossi Avneri, "Rabbi Abraham Isaac ha-Kohen Kook, Rabbi of Jaffa" (in Hebrew), *Cathedra* 37 (1986): 57.

68. For sources, see chap. 1, n. 54, and appendix, n. 6.

69. A. I. Kook, "Eulogy in Jerusalem," pp. 96–99.

70. Ibid., p. 97.

71. Luz, *Parallels Meet*, p. 141. I chose to exemplify this conventional view specifically through Luz's excellent book. Cf. M. Bernstein-Cohen and Y. Koren, *Sefer Bernstein-Cohen* (Tel Aviv, 1946), p. 122.

72. On Herzl's "messianic" image in his own generation, see Theodor Herzl, *Tagebucher* (Berlin, 1923), 2:458, 3:551; Joseph Nedava, "Herzl and Messianism," *Herzl Year Book* 7 (1971): 9–26; Shmuel Almog, "Messianism as a Challenge to Zionism" (in Hebrew), in Z. Baras, ed., *Meshihiyut ve-eskhatologiah* (Jerusalem, 1984), pp. 434–35.

73. A. I. Kook, *Iggerot ha-Reiyah*, letter 571, 2:208. In fact, Kook's criticism of Herzl was likewise leveled against the Mizrachi movement itself.

74. In his novel *Altneuland* ([Leipzig, 1902], p. 287), Herzl imaginatively uprooted the Temple from its original place (on the assumption that the Mosque of Omar would continue to stand on its site) and situated it elsewhere in Jerusalem.

75. See Ahad Ha-Am, *Al Parashat Derakhim* (Berlin, 1930), 3:158, 162. Ahad Ha-Am indeed reacted to Herzl's literary picture with mockery and criticism, seeing it as a further manifestation of Herzl's alienation from "all of the historical tradition that was deeply rooted in the heart of the people" (p. 162). For Rabbi Kook's understanding of the eternal holiness of the site of the Temple, see *Mishpat Kohen* (Jerusalem, 1937), responsum 96; idem, *Iggerot ha-Reiyah* 2:285.

It is worth noting, however, that, as against Ahad Ha-Am, who compared support of the Uganda plan to "public apostasy" (*Iggerot Ahad Ha-Am* [Tel Aviv, 1957], 3:136), Rabbi Kook was actually among the defenders of the plan, along with the people of Mizrachi (*Iggerot ha-Reiyah* 1:17).

76. A. I. Kook, *Iggerot ha-Reiyah* 1:209.

77. See Bein, *Herzl*, p. 412.

78. A. I. Kook, "Afikim Banegev," pp. 78–79; and see idem, "Etzot me-rahok," pp. 531–32.

79. A. I. Kook, *Orot*, p. 122. See also Kook's remarks in *Moriah*, 22 Tammuz 5671 (1911).

80. A. I. Kook, *Orot*, pp. 122–23.

81. Abraham Isaac Kook, *Orot ha-kodesh* (Jerusalem, 1964), 2:544.

82. Needless to say, in the past there were great individuals, prophets, and sages. We are speaking, however, of the collective human sphere. See ibid. 3:217–19.

83. Ibid. 2:545. See Shmuel Sperber, "'Continuity of the Generations' in the Teaching of Rabbi Kook" (in Hebrew), *Sinai* 57 (1965): 203–10.

84. On "the anarchy," see also A. I. Kook, *Iggerot ha-Reiyah* 1:177; idem, *Ma'amrei ha-Reiyah* 1:20; and see Benjamin Ish-Shalom, "Religion, Repentance, and Personal Freedom," in [B. Ish-Shalom, ed.], *The World of Rav Kook's Thought*, pp. 409–11.

85. See R. N. Niebuhr, *Faith and History* (London, 1949), pp. 1–14.

86. See Henry de Saint-Simon, *Oeuvres choisies* (Brussels, 1859), 2:328.

87. A. I. Kook, "Israel's Destiny," p. 45.

88. A. I. Kook, *Orot ha-kodesh* 1:374–76.

89. See S. H. Bergman, "The Doctrine of Development in the Teaching of Rabbi Kook" (in Hebrew), in his *Anashim u-derakhim* (Jerusalem, 1967), pp. 350–58; Nathan Rotenstreich, "Harmony and Return," in his *Jewish Philosophy in Modern Times: From Mendelssohn to Rosenzweig* (New York, 1968), pp. 219–38; idem, *Iyyunim ba-mahshavah ha-Yehudit ba-zeman ha-zeh* (Tel Aviv, 1978), pp. 41–56; S. H. Bergman, "All Reality Is in God," in *Faith and Reason* (New York, 1961), pp. 121–41.

90. Concerning these questions, see Yosef Ben-Shlomo, "Perfection and Becoming Perfected in the Theology of Rabbi Kook" (in Hebrew), *Iyyun* 33 (1984): 289–309; idem, "Spirit and Life in the Teaching of Rabbi Kook" (in Hebrew), *Divrei ha-Akademya ha-Leumit ha-Yisraelit la-Mada'im* 7, no. 11 (1988): 257–74; idem, "The Divine Ideals in the Teaching of Rabbi Kook" (in Hebrew), *Bar-Ilan* 22–23 (1988): 73–86; Tamar Ross, "Rabbi Kook's Concept of the Godhead" (in Hebrew), *Da'at* 8 (1982): 109–28.

91. In fact, this intellectual "transplanting" did not require any artificial effort. The modern idea of progress was itself originally none other than a secularized version of the belief in Divine Providence guiding history toward perfection.

92. See F. E. Manuel, *Shapes of Philosophical History* (Stanford, 1965), pp. 92–135; J. B. Bury, *The Idea of Progress* (New York, 1932); Karl Löwith, *Meaning in History* (Chicago, 1949). 93. See especially Kook's essay "Brooks in the Negev," pp. 656–59. On the fear of religious antinomianism underlying these warnings, see Goldman, "Secular Zionism," p. 124.

94. A. I. Kook, "Israel's Destiny," p. 225.

95. A. I. Kook, "Brooks in the Negev," end.

96. Thereafter, Rabbi Kook never stopped demanding restrained progress and warning against premature messianic antinomianism. See, for example, *Iggerot ha-Reiyah* 1:173–74; *Olat Reiyah* (Jerusalem, 1963), 2:262–64.

97. A. I. Kook, *Arpelei tohar* (unbound, Jerusalem, 1934), p. 13; idem, *Arpelei tohar*, p. 15. (The edition currently in print softens this text in accordance with the views of the editor and his mentors.)

98. A. I. Kook, *Iggerot ha-Reiyah* 1:85.

99. A. I. Kook, *Orot ha-kodesh* 1:194.

100. Eliezer Goldman, "Rav Kook's Relation to European Thought," in *The World of Rav Kook's Thought*, pp. 139, 146; idem, "The Formation of Rabbi Kook's Central Ideas" (in Hebrew), *Bar-Ilan* 22–23 (1988): 78–120; idem, "Responses to Modernity in Orthodox Jewish Thought," *Studies in Contemporary Jewry* 2 (1986): 64. See also Adin Steinsaltz, "The Problematic Nature of *Orot ha-*

kodesh" (in Hebrew), *Sinai* 57 (1965): 266–69; Ross, "Rabbi Kook's Concept"; Benjamin Ish-Shalom, *Rav Avraham Itzhak ha-Cohen Kook: Between Rationalism and Mysticism* (Albany, 1993), pp. 6–11, 244 n. 17; Mordecai Pechter, "Circles and Straightness: The History of an Idea" (in Hebrew), *Da'at* 18 (1987): 78–90; Yehudah L. Ashkenazi, "The Use of Kabbalistic Conceptions in Rav Kook's Teaching," in *The World of Rav Kook's Thought*, pp. 123–28; Eliezer Schweid, *Hashivah me-hadash* (Jerusalem, 1991), pp. 283–84.

101. Compare, for example, Kook's remarks in "Brooks in the Negev," p. 662, where he utilizes the Kabbalistic doctrine of *shemitot* (eons) specifically to emphasize the idea of gradual ascent.

102. Rivka Schatz-Uffenheimer, "Utopia and Messianism in the Thought of Rabbi Kook" (in Hebrew), *Kivvunim* 1 (1979): 25.

103. See Gershom Scholem, *Major Trends in Jewish Mysticism* (New York, 1941), pp. 244–86; idem, *Shabbatei Sevi,* pp. 44–51; idem, *Devarim be-go* (Tel Aviv, 1975), pp. 201–2.

104. See Moshe Idel, *Kabbalah: New Perspectives* (New Haven and London, 1988), pp. 264–66; Yehudah Liebes, "New Directions in the Study of Kabbalah" (in Hebrew), *Pe'amim* 50 (1992): 161–67.

105. A. I. Kook, *Orot ha-kodesh* 2:526. See Ben-Shlomo, "Perfection and Becoming Perfected," p. 97.

106. A. I. Kook, *Orot ha-kodesh* 2:526. See also Yehudah Gelman, "Evil and Its Justification in the Thought of Rabbi Kook" (in Hebrew), *Da'at* 119 (1987): 147–55.

107. Abraham Isaac Kook, *Eder ha-yakar ve-ikvei ha-tzon* (Jerusalem, 1967), p. 108.

108. Elhanan Bunem Wasserman, *Ikveta di-meshiha* (Jerusalem and Tel Aviv, 1952), pp. 6 ff. On a parallel approach attributed to Rabbi Elijah, the Gaon of Vilna, see Aryeh Morgenstern, *Ge'ulah be-derekh ha-teva* (Elkana, 1989), p. 54.

109. Abraham Isaac Kook, *Orot,* p. 83; idem, *Hazon ha-ge'ulah,* pp. 140–41. See also idem, *Orot ha-emunah* (Jerusalem, 1985), p. 29; idem, *Arpelei tohar,* pp. 12, 29; idem, *Orot ha-teshuvah,* ed. Y. Filber (Jerusalem, 1977), sec. 4, p. 30. The impact of this viewpoint is clearly felt in the writings of Rabbi Jacob Moses Harlap, the disciple of Rabbi Kook. See *Mei marom* (Jerusalem, 1977), 3:60–62.

110. A. I. Kook, *Orot ha-kodesh* 1:152 (corrected according to the manuscript, as cited by Ish-Shalom, *Rav Kook,* p. 59).

111. A. I. Kook, *Orot ha-kodesh* 2:541–42.

112. A. I. Kook, *Iggerot ha-Reiyah* 3:143. See also idem, *Arpelei tohar,* p. 46; and Rabbi Kook's notes published in *Ma'or* 1 (1984): 22–23.

113. See Eliezer Schweid, *Ha-yahadut veha-tarbut ha-hilonit* (Tel Aviv, 1981), pp. 122–25.

114. See S. B. Urbach, "Religious Zionism in a Messianic Perspective" (in Hebrew), in Y. Tirosh, ed., *Ha-Tzionut ha-datit: Kovetz ma'amarim* (Jerusalem, 1974), p. 169. This article demands critical study. See Alexander Barzel, *Lihyot Yehudi* (Tel Aviv, 1978), p. 19.

115. A. I. Kook, *Orot,* pp. 13–15. Compare Oswald Spengler, *The Decline of the West* (New York, 1926).

116. Shlomo Aviner, ed., *Sihot ha-Rav Zvi Yehudah* (Keshet, 1980), p. 11.

117. Z. Y. Kook, *Le-netivot Yisrael* 1:82.

118. See Abraham Mordekhai Alter, *Mikhtavim u-ma'amarim* (Warsaw, 1936), pp. 66–69; A. I. Kook, *Iggerot ha-Reiyah* 4:102–3.

119. See Menachem Friedman, *Ḥevrah ve-dat* (Jerusalem, 1978), p. 278.

120. On the significance of this expression as used by the rebbe, see Hayyim Lifschitz, *Shivḥei ha-Reiyah* (Jerusalem, 1979).

121. See David Tamar, "The Crowning Glory of Hasidism" (in Hebrew), *Ha-Tzofeh*, 20 May 1988.

122. See the beginning of Judah Halevi, *The Book of the Kuzari;* compare Rabbi Kook's remarks in *Iggerot ha-Reiyah* 1:348.

123. Neilah prayer for Yom Kippur.

124. Mussaf prayer for festivals. See Lam. 1:10.

125. S. Buber, ed., *Pesikta de-Rav Kahana*, sec. ha-Omer, p. 68b; and see BT Shabbat 30b, etc. The quotation is from A. M. Alter, *Mikhtavim u-ma'amarim*, pp. 66–68.

126. The rebbe of Munkács even attacked the rebbe of Gur for "what he wrote to honor the name of Rav Kook, who seduces and misleads by his impure writings." See Moshe Goldstein, ed., *Tikkun olam* (Munkács, 1933), pp. 18–19.

127. A. I. Kook, *Hazon ha-ge'ulah*, pp. 201.

128. Shlomo Avineri, *The Making of Modern Zionism: The Intellectual Origins of the Jewish State* (New York, 1981), pp. 192–94.

129. A. I. Kook, *Ḥazon ha-ge'ulah*, pp. 201–2; idem, *Iggerot ha-Reiyah* 3:158. It is interesting to compare this with the words of certain ultra-Orthodox authors concerning the status of the Zionist enterprise, which were said in a different spirit, however: "Even though the intention of the builders was not for the sake of heaven, of such a thing it is said, 'the wicked shall prepare but the righteous shall wear it' " (see Aryeh Leib ha-Kohen, son of the Hafetz Hayim, *Toldot ha-Hafetz Hayim*, p. 43; Menahem Mendel Kasher, *Ha-tekufah ha-gedolah* [Jerusalem, 1967], p. 172); "Let them build! Do they not build for us, the people of the Torah?" (Isaac Breuer, quoting Rabbi Joseph Hayyim Sonnenfeld, in his book *Tziyyunei derekh* [Jerusalem, 1982], p. 120). Compare Breuer's own interpretation of Kook's words in Horwitz, *Yitzhak Breuer*, p. 188. See also the remarks of Rabbi Hayyim Zimmerman in Paul Eidelberg, *Israel's Return and Restoration: The Secret of Her Conquest* (New York, 1987), p. 56.

130. A. I. Kook, *Ma'amrei ha-Reiyah*, p. 171.

131. A. M. Alter, *Mikhtavim u-ma'amarim*, pp. 66–68.

132. A. I. Kook, *Iggerot ha-Reiyah* 3:158.

133. A. I. Kook, *Ma'amrei ha-Reiyah*, p. 171. See also idem, *Iggerot ha-Reiyah* 3:348.

134. A. I. Kook, *Ḥazon ha-ge'ulah*, p. 199.

135. See David Canaani, *Ha-aliyah ha-sheniyah ha-ovedet ve-yahasah le-dat vela-masoret* (Tel Aviv, 1976), pp. 112–21; Avraham Zivyon, *Diyokno ha-Yehudi shel Berl Katzenelson* (Tel Aviv, 1984), p. 276; Yaakov Hadani, *Ha-Rav Kook veha-hityashvut ha-ḥilonit* (Jerusalem, 1980); Eyal Kafkafi, "At the Crossroad" (in Hebrew), *Nekudah* 101 (1986): 25; Tamar Shinar, "Rabbi Kook: How Did the Image Emerge?" (in Hebrew), *Nekudah* 135 (1990): 40–43; *Ha-Po'el ha-Tza'ir* 27 (1930); 40 (1909); David Tamar, "The Poet of Judaism" (in Hebrew), *Ma'ariv*, 24 August 1990.

136. A. I. Kook, *Orot*, p. 63. Compare also *Orot*, p. 79; idem, *Orot ha-kodesh* 3:24; idem, *Ḥazon ha-ge'ulah*, p. 184; idem, *Iggerot ha-Reiyah* 1:143; idem, *Musar avikha*, p. 85.

137. A. I. Kook, *Orot ha-teshuvah*, sec. 17, p. 158. As stated in chapter 1, this idea had already appeared in the writings of Rabbi Isaac Jacob Reines.

138. A. I. Kook, *Orot*, p. 135. See Sarah Strassberg, "The Image of Man in the Teachings of A. D. Gordon and Rabbi A. Y. Kook" (in Hebrew), doctoral dissertation, Hebrew University, Jerusalem, 1989.

139. A. I. Kook, Orot, pp. 63–64. Compare Kook's remarks in *Mishpat Kohen*, p. 328.

140. A. I. Kook, *Iggerot ha-Reiyah* 2:186. See Eliezer Don-Yehiya, "Understandings of Zionism in Orthodox Jewish Thought" (in Hebrew), *Ha-Tzionut* 9 (1984): 88; Charles Liebman and Eliezer Don-Yehiya, *Religion and Politics in Israel* (Bloomington, Ind., 1984), p. 72.

141. See Martin Buber, *On Zionism: The History of an Idea* (London, 1973), pp. 147–53.

142. See Eliezer Schweid, *Ha-Yehudi ha-boded veha-yahadut* (Tel Aviv, 1974), pp. 178–92; idem, *Ha-yahadut veha-tarbut ha-ḥilonit*, pp. 110–42.

143. Cf. Yehudah Alkalai, *Goral la-shem* (Vienna, 1857), sec. 7; Judah Alkalai and Zevi Hirsch Kalischer, *Mivhar kitvehem*, ed. G. Kressel (Eretz Israel, 1953), p. 43; Isaac Jacob Reines, *Or ḥadash al Tzion* (Vilna, 1902), p. 252.

144. A. I. Kook, *Iggerot ha-Reiyah* 1:143, 58. See idem, *Ḥazon ha-ge'ulah*, p. 36. Isaac Breuer presents a view diametrically opposed to the above. According to him, intention and personal awareness are the decisive elements in the religious view on life. See his *Nahaliel* (Tel Aviv, 1961), pp. 312–13. In the present generation, Yeshayahu Leibowitz represented this Kantian outlook in its full severity.

145. See R. J. Z. Werblowsky, *Beyond Tradition and Modernity* (London, 1976), pp. 56–57.

146. See Rabbi Kook's remarks in *Arpelei tohar*, pp. 90, 132.

147. M. M. Gerlitz, *Mara de-ara de-Yisrael* (Jerusalem, 1974), pt. 2, p. 176; M. Friedman, *Ḥevrah ve-dat*, pp. 97–98.

148. Haggi Segal, *Aḥim yekarim* (Jerusalem, 1987), p. 219.

149. Amos Oz, *In the Land of Israel* (New York, 1983), pp. 149–50.

150. Yirmiyahu Yovel, "Introducing Secularism" (in Hebrew), *Emdah* 6 (Elul 5745 [1985]): 12–13; idem, "Messiah Is Phoning" (in Hebrew), *Politikah* 24 (1989): 8–9; Ehud Ben-Ezer, *Ein sha'ananim be-Zion* (Tel Aviv, 1986), pp. 23–25.

151. From a statement made by Lichtenstein at a conference held in Jerusalem to mark the fiftieth anniversary of the death of Rabbi Kook, August 1985.

152. See Gideon Aran, *Ḥevel Yamit Tashmab*, Studies of the Jerusalem Foundation for Israel Studies, no. 18 (Jerusalem, 1988), pp. 28, 32, 43, 499–511.

153. A. I. Kook, *Orot ha-kodesh* 2:314.

154. Ibid. Compare A. I. Kook, *Arpelei tohar*, pp. 57–58; and see Ben-Shlomo, "Spirit and Life," p. 273. It is interesting to note that Rabbi Jacob Moses Harlap, one of the outstanding disciples of Rabbi Kook, applied the same dialectical categories to the ultra-Orthodox rabbis as used by his mentor regarding the freethinking pioneers—that is, he attempted to expose the dialectical tendency underlying their opposition to Zionism. The Zionist attempt to bring about redemption through

natural means, wrote Rabbi Harlap, aroused "great opposition among the great rabbis of our generation, even though they themselves did not understand the real quest of their inner souls." They too represented a partial, necessary moment within the messianic process—loyalty to the traditional hope for a complete and miraculous redemption at its most sublime. For "the nature of the redemption of Israel depends upon the nature of their longing for salvation. The more they will know how to uplift their anticipation to a more wondrous and sublime level . . . thus will be the result" (*Hed harim* [Jerusalem, 1953], pp. 60–61).

155. Abraham Isaac Kook, *Orot ha-kodesh* (Jerusalem, 1990), 4:402, and see 3:130.

156. Compare Canaani, *Ha-aliyah ha-sheniyah*, p. 119.

157. Yossi Avneri, "Rav Kook's Relationship with the Old Yishuv at the Period of the Second Aliyah," *Shragai* 2 (1985): 11–30; idem, "Rav A. Y. Kook and His Contacts with People of the Second Aliyah," *Be-Shevilei ha-Tehiyah* 1 (1983): 59–80; idem, "Rav Kook as Chief Rabbi of Palestine, 1921–1935: The Man and His Activity," doctoral dissertation, Bar-Ilan University, Ramat Gan, 1989; Michael Zvi Nehorai, "Notes concerning Rav Kook's Way in Halakhic Rulings," *Tarbitz* 59 (1990): 481–505.

158. *Shulḥan Arukh*, Yoreh De'ah, chapter 340, subsection 5.

159. See A. I. Kook, *Ma'amrei ha-Reiyah*, pp. 89–93. It is not surprising that one of Kook's followers recently mistakenly ascribed this reaction to the earlier period of Rabbi Kook. See *Nekudah* 84 (1985): 18, and the response by David Hanshke, *Nekudah* 85 (1985): 4.

160. A. I. Kook, *Iggerot ha-Reiyah* 1:146. See also Yosef Salmon, "Between Judaism and Zionism," *Zemanim* 30–31 (1989): 187; Zuriel, *Otzrot ha-Reiyah* 1:24.

161. A. I. Kook, *Orot ha-kodesh* 2:544. And see idem, *Orot*, p. 71; idem, *Arpelei tohar*, p. 32.

162. Ish-Shalom, *Rav Kook*, pp. 87–88.

163. Isaac Breuer, "Remarks in Memory of the Chief Rabbi, Avraham Yitzhak ha-Kohen Kook," in Horwitz, *Yitzhak Breuer*, p. 188.

164. A. I. Kook, *Moriyah*, 8 Tammuz 5671 (1911). See Avneri, "Rav Kook and His Contacts," p. 60.

165. I found living testimony to this tendency at a gathering called in 1985 at Merkaz Harav Yeshivah to commemorate the fiftieth anniversary of the death of Rabbi Kook. One after another, the speakers rose to make their declarations: one proclaimed that only scholars from their yeshivah were fit to serve in the Chief Rabbinic Council, as only they represented an "all-Israelite" spirit; the second claimed that only one who came out of their own school was qualified to speak publicly about the teaching of Rabbi Kook; all others can only spread "confusion"; and so on.

166. Needless to say, such a danger affects every monistic, all-encompassing viewpoint, in every culture or religion. See Isaiah Berlin, *The Crocked Timber of Humanity* (New York, 1991); Peter L. Berger, *The Sacred Canopy: Elements of a Sociological Theory of Religion* (New York, 1967); Karl Mannheim, *Diagnosis of Our Time* (London, 1943).

167. Schweid, *Ha-yahadut veha-tarbut ha-ḥilonit*, p. 139. See also the internal

criticism found in an article by Dan Beeri, "Zionism More Than Ever," *Nekudah* 95 (1985): 8–10.

168. A. I. Kook, "On Zionism," pp. 28, 33.

169. Thus far it has been deleted in the printed version. The editor, Rabbi David Cohen, "the Nazir," added it in his own hand in his personal copy, which I examined. I have also found there many other additions and corrections to the printed verion.

170. A. I. Kook, *Orot ha-kodesh* 1:157–58.

171. A. I. Kook, *Iggerot ha-Reiyah* 1:39, 113, 123, 158, 304; idem, *Orot ha-kodesh* 1:23, 298, 3:355, 367; idem, *Arpelei tohar*, pp. 15–16; idem, *Orot*, pp. 78, 98; idem, *Hazon ha-ge'ulah*, p. 84. See also Harlap, *Hed harim*, pp. 65–66, 69–70; Ish-Shalom, *Rav Kook*, pp. 54–55, 261 n. 122; Aran, "Religious Zionism," p. 131; Yoninah Dishon, "Four Motifs in *Orot ha-kodesh*," *Da'at* 24 (1990): 50–54; Dov Schwartz, "The Intellectual Innovation in the Memoirs of the Nazir," in *Yonati be-hagvei ha-sela'* (Jerusalem, 1987), pp. 197–222; idem, "Rav Kook and the Nazir," *Barqai* 5 (1989): 219–21; Haggi Segal, " 'Lights' in the Darkness," *Nekudah* 113 (1987): 25; Shlomo Aviner, *Shalhevetyah* (Jerusalem, 1989), pp. 20–24; Menahem Klein, "The Principles of Rav Kook's Theoretical Understanding of the Halakhah," in H. Y. Hamiel, ed., *Be-oro* (Jerusalem, 1986), pp. 154–58.

172. A. I. Kook, *Iggerot ha-Reiyah* 3:256–57. See also Yehudah Etzion, "From 'Degel Yerushalayim' to 'Movement of Redemption,'" *Nekudah* 94 (1986): 9.

173. A. I. Kook, *Orot*, p. 14, and see p. 104.

174. Shalom Rosenberg, "Contradictions and Dialectics in Social Ethics," in Y. Cohen, ed., *Hevrah ve-historyah* (Jerusalem, 1980), p. 154; Eliezer Goldman, "The State of Israel in the Test of Judaism" (in Hebrew), *Amudim* 364 (1976): 64–65. One of the sharpest critiques ever written against the worldview of Rabbi Kook is that of Harold Fisch, *The Zionist Revolution: A New Perspective* (London, 1978), pp. 62–65.

175. Abraham Isaac Kook, *Shabbat ha-aretz* (Jerusalem, 1937), introduction, p. 13.

176. A. I. Kook, *Hazon ha-ge'ulah*, p. 105.

177. A. I. Kook, *Iggerot ha-Reiyah* 3:175. See also the article written by Rabbi Zvi Yehudah Kook in his youth (in 1913!) under the guidance of his father: *Le-netivot Yisrael* 1:14–15.

178. One must emphasize that this utopianism does not characterize the Zionist perspective of Rabbi Kook alone. "The spiritual climate in which the Zionist movement was born was filled with nearly eschatological enthusiasm of movements striving to bring about the kingdom of heaven upon earth." See Anita Shapira, "Zionism and Political Messianism" (in Hebrew), in *Temurot be-historyah ha-Yehudit ha-hadashah* (Jerusalem, 1988), p. 151; E. A. Balfer, *Malkhut shamayim u-medinat Yisrael* (Ramat Gan, 1991).

179. See Jacob Katz, "Orthodoxy in Historical Perspective," *Studies in Contemporary Jewry* 2 (1986): 16–17.

180. See my remarks in an interview with Seffi Rakhlevski, "Knit Kipah, Dome of the Rock" (in Hebrew), *Devar ha-shavu'a*, 5 June 1987; and see Yovel, "Messiah Is Phoning," p. 10; Shlomo Deshen, "Two Trends in Israeli Orthodoxy," *Judaism* 27 (1978): 379–409.

181. Yosef Ben-Shlomo compared the concrete influence of the writings of Rabbi Kook, which was only realized after his death, with that of Karl Marx's *Capital*. See his article "Ideological Struggle with Right and Left," *Nekudah* 85 (1985): 20.

182. See the articles gathered in the collection David Newman, ed., *The Impact of Gush Emunim* (London, 1986); Amnon Rubinstein, *Me-Herzl ad Gush Emunim uve-ḥazarah* (Jerusalem and Tel Aviv, 1980).

183. See Gideon Aran, "Religious Zionism," pp. 1–99; idem, "From Religious Zionism to Zionist Religion: The Roots of Gush Emunim," *Studies in Contemporary Jewry* 2 (1986): 116–43. Compare Karl Mannheim, *Studies in the Sociology of Knowledge* (London, 1952), pp. 304–12.

184. Ya'akov Ariel, "The Father of Gush Emunim," *Nekudah* 147 (1991): 24.

185. See Zvi Raanan, *Gush Emunim* (Tel Aviv, 1980), pp. 60–75; Eliyahu Blitzki, *Bakesh shalom ve-rodfehu* (Tel Aviv, 1984), pp. 160–65; Yosef Salmon, "Traditional Messianism and Modern Nationalism: Continuation or Revolution?" *Kivvunim* 23 (1984): 101–2; Aryeh Fishman, *Bein dat le-ideologia* (Jerusalem, 1990), p. 24.

186. Z. Y. Kook, *Le-netivot Yisrael* 1:125. See also Jacob Moses Harlap, *Ma'ayanei ha-yeshuah* (Jerusalem, 1963), p. 227.

187. *Tanhuma: Shoftim* 9. See Nissenboim, *Masoret ve-ḥerut*; Avraham Rubinstein, "The Footsteps of Messiah and the Birthpangs of Messiah in His Teaching," *Sefer Shragai*, pp. 118–26.

188. See David Hartman, *A Living Covenant* (London, 1985), p. 286.

189. Maimonides, *Guide of the Perplexed* 2:29. See BT Pesahim 116b, Tosafot s.v. "ve-ne'emar"; Maharsha on BT Nazir 32b; and compare *Sefer ha-Zohar* 3:221.

190. Z. Y. Kook, *Le-netivot Yisrael* 1:188–95 (the essay was written in 1951). Compare idem, *Or le-netivati*, sec. 47, p. 97; H. E. Schwartz, ed., *Mi-tokh ha-Torah ha-goelet* (Jerusalem, 1983), pp. 148, 217; Shlomo Aviner, "Mitzvat Yishuv ha-aretz," in S. Aviner, ed., *Siḥot ha-RZY* (Jerusalem, 1982), pp. 13–14; Bramson, ed., *Ba-ma'arakhah ha-tzibburit*, pp. 52, 79, 86, 91, 97.

191. Jacob Katz has noted that during a number of phases in the history of Zionism there appeared a "messianic determinism," which assumed ab initio the predestined connection between the people and its land. See Jacob Katz, "Israel and the Messiah," *Commentary* 36 (1988): 31–34; and compare his *Leumiyut Yehudit*, pp. 3, 8. See also Luz, *Parallels Meet*, pp. 196–98; A. Shapira, "Zionism and Political Messianism," pp. 149–58; David Sidorsky, "The End of Ideology and Zionism in America," *Pirsumei ha-Hug le-Yedi'at Am Yisrael ba-tofutzat* 8, no. 4 (1974); Eliezer Schweid, *Mi-yahadut le-Tzionut, mi-Tzionut le-yahadut* (Jerusalem, 1984), pp. 107–20; Michael Graetz, "Secular Messianism in the Nineteenth Centry as a Means of Return to Judaism," in Baras, *Meshiḥiyut ve-eskhatologiah*, p. 401; Shmuel Almog, *Zionism and History* (New York and Jerusalem, 1987), pp. 67–80. See also Yeshayahu Aviad-Wolfsberg, "The Consciousness of Mizrachi," in Tirosh, *Ha-Tzionut ha-datit*, p. 138.

192. Fisch, *Zionist Revolution*, pp. 63–64.

193. Yosef Ben-Shlomo, *Shirat ha-Ḥayyim* (Tel Aviv, 1989), p. 88 n. 3.

194. Zvi Yehudah Kook, "Yom ha-Shoah 5733 (1973)," in S. Aviner, *Siḥot ha-RZY*, p. 11.

195. Zvi Yehudah Kook, "Yom ha-Shoah 5727 (1967)," in S. Aviner, *Sihot ha-RZY*, p. 21.

196. See Leo Strauss, *Spinoza's Critique of Religion* (New York, 1965), p. 6.

197. See Amnon Rubinstein, *Me-Herzl ad Gush Emunim ve-hazarah*, pp. 100–110.

198. Compare Menachem Friedman, "The Haredim and the Holocaust," in *Jerusalem Quarterly* 53 (1990): 87–123.

199. See Mordecai Attia, *Mahshavot shalom* (Jerusalem, 1948), p. 50; idem, *Simhat olam* (Mexico City, 1951), p. 34; idem, *Mahaseh va-oz* (Jerusalem, 1955), p. 18; idem, *Lekh Lekha* (Jerusalem, 1963), p. 29; idem, *Sod ha-shevu'ah* (Jerusalem, 1965), pp. 10, 24; Hayyim Kolitz, *Sarvanei ge'ulah* (Jerusalem, 1987), pp. 25–26.

200. S. Aviner, *Sihot ha-RZY*, Yom ha-Shoah 5727 (1967), p. 21.

201. While this approach is based on traditional sources, the very choice of these, rather than other, sources reflects a certain ideological choice.

202. Eliyahu Avihayil, *Le-or ha-shahar* (Jerusalem, 1982), pp. 107, 118–19; and see idem, "Who's Afraid of Our Righteous Messiah?" *Zera'im*, Adar II 5736 (1976).

203. Waldman alluded to the criticism by Amos Oz, published in *Nekudah* 53 (1983). Oz's remarks were subsequently published in his book *In the Land of Israel*, p. 146: "The sin of arrogance is absent from a religious man's belief in a divine plan . . . The sin of arrogance enters in when that man presumes to understand this plan better than his fellow man, to become its certified interpreter, its earthly representative."

204. Waldman, *Al da'at ha-zeman veha-makom*, pp. 108–10. Compare also the chapter "Builders of the Third Temple," in Amos Elon, *Habet ahorah be-vehala mesuyemet* (Tel Aviv, 1988).

205. Shlomo Aviner, "Concerning Our Redemption and Gush Emunim" (in Hebrew), *Amudim* 366 (1976): 276–77. See also his remarks in *Morashah* 9 (1975): 61–65; Yehuda Amital, *Ha-ma'alot mima'amakim* (Jerusalem and Alon Shevut, 1974), pp. 27, 31; idem, in Moshe Davis, ed., *Hizdahut ha-umah im ha-medinah* (Jerusalem, 1976), p. 366; Yaakov Filber, *Ayelet ha-shahar* (Jerusalem, 1975), pp. 117–26. And see also Moshe Zuriel, "An Irreversible Process" (in Hebrew), *Nekudah* 129 (1989): 6. For a radical expression of the understanding of the "train of redemption that strides confidently toward its desired destination," see Shlomo Ohanah, *Or hadash* (Jerusalem, 1974); idem, *Sihu bekhol nifle'otav* (Jerusalem, 1971). A rich literature concerning these issues was published in *Morashah* (Tel Aviv, 1975) and in *Eretz nahalah* (Jerusalem, n.d.). Rabbi Shlomo Goren, who at one time entertained the possibility of a legitimate Jewish state that "does not partake in the messianic process" (*Torat ha-mo'adim* [Tel Aviv, 1964], p. 563), changed his mind in the wake of the Six-Day War, claiming that "the first stage of the messianic vision is taking shape before our eyes." After the Yom Kippur War, he stated explicitly: "Everything is going according to the heavenly plan. We need fear no person, we must be confident that we shall ultimately realize the third redemption" (*Ha-Tzofeh*, 14 Shevat 5735 [1975]). See also the response of Uriel Simon, "Biblical Destinies: Conditional Promises" (in Hebrew), *Petahim* 2 (1975): 34; Uriel Tal, "The Land and the State of Israel in Israel Religious Life," *Proceed-*

ings of the Rabbinical Assembly of America 38 (1976), pp. 1-22; Immanuel Jako-bovits, *If Only My People* (London, 1984), pp. 243–60, and cf. pp. 129–55.

206. Zefaniah Derori, *Ma'ariv,* 18 July 1974. See Janet O'Dea, "Gush Emunim: Roots and Ambiguities," *Forum* 25 (1976): 47.

207. See Aviezer Ravitzky, "The Anticipated and the Permission Given" (in Hebrew), in A. Hareven, ed., *Yisrael likrat ha-me'ah ha-esrim ve-aḥat* (Jerusalem, 1984), pp. 135–97; David Henshke, "What Happened to *Orot ha-Reiyah?*" (in Hebrew), *Nekudah* 78 (1985): 12–13, 28.

208. Rakhlevski, "Knit Kipah," p. 13; Raanan, *Gush Emunim,* p. 64.

209. Hanan Porat, cited in *Amudim* 366 (1976): 276. See also his remarks in *Petaḥim* 32 (1975): 3–12.

210. See Jacob Talmon, *Ha-meshihiyut ha-medinit,* pp. 1, 9–10; idem, *The Origin of Totalitarian Democracy* (London, 1961), pp. 17–21; idem, *The Myth of the Nation and the Vision of Revolution* (London and Berkeley, 1982), p. 549. See also Werblowsky, *Beyond Tradition and Modernity,* p. 4.

211. On such tendencies in classical Zionism, see A. Shapira, "Zionism and Political Messianism."

212. See F. Ventury, *Roots of Revolution* (New York, 1960), pp. 402–8.

213. My views on this issue, which appeared in "The Anticipated and the Permission Given," were thereafter copied in Yohanan Rudick, *Eretz ge'ulah* (Jerusalem, 1989), pp. 107–8.

214. Dan Tor, "To Continue to Force the End" (in Hebrew), *Nekudah* 96 (1986): 28.

215. Hanan Porat, cited by Aran, "Religious Zionism," p. 549; and see idem, *Hevel Yamit Tashmab,* pp. 12, 51; Julien Bauer, "A New Approach to Religious-Secular Relationships?" in Newman, *Impact of Gush Emunim,* p. 107.

216. Compare *Tanhuma: Be-Hukkotai* 13.

217. See Judah Löw ben Bezalel of Prague, *Netzaḥ Yisrael* (Jerusalem, 1971), pp. 133, 148, 180. For further sources, see Amit Kula, "Redemption and Repentance" (in Hebrew), *Teḥumin* 6 (1985): 474. See the remarks of Rabbi Shem Tov ibn Shaprut, cited by Isaac Abrabanel, *Yeshu'ot meshiḥo* (Königsberg, 1861), p. 25a.

218. This idea is also cited in the name of Rabbi Hayyim ben-Attar (*Or ha-Hayyim*); see Attia, *Maḥshevot shalom,* p. 3. For the development of this idea during the nineteenth century, see Aryeh Morgenstern, *Meshiḥiyut ve-yishuv Eretz Yisrael* (Jerusalem, 1985), p. 182 (on Rabbi Eliezer Bergman); Judah Leib Fishman (Maimon), ed., *Sefer Shmuel* (Jerusalem, 1923), pp. 153–56 (on Rabbi Shmuel Mohilewer). See also Shmuel Sperber, "The Beginning of the Flowering of Our Redemption" (in Hebrew), in Y. Tirosh and A. Tirosh, eds., *Ha-Tzionut ha-datit veha-medinah* (Jerusalem, 1978), p. 67; H. S. F. Frank, "The Time of Remembering Has Come" (in Hebrew), *Ha-Ma'ayan* 8 (1968): 1–8; Eidelberg, *Israel's Return and Restoration,* p. 40.

219. Uzi Kalcheim, "The Vision of the 'Revealed End' over the Generations" (in Hebrew), in Y. Raphael and S. Z. Shragai, eds., *Sefer ha-Tzionut ha-datit* (Jerusalem, 1977), 1:103. For detailed sources concerning this issue, see Kasher, *Ha-tekufah ha-gedolah;* Yehuda Kiel, *Yisrael u-geulato* (Jerusalem, 1975); Samuel ha-Cohen Weingarten, "The Beginning of Redemption" (in Hebrew), in Raphael and Shragai, *Sefer ha-Tzionut ha-datit,* pp. 151 ff.

220. See Isaiah Berlin, *Historical Inevitability* (Oxford, 1954); Ernest Nagel, "Determinism in History," *Philosophy and Phenomenological Research* 20, no. 3 (1960): 291–317; Nathan Rotenstreich, *Sugyot be-filosophia* (Tel Aviv, 1962), pp. 78–94.

221. See Shulamit Haeven, *Mashiaḥ o kenneset* (Tel Aviv, 1987), p. 76; idem, *Ivrim be-Azah* (Tel Aviv, 1991), pp. 91–92.

222. S. Aviner, *Am ke-lavi* 2:195.

223. Zvi Yehudah Kook, *Ba-ma'arakhah ha-tzibburit*, p. 112. Compare idem, *Le-hilkhot tzibbur*, p. 246; idem, "Between a People and Its Land" (in Hebrew), *Artzi* 2 (1982): 21; idem, "To the Myriads of Our People Israel" (in Hebrew), *Artzi* 1 (1982): 3.

224. Z. Y. Kook, *Ba-ma'arakhah ha-tzibburit*, pp. 244–46; and see Tau, *Siḥot be-et milḥamah*, p. 45.

225. Yaakov Filber, "Our Period as Mirrored in the Sources" (in Hebrew), *Morashah* 1 (1971): 33.

226. Ibid., pp. 31, 37, 70.

227. S. Aviner, *Am ke-lavi* 2:190.

228. Aran, "Religious Zionism," introduction, p. 8.

229. Aran, *Ḥevel Yamit Tashmab*, pp. 68–69.

230. See Rudick, *Eretz ge'ulah*, p. 185; D. C. Rapoport, "Messianism and Terror," *Center Magazine* 19 (1986): 30–39; and the remarks of Ben-Yishai, quoted in Rakhlevski, "Knit Kipah," p. 6.

231. Harlap, *Ma'ayanei ha-yeshuah*, p. 29; and see S. Aviner, *Am ke-lavi* 2:188.

232. Segal, *Aḥim yekarim*, p. 216; compare p. 232, the condemnation by Chief Rabbi Abraham Shapira. For similar reactions, see Yoel Bin-Nun, "Not Faith without Common Sense" (in Hebrew), *Nekudah* 43 (1982); Yehuda Shaviv, "Go to the Halakhah" (in Hebrew)," *Nekudah* 45 (1982).

233. See Yo'el Bin-Nun, "On Behalf of Trust and Faith and against Cries of Despair" (in Hebrew), *Nekudah* 85 (195): 10–11; Menahem Froman, "It Is Not in Heaven" (in Hebrew), *Emdah* 16 (1987): 10; C. I. Waxman, "Messianism, Zionism, and the State of Israel," *Modern Judaism* 7 (1987): 175–92.

234. Michael Zvi Nehorai, "The State of Israel in the Teaching of Rabbi Kook" (in Hebrew), *Amudim* 358 (1975): 409–17; Z. Y. Kook, "To Clarify Basic Things," p. 40.

235. A. I. Kook, *Ḥazon ha-ge'ulah*, p. 134. One must also take into account the responsibility of the leader for strengthening the hearts of his community. See pp. 95–96.

236. A. I. Kook, *Orot*, p. 158.

237. See, for example, A. I. Kook, *Ma'amrei ha-Reiyah*, pp. 166–67; and see S. B. Urbach, "In a Messianic Light" (in Hebrew), *Shevilin* 20 (1968): 145–46 (note on *Orot ha-kodesh* 1:217).

238. See, for example, A. I. Kook, *Mishpat Kohen*, p. 328; and see Yehoshua Zuckerman, "Realization as a Surety for Faith" (in Hebrew), *Nekudah* 43 (1982); Elisha Aviner, "The Birth Pangs of Messiah" (in Hebrew), *Emdah* 4 (1985): 16–18.

239. See 1 Cor. 15:10; Donald Baille, *God Was in Christ* (London, 1948).

240. Henshke, "What Happened to *Orot ha-Reiyah?*" pp. 12–13. See, however,

Menachem Kellner, "Messianic Postures in Israel Today," *Modern Judaism* 8 (1988): 209.

241. Concerning the "midst of redemption," see Z. Y. Kook, *Le-netivot Yisrael*, pp. 196–98; idem, *Ba-ma'arakhah ha-tzibburit*, pp. 11, 28; Shmuel Federbush, *Torat ha-melukhah* (Jerusalem, 1971), p. 102; Menachem Friedman, "The State of Israel as a Religious Dilemma" (in Hebrew), *Alpayyim* 3 (1991): 65; Uriel Tal, *Mithos u-tevunah be-yahadut yameinu* (Tel Aviv, 1987), p. 115.

242. S. Aviner, ed., *Siḥot ha-RZY*, p. 1.

243. Ibid., p. 3.

244. Yitzhak Shilat, *Nekudah* 93 (1985): 12; David Setav, "The 'Lights' Have Not Been Extinguished" (in Hebrew), *Nekudah* 84 (1985): 20.

245. A. I. Kook, *Orot*, p. 149; idem, *Mishpat Kohen*, p. 328. See Zvi Tau, *Kelal u-perat: Yisrael veha-amim*, lectures (Jerusalem, n.d.), pp. 8–9; Eli Sadan, "The Desire for Peace and Our National Ethic" (in Hebrew), *Artzi* 2 (1982): 40–41. In fact, Rabbi Kook's statement was rooted in the Kabbalistic viewpoint, which identifies the supernal collectivity of Israel with a divine being.

246. See Amos Funkenstein, "Passivity as the Sign of Galut Jewry" (in Hebrew), in *Tadmit u-te'udah historit* (Tel Aviv, 1991), pp. 232–42.

247. Z. Y. Kook, *Le-netivot Yisrael* 1:81–93; S. Aviner, *Shalhevetyah*, p. 54; Blitzki, *Bakesh shalom ve-rodfehu*, p. 167; Jakobovits, *If Only My People*, p. 250.

248. Moshe Zuriel, "On Behalf of Redemptive Initiatives" (in Hebrew), *Nekudah* 105 (1987): 14. See C. D. Dubois, "Problemes de l'utopie," *Archives des Lettres Modernes* 85, no. 4 (1968): 12–18; compare Naomi Gal-Or, "*Ha-maḥteret ha-Yehudit*" bi-shenot ha-shemonim: Ḥiddush o hemshekhiyut, Ha-merkaz ha-beinleumi le-shalom be-mizraḥ ha-tikhon (Tel Aviv, 1986), pp. 34–35.

249. Waldman, *Al da'at ha-zeman veha-makom*, p. 96.

250. Moshe Levinger, "The Comprehensive Perfection of the State of Israel" (in Hebrew), *Nekudah* 125 (1989): 20–21.

251. Yisrael Ariel, "Indeed Rebellion against the Kingdoms?" (in Hebrew), *Nekudah* 73 (1984): 16–17, 28; idem, "Love Upsets Routine" (in Hebrew), *Nekudah* 79 (1985): 22–24. See also Z. Y. Kook, *Le-hilkhot tzibbur*, p. 52: "This government exists for the people, not the people for the government. How much more so that the living, sensitive people has no connection to the government when it betrays the people and its homeland." And see also Shlomo Aviner, "And We Have Not Been False to Your Covenant" (in Hebrew), *Artzi* 1 (1982): 38–39; Ehud Sprintzak, *Ish ha-yashar be-einav* (Tel Aviv, 1986), pp. 121–45; Yehuda Zuldan, "Suffering of Redemption" (in Hebrew), *Nekudah* 76 (1984): 22–23.

252. Barukh Lior, "To Prepare for Gift, Prayer, and War" (in Hebrew), *Nekudah* 85 (1985): 12. Compare the publications of the followers of Meir Kahana, such as: "We must gather round in order to establish a truly Jewish state in every region of the land in which the State of Israel will renege . . . a truly Jewish state with a kingdom, and not an alienated government" (*Or ha-ra'ayon ha-Yehudi*, Sukkot 5753 [1992]). On the ideology of Meir Kahana, see Aviezer Ravitzky, "The Roots of Kahanism: Consciousness and Political Reality," *Jerusalem Quarterly* 39 (1986): 98–118.

253. See Yo'el Bin-Nun's articles in *Nekudah* 72 (1984): 28–36; 141 (1990):

24–25; 149 (1991): 26–27; and see the response of Michael Ben-Horin, *Nekudah* 151 (1991): 45. See also Yohai Rudick, " 'The Jewish Underground' " (in Hebrew), *Kivvunim* 36 (1987): 84–95.

254. The decision of the Council of Settlements in Judah, Samaria, and Gaza, on 2 Heshvan 5747 (1986), taken from Moshe Shapira, "The State of Israel vs. the State of Judaea and Samaria" (in Hebrew), *Nekudah* 93 (1986).

255. Ibid., p. 11.

256. After the political upset brought to power a leftist government in Israel (in 1992), Rabbi Shaul Yisra'eli, *rosh yeshivah* at Merkaz ha-Rav, was no longer able to control himself and "proposed" to delete from the prayer for the welfare of the State of Israel recited in the synagogues the sentence "Send your light and truth to [the state's] heads, ministers, and advisers." He of course did not advocate omitting the opening petition of the prayer: "Bless the State of Israel, the beginning of the blossoming of our redemption," as this refers to an "essence," to the idea of the state, and not to a concrete government. This was primarily an expression of fury in a personal conversation with the Chief Rabbi of Israel, but one should not at all discount its symbolic significance. In 1994, following the Oslo agreements and the Israeli Defense Forces' withdrawal from certain territories of the land, he was followed in this by a few other rabbis.

257. See S. Aviner, *Shalhevetyah*, p. 85; Menahem Froman, "To Wait in Silence for Divine Grace" (in Hebrew), *Ha-Aretz*, 4 January 1991.

258. See Yehudah Etzion, "To Finally Wave the Banner of Jerusalem" (in Hebrew), *Nekudah* 85 (1986): 23–24; idem, "From 'Degel Yerushalayim.' " Compare the stenogram of his remarks at the beginning of his trial (12 May 1985), published in *Nekudah* 88 (1985): 24–25.

259. See Aran, "Religious Zionism," p. 560; Amnon Rubinstein, *Me-Herzl ad Gush Emunim uve-ḥazarah*, p. 121.

260. Yaʿakov Ariel, "The Land of Israel and Peace" (in Hebrew), in *Olah min ha-midbar* (Yeshivat Yamit, 1985), p. 101.

261. Hanan Porat, remarks in a symposium in *Petaḥim* 2 (1975): 9; Raanan, *Gush Emunim*, p. 126.

262. Yo'el Bin-Nun, quoted in Aran, "Religious Zionism," p. 560. See Hayyim Druckman, "The Cry of the Land of Israel" (in Hebrew), *Artzi* 1 (1982): 36.

263. On the utopian understanding of peace in Jewish sources, see Aviezer Ravitzky, "Peace," in A. A. Cohen and P. Mendes-Flohr, eds., *Contemporary Jewish Religious Thought* (New York, 1986), pp. 658–702; A. Ravitzky, *Al daʿat ha-makom*, pp. 32–33.

264. Blitzki, *Bakesh shalom ve-rodfehu*, pp. 167, 190.

265. See David Henshke, "The Blind Alley" (in Hebrew), *Nekudah* 134 (1990): 30–32; David Hartman, *Conflicting Visions* (New York, 1990), pp. 42–43.

266. Zefaniah Derori, *Maʿariv,* 18 July 1984.

267. It is interesting to note the transformations that have taken place over recent generations regarding the center of gravity of the messianic tension and effort. Rabbi Zevi Hirsch Kalischer, a Harbinger of Zionism, saw the renewal of sacrifices as an essential key in hastening the redemption (Katz, *Leumiyut Yehudit*, p. 294). The young Rabbi Kook, and even more so Rabbi Y. L. Maimon, made the renewal of the Sanhedrin the central axis in the messianic process (see above, at the begin-

ning of this chapter; Y. L. Maimon, *Ḥiddush ha-Sanhedrin,* pp. 23–29). Some Haredi groups, first and foremost Habad, strive to bring the End, primarily by campaigns of reaching out to nonobservant Jews and spreading the teaching of Hasidism (below, chapter 5). Finally, contemporary radical religious Zionism makes settlement throughout the Land of Israel the essential catalyst of redemption (see Katz, "Israel and the Messiah," pp. 34–41). The common denominator is the activist effort that seeks new avenues by which to accomplish the historical breakthrough.

268. S. Aviner, *Siḥot ha-RZY,* additions to Deuteronomy, p. 21. This approach, which separates redemption from voluntary repentance, attempts to base itself on the opinion of Rabbi Yehoshua, BT Sanhedrin 97b. See, however, the opposed view of Rabbi Joseph B. Soloveitchik (*On Repentance,* ed. P. Peli [Jerusalem, 1980], pp. 132–37), according to which Maimonides followed the approach of Rabbi Eliezer, BT Sanhedrin 97B, making redemption dependent on repentance. See also Lawrence Kaplan, "Divine Promises: Conditional and Absolute," *Tradition* 18, no. 1 (1979): 41–42; Eliezer Goldman, "Messianic Interpretations of Current Events," *Forum* 26 (1976): 38.

269. See David Schnall, "An Impact Assessment," in Newman, *Impact of Gush Emunim,* p. 16.

270. Shlomo Aviner, "Repentance and Redemption" (in Hebrew), *Amudim* 376 (1977): 150.

271. Oded Walensky, *Even Yisrael* (Jerusalem, 1985), p. 80.

272. Zalman Melamed, "A Further Stage in the Process of Redemption" (in Hebrew), *Nekudah* 119 (1988): 20–21.

273. A. I. Kook, *Orot,* pp. 16–17.

274. See Eliezer Goldman, "The State of Israel in tbe Test of Judaism" (in Hebrew), *Amudim* 360 (1976): 64–65; Fisch, *Zionist Revolution,* pp. 59–66; Herzl Fishman, *Ḥazon ve-shivro, (Jerusalem, 1987)* p. 367.

275. See Avineri, *Making of Modern Zionism,* pp. 192–94.

276. S. Aviner, *Siḥot ha-RZY,* Pinhas, 5736 (1976), addition at the end.

CHAPTER FOUR

1. [Shlomo Volbe], *Alei shur* (Be'er Ya'akov, 1978), pt. 1, p. 287.

2. Only ideological and philosophical differences will be mentioned here, though it is possible to distinguish among various groups on the basis of sociological, cultural, or other characteristics. See, for example, Jacob Katz, *Leumiyut Yehudit* (Jerusalem, 1983), pp. 88–90; Charles Liebman, "Judaism and the Chaos of Modernity," in J. Neusner, ed., *Take Judaism for Example* (Chicago, 1983), pp. 147–64; Eliezer Schweid, *Bein ortodoksiah le-humanism dati* (Jerusalem, 1977), pp. 6–24; Shalom Rosenberg, "Religion and Zion" (in Hebrew), *Sekirah Ḥodshit,* no. 2 (1987): 23–30.

3. See Moshe Samet, "Judaism in the Modern Era" (in Hebrew), *Mahalkhim* 1 (1969): 29–40; 3 (1970): 15–27; idem, *Ha-konflikt odot misud erkei ha-yahadut bi-medinat Yisrael* (Jerusalem, 1969), pp. 39–60; Menachem Friedman, "Haredim Confront the Modern City," *Studies in Contemporary Jewry* 2 (1986): 75–76; idem, "Jewish Zealots: Conservative versus Innovative," in E. Sivan and M. Fried-

man, eds., *Religious Radicalism and Politics in the Middle East* (New York, 1990), pp. 131–32.

4. The combination of the metaphysical with the political dimension of exile is of course a classical motif in Jewish thought. See Arnold Eisen, *Galut* (Bloomington, Ind., 1986), pp. xiv–xviii, 203. Liberal Jewish thought down to the present day has placed a strong emphasis upon the metaphysical dimension of Galut; see, for example, Arthur Cohen, *The Natural and Supernatural Jew* (New York, 1962); Nathan Rotenstreich, "Jewish Exile in American Jewish Thought" (in Hebrew), in *Publications of the Study Circle on World Jewry in the House of the President of Israel* (Jerusalem, 1967); Jacob Neusner, *Stranger at Home* (Chicago, 1981), p. 161. For the parallel discussion in the Orthodox press in the United States, see Shimon Glick, "Missing a Feeling of Galut," *Jewish Observer*, October 1978, October 1979; editorial, "On the Many Dimensions of Galut," *Jewish Observer*, December 1979.

5. Maimonides, *Mishneh Torah*, Teshuvah 7:5. Leo Strauss delved deeply into the problem of exile in the Holy Land. See his *Spinoza's Critique of Religion* (New York, 1965), p. 6.

6. Menachem Mendel Schneersohn, quoted in Shalom Dov Volpe, ed., *Da'at Torah be-inyanei ha-matzav be-eretz ha-kodesh* (Kiryat Gat, 1982), pp. 30, 36.

7. Eliezer Menahem Schach, *Mikhtavim u-ma'amarim* (B'nai Berak, 1980), p. 9.

8. Haredi denial of the current process of redemption distinguishes the Haredim from messianic religious Zionists; their claim of exile distinguishes them from any religious-Zionist position. See Shlomo Zalman Shragai, "The State of Israel Is Not Galut" (in Hebrew), in his *Pa'amei ge'ulah* (Jerusalem, 1963), pp. 70–74; Meir Eidelbaum, "Between Mizrachi and Agudat Israel" (in Hebrew), in Y. Raphael and S. Z. Shragai, eds., *Sefer ha-Tzionut ha-datit* (Jerusalem, 1977), 1:145. See also Moshe Samet, ed., *Ha-dat veha-medinah* (Jerusalem, 1977), pp. 45–46.

9. Binyamin Mendelssohn, *Kuntres iggeret ha-Rav* (Komemiyyut and Jerusalem, 1973), 49.

10. Yisrael Eichler, in *Ha-Mahaneh ha-Haredi*, 23 April 1985.

11. See Emanuel Sivan, "Nikmato shel ha-Hazon Ish," *Ha-Aretz*, 29 May 1990.

12. The statement "This is not the beginning of the redemption, but rather the end of the Exile" is attributed to Rabbi Avraham Yeshayahu Karelitz (the Hazon Ish). See S. Cohen, ed., *Pe'er ha-dor: Hayyei he-Hazon Ish* (Tel Aviv, 1967), pt. 4, p. 236; Moshe Schonfeld, in *Jewish Observer*, October 1974. Isaac Breuer developed an original formulation regarding this question. For a summary of his approach, see Pinhas Peli, "Isaac Breuer: Torah with Worldliness" (in Hebrew), in R. Horwitz, ed., *Yitzhak Breuer: Iyyunim be-mishnato* (Ramat Gan, 1988), pp. 114–15.

13. Rabbi Elhanan Bunem Wasserman was the outstanding pupil of the Hafetz Hayim and one of the leading *rashei yeshivah* in the pre-Holocaust generation. See *Hashkafatenu* (B'nai Berak, 1978), pt. 1, p. 109 (cited under the heading "a pure outlook on the notorious Zionist state"); Elhanan Bunem Wasserman, *Kovetz ma'amarim* (Tel Aviv, 1963), p. 92. See also Gershon Bacon, "Da'at Torah and the Birth Pangs of Messiah: On the Ideology of Agudat Israel in Poland" (in Hebrew), *Tarbitz* 52 (1983): 503; Menachem Friedman, "Israel as a Religious Dilemma," in B. Kimmerling, ed., *The Israeli State and Society: Boundary and Frontier* (New

York, 1989), chap. 3. The Yevsektsia (Jewish section of the Communist Party of the USSR) took an active hand in repressing Jewish religion in Russia in the 1920s.

14. Rabbi Moshe Blau published his articles in the Agudah weekly *Kol Yisrael;* they have been collected in *Kitvei Rabbi Moshe Blau* (Jerusalem, 1983). It should be noted that, on the eve of the Holocaust, Rabbi Blau viewed the persecutions of the Jews as the final undermining of exilic existence, and foresaw a widespread abandonment of the countries of the Diaspora by the Jews (pp. 190–93). Regarding the conventional Haredi argument that the Zionists angered Hitler by openly declaring war on him and thus made the entire Jewish people his enemy, special attention should be given to a previously unknown 1939 article written by Rabbi Blau in which he states: "If war were to occur now, it will be the first time in the history of Israel since it was exiled from its land that the Jewish people will be a party to the battle, *that the entire people of Israel will stand on the side of one of the combatants* . . . May the Lord strengthen the non-Jewish nations who are waging a righteous war, to conquer the kingdom of wickedness" (pp. 202–4, emphasis added). Five years later, however, in response to the Zionist criticism of those rabbis who dissuaded their students from immigrating to Eretz Israel on the eve of the Holocaust, Rabbi Blau responded by attributing some responsibility for the oppressor's lust for revenge to the Zionist. In this regard, he specifically mentioned "the *economic* war that the Zionists had publicly declared against Hitler *at the beginning of his persecutions* of the Jews" (pp. 250–51, emphasis added).

15. The quotation from Blau is taken from *Kitvei,* pp. 265–66. See also the pamphlet by Nathan Birnbaum, "In Golus bei Yiddn" (n.p., 1920). Gordon is quoted in Ehud Luz, *Parallels Meet* (Philadelphia, 1988), pp. 37–39; and Shmuel Almog, *Zionism and History* (New York and Jerusalem, 1987), pp. 171–72.

16. Some authors went even further in this point, expressing the fear that return to the Land of Israel would bring about a new "age of Torquemada." See Luz, *Parallels Meet;* Almog, *Zionism and History,* pp. 171–72, 239, 264, 273.

17. Dov Berish Tursch, *Bar hedyah o halom Herzl* (Warsaw, 1900), p. 41. Tursch mentions a letter he received from the Hakham Bashi in Constantinople, stating that the Zionist initiative threatened to arouse the ire of the Turkish sultan against the entire Jewish Yishuv in Eretz Israel (*Setirat Zekenim* [Warsaw, 1899]; see Yosef Salmon, "The Stance toward Zionism of Ultra-Orthodox Society in Russia and Poland" [in Hebrew], *Eshel Be'er Sheva* 1 [1976]: p. 391; idem, *Dat ve-Tzionut* [Jerusalem, 1990], p. 262).

18. See Menachem Friedman, *Hevrah ve-dat* (Jerusalem, 1978), p. 33. On Zionism as an illusion, see also the remarks of the rabbis collected by A. B. Steinberg, *Divrei ha-rabbanim* (Warsaw, 1902), p. 38; Joseph Isaac Schneersohn, *Mikhtav oz shel Torah* (n.p., n.d.), p. 11 (reprinted in Moshe Goldstein, ed., *Tikkun olam* [Munkács, 1933], p. 532).

19. See Isaac Breuer, "A Memorandum on Agudat Israel's Relation to the Jewish State" (in Hebrew), in Yitzhak Meir Levin, *Homer li-she'elat hitkonnenut ve-siddur ha-medinah ha-Yehudit al-pi ha-Torah* (New York, 1948), p. 5, clause 3; Y. Gitlin, *Yahadut ha-Torah veha-medinah* (Jerusalem, 1974), p. 41.

20. Raphael Reuven Grozovsky, *Be'ayot ha-zeman* (B'nai Berak, 1960), pp. 33–34. The distinction between Zionism and the State of Israel was on occasion formulated in a mood of excitement at the rebirth of the state (chiefly during its early

years). See, for example, *Ha-Modi'a*, 22 Av 5711 (1951): "The basic Agudah worldview is that the establishment of the state is one of the wonders of Providence over us, and it is an independent creation, with no connection to secular Zionism. For this reason, Agudat Israel does not view the state as a Zionist matter, but rather as a general Jewish one, which obligates every Jew to aid in its maintenance and fortification."

21. Yosef Avraham Wolf, *Ha-tekufah u-va'ayoteha* (B'nai Berak, 1983), 1:15.

22. Moses b. Ḥayyim Alsheikh, *Teshuvot Lev Avraham*, ed. Avraham Weinfeld (Brooklyn, 1961), sec. 129; Yo'el Schwartz, *Yalkut yemot olam* (Jerusalem, 1980), pp. 113–18.

23. Oral communication from Rabbi Avraham Stockhammer.

24. See I. Breuer, "Memorandum," p. 5, clause 3; p. 6, clause 6; Grozovsky, *Be'ayot ha-zeman*, pp. 14–15. See also the article by Eliezer Don-Yehiya, "Understandings of Zionism in Orthodox Jewish Thought" (in Hebrew), in *Ha-Tzionut* 9 (1984): 9, 75.

25. Regarding this approach as characteristic of conservative stances, see Karl Mannheim, *Ideology and Utopia* (New York, 1936), p. 30. See Bacon, "Da'at Torah and the Birth Pangs of Messiah," p. 507. It should be noted that the distinction between principle and essence, on the one hand, and tools and material fruits, on the other hand, likewise serves the Haredi society in its stance vis-à-vis basic characteristics of Western modernity in general, such as democracy, science, and economic method. Regarding the issue of the consistency and morality of this separation, see Jacob Neusner, *Why No Science in Judaism?* (New Orleans, 1987), p. 1 n. 1.

26. I remember the response of my grandfather, of blessed memory, the Hasidic rabbi Abraham Roest, when as a child I asked him why the prayer for the welfare for the State of Israel was not recited in the synagogue of the Gur Hasidim. His response: "The state belongs to Mapai!" That is to say, because it was controlled and led by secularists, but not because of its inherent nature as a state.

27. See, for example, Eliezer Waldman, *Al da'at ha-zeman veha-makom* (Kiryat Arba, 1983), p. 62; Ya'akov Ariel, "For What Was the Land Lost?" (in Hebrew), in *Olah min ha-midbar* (Yeshivat Yamit, 1985), pp. 93–95. Hanan Porat spoke of "the national will" that had disappointed instead of acting courageously.

28. This is also true regarding the Golan Law, the production of the Lavi aircraft, and other such issues.

29. See Rabbi Schach's statement cited in S. D. Volpe, *Da'at Torah*, pp. 24, 30, 35–37.

30. See the commentary of Rashi on BT Ketubbot 111a, s.v. "she-lo yirhaku et ha-ketz."

31. Binyamin Y. Silber, "Halifat mikhtavim," in *Mekor halakhah* (B'nai Berak, 1961), p. 88. Rabbi Menahem Mendel Kasher disputed this statement without mentioning the author ("and I saw [a work] by an important author in Eretz Israel"). See *Ha-tekufah ha-gedolah* (Jerusalem, 1967), p. 221.

32. Weinfeld, *Teshuvot Lev Avraham*, sec. 129.

33. Joseph David Epstein, *Mitzvat ha-shalom* (New York, 1970), p. 605. And see also Grozovsky, *Be'ayot ha-zeman*, p. 14; Gitlin, *Yahadut ha-Torah*, p. 28.

34. Rabbi Kalman Kahana, the leader of Po'alei Agudat Israel, adopted another

view that imparts positive religious significance to the very fact of political rebirth, thereby drawing closer to the position of religious Zionism. See his article "The Torah and the State: The General Problem" (in Hebrew), *Ha-Ma'ayan*, Tishri 5715 (1954).

35. On a later variant of this idea, specifically among the radical group in Neturei Karta, see Amnon Levi, *Ha-Haredim* (Jerusalem, 1988), p. 200.

36. See Yosef Eliyahu Henkin, *Lev Ibrah* (New York, 1957); Yisrael Schizipansky, "The Redemption from Egypt, the Redemption from Babylonia, and the Future Redemption" (in Hebrew), *Or ha-Mizrah* 22, no. 77 (Tishri 5733 [1972]): 205n.

37. Joseph Baer Soloveichik, *Divrei hagut veha'arakhah* (Jerusalem, 1982), p. 89.

38. See Gitlin, *Yahadut ha-Torah*, p. 30.

39. Jacob Katz, "Orthodoxy in Historical Perspective," *Studies in Contemporary Jewry* 2 (1986): 15.

40. Histadrut Agudat Israel, *Lehasir masveh* (Jerusalem, 1951), p. 12.

41. Grozovsky, *Be'ayot ha-zeman*, p. 15. Compare the remark of the present Belzer rebbe, Issachar Dov Rokah, "Masa Hitva'adut," in *Ve-zarah ha-shemesh: Yisudah shel degel ha-Torah* (B'nai Berak, 1989), p. 223.

42. Katz, "Orthodoxy in Historical Perspective," p. 15.

43. Yitzhak Meir Levin, *Neumim*, (Jerusalem, 1952), pp. 27–28, 35, 42, 77, 93. For Levin's response to the Six-Day War, see also the biography written by his associates, *Ha-ish u-foalo* (Jerusalem, 1972), p. 71. The Agudah press contained an inordinate number of responses such as this in the wake of the Six-Day War, which was depicted as a "chain of miracles, a combination of one miracle with another, the wondrous beyond all wonder" (*Ha-Modi'a*, 12 Tammuz 5727 [1967]; see *Diglenu*, Tammuz 5727; *Beit Ya'akov*, Tammuz 5727, Elul 5727). See also the statement made in this press about the miracles revealed during the War of Independence (e.g., *Ha-Modi'a*, 22 Av 5711 [1951]) and during the Sinai campaign (e.g., *Ha-Modi'a*, 1 and 5 Kislev 5717 [1957]; *Ha-Kol*, Heshvan 5717).

44. For Neturei Karta criticism and Agudat Israel's later "disavowal" of Levin's statements, see Edah Haredit, *Lehasir masveh* (Jerusalem, 1950). See also the harsh attacks that were delivered later by one of the leading spokesmen of this circle, Rabbi Yerahmiel Domb, in *Kuntres al ha-nissim* (Jerusalem, 1957) and *Kuntres et nisayon* (Jerusalem, 1972), pp. 96–101. Most recently, the small number of strikes and injuries resulting from the Iraqi missiles during the Gulf War has been depicted as a manifest miracle.

45. Histadrut Agudat Israel, *Lehasir masveh*, p. 68.

46. Levin, *Ne'umim*, pp. 27–28.

47. Kasher, *Ha-tekufah ha-gedolah*, pp. 204–10; Harry Rabinowicz, *Hasidism and the State of Israel* (London and Toronto, 1982); *Yarhon Beit Ya'akov*, Tevet 5726 (1966).

48. There has been a certain questioning of the authenticity of these signatures within Haredi circles. See Zvi Weinman, "Ha-ziyuf," *Yom Ha-shisi*, 22 April 1988. As against that, see David Tamar, "Keter Torah," *Ha-Tzofeh*, 21 July 1989.

49. S. D. Volpe, *Da'at Torah*, pp. 23–24.

50. Shalom Dov Volpe, *Shalom shalom ve-ein shalom* (Kiryat Gat, 1982), p. 34;

Gershon Yacobson, *Yediot Aḥaronot*, 24 July 1967. The statement by the rebbe on the miracle of Entebbe: S. D. Volpe, *Shalom shalom*, p. 117; *Ha-Tzofeh*, 28 August 1976.

51. It seems that the rebbe intentionally refrained from using the term "independence."

52. S. D. Volpe, *Da'at Torah*, pp. 23–24.

53. See chapter 1. Pessimistic predictions concerning the future failure of Zionism were also attributed to the Hazon Ish and the Hafetz Hayim. See Yosef Avraham Wolf, *Ha-tekufah u-ve'ayoteha: Eretz Yisrael* (B'nai Berak, 1982), pp. 298–99; Paul Eidelberg, *Israel's Return and Restoration* (New York, 1987), p. 50.

54. Testimony of Israel Meir ha-Kohen's son, in Shmuel Grainemann, ed., *Ḥafetz Ḥayim al ha-Torah* (B'nai Berak, n.d.), p. 101. For the religious excitement that the Balfour Declaration caused among eastern Jewry, see Yosef Yo'el Rivlin, "Footsteps of Redemption" (in Hebrew), in *Minḥah le-Avraham [Almaliah Festschrift]* (Jerusalem, 1959), pp. 40–48. And see the remarks of Rabbi Moshe Khalfon of Djerba in his *Darkei Moshe* (Djerba, 1935), cited by Joseph Tubi, "The Roots of the Attitude of Oriental Jewry to the Zionist Movement" (in Hebrew), in *Temurot ba-historyah ha-Yehudit ha-hadashah* (Jerusalem, 1988), n. 65.

55. According to the testimony of Isaac Breuer in his book *Moriah* (Jerusalem, 1980), p. 104.

56. Kasher, *Ha-tekufah ha-gedolah*, p. 202. See also the statement by Isaac Breuer, "I had already earnestly requested, at the third Great Assembly [i.e., of the Agudah, 1937]: Tell us openly if the Mandate is from God or the work of the devil, for otherwise this is impossible; but I did not receive a reply" (*Moriah*, p. 215). And indeed, Breuer's book *Messiasspuren* was published about the time of the Balfour Declaration (Frankfurt am Main, 1918). See also Gitlin, *Yahadut ha-Torah*, p. 27.

57. See Shlomo Volbe, *Ben sheshet le-asor* (Jerusalem, 1976), p. 145.

58. Within the Gur Hasidic court as well, the Balfour Declaration was viewed as a "hint from Divine Providence." See the statement by Rabbi Yitzhak Meir Levin in *Kol Yisrael*, 16 Kislev 5693 (1933). See Yitzhak Alfasi, "Rabbi Abraham Mordecai Alter of Gur and His Relation to the Settlement of the Land of Israel" (in Hebrew), *Bi-Shevilei ha-Tehiyah* 2 (1987): 121. On ferment in other Hasidic courts, see Mendel Piakarz, *Ḥasidut Polin* (Jerusalem, 1990), pp. 233–39.

59. A direct parallel between the Balfour Declaration and Cyrus's proclamation was drawn by Shmuel Bornstein, the Sochaczew rebbe. See Zvi Yehudah Mamlak, *Abir ha-ro'im* (Piotrkow, 1935), pt. 1, p. 106. See Yosef Eliyahu Henkin, *Kitvei ha-Gria Henkin* (New York, 1981), 1:158.

60. On the other hand, as mentioned, God adjured the nations that "they not subjugate Israel overly much" (BT Ketubbot 111a).

61. The allusion apparently refers to versions of religious Zionism.

62. Elijah Dessler, *Mikhtav me-Eliyahu*, pt. 3, p. 218. (The original punctuation has been altered in the interests of clarity.)

63. Gershon Weiler, *Teokratiah Yehudit* (Tel Aviv, 1977).

64. A. B. Yehoshua, *Bi-zekhut ha-normaliyut* (Jerusalem and Tel Aviv, 1980). See Perat [Avigdor Levinton], *Boker va-erev* (Jerusalem, 1991).

65. Regarding the universal application of the halakhic rule, "the law of the

kingdom is law"—to both Jewish and non-Jewish governments—see Shmuel Shiloh, *Dina de-malkhuta dina* (Jerusalem, 1975), pp. 77–78, 104; Yaakov Blidstein, *Ekronot medini'im be-mishnat ha-Rambam* (Ramat Gan, 1983), pp. 131, 152–53.

66. Add to this the drop in political power of religious Zionism and its loss of confidence. See Eliezer Schweid, "Which Way Is the Religious Public Headed?" (in Hebrew), *Kivvunim* 13 (1982): 15–28; Nahum Arieli, "The Religious Zionist Idea: The Glory and the Failure" (in Hebrew), *Kivvunim* 29 (1986): 25–46; Michael Zvi Nehorai, "The Shattering of the Religious Zionist Movement" (in Hebrew), *Nekudah* 83 (February 1985).

67. Yo'el Schwartz, *Binu shenot dor va-dor* (Jerusalem, 1984), pp. 96–99; Yisrael Rosen, "The New Religious Zionism" (in Hebrew), *Emdah* 11 (June 1986): 14–15; Amnon Levi, *Ha-Ḥaredim*, p. 219.

68. See *Lehasir masveh*, pp. 6–12.

69. "Saviv la-hishtafut ba-memshalah," in *Lehasir masveh*, p. 26.

70. See S. Zalman Abramov, *Perpetual Dilemma* (Rutherford, N.J., 1976), p. 157; M. Friedman, "Religious Dilemma," chaps. 4–5.

71. See the memorandum by Rabbi Moshe Blau regarding the question of a constitution for the State of Israel, in Levin, *Ḥomer li-she'elat*, p. 19.

72. Moshe Sheinfeld, in *Diglenu*, Tishri 5711 (1951); also published in *Hashkafatenu*, sec. 1.

73. "Because of collective responsibility . . . because of the educational harm, because each member of the government must naturally justify all actions of the government" (Aharon Yeshaya Rotter, in *Hashkafatenu*, sec. 1).

74. Abramov, *Perpetual Dilemma*, p. 162.

75. Schach, *Mikhtavim u-ma'amarim*, p. 46. See also Abramov, *Perpetual Dilemma*, p. 160, regarding the sharp criticism by M. K. Moshe Lorencz of Agudat Israel (in 1960) concerning the coalition responsibility assumed by the National Religious Party; Uri Milstein, "Ideological Positions of Political Parties in Relation to Religion and State in Israel" (in Hebrew), *Medinah, Mimshal ve-Yaḥasim bein-Leumi'im* 7 (spring 1975): 98; Eliezer Don-Yihya, *Tefisot shel ha-Tzionut* (Tel Aviv, 1984), p. 93.

76. We should not overlook the fact that Rabbi Obadiah Yosef, the head of this movement's Council of Torah Sages, served in the past as chief rabbi (a statesanctioned office), and that the political leader of this movement, Rabbi Yitzhak Peretz, also studied in religious-Zionist educational institutions.

77. See Rosenberg, "Religion and Zion," p. 28; Shlomo Deshen, "To Understand the Special Attraction of Religiosity for Oriental Jews" (in Hebrew), *Politikah* 24 (January 1989): 40–43. See the afterword below.

78. The article was written by Y. A. Schneider. He added: "We are anti-Zionists, and no one can do anything about this . . . Our central struggle with Zionism is still unfinished. It is still underway, it still exists." See also Yisrael Volman, "Everything Is Holy" (in Hebrew), *Emdah* 5 (February 1985).

79. This phenomenon is naturally noticeable among Haredim in Israel, but not among those abroad. See Aharon Lichtenstein, "The Relationship to Israel of Jewish Religious Groups: Orthodoxy," in *Publications of the Study Circle on World Jewry in the Home of the President of Israel* (Jerusalem, 1984). According to Lich-

tenstein, the very fact of shared life in Eretz Israel, "in the same boat," leaves its mark. A clear example of this is contained in the statement during the Six-Day War by Rabbi Yehezkel Levinstein, the *mashgiah ruhani* (spiritual supervisor) of the Ponevezh Yeshivah, who stressed the feeling of fraternity of all Israel at such a time, the shared danger and the shared sense of salvation that followed. See Yehezkel Levinstein, *Kovetz inyanim she-hishmiʿa maran ha-mashgiah bi-Yeshivat Ponevezh be-et ha-tzarah ha-milhamah veha-yeshuah* (Bʿnei Berak, 1967), pp. 9, 15, 20; Yehezkel Levinstein, *Kovetz inyanim she-hishmiʿa maran ha-mashgiah be-Yeshivat Ponevezh bi-yemei Elul 5727–Tishri 5728*, (Bʿnei Berak, 1918), p. 3; and elsewhere.

80. Gitlin, *Yahadut ha-Torah.*

81. See Maimon ha-Dayan, *Iggeret nehamah* (Jerusalem, 1945), pp. 43–44.

82. S. D. Volpe, *Daʿat Torah*, p. 30.

83. Maimonides, *Mishneh Torah*, Melakhim 11:4. See Aviezer Ravitzky, *Al daʿat ha-makom* (Jerusalem, 1991), pp. 78–79, 87–90; idem, " 'To the Utmost of Human Capacity': Maimonides on the Days of the Messiah," in J. L. Kraemer, ed., *Perspectives on Maimonides: Philosophical and Historical Studies* (Oxford, 1991), pp. 236–40.

84. Isaac Breuer differed from his colleagues on this issue, as on other issues. See, for example, *Moriah*, p. 224. See also Yaakov Levinger, "The Zionist Makes War on Zionism" (in Hebrew), in *Sefer Barukh Kurzweil* (Tel Aviv, 1975), pp. 151–68.

85. See Peter L. Berger, *A Rumour of Angels* (New York, 1969), p. 32.

86. See Yeshayahu Wolfsberg, "The Mizrachi and Its Stance concerning Non-Zionist Orthodoxy" (in Hebrew), in Y. L. Maimon, ed., *Yovel ha-Mizrahi* (Jerusalem, 1982), pp. 256–68; and see Boaz Shapira, "Portfolio of the Religious: A Picture of the Situation" (in Hebrew), *Politikah* 24 (January 1989): 31–35.

87. Gershom Scholem, *The Messianic Idea in Judaism and Other Essays on Jewish Spirituality* (New York, 1971), pp. 35–36. See also Arieli, "Religious Zionist Idea," p. 29.

88. Ironically, the last section of the mishnah, which teaches passivity (i.e., reliance on the salvation of the Lord), was interpreted as a curse, not as a blessing: "And they say in the name of the author of *Nefesh ha-Hayyim* [Rabbi Hayyim of Volozhin] . . . that the last things in this mishnah are a curse as well . . . For the God-fearing in those days will despair and their will to wage the war of the Lord will be weakened." See Wasserman, *Kovetz ma'amarim*, p. 92.

89. Shmuel Bornstein of Sochaczew, *Shem mi-Shmuel* (Piotrkow, 1928), Parashat Bo, 5678 (compare *Sefer ha-Zohar* 2:184a). And see also Piakarz, *Hasidut Polin*, pp. 21, 236, 262.

90. Elhanan Bunem Wasserman, *Ikveta di-meshiha* (Jerusalem and Tel Aviv, 1952), pp. 6 ff. (this essay was also published in *Kovetz ma'amarim*, pp. 106 ff., in two different versions). On a parallel approach attributed to Rabbi Elijah, the Gaon of Vilna, see Aryeh Morgenstern, *Ge'ulah be-derekh ha-teva* (Elkana, 1989), p. 54.

91. See Moshe Prager, ed., *Le-or ha-emunah* (New York, 1958), pp. 6, 12; Grainemann, *Hafetz Hayim al ha-Torah*, p. 228. *Le-or ha-emunah* cites the words of numerous sages of the previous generation who, in their time—in the depths of evil and despair—found signs of the "birth pangs of the Messiah." See also Bacon,

"Da'at Torah and the Birth Pangs of Messiah," pp. 505–7; Eliyahu Lapian, *Lev Eliyahu* (Jerusalem, 1972), pp. 76–77; Levin, *Ne'umim*, pp. 109–12.

92. See Yehezkel Levinstein, "The Obligation to Strengthen Oneself during the Birth Pangs of Messiah" (in Hebrew), published together with the work by the Hafetz Hayim, *Kuntres "tzipita li-yeshuah?"* (Jerusalem, 1978), p. 27.

93. Schach, *Mikhtavim u-ma'amarim*, p. 6. (Schach stresses that changes of government in Israel change matters neither for better nor worse.) The phrase "footsteps of the Messiah" also appears in the writings of the Lubavitcher rebbe, but used in a different sense. See S. D. Volpe, *Da'at Torah*, p. 38; and see the appeals by his predecessor, in "For Immediate Redemption" (in Hebrew), in *Arba'ah kol ha-korei meha-admor shelita mi-Lubavitch* (Jerusalem, 1943); see also Prager, *Le-or ha-emunah*, p. 82.

94. *Hashkafatenu*, sec. 4, p. 109.

95. Schach, *Mikhtavim u-ma'amarim*, p. 6.

96. Goldstein, *Tikkun olam*, p. 46; J. I. Schneersohn, *Mikhtav oz shel Torah*, p. 6.

97. Goldstein, *Tikkun olam*, p. 51; J. I. Schneersohn, *Mikhtav oz shel Torah*, p. 9. See also "Mikhtav katzar," printed in *Mikhtav Oz:* "I request that it be made known in the Hebrew newspapers, that the claim that [Hasidic] rebbes and rabbis of Poland held fast to the Land of Israel simply to extend its industry and [other] practical deeds, is false." In this matter, Schneersohn's stance resembled that of the rabbi of Munkács (see chapter 2). On the central role played by the above-mentioned rebbe of Lubavitch in the opposition to Zionism in (Soviet) Georgia, see Nathan Alihasvilli, *Ha-Yehudim ha-geruzim be-Geruziah uve-Eretz Yisrael* (Tel Aviv, 1975), pp. 60–63; Tubi, "Roots of the Attitude." Rabbi Menahem Mendel Kasher attributed to the rebbe a positive attitude to the creation of the State of Israel (*Ha-tekufah ha-gedolah*, p. 209), but see the response of Rabbi Moshe Sternbuch in his book *Be'ayot ha-zeman be-hashkafat ha-Torah* (Jerusalem, 1969), p. 38. See also Rabbi Tuviah Blau, a leader of Habad in Israel, in *Kefar Habad* 24 (Iyyar 5745 [1985]), who holds it to the credit of the rebbe that, unlike other rabbis, he never saw the state as "the beginning of the redemption," but rather as "the darkness of exile." And see the newsletter *Torah va-Avodah* 13 (Nisan 5747 [1987]).

98. The village was already established in the final days of his predecessor!

99. S. D. Volpe, *Shalom shalom*, p. 34.

100. Yeshayahu Binyamin Holzer, *Yelamed da'at* (New York, 1988), p. 15.

101. M. M. Schneersohn, quoted in S. D. Volpe, *Da'at Torah*, pp. 30, 36. Only the Messiah will ingather the dispersed of Israel; therefore, an entire Diaspora, even one such as that in South Africa, is not to be uprooted from its location. This is not the case in regard to the settlement of individual Jews in Eretz Israel, which is to be encouraged.

102. Aharon Dov Halperin, *Kefar Habad*, 20 Adar I 5743 (1983).

103. It should be mentioned that the messianic tension now present in Habad Hasidism and that manifest in redemptionist religious Zionism are based directly on Maimonides. These phenomena pose a question against the claim of those scholars who find in Maimonides' works elements explicitly neutralizing the actual messianic tension. See Amos Funkenstein, *Tadmit u-te'udah historit* (Tel Aviv, 1991), p. 239; Ravitzky, *Al da'at ha-makom*, pp. 90–92.

104. S. D. Volpe, *Shalom shalom,* p. 20. The messianic tension noticeable today among Habad circles, which also revolves around the personality of the rebbe, was sharply criticized by Rabbi Schach in various contexts. See Schach, *Mikhtavim u-ma'amarim,* letter from 1980, p. 18. In the remarks of Rabbi Schach, unlike those of his predecessors, the Hafetz Hayim and Rabbi Wasserman, one finds a clear neutralization of messianic tensions. This reflects his opposition to the messianic views of the disciples of Rabbi Kook, on the one hand, and those of Habad Hasidim, on the other. The devotees of Habad, for their part, attacked Rabbi Schach in strident terms (*Yir'eh ha-kahal ve-yishpot* [Kefar Habad, 1982]), condemning any "zealotry" and "self-righteous approach" that negates their appeals for "Messiah Now!" (*Kefar Habad,* no. 100 [1983]). The controversy extends to other subjects as well: a hawkish political stance (Lubavitch) against a more dovish stance (Rabbi Schach; see below, and see Schach's criticism of Habad in *Mikhtavim u-ma'amarim,* p. 18: "Their words in this matter are not based upon Torah opinion, and are alien to the spirit of Old Israel"; see his letter published by S. D. Volpe, *Shalom shalom,* pp. 564–72, accompanied by Volpe's sharp reaction). Similarly, the Hasidic rebbe called for educational populism. He took upon himself responsibility for the religious behavior of the entire Jewish people, even calling upon yeshivah students to temporarily abandon their studies so as to enable nonobservant Jews to perform a mitzvah. The Lithuanian *rosh yeshivah,* by contrast, advocates an elitist approach: he focuses upon the way of life and studies of a select few, of Torah students "upon whom the world [spiritually] stands." Also underlying these debates is the difference between the approach of the mystic and that of the Halakhist, as well as, of course, differences in individual personality. In recent years, prior to the illness and death of the rebbe, the controversy flared up with greater intensity; Rabbi Schach has designated Habad as "the known sect" and issued warnings against its false messianism. This deep split brought about, at the time, a split within Agudat Israel and the creation of a separate party, Degel ha-Torah. See my remarks on this subject in an interview by Nadav Shragai, *Ha-Aretz,* 6 March 1987.

105. See Aryeh Leib Alter's letter written in 1891, appended to the end of the book of his predecessor, Yisrael Meir Alter, *Hiddushei ha-Rim ve-Gur Aryeh Yehudah* (Warsaw, 1892); Goldstein, *Tikkun olam,* secs. 60, 72–73.

106. See Yisrael Meir Alter, *Osef mikhtavim* (Augsburg, 1947), pp. 63–67; Joseph Friedman, *A History of Agudath Israel* (New York, 1970), p. 26.

107. Alfasi, "Rabbi Avraham Mordechai Alter," p. 130.

108. Aryeh Leib Alter, "Letters from Warsaw" (in Hebrew), *Ha-Melitz* 133 (1900).

109. See Aryeh Leib Alter's letter of 1891 in Y. M. Alter, *Hiddushei ha-Rim ve-Gur Aryeh Yehudah.*

110. Y. M. Alter, *Osef mikhtavim,* p. 26.

111. See *Ha-ish u-foalo,* p. 44.

112. An interview in the weekly *Erev Shabbat,* cited in Volman, "Everything Is Holy."

113. The sympathy toward the Zionist enterprise of Rabbi Joseph Dov Soloveichik, Rabbi Hayyim's grandson, is not relevant, because he left the Haredi circles and led American modern Orthodoxy.

114. Schach, *Mikhtavim u-ma'amarim*, p. 20.

115. *Yated Ne'eman*, 20 April 1986. The style of the mouthpiece of the Belzer Hasidim, *Ha-Mahaneh ha-Haredi*, is also very strident: for example, the language of the editor, Israel Eichler: "Not only is this state not at all deserving to be called Jewish, but it is not even deserving to be called human"; "It is impossible to bridge between the Jewish viewpoint and its Zionist enemy"; and so forth (as in the remarks quoted early in this chapter.

116. See *Hashkafatenu*, sec. 1; Aaron Yeshaya Rotter, *Sha'arei Aharon* (B'nai Berak, 1982), p. 158.

117. This policy of exile was recommended by Rabbi Schach's predecessors, who directly criticized the new winds of activism affecting the Zionists. See Grainemann, *Hafetz Hayyim*, Deuteronomy; Wasserman, *Kovetz ma'amarim*, pp. 124–25; Schach, *Mikhtavim u-ma'amarim*, p. 910; idem, "Masa Maran ha-Gram Schach al Hok ha-Golan," stenciled sheet.

118. Schach, *Mikhtavim u-ma'amarim*, pp. 6, 13, 34–35.

119. Nathan Ze'ev Grossman, *Yated Ne'eman*, 24 May 1991. Compare the remarks of Rabbi Grozovsky, *Be'ayot ha-zeman*; and see Rotter, *Sha'arei Aharon*, p. 135; A. M. Alter, *Osef mikhtavim*, p. 28; Piakarz, *Hasidut Polin*, p. 27.

120. Schach, *Mikhtavim u-ma'amarim*, pp. 6, 13.

121. See Lichtenstein, "Relationship to Israel," p. 14; Rosen, "New Religious Zionism."

122. See Isaac Arama, *Akedat Yitzhak*, on Gen. 20; Maimonides, *Guide of the Perplexed* 3:51.

CHAPTER FIVE

This chapter is substantially based upon a paper prepared for the Fundamentalism Project of the American Academy of Arts and Sciences, published in *Accounting for Fundamentalisms: The Dynamic Character of Movements*, ed. M. E. Marty and R. S. Appleby, Fundamentalism Project, vol. 4 (Chicago, 1994), pp. 303–27.

1. H. M. Heilman, *Bet Rebbi* (Jerusalem, 1953), pp. 92–94.

2. This "paradox" thereafter appeared repeatedly, in various guises, among different Hasidic populations. For example, according to a Hasidic tradition, when Rabbi Menahem Mendel of Kotsk heard that "the government had decided to give the Jews equal rights, [he] burst into bitter tears" (Yehezkel Rotenberg and Moshe Sheinfeld, *Ha-Rabbi mi-Kotsk ve-shishim gibborim saviv lo* [Tel Aviv, 1959], pt. 1, p. 71). From his point of view, "when Jews are dwelling in a foreign land, they should be aliens, not citizens" (Shimon Federbusch, *Ha-Hasidut ve-Tzion* [New York, 1963], p. 96). That is, he perceived that conditions of prosperity and equality severely diminish the Jewish consciousness of exile, upsetting the feeling of strangeness and separateness the Jew should cultivate in premessianic times in the lands of dispersion. For detailed sources and other examples, see Mendel Piakarz, *Hasidut Polin* (Jerusalem, 1990), p. 269.

3. Shalom Dov Baer Schneersohn, "the Maharshab," *Iggerot kodesh* (New York, 1982), p. 130. Cf. Aviezer Ravitzky, "Exile in the Holy Land: The Dilemma of Haredi Jewry," in P. Y. Medding, ed., *Israel, State, and Society, 1948–1988*, Studies in Contemporary Jewry, no. 5 (Oxford and New York, 1989), pp. 113–14.

4. Of course, one might argue that Rabbi Schneersohn referred here only to the total, messianic ingathering of exiles of all of Israel. In any event, the rebbe was a staunch opponent—perhaps the staunchest—of the Zionist enterprise as such.

5. Concerning the theology of Ḥabad during its early generations, see Moshe Halamish, "The Theoretical Doctrine of Rabbi Shneur Zalman of Lyady" (in Hebrew), doctoral dissertation, Hebrew University, Jerusalem, 1976; Rachel Elior, *The Paradoxical Ascent to God: The Kabbalistic Theosophy of Ḥabad* (Albany, 1992); idem, *Torat ha-elohut ba-dor ha-sheni shel Ḥasidut Ḥabad* (Jerusalem, 1982); idem, "ḤaBaD: The Contemplative Ascent to God," in A. Green, ed., *Jewish Spirituality*, World Spirituality, no. 14 (New York, 1987), 2:157–205; Louis Jacobs, *Seeker of Unity* (New York, 1966); Naftali Loewenthal, *Communicating the Infinite* (Chicago, 1990); Yoram Jacobson, "Rabbi Shneur Zalman of Lyady's Doctrine of Creation" (in Hebrew), *Eshel Be'er Sheva* 1 (1976): 307–68; Rivka Schatz, "Ḥabad: Anti-Spiritualism as a Quietistic Value," in *Hasidism as Mysticism* (Princeton and Jerusalem, 1993), pp. 255–89; Isaiah Tishby and Joseph Dan, "Hasidic Doctrine and Literature" (in Hebrew), in *Ha-entzeklopediah ha-ivrit* (Jerusalem, 1965), vol. 17, cols. 776–78; Amos Funkenstein, "Imitatio Dei and the Concept of Tzimtzum in Ḥabad Teaching" (in Hebrew), *Sefer ha-yovel le-Raphael Mahler* (Tel Aviv, 1974), pp. 83–88.

6. This call was already proclaimed in the third generation of Ḥabad Hasidism. Rabbi Menachem Mendel Schneersohn was in the habit of issuing it from time to time; see, for example, the *Iggerot ha-Kodesh*, which he sent prior to Rosh Ha-shanah 5751 (fall 1990), published in the Israeli press (e.g., in *Yedi'ot Aḥaronot*, 17 September 1990). See Menachem Mendel Schneersohn, *Siḥot kodesh: Tashla* (Brooklyn, 1986), pt. 1, p. 63; idem, *Sha'arei geulah* (Jerusalem, 1991), pp. 168–74. But cf. Moshe Halamish, "Rabbi Shneur Zalman of Lyady in the Land of Israel" (in Hebrew), *Hebrew Union College Annual* 61 (1990): i–xiii (Hebrew sec.).

7. See Zvi Yehudah Kook, *Le-hilkhot tzibbur* (Jerusalem, 1987), p. 33.

8. See Moshe Idel, "Some Conceptions of the Land of Israel in Medieval Jewish Thought," in R. Link-Selinger, ed., *A Straight Path: Studies in Medieval Philosophy and Culture in Honor of Arthur Hyman* (Washington, D.C., 1988), pp. 124–41; cf. *Yalkut Shimoni*, vol. 2, sec. 503.

9. Menachem Mendel Schneersohn, *Sefer ha-ma'amarim: Tashmav* (Brooklyn, 1986), p. 215.

10. In Schneersohn's talk on Parashat Mishpatim, 5744 (1984), cited in Joseph Weinberg, *Shiurim be-Sefer ha-Tanya* 3:vii. The idea that modern innovations reflect the strength and power of the Creator has long been known in Hasidic tradition. See also the Rebbe's remarks concerning the use of the telephone for disseminating Torah (*Siḥot kodesh: Tashla*, pp. 62–65).

11. See the remarks of the fifth rebbe of Ḥabad, Shalom Dov Baer Schneersohn, *Sefer ha-ma'amarim: Taras* (Brooklyn, 1985), p. 183.

12. Weinberg, *Shiurim be-sefer ha-Tanya* 3:xlii.

13. See Hermann Lübbe, *Säkularisierung: Geschichte eines ideenpolitischen Begriffs* (Freiburg, 1965); Jacob Katz, *Jews and Freemasons in Europe, 1739–1772* (Cambridge, Mass., 1970).

14. *Kifshuto*, "literally," means "as interpreted in earlier generations," first and foremost in Ḥabad literature.

15. Menachem Mendel Schneersohn, *Emunah u-mada: Iggerot kodesh* (Kefar Ḥabad, 1974), pp. 93–99, 47, 131.

16. See Edmond Gosse, *Father and Son* (London, 1907), chaps. 5–16; Hava Lazarus-Yafeh, "Contemporary Fundamentalism: Judaism, Christianity, Islam," *Jerusalem Quarterly* 47 (1988): 33.

17. See Menachem Mendel Schneersohn, *Hitva'aduyot: Tashmav* (New York, 1986), 3:291; idem, *Emunah u-mada*, pp. 103–6, 143; Y. Y. Havlin, ed., *Sha'arei emunah*, based on the rebbe's words (Jerusalem, 1986), pp. 193–94.

18. M. M. Schneersohn, *Emunah u-mada*, pp. 131–33.

19. See M. M. Schneersohn, *Sha'arei emunah*, pp. 210–21. The methods of healing mentioned in the Talmud and in medieval Halakhic literature likewise represent an eternal truth. See Menachem Mendel Schneersohn, *Likkutei siḥot* (Brooklyn, 1984), 23:33–41. However, in everyday life the Rebbe advises his followers to obey their physicians "precisely," and "not to interfere with the instructions of a doctor." See idem, *Iggerot kodesh*, vol. 18 (Brooklyn, 1959), letter 6, p. 574.

20. M. M. Schneersohn, *Emunah u-mada*, pp. 7, 32, 46–49, 89–93, 131. Cf. Aryeh Carmell and Cyril Domb, *Challenge: Torah Views on Science and Its Problems* (Jerusalem and New York, 1976), pp. 142–49.

21. M. M. Schneersohn, *Emunah u-mada*, pp. 51, 146; idem, *Hitva'aduyot: Tashmav* 3:291.

22. M. M. Schneersohn, *Emunah u-mada*, pp. 136, 139–40.

23. See Yeshayahu Leibowitz, *Yahadut: Am Yehudi u-medinat Yisrael* (Jerusalem and Tel Aviv, 1976), pp. 337–84.

24. Charles S. Liebman, *Deceptive Images* (New Brunswick, N.J., and Oxford, 1988), pp. 43–60; idem, "Judaism and the Chaos of Modernity," in J. Neusner, ed., *Take Judaism for Example* (Chicago, 1983), pp. 143–64; Peter L. Berger, *The Heretical Imperative* (New York, 1979).

25. M. M. Schneersohn, *Hitva'aduyot: Tashmav*, pp. 136, 383; idem, *Siḥot kodesh: Tashmat* (Brooklyn, 1989), 1:132; idem, *Ma'ayenei ha-yeshuah* (Brooklyn, 1988), p. 204: "To that outside, than which there is nothing farther outside . . . to that lowly place, than which there is nothing lower." On the significance of the mission to other Jews, see idem, *Sefer ha-sheliḥut* (Brooklyn, 1987); idem, *Sefer ha-sheliḥut: Tashma-Tashan* (Brooklyn, 1991); idem, *Sefer ha-siḥot: Tismaḥ* (Brooklyn, 1988), vol. 22, pt. 2, pp. 585–86.

26. See Mordecai Wilensky, "The Hasidic Settlement in Tiberias at the End of the Eighteenth Century" (in Hebrew), *Proceedings of the American Academy for Jewish Research* 48 (1981): i–xvii (Hebrew sec.); Rachel Elior, "The Minsk Disputation" (in Hebrew), *Meḥkerei Yerushalayim be-Maḥshevet Yisrael* 4 (1982): 194; Emanuel Etkes, "Rabbi Shneur Zalman of Lyady's Path as a Hasidic Leader" (in Hebrew), *Zion* 50 (1985): 324–54.

27. Shneur Zalman of Lyady, *Iggerot kodesh* (New York, 1980), 51, 124.

28. Asher of Stolin, in D. Z. Heilman, ed., *Iggerot ba'al ha-Tanya u-venei doro* (Jerusalem, 1953), p. 185.

29. A. H. Glitzenstein, *Sefer ha-toladot: Rabbi Shneur Zalman mi-Ladi* (Brooklyn, 1976), p. 3; Elior, "Minsk Disputation," p. 193.

30. Elior, "Minsk Disputation," pp. 217–18.

31. Ibid., p. 186.

32. M. M. Schneersohn, *Hitva'aduyot: Tashmav* 3:678. Cf. M. M. Schneersohn, *Iggerot kodesh*, vol. 9 (1954), letters 2622, 2684, 2854, 2887; vol. 10 (1955), letters 2973, 3110; idem, *Devar malkhut* 17 (Parashat Naso, 5751 [1991]): 18–19; idem, *Kuntres veha-hai yitten el libo* (Brooklyn, 1988), p. 76; idem, *Sefer ha-ma'amarim* (Brooklyn, 1989), 2:101. For the theological basis of this idea, see idem, *Sefer ha-ma'amarim: Bati le-gani* (Brooklyn, 1991), 2:251–52.

33. See Menachem Mendel Schneersohn, *Sihot kodesh: Tasham* (Brooklyn, 1986), 1:387–94; idem, *Likkutei sihot*, vol. 19 (1983), pp. 249–44; idem, *Sefer ha-ma'amarim: Tashmav*, p. 185.

34. Elimelech of Lyzhansk, *No'am Elimelekh* (Jerusalem, 1960), p. 35. Cf. Yoram Jacobson, *Toratah shel ha-Hasidut* (Tel Aviv, 1985), pp. 138–42.

35. See, for example, M. M. Schneersohn, *Hitva'aduyot: Tashmav* 3:89; idem, *Sihot kodesh: Tashmat*, pp. 272–74.

36. Levi Levinson, *Kefar Habad*, 13 Tammuz 5743 (1983).

37. See *Tanya*, chap. 42: "In every generation sparks of the soul of our teacher Moses, of blessed memory, descend, and they are embodied in the body and soul of the sages of the generation"; cf. *Tiqqunei Zohar*, sec. 112. M. M. Schneersohn said this concerning his predecessor (e.g., in *Sihot kodesh: Tashmat*, p. 277) and, appropriately, his followers say the same about him. See Yehezkel Sofer, "Moses Our Teacher of the Eighties" (in Hebrew), *Kefar Habad*, 7 Nisan 5742 (1982).

38. Dov Halperin, *Kefar Habad*, 22 Adar 5742 (1982). See the severe attack on these positions by other schools within ultra-Orthodox Jewry—by the Satmar Hasidim, Mordecai Moshkowicz, *Kuntres ha-emet al tenuat Habad bi-shenot ha-80* (Brooklyn, n.d.); by the Mitnaggedim in Israel, loyal to Rabbi Eliezer Menahem Schach, *Yated Ne'eman*, 4 Shevat 5787 (13 February 1987).

39. This authentic Judaism reached the height of its creative expression in the Hasidic movement, while Habad is in turn the authentic expression of this movement (the Ba'al Shem Tov, founder of Hasidism, is considered the first leader of Habad).

40. See, for example, *Hitva'aduyot: Tashmav* 3:366, 420, 431, 460, 486.

41. Ibid., p. 515.

42. Maimonides, *Mishneh Torah*, Melakhim 8:10.

43. M. M. Schneersohn, *Hitva'aduyot: Tashmav*, pp. 63, 113, 525, 658; idem, *Emunah u-mada*, pp. 32, 81. But cf. idem, *Iggerot kodesh*, vol. 19 (1959), letter 6474.

44. M. M. Schneersohn, *Hitva'aduyot: Tashmav*, pp. 168, 184, 525.

45. Similarly, Reform Jewish leaders have recently protested the practice of Habad Hasidim of placing Hanukkah menorahs on American public buildings, seeing this as a breach in the wall of separation between church and state.

46. See Gershom Scholem, *The Messianic Idea in Judaism and Other Essays on Jewish Spirituality* (New York, 1971), pp. 176–202; idem, *Major Trends in Jewish Mysticism* (New York, 1941), pp. 328–30; Rivka Schatz, *Hasidism as Mysticism*, chap. 15; idem, "The Messianic Element in Hasidic Thought" (in Hebrew), *Molad*, n.s., 1, no. 1 [24/211] (1967/68): 105 ff. Cf. Isaiah Tishby, "The Messianic Idea and Messianic Tendencies in Early Hasidism" (in Hebrew), *Tzion* 32 (1967): 1–45.

47. See, for example, Shneur Zalman of Lyady, *Iggeret ha-kodesh*, printed in

standard editions of *Tanya* (e.g., Kefar Ḥabad, 1976), sec. 4:210. But see also *Tanya*, chaps. 36–37, pp. 90–98.

48. See Shalom Dov Baer Schneersohn, *Torat shalom* (Brooklyn, 1983), pp. 15, 72, 74; idem, *Ha-ketav veha-mikhtav* (New York, 1917); idem, *Kuntres u-maʿayan mi-beit ha-shem* (New York, 1943), pp. 46–51; idem, *Iggerot kodesh* (Brooklyn, New York, 1982), vol. 1, secs. 122, 130, 222, 292, 309–10; vol. 2, secs. 337, 459, 490; S. D. Landau and Joseph Rabinowitz, eds., *Or la-yesharim* (Warsaw, 1900), pp. 57–61; cf. Yosef Salmon, *Dat ve-Tzionut* (Jerusalem, 1990), pp. 265–72. It is interesting to note that Rabbi Shmuel Schneersohn, the father of Rabbi Shalom Dov Baer, declared in his day that, had the first Zionist settlers in Palestine (Bilu) during the early 1880s in fact followed "in the light of God," he himself would have immigrated with them to the Land of Israel. See *Sefer ha-toladot shel ha-admor Maharash* (New York, 1947), p. 38; Yitzhak Alfasi, *Ha-Ḥasidut ve-shivat Tzion* (Tel Aviv, 1986), p. 22.

49. Landau and Rabinowitz, *Or la-yesharim*, p. 57. See above, chapter 1.

50. Menachem Mendel Schneersohn, *Arbaʿah kol ha-korei meha-admor shelita mi-Lubavitch;* idem., *Ha-Keriah ha-Kedoshah*, nos. 9–11 (5701 [1941]); no. 25, (5702 [1942]); idem, *Netzaḥ Yisrael* (Munich, 1948); see also the collections idem, *Siḥot kodesh: Tasha* (Kefar Ḥabad, 1981), p. 95; idem, *Iggerot kodesh,* vol. 5 (1981), pp. 377, 385, 408. Cf. Gershon Greenberg, "Redemption after the Holocaust according to Mahane Israel: Lubavitch, 1940–1945," *Modern Judaism* 12 (1992): 61–84.

51. M. M. Schneersohn, *Hitvaʿaduyot: Tashmav* 3:194. Cf. pp. 369, 450.

52. See, for example, Menachem Mendel Schneersohn, *Sefer siḥot: Tishmah* 2:533; idem, *Yein malkhut* (Brooklyn, 1988), 2:517–18.

53. *Kefar Ḥabad,* 10 Tammuz 5744 (1984). Cf. M. M. Schneersohn, *Shaʿarei geʾulah,* pp. 101–2.

54. M. M. Schneersohn, talk on 2 Tevet 5751 (19 January 1991), published in *Devar malkhut,* Parashat Va-Era, 1991. Cf. idem, *Sefer ha-maʿamarim: Tismaḥ* (Brooklyn, 1988), p. 171. These remarks were made in the context of a polemic with Rabbi Eliezer Menahem Schach, leader of the "Lithuanian" or "Mitnaggedic" stream in Israel, who warned, on the eve of the Gulf War, of a new holocaust in punishment for the abandonment of religion and desecration of the Sabbath in Israel. See the reactions of those loyal to Rabbi Schach, published in *Yeted Neʿeman,* 18 Tevet 5751 (1 April 1991).

55. M. M. Schneersohn, *Siḥat ha-shavuʿa,* no. 238, Devarim, 5751 (27 July 1991).

56. M. M. Schneersohn, *Devar malkhut* 24 (Pinhas, 5731 [1971]): 9.

57. See, for example, *Kovetz ḥiddushei Torah: Ha-melekh ha-mashiaḥ veha-geʾulah ha-shelemah* (n.p., 1983). Many Ḥabad Hasidim deny their authorship of this treatise, in which the rebbe is openly declared to be "the King Messiah."

58. M. M. Schneersohn, *Hitvaʿaduyot: Tashmav* 3:194.

59. In many cases, the Hasidim say of their Rebbe only what they heard him say about his own predecessor.

60. M. M. Schneersohn, *Siḥat ha-Shavuʿa,* no. 244, Parashat Ki Tavo, 5751 (30 August 1991). Compare to this the remarks of the compilers of the book *Oro shel mashiaḥ* (Kefar Ḥabad, 1991), p. 5; idem., *Siḥat ha-shavuʿa,* no. 238, Devarim,

5751 (19 July 1991); cf. the remarks of the rebbe concerning his predecessor, M. M. Schneersohn, *Hitva'aduyot: Tashmav* 1:374–75. Moreover, compare the remarks of Rabbi S. D. Wolpa, *Kefar Ḥabad*, 19 Shevat 5745 (1985): "The Rebbe, *shelita*, incorporates the seven heavens, the earth, and the four corners of the world"; and the words of Rabbi Hanoch Glitstein, *Kefar Ḥabad*, 12 Tammuz 5743 (1983): "There has never yet arisen within the Jewish people a man of his great intellectual abundance . . . He is unique in his generation; and not only in his generation, but sui generis, over many generations of great *ge'onim* in Israel, holy ones and great *Tzaddikim*—[he is] the wonder of the generations!"

61. Shneur Zalman of Lyady, *Torah or* (Brooklyn, 1972), p. 106b.

62. Shneur Zalman of Lyady, *Ma'amarei admor ha-zaken: Taksah* (Brooklyn, 1980), p. 106. Cf. idem, *Ma'amarei admor ha-zaken ha-ketzarim* (Brooklyn, 1981), p. 539; idem, *Ma'amarei admor ha-zaken: Inyanim* (Brooklyn, 1983), p. 431.

63. Menahem Mendel ben Baruch, "Tzemaḥ Tzedek," *Or ha-Torah* (Brooklyn, 1972), 6:1083. See also the remarks of his predecessor, the "Mittler Rebbe," Dov Baer ben Shneur Zalman, *Sha'arei teshuvah* (Brooklyn, 1984), 2:45a; *Ma'amarei ha-admor ha-emtzai* (Brooklyn, 1986), p. 68a.

64. S. D. B. Schneersohn, *Torat shalom*, p. 74.

65. M. M. Schneersohn, *Devar malkhut* 13 (Parashat Emor, 5751 [1991]): 8–10; idem, *Sha'arei geulah*, pp. 270–73.

66. See *Oro shel mashiaḥ*, pp. 5–13.

67. See, for example, M. M. Schneersohn's remarks from 1979, published in *Likkutei sihot*, vol. 22 (1983), p. 334: "The painful question of the flight from neighborhoods populated by Jews [in New York City] . . . and in a similar way [!] the painful and astonishing 'question' of the return of territories in the Holy Land."

68. See Yair Sheleg, " 'Even though He Tarry' " (in Hebrew), *Kol ha-Ir*, 14 February 1992.

69. See "A False Messiah in the Gate" (in Hebrew), *Yated Ne'eman*, 24 February 1992.

70. S. Zalman, *Iggerot kodesh*, p. 56.

71. See Tishby and Dan, "Hasidic Doctrine and Literature," cols. 783–84; Moshe Halamish, "The Relation between Leader and Community in the Teaching of R. Shneur Zalman of Lyady," in Y. Cohen, ed., *Ḥevrah ve-historyah* (Jerusalem, 1980), pp. 79–92; Elior, "Minsk Disputation"; Emanuel Etkes, "Rabbi Shneur Zalman's Path"; idem, "The Ascent of Rabbi Shneur Zalman of Lyady to a Position of Leadership" (in Hebrew), *Tarbitz* 54 (1985): 435.

72. Menahem Mendel of Vitebsk, *Peri ha-aretz* (Jerusalem, 1974), p. 50.

73. See Elior, "Minsk Disputation," p. 193.

74. Rabbi Tuviah Blau is the author of several books on Hasidim and one of the Ḥabad leaders in Israel. I wish to thank Rabbi Blau for his interesting and illuminating conversation.

APPENDIX

1. Benjamin of Tudela, *Travels*, ed. Nathan Adler (London, 1907), p. 72.

2. Scholars are divided as to whether this document was written by Rabbi Ben-

jamin himself or whether it found its way into his book from elsewhere. See S. Schechter, "Jewish Saints in Medieval Germany," in *Studies in Judaism,* 3d ser. (Philadelphia, 1945), pp. 6–8.

3. Thus the language of the document. Concerning the mourners of Zion in Franco-Germany, see Yaakov Gartner, "The Consciousness of the Mourners of Zion as a Factor in the Development of the Customs for Tisha be-Av" (in Hebrew), *Milet* 2 (1984): 204–7.

4. Rashi's comment: " 'not to ascend,' together, by force." Rabbi Jacob Emden and Rabbi Samuel Strashun suggested the reading *ka-homah* (as a wall), based on the language of the Talmud in BT Yoma 9b (cf. Cant. R. 8:11; the novellum of Yavetz and Rashash on Ketubbot 111a in various editions of the Talmud). Salomon Buber suggests the reading *ba-homah,* based on the text brought in his edition of Midrash Tanhuma (Vilna, 1885), Devarim, chap. 4: "That they not go up as multitudes."

5. *Mekhilta de-Rabbi Yishmael,* ed. Horovitz-Rabin (Frankfurt am Main, 1931), Masekhta de-Vayehi, Petihta.

6. See, for example, Tanhuma: Devarim, chap. 4; Targ. Ps.-Jon. to Exod. 13:17. For explanations and detailed sources, cf. Joseph Heinemann, *Aggadot ve-toldotehen* (Jerusalem, 1974), pp. 137–47; Yaakov Blidstein, "The Exodus from Egypt of the Children of Ephraim: Further Discussion" (in Hebrew), *Mehkerei Yerushalayim be-Mahshevet Yisrael* 5 (1986): 12–13; Louis Ginzberg, *The Legends of the Jews* (Philadelphia, 1968), 6:2; David Berger, "Three Typological Themes in Early Jewish Messianism," *AJS Review* 10 (1985): 141 ff.

7. Mordecai Breuer, "The Discussion concerning the Three Oaths in Recent Generations" (in Hebrew), in *Ge'ulah u-medinah* (Jerusalem, 1979), pp. 49–57.

8. Ehud Luz, *Parallels Meet* (Philadelphia, 1988), pp. 215–17. Cf. Yosef Salmon, *Dat ve-Tzionut* (Jerusalem, 1990), pp. 314–15.

9. During the last generation, extensive rabbinic literature regarding the question of the oaths has been written, primarily in response to the book *Va-Yo'el Moshe* by Joel Teitelbaum, the late Rebbe of Satmar. See Menahem Mendel Kasher, *Ha-tekufah ha-gedolah* (Jerusalem, 1967), pp. 150, 174–78, 195–97, 221, 272–81; Samuel ha-Cohen Weingarten, *Hishba'ti etkhem* (Jerusalem, 1966); Shlomo Aviner, "Clarifications regarding 'That They Not Ascend as a Wall' " (in Hebrew), *No'am* 20 (1980): 4–28; Hayyim Zimmerman, *Torah l'Israel* (in English) (Jerusalem, 1978), pp. 9–35; Meir Blumenfeld, "Concerning the Oath That They Not Ascend as a Wall" (in Hebrew), in *Shanah be-shanah* (Jerusalem, 1974), pp. 148–53; A. Y. Waldenberg, *Tzitz Eliezer* (Jerusalem, 1970), vol. 10, sec. 1, "Completions"; Yisrael Stipanski, "The Redemption from Egypt, the Redemption from Babylonia, and the Future Redemption" (in Hebrew), in *Or ha-mizrah* (1973), pp. 200–25; S. P. Frank, *Toldot Ze'ev* (Jerusalem, 1964), pt. 2, sec. 24. Cf. Zvi Yehudah Kook, *Mitokh ha-Torah ha-goelet* (Jerusalem, 1982), p. 190.

10. Joseph Yahalom, *Piyyutei Shimon ben Nagas* (Jerusalem, 1984), p. 241.

11. The *piyyut* is published in *Ginzei Schechter* (New York, 1928), pt. 2, pp. 65, 70.

12. See Moshe Gil, *Eretz Yisrael ba-tekufah ha-Muslemit ha-Rishonah, 634–1099* (Tel Aviv, 1983), 1:499–508; idem, "Aliyah and Pilgrimage during the Period

of the First Muslim Conquest, 634–1099" (in Hebrew), *Cathedra* 8 (1978): 124–33; Avraham Grossman, "Aliyah to the Land of Israel during the Period of the First Muslim Conquest" (in Hebrew), *Cathedra* 8 (1978): 136–44. See also the reactions of Shmuel Safrai and Haggi Ben Shammai, in A. Grossman, "Aliyah to the Land of Israel," pp. 134–35, 145.

13. See Jacob Mann, "An Early Karaite Text," *Jewish Quarterly Review* 92 (1922): 285.

14. Maimonides, *Iggerot ha-Rambam* (Jerusalem, 1960), p. 189. See the commentary of Ibn Ezra on Song of Songs 8:7: "Solomon said in his Holy Spirit: I have adjured you that you are not to awaken until there comes the End."

15. English translation from Abraham Halkin and David Hartman, *Crisis and Leadership: Epistles of Maimonides* (Philadelphia, 1985), pp. 130–31.

16. Regarding the rhetorical nature of Maimonides' *Epistle* and its goals, see Abraham Halkin's introduction to his edition of *Iggeret Teman* (New York, 1952), pp. 27–30; Aviezer Ravitzky, *Al da'at ha-makom* (Jerusalem, 1991), p. 54 n. 52; Halkin and Hartman, *Crisis and Leadership*, pp. 150–200.

17. In both these works, the Song of Songs is interpreted as a metaphysical allegory of the relationship between man and God (or the Active Intellect). See Joseph Baer Soloveitchik, "U-vikashtem mi-sham," in his *Ish ha-halakhah: Galuy ve-nistar* (Jerusalem, 1979), pp. 119–20; Joseph Kapah, *Kovetz ketavim* (Jerusalem, 1989), 2:619–20; Ravitzky, *Al da'at ha-makom*, p. 54 n. 52.

18. Elhanan Reiner, "Aliyah and Pilgrimage to the Land of Israel, 1517–1909" (in Hebrew), doctoral dissertation, Hebrew University, Jerusalem, 1988, pp. 39–118.

19. Ephraim Kanarfogel, "The Aliyah of 'Three Hundred Rabbis' in 1211: Tosafist Attitudes towards Settling in the Land of Israel," *Jewish Quarterly Review* 76 (1986): 191–212.

20. MS Bodlaiaen Opp. 202, fol. 106b.

21. Israel Ta-Shma, "A Note concerning the Attitude of the Early Ashkenazic Scholars to Aliyah" (in Hebrew), *Shalem* 6 (1992): 315–18.

22. Israel Ta-Shma, "Matters of the Land of Israel" (in Hebrew), *Shalem* 1 (1974): 81–82.

23. Gershom Scholem, "A New Document concerning the History of the Early Kabbalah" (in Hebrew), in *Sefer Bialik [Knesset]* (Tel Aviv, 1934), pp. 161–62; Moshe Idel, "The Land of Israel in Medieval Kabbalah," in L. A. Hoffman, ed., *The Land of Israel: Jewish Perspectives* (Bloomington, Ind., 1986), pp. 170–87.

24. Haviva Pedaya, "Land of Spirit and Land of Reality" (in Hebrew), in A. Ravitzky and M. Halamish, eds., *Eretz Yisrael ba-mahshevet ha-Yehudit be-yemei ha-beinayim* (Jerusalem, 1991), pp. 244–49.

25. Isaiah Tishby, *Hikrei Kabbalah u-sheluhoteha* (Jerusalem, 1982), pp. 3–10.

26. Azriel, *Perush ha-aggadot*, ed. I. Tishby (Jerusalem, 1945), pp. 29–30.

27. Ezra, *Perush shir ha-shirim* (attributed to Nahmanides), in H. D. Chavell, ed., *Kitvei ha-Ramban* (Jerusalem, 1964), 2:514.

28. Haviva Pedaya, "Land of Spirit and Land of Reality," n. 71; idem, "'Flaw' and 'Correction' in the Concept of the Godhead in the Teachings of Rabbi Isaac the Blind" (in Hebrew), *Mehkerei Yerushalayim be-Mahshevet Yisrael* 9 (1987): 212.

29. Ezra, *Perush shir ha-shirim*, p. 519.

30. Nahmanides, addenda to *Sefer ha-mitzvot* of Maimonides, Mitzvat Aseh 4 (printed with Maimonides' *Sefer ha-mitzvot* [Jerusalem, 1959], 2:42).

31. Ibid.

32. See Aviezer Ravitzky, " 'Set Yourself Markers' for Zion: The Development of an Idea" (in Hebrew), in M. Halamish and A. Ravitzky (eds.), *Eretz Yisrael be-hagut ha-Yehudit* (Jerusalem, 1991), pp. 8–13, and the sources quoted there.

33. Nahmanides nevertheless wished to attribute the small numbers in the aliyah following Cyrus's proclamation to the fact that "they did not wish to press the End" (Chavell, *Kitvei ha-Ramban* 1:274).

34. Tishby, *Ḥikrei Kabbalah u-sheluḥoteha*, pp. 6–7. Idel and Pedaya have already noted the opposition between Rabbi Ezra and Nahmanides concerning the question of *aliyah*.

35. According to Buber's reading of Midrash Tanhuma (above, n. 4): "that they should not press the End, and that when they ascend from exile they not come en masse."

36. Estori [Isaac ben Moses] ha-Parhi, *Kaftor va-feraḥ* (Jerusalem, 1897), p. 197.

37. Ibid., p. 2.

38. Isaac ben Sheset Perfet, *Teshuvot ha-Ribash* (Constantinople, 1546), sec. 101. Cf. Shaul Yisraeli, *Eretz ḥemdah* (Jerusalem, 1988), p. 17; Eliezer Bashan, "Does Military-Political Struggle for Redemption Suit the Jewish Tradition?" (in Hebrew), *Petaḥim* 32 (1975): 13–14.

39. Yisrael Stipanski suggested the reading "It is withheld from the collectivity." See his *Eretz Yisrael be-sifrut ha-yeshuvot* (Jerusalem, 1967), 1:133 n. 3.

40. Rashbash, *Teshuvot Yakhin u-Voaz* (Livorno, 1872), vol. 2, sec. 2. In another responsum, Rashbash opposed the philosophical-spiritualistic position that ignored the value of the Land of Israel (and of the earthly dimension generally) in religious life. Rashbash sought to avenge the insult to the concrete religious act.

41. Cf. the commentary of Rabbi Levi Gersonides to the Song of Songs (Königsberg, 1860). In his view, the oath requires Israel "to go toward redemption in the proper order, stage by stage."

42. See B. Z. Dinur, "The Aliyah Movement from Spain to the Land of Israel following the Pogroms of 1391" (in Hebrew), *Zion* 32 (1967): 161–74. Joseph Hacker has shown that the date of this awakening should be the second half of the century. See his paper "The Relation of Spanish Jews to the Land of Israel and Their Aliyah" (in Hebrew), *Cathedra* 36 (1985): 20–28. Cf. E. E. Urbach, "Aliyah and Abandonment of the Land in Historical Perspective" (in Hebrew), in *Al Tzionut ve-yahadut: Iyyunim u-masot* (Jerusalem, 1985), pp. 152–54.

43. Dinur, "Aliyah Movement," pp. 161–74.

44. At the end of the nineteenth century Rabbi Yeruham Perlman, "the Minsker Gadol," made unusual use of the idea of the oaths. According to him, the edict was specifically intended to restrain the yearning of many individuals to go up to the Land of Israel: "All of the commandments are incumbent personally and categorically . . . Each Jewish individual is obligated to perform them without any conditions or limitation. The commandment of dwelling in the Land of Israel, however,

is incumbent only upon the people as a whole. The rabbis anticipated in their holy spirit that if this commandment would be imposed upon each individual, the people would break through any bounds, and would flow to the land by the thousands from the four corners of the earth . . . Therefore our rabbis informed us that the Holy One adjured Israel that they not ascend the wall and not rebel against the nations . . . The power of the commandment is thus weakened . . . because of the need of the hour" (see *Sinai* 6 [1940]: 210–21).

45. Isaac de Leon, *Megillat Esther* on Maimonides' *Sefer ha-mitzvot, Mitzvat Aseh* 4 (Jerusalem, 1959), pt. 2, p. 42.

46. Samuel Yaffe, *Yefeh kol* (Izmir, 1739), fol. 71a. The primeval myth of the children of Ephraim, who went up from Egypt prematurely, served Yaffe as an archetype for the dangers of forcing the End: "They thought to go out by force . . . they did not trust God, but their own sword and arm . . . they did not fear the oath not to arouse until God wishes it; thus they violated [the prohibition not to go before] the End."

47. Galante's interpretation is printed in *Bet Avot* (Belgraye, 1911), i, x, p. 91.

48. Compare the demand of the anonymous fifteenth-century Kabbalist to refrain from any mystical or magical activity to hasten the redemption (*Perush le-shir ha-shirim*, MS Schocken, Kabbalah 10, fol. 42a). Moshe Idel observed that this Kabbalist rejected the activist-messianic approach of Kabbalists from the circle of *Sefer ha-Meshiv*, who attempted to overcome the powers of evil by magical means. See Idel's introduction to A. Z. Escoly, *Ha-tenu'ah ha-meshihit be-Yisrael* (Jerusalem, 1987), p. 19.

49. See Rivka Schatz, "Existence and Eschatology in the Teachings of the Maharal," *Immanuel* 14 (1982): 86–97; 15 (1982/83): 62–72; Benjamin Gross, *Netzah Yisrael* (Jerusalem and Tel Aviv, 1974), pp. 128–69; Shalom Rosenberg, "Exile and Redemption in Jewish Thought in the Sixteenth Century: Contending Conceptions," in B. D. Cooperman, ed., *Jewish Thought in the Sixteenth Century* (Cambridge, Mass., 1983), pp. 399–430; André Neher, *Le puits de l'exile* (Paris, 1966); B. L. Sherwin, *Mystical Theology and Social Dissent* (London and Toronto, 1982).

50. Judah Löw ben Bezalel of Prague, *Netzah Yisra'el* (Jerusalem, 1971), chap. 16, p. 89.

51. Ibid., chap. 1, p. 9; chap. 24, p. 121. Cf. A. D. Kulka, "The Historical Background of the National Doctrine of the Maharal of Prague" (in Hebrew), *Zion* 50 (1985): 281–82.

52. See Rashi on BT Ketubbot 111a. The prohibition against forcing the End by means of prayer was strongly emphasized in Hasidic literature. See also the remarks of Rabbi Moshe Sofer (the Hatam Sofer) in *Eleh divrei ha-berit* (Altona, 1819), p. 42.

53. Judah Löw, *Netzah Yisra'el*, chap. 24, pp. 122–34.

54. Ibid., p. 124.

55. Kasher, *Ha-tekufah ha-gedolah*, pp. 272–81.

56. Judah Löw ben Bezalel, *Be'er ha-Golah* (Jerusalem, 1971), sec. 7, p. 147.

57. Yo'el Teitelbaum, *Va-Yo'el Moshe* (Jerusalem, 1978), Ma'amar Shalosh Shevu'ot, secs. 20, 32, 76, 83, 86.

58. Judah Löw, *Netzah Yisrael*, chap. 24, p. 124.

59. Isaiah Horowitz, *Shenei luḥot ha-berit* (Warsaw, 1863; reprinted, Jerusalem, 1963), pt. 3, p. 48b.

60. Ibid., pt. 1, p. 56a; cf. p. 75b.

61. Ibid., pt. 3, p. 24a. Cf. p. 49a, where the idea was directly connected to the subject of the oaths.

62. Bahya ben Asher, *Perush al ha-Torah* (Jerusalem, 1958), Va-Yishlah, Gen. 32:7.

63. See below, n. 100.

64. I. Horowitz, *Shenei luḥot ha-berit*, pt. 2, p. 73a. Cf. p. 77a.

65. See Meir Benayahu, "The 'Holy Society' of Rabbi Judah he-Hasid" (in Hebrew), in *Sefer yovel le-Shneur Zalman Shazar* (Jerusalem, 1960), pp. 133–82; Yaakov Barnai, *Yehudei Eretz-Yisrael ba-meah ha-YH* (Jerusalem, 1982), p. 28, and bibliography there.

66. See above, n. 4.

67. Jacob Emden, *Torat ha-kena'ot* (Amsterdam, 1752; reprinted, Jerusalem, 1971), p. 48. See B. Z. Dinur, *Be-mifneh ha-dorot* (Jerusalem, 1972), p. 29.

68. Jacob Emden, *Siddur bet Ya'akov* (Warsaw, 1882), p. 80b.

69. Emden, *Torat ha-kena'ot*, p. 2. See Yehudah Liebes, "The Messianism of Rabbi Jacob Emden and His Relation to Sabbateanism" (in Hebrew), *Tarbitz* 49 (1980): 125.

70. Emden, *Torat ha-kena'ot*, p. 132. In this spirit one should understand the emphasis placed by Emden upon the Talmudic aphorism that makes the removal of one's mind from messianic concerns a precondition for the coming of the Messiah (BT Sanhedrin 97b). See Jacob Emden, *Ḥiddushim ve-Hagahot on the Talmud* (printed in standard editions of the Talmud), on Ketubbot 111a.

71. Moses Hagiz, *Shever posh'im* (Amsterdam, 1719), p. 6.

72. However, it was Emden who condemned the massive *aliyah* of the circle of Rabbi Judah he-Hasid, also blaming Rabbi Jonathan Eybeschütz for supporting this *aliyah*. See *Shevirat luḥot ha-berit* (Altona, Germany, 1756), p. 476a: "Several times he [Eybeschütz] spoke before them in praise of the suspect sect of Rabbi Judah Hasid, who had gone up to the Land of Israel."

73. See Ravitzky, "Set Yourself Markers," pp. 30–35.

74. Jonathan Eybeschütz, *Ahavat Yehonatan* (Warsaw, 1872), Va-Ethannan, fol. 74a. Samuel ha-Cohen Weingarten, *Hishba'ti etkhem*, claims, in light of parallels in Eybeschütz's writings, that the national passivity is not presented here as a norm but as a fact, that it does not reflect a divine decree but the Jewish refusal to go up to the Land of Israel. Examination of these texts does not confirm his interpretation. On the contrary, God Himself is portrayed by them as postponing the return of the people to Zion to days in which "the Evil Urge will be uprooted from the earth"— that is, to a metahistorical era.

75. Some Talmudic and midrashic sayings condemn the Babylonian exiles for not ascending "as a wall" to the Second Commonwealth (see above, n. 4). This motif appears frequently in Jewish literature; Eybeschütz's opponent, Rabbi Jacob Emden, likewise used it. Cf. above, n. 33; and chapter 1, n. 58.

76. Eybeschütz, *Ahavat Yehonatan*, Mi-Kets, p. 19a.

77. Ibid., Ki Tetse, p. 84a.; and cf. Shofetim, p. 82a.

78. A wealth of similar sources is cited by Mendel Piakarz in *Hasidut Polin* (Je-

rusalem, 1990). Cf. Yitzhak Alfasi, *Ha-Hasidut ve-shivat Tzion* (Tel Aviv, 1986); Levi Yitzhak of Berdichev, *Kedushat Levi* (Jerusalem, 1964), pt. 1, pp. 103, 165; Shmuel Shemaryah of Strazov, *Zikhron Shemuel* (Warsaw, 1908), p. 13a.

79. Ya'akov Yosef of Polonnoye, *Toldot Ya'akov Yosef* (Koritz, 1780), p. 165c.

80. Elimelech of Lyzhansk, *No'am Elimelekh* (Lvov, 1786), p. 54b. Cf. Gershom Scholem, "The Neutralization of the Messianic Element in Early Hasidism," *Journal of Jewish Studies* 44 (1969–70): 44, reprinted in idem, *Messianic Idea in Judaism*, pp. 176–202.

81. Yitzhak Ya'akov of Lublin, *Zikhron zot* (Warsaw, 1869), p. 65d. Cf. the remarks of his disciple, Ya'akov of Mialiscz, *Kol Ya'akov* (Jerusalem, 1989), p. 361: "'He may not treat as first-born the son of the loved one' [Deut. 21:16], that is, the congregation of Israel, which is beloved to God, 'in disregard of the son of the unloved one,' so long as the rule of the hated one continues. For our Creator has adjured us not to force the End."

82. I have not found the edict of the oaths directed against the Hasidic aliyot to the Land of Israel. See Israel Halperin, *Ha-aliyot ha-rishonot shel ha-Hasidim le-Eretz Yisrael* (Jerusalem and Tel Aviv, 1947); Yaakov Barnai, *Iggerot Hasidim mi-Eretz Yisrael* (Jerusalem, 1980); Hayyah Steinman-Katz, *Reshitan shel aliyot Hasidim* (Jerusalem, 1987).

83. Abraham Loewenstamm, *Tzeror ha-Hayyim* (Amsterdam, 1820), pp. 61–62.

84. Samson Raphael Hirsch, *Horeb* (London and New York, 1962), sec. 608, p. 461, discussion of three oaths.

85. See chapter 1. Only faint traces of this view appeared among eastern Jewry. See, for example, in the words of Rabbi Hayyim Palaggi, a great Sephardic sage in Turkey: "the Holy One, blessed be He, adjured Israel that they not go up the wall . . . for God, may He be blessed, has scattered us to the four corners" (*Otzrot ha-Hayyim* [Jerusalem, 1872], p. 37). But cf. his *Nishmat kol hay* (Salonika, 1832–37), Yoreh De'ah, secs. 49, 85.; cf. Joseph Tubi, "The Roots of the Attitude of Oriental Jewry to the Zionist Movement" (in Hebrew), in *Temurot ba-historyah ha-Yehudit ha-hadashah* (Jerusalem, 1988), p. 182.

86. Zvi Hirsch Lehren, sources in *Iggerot ha-pekidim veha-amarkalim me-Amsterdam*, MS Jerusalem, Ben-Zvi Archives. Cf. Aryeh Morgenstern, "Messianic Anticipations Preceding the Year 5600 (1840)" (in Hebrew), in Z. Baras, ed., *Meshihiyut ve-eskhatologiah* (Jerusalem, 1984), pp. 351–52.

87. See Aryeh Morgenstern, *Meshihiyut ve-Yishuv Eretz Yisrael* (Jerusalem, 1985), p. 107. Cf. pp. 25, 130, 182.

88. Moshe Teitelbaum, *Yismah Moshe* (New York, 1947), pt. 1, end; cf. Alfasi, *Ha-Hasidut ve-shivat Tzion*, p. 17.

89. Morgenstern, *Meshihiyut ve-Yishuv Eretz Yisrael*, pp. 104–7.

90. Israel of Shklov, *Pe'at ha-shulhan* (Jerusalem, 1959), 1.3. Cf. in a letter of his: "The proscription of the oaths does not apply to individuals" (Avraham Yaari, ed., *Iggerot Eretz Yisrael* [Tel Aviv, 1943], p. 355). Shklov also rejected the approach of Rabbi Isaac de Leon (*Megillat Esther*, pt. 2, p. 42), cited above. See *Pe'at ha-shulhan*, 1.14.

91. Shmuel Idels, *Hiddushei halakhot va-aggadot Maharsha*, in standard editions of the Talmud, on BT Ketubbot 111a.

92. Joshua Heshel Falk of Cracow, *Penei Yehoshua,* on BT Ketubbot 111a.

93. Cf. the remarks of Rabbi Ze'ev Wolf Einhorn of Grodno, "the Maharzu," from the mid–nineteenth century, in his commentary on Cant. R. 2:7: "King Messiah will bring all of Israel out of the Exile; if they do so by themselves, however, they will miss the messianic redemption." I wish to thank Dr. Hananel Mack for bringing this source to my attention.

94. See Kasher, *Ha-tekufah ha-gedolah,* pp. 174–75. Cf. the letters in praise of settlement of the land (from 1891) gathered in A. J. Slutzki, *Shivat Tzion* (Warsaw, 1900). The struggle with the edict of the oaths repeatedly appears as a motif in these letters: see 1:9, 35, 43, 51, 74, 2:16, 53, 84.

95. A letter of Rabbi Meir Simhah ha-Kohen of Dvinsk from 1922. Cf. Shimon Federbusch, *Torah u-melukhah* (Jerusalem and New York, 1961), pp. 91–92.

96. Hayyim Vital, *Etz Hayyim* (Warsaw, 1931), introduction.

97. Pinhas Halevi Horowitz, *Sefer ha-Hafla'ah,* pt. 1 (Offenbach, 1787), on BT Ketubbot 111a.

98. Elijah, Gaon of Vilna, *Siddur ha-Gera* (Jerusalem, 1891), pt. 2, p. 48a. For further sources see Aviner, "Clarifications."

99. Moses Hagiz, *Sefat emet* (Vilna, 1876; reprinted, Jerusalem, 1968), p. 65.

100. Some rabbinical authorities have argued that, from the moment the nations of the world violated their oath "not to oppress Israel overly much," the people of Israel too have been free of their oath. This view was raised in light of the 1929 Arab riots (see Y. M. Toledano, *Teshuvot Yam ha-gadol* [Cairo, 1931], sec. 97, p. 183), and especially in light of the Holocaust (see Y. A. ha-Levi Herzog, "The Establishment of a State Prior to the Coming of the Messiah" [in Hebrew], in *Sefer ha-Tzionut ha-datit* [Jerusalem, 1977], vol. 1, p. 62). Some authorities have limited the prohibition of the oaths specifically to a military conquest of the land. See Shmuel Mohilever, *Shivat Tzion,* pt. 1, p. 9; Isaac Jacob Reines, *Or hadash al Tzion* (Vilna, 1902), 19b; Azriel Hildesheimer, *Gesammelte Aufsatze,* ed. M. Hildesheimer (Frankfurt am Main, 1923), p. 216. There are yet other rabbis who suggested a spiritualistic interpretation of the oaths, removing them entirely from the political-historical arena. See Abraham Bornstein of Sochaczew, *Avnei Nezer,* Yoreh De'ah, sec. 456, p. 3: "The oath was directed to the root of their souls up above."